大学实用英语
语法教程

詹丽芹 张婷 主编

清华大学出版社
北京

内容简介

本书涵盖了《大学英语教学大纲》中所有的语法项目，全书按照"实践—理论—再实践"的编写思路，即课前热身训练—课中理论讲解—课后巩固练习。本书具有条理性强、针对性强、操作性强的特点，且富含思政元素，在培养学生英语能力的同时，让学生逐渐形成正确的价值观，充分体现课堂教书育人功能。

本书既适用于参加全国大学英语四、六级考试和全国硕士研究生招生考试及其他各类英语考试的学生，也适用于英语专业的学生。同时还是广大英语教师以及英语爱好者的必备参考书。

本书封面贴有清华大学出版社防伪标签，无标签者不得销售。
版权所有，侵权必究。举报：010-62782989，beiqinquan@tup.tsinghua.edu.cn。

图书在版编目（CIP）数据

大学实用英语语法教程/詹丽芹，张婷主编. —北京：清华大学出版社，2022.8(2024.8重印)
ISBN 978-7-302-61119-6

Ⅰ.①大… Ⅱ.①詹… ②张… Ⅲ.①英语－语法－高等学校－教材 Ⅳ.①H319.35

中国版本图书馆 CIP 数据核字(2022)第 104330 号

责任编辑：聂军来
封面设计：刘　键
责任校对：刘　静
责任印制：杨　艳

出版发行：清华大学出版社
　　网　　址：https://www.tup.com.cn,https://www.wqxuetang.com
　　地　　址：北京清华大学学研大厦 A 座　　邮　　编：100084
　　社　总　机：010-83470000　　邮　　购：010-62786544
　　投稿与读者服务：010-62776969, c-service@tup.tsinghua.edu.cn
　　质量反馈：010-62772015, zhiliang@tup.tsinghua.edu.cn
　　课件下载：https://www.tup.com.cn,010-83470410
印　装　者：三河市天利华印刷装订有限公司
经　　销：全国新华书店
开　　本：185mm×260mm　　印　　张：20.25　　字　　数：512 千字
版　　次：2022 年 8 月第 1 版　　印　　次：2024 年 8 月第 2 次印刷
定　　价：59.50 元

产品编号：097301-02

本书编委会

主 编：

詹丽芹　张　婷

副主编：

黄银梅　周　楠　吕少勤　吴芳芳

卢剑文　刘　娟　余干龙

前言

语法赋予语言条理性和可理解性,在语言学习过程中起着重要的作用。根据《大学英语教学大纲》中对语法的要求,针对学生日常生活交际、英语教师资格证考试、从业上岗以及全国大学英语四、六级考试等各类英语考试的需要,编写了这本《大学实用英语语法教程》,供大学生及其他中高级英语学习者使用。

本书内容丰富,全书共有二十九章,涵盖了《大学英语教学大纲》的所有语法项目,并根据语言使用的实际情况增加了语法要点和惯用法方面的内容,既全面系统,又详略得当,重难点突出;同时,用加"注"的形式说明一些语法现象的特殊用法。全书遵循"实践—理论—再实践"的编写思路,即课前学生热身训练—课中教师理论讲解—课后学生巩固练习。本书有以下特征。

(1)条理性强。本书对大学英语教学中的各种句法和各类词法进行梳理、归纳,使各语法知识点概念清晰、重点显现,使学生对英语语法知识形成系统、完整的认识。

(2)针对性强。本书各章收集历年英语等级考试及其他相关英语考试试题中相关的语法类题目,让学生明确考试中相关语法的重点和动向,进而提高应试能力。

(3)操作性强。本书课前有热身改错练习,让学生能了解自己在每个版块中的不足,从而有针对性地学习;课后附有大量的专项强化训练题,以便学生在掌握每一章的理论基础上进行强化练习,达到融会贯通。

(4)融入思政元素。本书各章的例句中体现思想政治教育。运用课堂教学的优势,让思想政治教育合理融入大学英语语法课堂教学中,在培养学生英语能力的同时,让学生逐渐形成正确的价值观,坚定文化自信,充分体现课堂教书育人功能。

本书由詹丽芹、张婷担任主编,负责本书的设计、修改、统稿和定稿工作。参加编写的有:黄银梅(第一~三章),周楠(第四~六章),吕少勤(第七、十八、十九章),吴芳芳(第八、九、十、十二章),张婷(第十一、十三、十五、十七章),詹丽芹(第十四、十六、二十二、二十五、二十六、二十九章),卢剑文(第二十、二十一章),刘娟(第二十三、二十四章),余干龙(第二十七、二十八章)。

在编写本书过程中参阅了相关的专业书籍和资料，在此对这些作者致以深切的谢意。另外，还要特别感谢华东师范大学邹为诚教授为本书提出宝贵意见。

由于编者水平有限，书中不足之处在所难免，敬请广大读者批评、指正。

编者

2022 年 3 月

本书勘误及资源更新

目 录

第一章 名词 ·· 1
一、名词的分类 ·· 1
二、名词的数 ··· 2
三、名词的用法 ·· 6
四、名词的性 ··· 7
五、名词所有格 ·· 8
巩固练习 ·· 9

第二章 冠词 ·· 13
一、不定冠词 ··· 13
二、定冠词 ·· 15
三、零冠词 ·· 16
巩固练习 ·· 18

第三章 代词 ·· 21
一、人称代词 ··· 21
二、物主代词 ··· 23
三、反身代词 ··· 24
四、指示代词 ··· 25
五、不定代词 ··· 26
六、相互代词 ··· 31
七、疑问代词 ··· 32
巩固练习 ·· 32

第四章 数词 ·· 36
一、数词的构成和用法 ··· 36
二、数词的功能 ·· 38
三、常用数的表示法 ·· 39
巩固练习 ·· 42

第五章 形容词和副词 ·· 45
一、形容词 ·· 45
二、副词 ··· 49
三、形容词和副词的形式 ·· 52

巩固练习 ··· 55

第六章　介词 ··· 59
　　一、介词的分类 ··· 59
　　二、介词短语的构成及其句法功能 ··· 60
　　三、介词与其他词类的搭配 ··· 61
　　四、介词的省略 ··· 61
　　五、常用介词 ·· 62
　　六、常考介词 ·· 65
　　巩固练习 ··· 67

第七章　连词 ··· 70
　　一、并列连词 ·· 70
　　二、从属连词 ·· 72
　　三、部分连词的用法比较 ·· 74
　　巩固练习 ··· 75

第八章　动词概说 ··· 78
　　一、动词的分类 ··· 78
　　二、动词的变化形式 ·· 79
　　三、动词的限定形式和非限定形式 ··· 79
　　四、实义动词 ·· 80
　　五、连系动词 ·· 81
　　六、短语动词 ·· 82
　　巩固练习 ··· 84

第九章　动词的时和体 ··· 87
　　一、一般现在时 ··· 88
　　二、一般过去时 ··· 89
　　三、现在进行体 ··· 90
　　四、过去进行体 ··· 91
　　五、现在完成体 ··· 93
　　六、过去完成体 ··· 95
　　七、现在完成进行体 ·· 96
　　八、过去完成进行体 ·· 97
　　九、将来时间表示法 ·· 97
　　十、时态的呼应 ··· 100
　　巩固练习 ··· 101

第十章　被动语态 ··· 105
　　一、被动语态的各种时态形式 ·· 105
　　二、被动语态的用法 ·· 106
　　三、主动语态变被动语态 ·· 107

四、主动形式表示被动意义 ·································· 107
　　五、不可用被动语态的情况 ·································· 108
　　巩固练习 ·· 108

第十一章　助动词和情态动词 ································ 112
　　一、助动词 ·· 112
　　二、情态动词 ·· 114
　　三、情态动词+have done 的用法 ························· 121
　　四、情态动词+be doing 的用法 ···························· 122
　　五、情态动词+have been doing 的用法 ·············· 122
　　巩固练习 ·· 123

第十二章　动词不定式 ·· 127
　　一、动词不定式的特征 ··· 127
　　二、不定式的时式与语态 ····································· 128
　　三、不定式的句法功能 ··· 129
　　四、不定式的特殊用法 ··· 132
　　巩固练习 ·· 133

第十三章　动名词 ·· 136
　　一、动名词的时式和语态 ····································· 136
　　二、动名词的基本用法 ··· 138
　　三、动名词和现在分词的区别 ····························· 138
　　四、动名词和不定式的区别 ································· 139
　　巩固练习 ·· 140

第十四章　分词 ·· 143
　　一、现在分词 ·· 143
　　二、过去分词 ·· 148
　　三、分词的独立结构 ··· 150
　　四、现在分词和过去分词的区别 ·························· 151
　　五、现在分词和动名词的区别 ····························· 151
　　巩固练习 ·· 152

第十五章　虚拟语气 ·· 155
　　一、语气的分类 ·· 155
　　二、虚拟语气在条件状语从句中的应用 ············· 156
　　三、虚拟语气的另一种表达形式——(should)+动词原形 ·· 158
　　四、虚拟语气在其他结构中的使用 ····················· 159
　　巩固练习 ·· 161

第十六章　构词法 ·· 164
　　一、合成法 ·· 164
　　二、派生法 ·· 165

三、转化法 ··· 172
　　四、其他构词法 ·· 172

第十七章　句子 ·· 174
　　一、句子的成分 ·· 174
　　二、句子的种类 ·· 179
　　三、简单句的基本句型 ··· 186
　　巩固练习 ·· 187

第十八章　名词性从句 ··· 191
　　一、引导名词性从句的关联词 ····································· 192
　　二、名词性从句的种类 ··· 194
　　三、名词性从句注意事项 ··· 199
　　巩固练习 ·· 200

第十九章　直接引语和间接引语 ······································ 203
　　一、直接引语和间接引语的概念 ································· 203
　　二、直接引语和间接引语的转换 ································· 204
　　巩固练习 ·· 208

第二十章　定语从句 ··· 211
　　一、限制性定语从句与非限制性定语从句的区别 ······· 211
　　二、关系代词 ··· 212
　　三、关系副词 ··· 217
　　四、关系词的省略 ··· 218
　　五、关系词的选择 ··· 219
　　巩固练习 ·· 219

第二十一章　状语从句 ··· 222
　　一、时间状语从句 ··· 222
　　二、地点状语从句 ··· 226
　　三、原因状语从句 ··· 227
　　四、条件状语从句 ··· 228
　　五、方式状语从句 ··· 229
　　六、让步状语从句 ··· 230
　　七、目的状语从句 ··· 232
　　八、结果状语从句 ··· 233
　　九、比较状语从句 ··· 234
　　十、状语从句中的省略 ··· 235
　　巩固练习 ·· 236

第二十二章　一致关系 ··· 239
　　一、主语和谓语的一致 ··· 239
　　二、代词和名词的一致 ··· 245

三、平行结构中成分的一致 ·· 245
　　四、句子主语与状语逻辑主语的一致 ·· 245
　　巩固练习 ··· 246

第二十三章　附加疑问句 ··· 249
　　一、附加疑问句的结构 ·· 249
　　二、附加疑问部分的主语 ·· 249
　　三、附加疑问部分的动词 ·· 251
　　四、其他有关问题 ·· 253
　　巩固练习 ··· 253

第二十四章　there be 句型 ·· 256
　　一、there be 句型中的谓语形式 ··· 256
　　二、there be 句型的非限定形式 ··· 258
　　三、there be 句型中的附加部分 ··· 258
　　四、there be 句型的惯用结构 ··· 259
　　五、there be 句型其他注意事项 ··· 259
　　巩固练习 ··· 260

第二十五章　倒装与强调 ··· 262
　　一、倒装结构 ·· 262
　　二、强调结构 ·· 268
　　巩固练习 ··· 272

第二十六章　独立结构 ··· 276
　　一、独立结构的形式 ·· 276
　　二、独立结构的句法功能 ·· 278
　　巩固练习 ··· 279

第二十七章　as 的用法 ·· 282
　　一、as 用作副词 ··· 282
　　二、as 用作介词 ··· 282
　　三、as 用作关系代词 ··· 283
　　四、as 用作连词 ··· 284
　　五、含有 as 的习惯用语 ·· 285
　　巩固练习 ··· 285

第二十八章　否定结构 ··· 288
　　一、否定词 not 的位置和用法 ··· 288
　　二、否定的方式 ·· 289
　　三、肯定形式表示否定意义 ·· 291
　　四、否定形式表示肯定意义 ·· 293
　　五、容易混淆的否定结构 ·· 294
　　巩固练习 ··· 295

第二十九章　标点符号与分隔现象 ·································· 299
　一、标点符号 ··· 299
　二、分隔现象 ··· 305
　巩固练习 ··· 307
参考文献 ··· 309

第一章 01

名　　词

热身训练： 下列句子各有一处错误,请指出并改正。

❶ Last winter when I went there again, they had a big separate house to raise dozens of chicken.
❷ Besides, they often get some useful informations from the Internet.
❸ My uncle tells me that the key to his success is honest.
❹ The teenage year from 13 to 19 were the most difficult time for me.
❺ Mom has a full-time job, but she has to do most of the houseworks.
❻ When I was a young children, my father created a regular practice I remember well years later.
❼ The airs we breathe in is getting dirtier and dirtier.
❽ But one and a half year later, I now think English fun to learn.
❾ Thank to her help, I made great progress in my study.
❿ Mom, I know I have never expressed my thank to you before.
⓫ Tom was having much troubles getting up in the morning.
⓬ He agreed to read my story and give me some advices on how to write like a real writer.
⓭ In one test I got only 36 percent of the answer correct.
⓮ I looked at his other hands.
⓯ Your knowledges of Greece can help the whole class.

名词是表示人、事物以及抽象概念等名称的词。

一、名词的分类

根据名词的可数性,名词可分为可数名词和不可数名词两大类;根据词汇意义,名词可分为专有名词和普通名词。普通名词又可以分为个体名词、集体名词、物质名词、抽象名词。其中前两者属于可数名词,后两者属于不可数名词。名词的分类如表1-1所示。

表1-1　名词的分类

类　　别	意　　义	例　　词
专有名词	指个人、国家、地方、机构、组织等所专有的名称	Brown、China、Shanghai、the Great Wall

续表

类 别		意 义	例 词
普通名词	可数名词	个体名词 表示某一类人或物的个体	farmer、book、city、teacher
		集体名词 表示一群人或一类物的集合体	crowd、family、class、team
	不可数名词	物质名词 表示制作实物的材料的名词	water、air、cotton、iron、wood、wool
		抽象名词 表示品质、行为、状态、感情或其他抽象概念	spirit、courage、value、strength、love、beauty

1. 普通名词与专有名词

普通名词可以是一类人或事物所共有的名称，也可以表示一个抽象概念，如 teacher、farmer、farming 等。专有名词是个人、地方、国家、机构、组织等专有的名称，如 Beijing、Tian'anmen 等，其首字母一般要大写。例如：

She is a surgeon. 她是一名外科医生。

Every year the Great Wall attracts tourists from all over the world. 每年，长城吸引着来自世界各地的游客。

China is a country with her amicable and respectable people. 中国有可亲可敬的人民。

2. 个体名词与集体名词

个体名词表示单个的人或事物，如 student、chair 等；集体名词表示由若干个体组成的集合体，如 police、furniture、crowd 等。例如：

It's said that the essay contains a number of factual errors. 据说文章中有一些与事实不符的错误。

Try and push your way through the crowd. 试着从人群中挤过去。

3. 物质名词与抽象名词

物质名词是表示制作实物的材料的名词，一般是无法分为个体的，如 iron、copper、glass、wood、wool、cotton 等；抽象名词是表示动作、状态、情感或品质等抽象概念的名词，如 imagination、sorrow、aspiration 等。例如：

Wool is on the sheep. 羊毛出在羊身上。

To accomplish our great mission, we must always remain true to our original aspiration. 不忘初心，方得始终。（为了完成我们伟大的使命，我们必须始终忠于我们最初的愿望。）

Greater public involvement in winter sports also contributes to the Olympic Movement. 让更多人参与到冰雪运动中来，这也是奥林匹克运动的题中之义。

4. 可数名词与不可数名词

有些名词，如个体名词，可以用数目来计算，称为可数名词，如 book、child 等；有些名词，如物质名词和抽象名词，一般无法用数目来计算，称为不可数名词，如 information、air 等。

二、名词的数

（一）名词复数的构成

可数名词有单数和复数两种形式。可数名词复数的构成有规则和不规则两种情况。

1. 规则变化

（1）绝大多数名词的复数形式是在单数形式后加 s，如：sister—sisters；bag—bags；student—students 等。

词尾 s 在清辅音后读/s/，在浊辅音和元音后读/z/。以 ce、se、ge 结尾的名词加 s 后，-es 读作/iz/。

（2）以字母 s、x、ch、sh 结尾的名词在其后加 es，如：bus—buses；box—boxes；church—churches；dish—dishes 等。

注：① 词尾 es 读作/iz/。
② 以 ch 结尾的名词，多数加 es。但如果 ch 发/k/音时，其复数只加 s，如：stomach—stomachs；epoch—epochs（时期，时代）等。

（3）以辅音字母+y 结尾的名词，需把 y 变为 i，再加 es，词尾 ies 读作/iz/，如：ability—abilities；party—parties；family—families；university—universities 等。

注：以 y 结尾的专有名词，变为复数时，直接加 s。例如：the little Marys（小玛丽们）、the Henrys（亨利一家，亨利夫妇）等。

（4）以 f 或 fe 结尾的名词，一般把 f 或 fe 变成 v，再加 es，如：wolf—wolves；shelf—shelves；leaf—leaves；thief—thieves 等。

注：① 词尾 ves 读作/vz/。
② 以下以 f 或 fe 结尾的名词变为复数时，直接加 s，如：chief—chiefs；gulf—gulfs；cliff—cliffs；belief—beliefs；serf—serfs（农奴）；strife—strifes（争斗）；safe—safes；roof—roofs；proof—proofs（证明）等。
③ 有少数几个词，上述两种变法均可，如：handkerchief—handkerchiefs/handkerchieves；scarf—scarfs/scarvesk；hoof—hoofs/hooves（蹄）；beef—beefs/beeves；dwarf—dwarfs/dwarves；wharf—wharfs/wharves 等。

（5）以 o 结尾的名词包括以下四种情况。
① 以元音字母+o 结尾的名词，加 s，如：bamboo—bamboos；radio—radios；video—videos；zoo—zoos；studio—studios；kangaroo—kangaroos 等。
② 大部分以辅音字母+o 结尾的名词，加 s，如：casino—casinos；piano—pianos；memo—memos；photo—photos 等。
③ 少数以辅音字母+o 结尾的名词，加 es，读作/z/，如：tomato—tomatoes；potato—potatoes；hero—heroes；negro—negroes；echo—echoes 等。
④ 少数以 o 结尾的名词，加 s 或 es 均可，如：buffalo—buffaloes/buffalos；motto—mottoes/mottos（箴言）；volcano—volcanoes/volcanos（火山）；tornado—tornadoes/tornados（龙卷风）；mosquito—mosquitos/mosquitoes（蚊子）等。

（6）由字母、数字构成复数时，在其后加 's 或 s。例如：
There are three 3's/3s in 333. 在数字 333 中，有 3 个 3。
There are two t's/ts in the word "student". 在单词 student 中有两个 t。

（7）缩略词后一般加 s。例如：
Two Pros visited our school last week. 上周有两位教授参观了我们学校。

（8）表示年代或年龄几十多岁时，常用复数形式，一般在其后加 s 或 's。例如：

In the 1980s, ten thousand yuan households were people with a lot of money. 在 20 世纪 80 年代，万元户是指很有钱的人。

He became a famous entrepreneur in his twenties. 他二十多岁时就成为著名的企业家。

2. 不规则变化

（1）变内部元音字母，如：man—men；woman—women；foot—feet；tooth—teeth；goose—geese 等。

（2）变词尾，如：child—children；ox—oxen；mouse—mice 等。

（3）单复数同形，如：species、series、means、cattle、sheep、Chinese、Japanese、Lebanese 等。

（4）只有复数形式的名词，如：goods、clothes、trousers、glasses、shorts、scissors、scales、compasses（圆规）等。

> 注：① 以上名词要表示数量时，需要加上相应的单位名词。例如：a pair of glasses、a suit of clothes、two pairs of scissors 等。
> ② hair、fruit 等词通常用单数表示总称。但表示"若干根头发""若干种水果"时，则用复数。例如：a few white hairs、several juicy fruits 等。

（5）一些外来名词的复数形式。例如：bacterium—bacteria；penny—pennies/pence；medium—media；datum—data；phenomenon—phenomena 等。

（二）复合名词的单复数

1. 复合名词的构成

复合名词由单个名词加一个或一个以上的名词或其他词类的词组成。复合名词的表达形式有三种。

（1）两部分连写，如：raincoat、bookshop、eyesight、sunlight 等。

（2）两部分用连词符连接，如：coal-mine、shoe-maker 等。

（3）两部分分开写，如：bus stop、post office、man student、sports meeting 等。

2. 复合名词的复数

（1）以不可数名词结尾的复合名词无复数形式，如：homework、newspaper 等。

（2）以 man 或 woman 为前缀的名词变复数时，前后两个名词都变成复数，如：woman doctor—women doctors；man teacher—men teachers 等。

（3）以两个名词构成的复合名词（前面的名词为 man 或 woman 除外），一般将主体词变复数，如：boy friend(s)、paper bag(s)、mother(s)-in-law、looker(s)-on、fortune-teller(s) 等。

（4）没有主体词的复合名词，在词尾加 s，如：grown-up(s)、hang-up(s)（障碍）、get-together(s)（聚会）、good-for-nothing(s)（无用的人）等。

（三）集体名词单复数

集体名词从形式上有单数和复数两种。

（1）形式上虽是单数，意义上却是复数，如：people、cattle、police 等，这些词用作主语时，谓语动词要用复数。例如：

The police are investigating the matter. 警察正在调查这件事。

（2）形式上虽是单数，意义上却既可以是单数也可以是复数，如：family、team、class、audience 等集体名词，若视为整体，表示单数意义；若考虑其个体成员，表示复数意义。例如：

His family is large. 他的家庭是个大家庭。

Her family all like reading. 她的家人都喜欢阅读。

This delegation consists of 10 persons. 这个代表团由 10 个人组成。

This team are playing basketball. 这支球队的人正在打篮球。

（3）形式为复数，意义也为复数，如：goods、clothes 等，作主语时谓语动词用复数。例如：

These goods are about to expire. 这些商品快要过期了。

It is getting warmer, so the thick clothes are put away. 天气暖和，厚衣服收起来了。

Baby clothes are cotton goods. 婴儿的衣服都是棉织品。

（4）形式上为单数，意义上也为单数，如 luggage、furniture、poetry 等作主语时谓语动词用单数。例如：

That piece of luggage is mine. 那件行李是我的。

My furniture is made of solid wood. 我的家具是实木的。

（四）物质名词的数

物质名词一般为不可数名词，视为单数。但在下列情况下，物质名词也可用作可数名词。

（1）当物质名词表示该物质的不同种类时，可用作复数形式。例如：

His factory produces iron. 他的工厂生产铁。（物质名词，不可数）

Various irons are used for different purposes. 不同的铁有不同的用途。（表示种类，可数）

（2）当物质名词转化为具体的个体名词时，可用作复数形式。例如：

This bridge is made of stone. 这座桥是用石头造的。（物质名词，不可数）

Field threw a stone at the dog. 弗尔德朝那条狗扔了一块石头。（个体名词，可数）

（3）当物质名词表示份数时，可用作复数形式。例如：

Brazil is rich in coffee. 巴西盛产咖啡。（物质名词，不可数）

Two coffees, please. 请来两杯咖啡。（表示份数）

（4）表示数量巨大或范围较广时，可用作复数形式。如：

Water is made up of hydrogen and oxygen. 水是由氢和氧构成的。（物质名词，不可数）

The waters of the lake flow out over a large waterfall. 这个湖的水流出去之后形成了一个大瀑布。（waters 表示范围）

（五）抽象名词的数

（1）抽象名词是表示行为、状态、品质、情感等非实物的名词。一般是不可数，没有复数形式，如：responsibility、peace、warmth、equality、honesty、information、knowledge、patience 等。

（2）有些抽象名词可具体化，用作可数名词，有复数形式，词义改变了。这类词一般分为三类。

① 表示情感、情绪的词。例如：

I take pride in my homeland, China. 我为我的祖国——中国，感到骄傲。

Lily is a pride to her parents. 莉莉是父母的骄傲。

② 含有"种类"之意，常与动词连用构成短语，名词前有形容词修饰或名词后有短语修饰。如 a good education、a knowledge of English。例如：

It is very important for us to have a good knowledge of computer. 我们掌握计算机技术是非常重要的。

A Yellow River well harnessed is a millennia-long aspiration of the Chinese people. 黄河安澜是中华儿女的千年期盼。

③ 担当同源宾语的短语，通常名词表示具体化意义。例如：

Last night I dreamed a strange dream. 昨天晚上我做了个奇怪的梦。

He lives a simple life. 他过着简单的生活。

（六）不可数名词的计数问题

不可数名词是指表示不可以计数的事物的名词。不可数名词一般无单复数之分，不能与 a、an 直接连用。若要表示数量，需要加适当的单位名词或单位名词词组，如用"of"词组来表示其数的变化。例如：

Air here is very fresh. 这儿空气很新鲜。

I have eaten two pieces of bread. 我已经吃了两块面包。

常见的不可数名词有 water、beer、flour、coffee、work、money、time、news、soap、string、food 等。

不可数名词一般没有复数形式，在表示其数量时，常借助"单位词"。英语的单位词大体有以下几类。

（1）一般性的单位词有 piece、bit、article 等，可与大量的不可数名词连用。例如：a piece of advice、a bit of information、an article of luggage 等。

（2）表示形状的单位词有 bar、ball、block、loaf 等。例如：a loaf of bread、a block of ice、a ball of string 等。

（3）表示容器、度量的单位词有 bottle、glass、bag、spoonful、gallon 等。例如：a spoonful of salt、a bottle of ink、a gallon of wine 等。

（4）表示动态的单位词有 fit、burst、flash 等。例如：a fit of anger、a burst of applause、a flash of lightening 等。

三、名词的用法

名词在句子中可用作主语、宾语、补足语、表语、同位语、呼语、状语、定语等。

（1）作主语。例如：

Chinese people live on rice. 中国人以大米作为主食。

The struggle fully demonstrates the Chinese people's self-confidence, self-reliance and self-improvement. 斗争充分展现中国人的自信、自立、自强。

（2）作宾语。例如：

Americans like eating hamburgers. 美国人喜欢吃汉堡包。

Professor Wang made a wonderful speech yesterday. 王教授昨天做了一场精彩的演讲。

（3）作补足语（分为主语补足语和宾语补足语）。例如：

Lily is called a campus belle. 丽丽被称为校花。

We elected him our monitor. 我们推选他做我们的班长。
（4）作表语。例如：
That is a puzzle to me. 那个对我来讲是一个难题。
My niece became a nurse last year. 去年我外甥女成为一名护士了。
（5）作同位语。例如：
Bird flu, a new disease has no effective cure. 禽流感是一种新的疾病,没有特效疗法。
John, our new teacher, comes from USA. 约翰,我们的新老师,来自美国。
（6）作呼语。例如：
I'm coming to answer the door, Mum. 妈妈,我去开门。
（7）作状语。例如：
Please come this way. 请这边走。
Wait a minute, please! 请稍等。
（8）作定语。在通常情况下,名词作定语要用单数形式。例如：
All difficulties are all paper tigers. 一切困难都是纸老虎。
They are to send a trade delegation to Paris. 他们将派一个贸易代表团去巴黎。

四、名词的性

1. 名词的性的分类

英语名词的性在形式上没有特征和变化,主要由词义来区别。英语名词的性共分为四类。
（1）表示男性或雄性动物的名词,属于阳性。例如：boy、brother、cock、lion 等。
（2）表示女性或雌性动物的名词,属于阴性。例如：girl、sister、hen、lioness 等。
（3）可以表示两性的名词。例如：cook、scientist、doctor、guest 等。
（4）表示无生命事物的名词属于中性(neutral gender)。例如：post、office、sand、school 等。

2. 代词与名词的性的一致

由于名词表示的概念有了性的区别,所以在使用人称代词、物主代词、反身代词和关系代词时,就必须注意代词与性的一致。一般说来,阳性名词用 he 和 who 指代；阴性名词用 she 和 who 指；通性名词视具体情况来决定采用阳性或阴性的代词；而中性名词则用 it 和 which 指代。
（1）表示人的名词根据自然性别分阴阳性。例如：father—mother; son—daughter; gentleman—lady; nephew—niece; king—queen 等。
（2）在阳性名词前、后,加前、后缀,组成阴性名词。例如：poet—poetess; landlord—landlady; lad—lass; male—female; god—goddess; waiter—waitress; emperor—empress; master—mistress; hero—heroine; prince—princess; actor—actress; salesman—saleswoman 等。
（3）有些普通名词在其前面加 man、woman、boy、girl、male、female 等词用于区别阴阳性。例如：boy student、girl student、male baby、female baby、man servant、woman servant 等。
（4）某些动物根据其自然性别分为阴阳性,一般可用 it 指代,必要时用 he 或 she 指代。例如：bull—cow; cock—hen; stallion—mare; gander—goose 等。
（5）当不强调性别,泛指某生物时,多用阳性名词。例如：
Man proposes, god disposes. 谋事在人,成事在天。
（6）在拟人化的修辞手法里,往往用 she(her)而不是用 it(its)来指代前面的名词。例如：

Our mother land is famous for her long history. 我们的祖国以其悠久的历史而闻名。

五、名词所有格

名词所有格表示名词与名词之间的所属关系。它有"名词+'s""of+名词""双重所有格"三种不同的结构。

(一)"名词+'s"结构

"名词+'s"结构多用来表示有生命东西的所有格。

1."名词+'s"所有格的构成

(1) 一般来说,在单数名词和不以 s 结尾的复数名词词尾加"'s"。例如:
She is Lucy's friend. 她是露西的朋友。
Children's Day is on June 1st. 6月1日是儿童节。
The struggle demonstrates the Chinese nation's ambition, courage and integrity. 斗争彰显中华民族的志气、底气、骨气。

(2) 以 s 结尾的复数名词,在其后加"'";复合名词,则在最后的词的词尾加"'s"。例如:
On Teachers' Day I visited my primary school teacher. 教师节那天我拜访了我小学老师。
My brother-in-law's father is a doctor. 我姐夫的父亲是医生。
a day or two's stay. 一两天的逗留

(3) 表示店铺、某人的家、私人开的诊所、餐馆等所有格后的名词可省略,如:at Bill's(在比尔的家)、at the dentist's(在牙医诊所)等。

(4) 名词后有同位语时,所有格加在同位语后。例如:
My little daughter, YiYi's hair is very thick. 我小女儿依依的头发非常浓密。

> 注:表示两人共有的东西,在后面一个名词上加's;表示各自拥有的东西,需在各名词后分别加's。例如:
> She is Lucy and Lily's grandmother. 她是露西和莉莉的奶奶。(奶奶是同一人)
> Jack's grandmother and John's grandmother are both at the age of 85. 杰克的奶奶和约翰的奶奶都是85岁。

2."名词+'s"所有格的用法

(1) 表示所属关系,主要用于有生命的东西的名词词尾。如:the student's requirement(学生的要求),man's future(人类的未来),the horse's stable(马厩),Li Ping's new job(李萍的新工作)。

(2) 表示类别。如:a man's work(男人干的活),children's magazine(儿童杂志),a teacher's book(教师用书),a girl's school(女子学校),a doctor's degree(博士学位)。

(3) 表示时间、距离、国家、团体、度量、数量、价值等无生命名词后,也常用名词's所有格形式。如:four years' study(四年的学习),3 dollars' worth of meat(3 美元的肉),today's newspaper(今天的报纸),five minutes' walk(5 分钟的步行),China's mother river(中国的母亲河),the committee's decision(委员会的决定)。

应避免两个"'s"结构连用,如"他是我哥哥朋友的父亲",不能表述为 He is my brother's friend's father. 最好表述为 He is the father of my brother's friend。

英语中有一些含"'s"的固定短语,如:a stone's throw(一箭之遥)、out of harm's way(在安全的地方)、a bird's eye view(鸟瞰)、at death's door(〈生命〉危在旦夕)、a cat's paw(被人利用的人)、at one's wit's end(黔驴技穷)、at a snail's pace(缓慢地)、to one's heart's content(心满意足)、lead a dog's life(过着牛马不如的生活)、any body's guess(拿不准的事)、a wolf in sheep's clothing(披着羊皮的狼)等。

(二)"of+名词"所有格结构

"of+名词"所有格结构,多用于无生命和抽象概念的名词。of+名词构成所有格,修饰前面的名词。用于表示这两个名词之间的关系:所属关系、主谓关系、动宾关系、同位关系等。例如:

I can't remember the cover of the book. 我不记得那本书的封面。

We are waiting for the arrival of the next bus. 我们正在等下一班车的到来。

Loss of health is worse than loss of wealth. 没有健康比没有财富更糟糕。

The city of Beijing is the capital of China. 北京是中国的首都。

(三)双重所有格

1. 双重所有格的定义

由名词加"'s"和of结构(或of+名词性物主代词)构成的所有格称为双重所有格。双重所有格含有全体中的一部分的意思。例如:

This is a picture of my mother's. 这是我妈妈众多照片中的一张。

Liu Ling is a classmate of mine. 刘玲是我同班同学中的一个。

2. 双重所有格的用法

(1) of 短语所修饰的那个名词,通常不能带定冠词,但可带 a(n)、two、any、some、several、few、another、no、such、each、every 或 his、that、these、those 之类的修饰语。可以说:A toy of my daughter's costs me 100 yuan.(我女儿的一个玩具花了我一百元。)但不能表述为 The toy of my daughter's costs me 100 yuan.

(2) of 短语所修饰的名词不能是专有名词或具有独一无二性质的名词。例如:不能说:Lucy of Mr. Green's 或 a father of Tom;但可以说:Mr. Green's Lucy 和 Tom's father。

(3) of 短语后面的名词必须是指人的名词。例如:

He is a student of my father's. (√)

These are windows of the room's. (×)应改成 These are windows of the room.

巩 固 练 习

Complete the following sentences by choosing the items marked A,B,C,or D.

1. She is young for the job, but on the other _____ , she is well trained.
   A. way　　　　　B. situation　　　　C. chance　　　　D. hand

2. —I'd like _____ information about the management of your hotel, please.
   —Well, you could have _____ word with the manager. He might be helpful.
   A. some; a　　　B. an; some　　　　C. some; some　　D. an; a

3. He told me he had been offered a very well-paid _____.
   A. business   B. service   C. work   D. position
4. Each player must obey _____, who is the leader of the team.
   A. captain   B. a captain   C. the captain   D. captains
5. It was _____ that he had to ask for help.
   A. such big a work   B. a so big job
   C. a so big work   D. such a big job
6. He dropped the _____ and broke it.
   A. cup of coffee   B. coffee's cup
   C. cup for coffee   D. coffee cup
7. What _____! Where did you get them?
   A. big fish   B. a big fish   C. a piece of big fish   D. big a fish
8. He left _____ with my secretary that he would call again in the afternoon. He said he would keep _____.
   A. words; his words   B. word; his word
   C. word; word   D. the word; his words
9. The beach is a _____ throw.
   A. stone   B. stones   C. stones'   D. stone's
10. The new law will come into _____ on the day it is passed.
    A. effect   B. use   C. service   D. existence
11. We held a party in _____ of our Australian teacher, Megi.
    A. prize   B. honor   C. praise   D. pride
12. —Tom, will you boys play soldiers outside? There's not enough _____ for you boys here.
    —But we can play in the next _____, can't we?
    A. places; place   B. room; room   C. rooms; space   D. house; rooms
13. Last week I called at my _____.
    A. aunt   B. aunts   C. aunt's   D. aunts'
14. —Mum, I'm going to visit my aunt. What about a week?
    —A week is too long. Try to be back in a _____ of days.
    A. number   B. dozen   C. few   D. couple
15. Mrs. Green tried hard to find a job but she had no _____.
    A. luck   B. time   C. hope   D. chance
16. His daughter is always shy in _____ and she never dares to make a speech to _____.
    A. the public; the public   B. public; the public
    C. the public; public   D. public; public
17. Fast-food restaurants are _____ to us all.
    A. of many helps   B. a great help
    C. great helps   D. much help

18. These young people are now making an active _____ to beautify（美化）our city.
    A. part   B. effort   C. decision   D. plan
19. —What you like may not be what I like.
    —Yes, one man's meal is another man's _____.
    A. poison   B. medicine   C. meal   D. food
20. He said that two _____ would come to our school the next day.
    A. woman scientist   B. women scientist
    C. woman scientists   D. women scientists
21. My _____ all _____ hard for the people.
    A. family; work B. family; works   C. families; work   D. families; works
22. Dr. Jones ordered _____ for the laboratory.
    A. two equipments   B. two pieces of equipments
    C. two pieces of equipment   D. two equipment pieces
23. —Where have you been? —I've been to _____.
    A. the Turners   B. the Turner's   C. Mr. Turners'   D. the Turners'
24. Many children have to see the films for _____.
    A. grown-up   B. growns-up   C. grown-ups   D. growns-ups
25. I told about some of the terrible _____ I had had in the war.
    A. experience   B. experiences   C. experiencing   D. experienced things
26. The table is only _____ high.
    A. two-foot   B. two foot   C. two-feet   D. two feet
27. The employer will bear 80% medical _____ for the employee during the employment period.
    A. discount   B. fare   C. fee   D. fine
28. That's _____.
    A. James and Charles father   B. James and Charles's father
    C. James's and Charles's father D. James's and Charles father
29. _____ is published daily.
    A. *Time*   B. *Times*   C. *The Time*   D. *The Times*
30. There are many _____ in big _____.
    A. ladies driver; citys   B. lady drivers; cities
    C. ladies drivers; cities   D. ladies driver; city
31. The shirt isn't mine. It's _____.
    A. Mrs Smith   B. Mrs' Smith   C. Mrs Smiths'   D. Mrs Smith's
32. Mr Smith has two _____, both of whom are teachers in a school.
    A. brothers-in-law B. brother-in-laws C. brothers-in-laws D. brothers-in law
33. —How many _____ does a cow have?
    —Four.
    A. stomaches   B. stomach   C. stomachs   D. stomachies

34. Some _____ visited our school last Wednesday.
    A. German   B. Germen   C. Germans   D. Germens
35. The _____ of the building are covered with lots of _____.
    A. roofs; leaves   B. rooves; leafs   C. roof; leaf   D. roofs; leafs
36. When the farmer returned home he found three _____ missing.
    A. sheeps   B. sheepes   C. sheep   D. sheepies
37. That was a fifty _____ engine.
    A. horse power   B. horses power   C. horse powers   D. horses powers
38. My father often gives me _____.
    A. many advice   B. much advice   C. a lot of advices D. a few advice
39. Mary broke a _____ while she was washing up.
    A. tea cup   B. a cup of tea   C. tea's cup   D. cup tea
40. How far away is it from here to your school? It's about _____.
    A. half an hour's drive   B. half hours drive
    C. half an hour drives   D. half an hour drive

第二章

冠 词

热身训练： 下列句子各有一处错误，请指出并改正。

① During my last winter holiday, I went to countryside with my father to visit my grandparents.
② As the kid, I loved to watch cartoons, but no matter how many times I asked to watch them, my parents would not let me.
③ I still remember how hard first day was.
④ It takes them about a hour and a half to go to work every day.
⑤ My uncle says that he never dreams of becoming rich in the short period of time.
⑥ At the first, I thought I knew everything and could make decisions by myself.
⑦ Every time he arrived home at end of the day, we'd greet him at the door. He would ask who we were.
⑧ I asked Mom to stay in the sitting room and I cooked in kitchen.
⑨ I was always interested to see the drivers in hurry in the morning.
⑩ As result, the plants are growing everywhere.
⑪ There are all kinds of the flowers and trees around the classroom buildings.
⑫ There was Uncle Chen, gentleman living near my house, who was a very famous writer.
⑬ However, the popular teacher is at same time the one who should be strict with students.
⑭ A girl as she is, she is very fond of boxing.
⑮ I have already had the good knowledge of computer before.

冠词是位于名词前用于说明该名词含义的虚词，没有词义、数和格的变化。冠词可分为不定冠词(a, an)、定冠词(the)及零冠词三大类。不定冠词主要特点是表示"不确定"或"泛指"，用在单数可数名词前；定冠词之所以冠以"定"字，是因为它的主要特点是表示"确指"或"特指"，可用于单数名词、复数名词或不可数名词之前。

一、不定冠词

（一） a 和 an 的区别

不定冠词有 a 和 an 两个，含有"一"的意思。不定冠词 a 用在以辅音（读音）开头的单数可数名词前面,表示某类人或事物中的"一个/一种/一件"等,泛指某一类人或事物中的任意一个或首次提到的人或物;an 用在元音开头的单数可数名词前。不定冠词后,无论是字母还是数字,都应以第一个读音为依据来决定用 a 还是 an,如:a European man、a bus、an hour and a half、an honest boy 等。例如:

There is an "l" in the word "life". 单词 life 中有一个字母 l。

不定冠词修饰人时,如果这个人有多个身份,则只在第一个名词前加冠词,其他几个不再加冠词;但若指不同的人则各个名词前都需要加上冠词,如:a farmer and writer(农民兼作家)、a farmer and a writer(一个农民和一个作家)等。

(二) 不定冠词的用法

(1) 用于第一次提到的不表示特定的人或物的可数的单数名词之前。例如:

Conrad passed himself off as a senior psychologist. 康拉德冒充自己是一名资深心理学家。

An unknown bird has broken into my house. 一只不知名的小鸟闯进了我的家。

(2) 用在普通单数名词前,指一类人或物当中的一个。例如:

Geoffrey is a famous career adviser. 杰弗里是一位有名的职业规划师。

Students should master a foreign language. 学生应该掌握一门外语。

(3) 与时间或度量名词连用,表示"每一(个)",相当于 per。例如:

She recites 30 words a day. 她每天背诵 30 个单词。

A mile is 500 metres. 1 里等于 500 米。

(4) 常用在"of+a(an)+名词"结构中,表示"同一"。例如:

Things of a kind come together; people of a mind fall into the same group. 物以类聚,人以群分。

The cups are all of a size. 这些杯子都一样大小。

(5) 表示人或事物的类型,泛指,相当于 any。例如:

A person has two eyes. 人有两只眼睛。

A child needs love. 孩子需要爱。

(6) 用在某些专有名词前,可表示借喻,译为"像……那样的人或物"。例如:

I wish to become an Einstein. 我期望成为爱因斯坦那样的科学家。

He bought his daughter a Golf. 他给他的女儿买了辆高尔夫轿车。

(7) 用于某些物质名词和抽象名词前,此时已转化为可数名词。例如:

The English evening is a great success. 英语晚会获得了巨大的成功。

A soda, please. 请给我来杯苏打水。

The complete reunification of our motherland is an aspiration shared by people on both sides of the Taiwan Strait. 实现祖国的完全统一,是两岸同胞的共同心愿。

(8) 用于序数词前,表示"又一""再一",表示序数的递增。例如:

Please give me a third cup of tea. 请再给我来杯茶。

He has a second factory in Tuscany. 他在多斯卡纳还有一家工厂。

(9) 含不定冠词的习惯用语。一些固定短语,需用不定冠词,如:as a matter of fact、as a whole、all of a sudden、as a rule、at a loss、at a glance、for a while、have an eye for、in a hurry、in a word、make a fire、make a fortune、make a living、on a large scale、once upon a time、put an end to、

take a pride in、take an interest in、to a degree、turn a deaf ear to、with a view to 等。

二、定冠词

定冠词 the 用于特指或类指。

（一）特指用法

定冠词通常表示某个或某些特定的人或事物。

（1）用在世界上独一无二的事物的名词前，如：the moon、the sun、the sky、the earth、the world、the universe、the solar system（太阳系）、the Galaxy（银河系）等。

（2）特指说话双方都明白的人或物。例如：
Where is the teacher? 老师在哪儿？
Excuse me, could you please tell me where the post office is? 打扰了,你能告诉我邮局在哪里吗?

（3）特指上文提到过的人或事。例如：
He is studying in a room and the room is very small. 他在房间里学习,这房间非常小。
My brother has a daughter. The daughter is an actuary. 我哥哥有个女儿。她是一名精算师。

（4）用在表示山川、湖泊、海洋、海峡、群岛等名词之前，如：the West Lake、the Pacific Ocean、the Atlantic Ocean、the Yellow River、the Yangtze River、the Thames、the Suez(Canal)、the Dead Sea、the English Channel、the Taishan Mountains、the Bay of Bengal、the Sahara 等。

（5）用在形容词、副词最高级和序数词前面。例如：
He runs (the) fastest in his class. 他在班上跑得最快。
He is the first person who comes to school. 他第一个到达学校。

（6）用在限制性定语修饰的名词前,表示特指。例如：
This is the factory where I worked two years ago. 这是我两年前工作过的工厂。
The documents on the desk are Bertha's. 桌子上的文件是伯莎的。

（7）用在表示方向、方位的名词前时,分为以下两种情况。
① 在介词短语中,方向、方位名词前要用定冠词。例如：
The sun rises in the east. 太阳从东边升起。
② 指某个国家或世界的某一部分时,方位名词大写,前面要用定冠词。例如：
The North of China is colder than the South. 中国北方比南方冷。

（二）类指用法

（1）用于单数可数名词前表示一类人或物。例如：
The camel was a useful animal in the past. 过去骆驼是一种很有用的动物。
The computer has revolutionized office work. 计算机彻底改变了办公室的工作。

（2）用于某些形容词或分词前,表示一类人或事物,如：the wealthy、the strong、the weak、the sick、the old、the young、the dumb、the deaf、the dead、the rich、the poor、the wounded、the injured、the killed 等。

当它们作主语时,谓语动词用复数形式。例如：
The young are more receptive. 年轻人接受能力更强。

The beautiful always give us pleasure. 漂亮的东西总是让人们高兴。

（3）用在某些集体名词或复数名词前，表示民族、阶级、阶层等，如：the Chinese、the Europeans、the masses、the public、the audience、the intellectuals、the world、the working class、the upper class 等。

（三）其他用法

（1）用在演奏的西洋乐器名词前。例如：

My daughter enjoys playing the violin. 我女儿喜欢拉小提琴。

（2）用在姓氏的复数名词之前，表示"一家人"或"夫妇"。例如：

The Smiths like Yao Ming. 史密斯一家都喜欢姚明。

The Curies discovered radium in 1902. 居里夫妇1902年发现了镭元素。

（3）用于表示时间顺序、一天中的各段时间，如：the beginning、the middle、the end、the past、the present、the future、the following day、in the morning/afternoon 等。

（4）用于"by+the+计量单位名词"中，如：by the hour/day/week/year（按小时/日/星期/年计算）、by the pound/dozen（按磅/打计算）、by the foot/yard（按英尺/码计算）等。例如：

Meat is sold by the Jin. 肉论斤卖。

（5）用在某些由普通名词构成的国家名称、机关团体、阶级、党派、报刊书籍、历史时期和事件等专有名词前，如：the People's Republic of China、the Communist Party of China、the Forbidden City、the Summer Palace、the Red Cross、the Great Wall、the Stone Age、the Qing Dynasty、The New York Times 等。

（6）用在可数的单数名词前，指其属性、功能等抽象意义，如：from the cradle to the grave（从出生到死亡）等。例如：

Randy is fond of the bottle. 兰迪喜欢喝酒。

Camille took up the stage as a career. 卡米尔选择了演员职业。

The pen is mightier than the sword. 〈谚〉文字的力量胜过武力。（文胜于武。）

（四）习惯表达

带有定冠词的一些习惯表达，如：all the time、to tell the truth、all the year round、at the same time、at the end of、at the sight of、in the end、in the open、in the long run、on the average、on the contrary、on the spot、on the whole 等。

三、零冠词

零冠词是指那些不用冠词的情况，表示泛指或表示一般概念，主要有以下几种情况。

（1）复数名词泛指一类人或物。例如：

Masks must be worn when entering public places. 进入公共场所必须佩戴口罩。

Horses were used to carry things in the past. 过去马被用来驮东西。

（2）专有名词（人名、地名、国名、节日、星期、季节、月份等）前面。例如：

Spring follows winter. 冬去春来。

We have no classes on Sunday. 星期天我们不上课。

On July 1st, 2021, we solemnly celebrated the 100th anniversary of the founding of the Communist Party of China. 2021年7月1日,我们隆重庆祝了中国共产党成立一百周年。

National Day is on October 1st. 十月一日是国庆节。

(3) 物质名词和抽象名词表示泛指时。例如:

Some bridges are made of iron and steel. 有些桥是用钢铁造的。

Self-confidence is very important to success. 自信心对于成功是非常重要的。

(4) 名词表示人际关系或作称呼用时。例如:

What's wrong with my stomach, doctor? 医生,我的胃怎么了?

Mother bought me a present for my birthday yesterday. 妈妈昨天给我买了生日礼物。

(5) 在 as 引导的让步状语从句中。例如:

Child as he is, he can recite many poems. 虽然他是个孩子,但会背很多诗。

Manager as he is, he is unhappy. 尽管他是经理,他并不开心。

(6) 表示职位、身份、头衔的名词用作表语、补足语、同位语时。例如:

He is president of the USA. 他是美国总统。

He was appointed captain of the team. 他被任命为队长。

(7) 三餐、学科、球类和棋类运动的名称前。例如:

Mr.Ren, board chairman, ruled against the proposal. 董事长任先生否决了这项提案。

Let's have dinner, so we can talk at leisure. 咱们吃晚饭吧,边吃边谈。

They are playing chess. 他们正在下棋。

> **注:** ① 特指某餐饭时要用定冠词。例如:
> I had the first dinner with her yesterday. 昨天第一顿饭我和她一起吃的。
> ② 当表示某餐饭的名词前有形容词修饰时,常用不定冠词。例如:
> Yesterday I had a big lunch. 昨天我吃了顿丰盛的午餐。

(8) 表示语言的名词前。例如:

He speaks English very fluently. 他英语讲得很流利。

但是表示语言的名词与 language 连用时,需在该名词前加定冠词。例如:

The English language is her native language. 英语是她的母语。

(9) 在"by+交通工具或通信手段"结构中,名词前不用冠词。例如:

Traveling by plane is the most convenient for a long distance. 对于长距离,乘飞机是最便捷的。

If you know the reasons, please tell me by email. 如果你知道原因,请用电子邮件告诉我。

> **注:** 如果表示交通工具的名词前有定语,就不能用 by。例如:
> I came here on his old bike. 我是骑着他的旧自行车来这里的。

(10) 以 and 连接的"成对的人或物",如:day and night、heart and soul、husband and wife、father and son、sun and moon 等。

(11) 某些介词连接相同或相对的名词时,也不用冠词,如:face to face、little by little、side by side、step by step、from beginning to end、from door to door、from morning till night 等。

(12) 某些独立结构中的单数可数名词前。例如:

The teacher came in, book in hand. 老师手里拿着书,走进教室。

(13) 在 a kind of、a piece of、a slice of、a loaf of 等结构后的名词前。例如:

That's a new kind of game. 那是一种新游戏。

She bought a loaf of bread. 她买了一个面包。

（14）系动词 turn（成为……）后跟 traitor、informer 等名词作表语时，名词前用零冠词。例如：

That man turned traitor to his wife. 那个男人背叛了他的妻子。

He turned informer on the matter. 他成了这件事的告密者。

（15）有些名词如 man、fool、scholar 等抽象化时，相当于形容词。此时，前面用零冠词。例如：

He was not man enough to admit his mistakes. 他没有认错的勇气。

He was fool enough to make such a silly mistake. 他真傻，竟然犯如此低级的错误。

He is not scholar enough to appreciate Shakespeare. 他没有足够的学识水平去欣赏莎士比亚的作品。

（16）一些固定短语中不用冠词，如：at hand、attend school、at noon、at home and abroad、at top/full speed、by accident、by chance、catch fire、catch sight of、do harm to、for fear of、in debt、in search of、in secret、in use、kill time、lose face、out of order、out of date、take action、under repair 等。

（17）部分词前是否有冠词，会产生不同的意义。例如：

in front of 在外部的前方　　　　　in the front of 在内部的前方
in place of 代替　　　　　　　　　in the place of 在某地方
on earth 究竟；世上　　　　　　　on the earth 在地球上
out of question 没有问题　　　　　out of the question 根本不可能
in charge of 主管　　　　　　　　in the charge of 在……掌控下

巩固练习

Complete the following sentences by choosing the items marked A, B, C, or D.

1. Life is like _____ ocean; only _____ strong-willed can reach the other shore.
   A. an; the　　　B. the; a　　　C. the; /　　　D. /; a

2. I can't tell you _____ way to the Wilson's because we don't have _____ Wilson here in the village.
   A. the; a　　　B. a; /　　　C. a; the　　　D. the; /

3. The paper is due next month, and I am working seven days _____ week, often long into _____ night.
   A. a; the　　　B. the; /　　　C. a; a　　　D. /; the

4. They chose Tom to be _____ captain of the team because they knew he was _____ smart leader.
   A. a; the　　　B. the; the　　　C. the; a　　　D. a; a

5. _____ village where I was born has grown into _____ town.
   A. The; a　　　B. A; the　　　C. The; the　　　D. A; a

6. Jane's grandmother had wanted to write _____ children's book for many years, but one thing or another always got in _____ way.
   A. a; /　　　B. the; the　　　C. /; the　　　D. a; the

7. Jane is _____ European and Jack is _____ American.
   A. an; an   B. a; an   C. an; a   D. a; a

8. We will be traveling by _____ camel across the desert before we go to _____ university.
   A. /; the   B. the; /   C. /; /   D. the; a

9. _____ Europe and _____ American are separated by _____ Atlantic Ocean.
   A. /; /; the   B. the; the; the   C. /; /; /   D. the; the; /

10. When he left _____ college, he got a job as _____ reporter in a newspaper office.
    A. the; the   B. a; the   C. /; the   D. /; a

11. Throughout the entire day, there's not a minute when we're not on _____ run.
    A. /   B. a   C. the   D. to

12. _____ Suez Canal brought _____ East and _____ West closer.
    A. The; the; the   B. /; the; the   C. The; /; /   D. /; /; /

13. The policeman caught the thief by _____ arm.
    A. an   B. a   C. the   D. /

14. _____ Yellow River is _____ second longest river in our country.
    A. The; a   B. An; an   C. The; the   D. /; /

15. Many people are still in _____ habit of writing silly things in _____ public places.
    A. the; /   B. /; the   C. the; the   D. /; /

16. For a long time, they walked without saying _____ word. Jim was the first to break _____ silence.
    A. the; /   B. a; /   C. a; the   D. the; a

17. The Wilsons live in _____ A-shaped house near the coast. It is _____ 17th century cottage.
    A. the; /   B. an; the   C. /; the   D. an; a

18. _____ China of those years in the hit TV series—*The Legend of Miyue* is _____ China at war.
    A. The; /   B. The; a   C. /; a   D. /; /

19. What _____ it is to travel in _____ spaceship!
    A. a fun; the   B. a fun; a   C. fun; /   D. fun; a

20. What _____ wonderful time we had at _____ Smiths' then!
    A. a; /   B. a; the   C. /; the   D. the; the

21. We must pay special attention to the idioms of _____ English language.
    A. the   B. a   C. an   D. /

22. —How did you pay the workers?
    —As a rule, they were paid by _____.
    A. an hour   B. hours   C. a hour   D. the hour

23. _____ is hanging in the sky.
    A. New moon   B. A moon   C. The new moon   D. A new moon

24. What _____ interesting work he is doing!
    A. a   B. an   C. the   D. /

25. Einstein may be called _____ Newton of our times.
    A. a   B. the   C. /   D. an
26. It is a long time since I had _____ pleasure of seeing you.
    A. a   B. some   C. the   D. /
27. Almost all sorts of fruit are sold by _____ weight. Eggs are sold by _____ dozen.
    A. /; /   B. the; /   C. /; the   D. the; the
28. He, as _____ director of the company, attended the meeting.
    A. a   B. an   C. the   D. /
29. Lesson Twelve is _____ most difficult lesson, but it isn't _____ most difficult lesson in Book One.
    A. a; a   B. a; the   C. the; the   D. /;/
30. The cakes are delicious. I'd like to have _____ third one as _____ second one I ate was too small.
    A. The; the   B. a; the   C. the; a   D. a; a
31. On May 5th, 2005, at _____ World Table Tennis Championship, Kong Linghui and Wang Hao won the gold medal in men's with _____ score of 4 : 1.
    A. a; a   B. /; the   C. a; /   D. the; a
32. I knew _____ John Lennon, but not _____ famous one.
    A. /; a   B. a; the   C. /; the   D. the; a
33. When he left _____ college, he got a job as _____ reporter in a newspaper office.
    A. /; a   B. /; the   C. a; the   D. the; the
34. The most important thing about cotton in history is _____ part that it played in _____ Industrial Revolution.
    A. /; /   B. the; /   C. the; the   D. a; the
35. Tom owns _____ larger collection of _____ books than any other student in our class.
    A. the; /   B. a; /   C. a; the   D. /; the
36. I earn 10 dollars _____ hour as _____ supermarket cashier on Saturday.
    A. a; an   B. the; a   C. an; a   D. an; the
37. One way to understand thousands of new words is to gain _____ good knowledge of basic word formation.
    A. /   B. the   C. a   D. an
38. It is often said that _____ teachers have _____ very easy life.
    A. /; /   B. /; a   C. the; /   D. the; a
39. I can't remember when exactly the Robinson left _____ city; I only remember it was _____ Monday.
    A. the; the   B. a; the   C. a; a   D. the; a
40. After dinner, he gave Mr. John _____ ride to _____ Capital Airport.
    A. the; a   B. a; the   C. /; a   D. /; the

第三章 03

代　　词

热身训练： 下列句子各有一处错误,请指出并改正。

① The first time I went there, they were living in a small house with dogs, ducks and another animals.
② Mr. and Mrs. Zhang all work in our school.
③ My picture often brings back to me many happy memories of your high school days.
④ I think that it is a good idea. It does not cost many, yet we can still learn a lot.
⑤ At first, I thought I knew everything and could make decisions by yourself.
⑥ However, my parents didn't seem to think such.
⑦ Close to the school there was a beautiful park with many trees around them.
⑧ I wanted to do anything special for him at his retirement party.
⑨ Then everyone in the carriage began searching for the ticket, which was eventually found under a seat several rows from his owner.
⑩ I'm sorry that I am abroad and can't send your flowers, so I'm writing to you.
⑪ With the help of Kate, a roommate of me, I have soon got used to living abroad.
⑫ Before I could answer him, he continued to ask me the name of the fish on another one plate.
⑬ Just at that time I woke up and found me still in bed!
⑭ It is clear that your life in your country is different from me.
⑮ In our Greece unit, we have been learning about it's rich culture and long history.

　　代词是代替名词以及相当于名词的短语或句子的词。代词根据其意思和用法可分为人称代词、物主代词、指示代词、反身代词、相互代词、疑问代词、不定代词、连接代词和关系代词。代词的使用必须和它所代替的名词在人称、数、性、格上一致。

一、人称代词

　　人称代词是用来指人、动物或事物的代词。它有数和格的变化,数是指人称代词的单数和复数,格是指人称代词有主格和宾格之分。

1. 人称代词用作主语、表语

　　人称代词主格用作主语、表语。例如:

He was absent for five consecutive days. 他一连缺席了五天。

—Who is knocking at the door? 谁敲门？

—It is I(口语中常用 me). 是我。

2. 人称代词用作宾语

人称代词宾格用作及物动词的宾语、介词的宾语。例如：

Varga, the Origo Film Group CEO, appreciates him. 欧瑞格电影集团首席执行官瓦尔加很欣赏他。

The other three students also worked out the problem besides him. 除了他另外三个同学也解出了这道题目。

3. 人称代词的排序

人称代词的排列顺序,一般情况下,当几个不同的人称代词并列使用时,I 总是放在最后一位,表示礼貌。例如：

单数：you and I、you and he/she、you、he/she and I(二三一顺序)。

复数：we and you、we and they、you and they、we、you and they(一二三顺序)。

男女并用：he and she(男先女后)。

> 注：在下列情况下,第一人称放前面。
> ① 承认错误、承担责任时,则把第一人称放在其他人称代词之前。例如：
> It was I and she that made our teacher angry. 是我和她惹我们的老师生气了。
> ② 与 I 并列的词前面被不定代词修饰时,应将第一人称排到最前面。例如：
> I and some other teachers have discussed the problem. 我和其他几个老师讨论了这个问题。
> ③ 与 I 并列的词有后置定语修饰时,应将 I 排在最前面。例如：
> I and the students who made great progress checked the answer. 我和那些取得巨大进步的学生核对了答案。

4. 人称代词 it 的用法

(1) 当不知道所指对象的性别或指代婴儿时一般用 it。例如：

Someone must have come here, but I don't know who it is. 一定有人来过这儿,但我不知道是谁。

It is a newly born baby. 那是个新生儿。

(2) 用来表示时间、天气、距离、季节、日期、温度等。例如：

It is the Spring Festival today. 今天是春节。

If it is fine tomorrow, I will go climbing. 如果明天天气好,我将去爬山。

It's five degrees Celsius hotter than it was yesterday. 今天气温比昨天高 5℃。

It's April 17th, 2021 today. 今天是 2021 年 4 月 17 日。

(3) it 作引导词,用于强调结构"It is/was...that/who..."中,可强调除谓语之外的其他句子成分,包括主语、状语或宾语等。例如：

It was Thomas Edison who invented the electric light. 是爱迪生发明了电灯。

It is only through working hard that one can make great progress. 只有通过努力学习,才能取得巨大进步。

(4) 作形式宾语(真正的宾语是不定式、动名词或从句)。例如：

I think it important for college graduates to master certain interview skills. 我觉得掌握一定的面试技巧对大学毕业生很重要。

We all thought it a pity that he gave up his studies. 他放弃他的学业，我们都觉得很遗憾。

（5）作形式主语。例如：

It is important for the staff working here to be able to communicate with others fluently in English. 在这里工作的员工能用英语流利地与他人交流很重要。

It is a pity that you have a fever. 真遗憾你发烧了。

5. 人称代词的指代用法

（1）英语中常用 we、you、they 来指代一个集体或泛指"大家"。例如：

We must not make a lot of noise in public. 我们不应该在公共场合大声喧哗。

You should keep quiet in the hospital. 在医院里你应该保持安静。

（2）she（her）还可指国家、地球、月亮和船等。例如：

China is a developing country. She stands in the east of the world. 中国是一个发展中国家，她屹立于世界的东方。

The earth is our mother and we should protect her. 地球是我们的母亲，我们要保护她。

The moon shed her mild light upon the little baby's face. 月光轻柔地照在小婴儿的脸上。

When the ship fills with people, she will leave. 当船上满员的时候，她就可以离开了。

（3）glasses、trousers、scissors、clothes 等复数名词的指代词为 they（them、their、themselves）。例如：

Keep the scissors away from the children because they are very sharp. 不要让孩子摸到剪刀，因为它很锋利。

（4）and 连接的两个名词，如指同一事物，可视为一个集合体，其指代词往往用 it。例如：

Please give me a lock and key. I need it badly. 请给我一把带钥匙的锁，我非常需要它。

二、物主代词

物主代词是表示所有关系的代词。物主代词分为形容词性物主代词和名词性物主代词两大类，而且有人称和数的区别。

（一）形容词性物主代词

形容词性物主代词用来说明与后面的名词的所属关系，形容词性物主代词具有形容词的特征，在句子中用作定语，后面接所修饰的名词。例如：

My bed is made of wood. 我的床是用木头制作的。

This is your pencil. Mine is over there. 这是你的铅笔。我的在那儿。

（二）名词性物主代词

名词性物主代词具有名词的特征，在句子中可以作主语、宾语、表语等成分。名词性物主代词相当于"形容词性物主代词+名词"，它只能单独使用，其后不能跟名词。例如：

This is my umbrella and yours is over there. 这是我的伞，你的在那边。（主语）

My telephone is out of power. Can I use yours? 我的手机没电，我可以用你的吗？（宾语）

There is a red watch on the desk. Is it yours? 桌子上有块红色手表,它是你的吗?（表语）

(三) 物主代词需要注意的地方

（1）物主代词不可与 a、an、this、that 等词一起修饰名词。名词性物主代词加 of 结构,可以构成双重所有格。例如：

That friend of yours whom you mentioned is my classmate. 你提到的你那个朋友是我的同班同学。

I know each classmate of hers. 我认识她的每一个同学。

（2）形容词性物主代词常与 own 连用,相当于 one's own。例如：

Everyone has his own habit. 每个人有自己的习惯。

I want to solve the problem in my own way. 我想用自己的方法解决这个问题。

> 注：在这种结构里,own 后不宜接前文提到的名词,如：我碰到了我的一个朋友。翻译为 I met a friend of my own friends. 是错误的；正确译法是：I met a friend of my own. 或 I met a friend of mine. 或 I met one of my friends.

（3）书信等礼貌用语。例如：

Yours faithfully./Faithfully yours. 谨上。（信尾用语）

Give my greetings to her and hers. 请代我向她和她的家人问好。

三、反身代词

反身代词又称自身代词,是用来表示"我自己、你自己、她自己、我们自己"等意义的代词。

（1）反身代词在句子中可以充当宾语、表语和同位语。例如：

You must look after yourselves. 你们应该照顾好自己。

Jack himself finished the statistical report. 杰克他自己完成了统计报表。

I will be myself in no time. 我很快就会好的。

Athletes outdo themselves to excel on the sports field. 运动健儿激情飞扬、奋勇争先。

（2）反身代词一般不作主语,但在 and、or、nor 连接的并列主语中,第二个主语可用反身代词。例如：

His wife and himself were invited to the party. 他和他的妻子应邀参加这个晚会。

（3）反身代词作宾语常用于某些习惯用语中。例如：

Help yourself! 请随便吃!

Make yourself at home! 别客气!

Don't upset yourself. 别自寻烦恼。

英语有许多惯用语中含有反身代词,如：enjoy oneself、say to oneself、make oneself at home、introduce oneself、give oneself away、teach oneself、come to oneself、keep something to oneself、not be/feel oneself、express oneself、behave oneself、devote oneself to 等。

（4）反身代词也可以跟在介词之后表示多种意义,如：by oneself、for oneself、in oneself、beside oneself、to oneself、between ourselves 等。例如：

Work out the problem by/for yourself. 自己解决这个问题。

Hearing the good news, he was beside himself. 听到这个好消息,他欣喜若狂。
He cooked the delicious food only for himself. 他给自己一人做美食。

四、指示代词

指示代词是指起指示作用的、将事物与同类中其他事物分开的一种代词。指示代词有单复数两种形式,除了 this、that、these 和 those 外,such、so 和 the same 也可用作指示代词。

(一) this、these、that、those 的用法

(1) this、these 指较近的人或事物;that、those 指较远的人或事物。例如:
These succulents are mine. 这些多肉植物是我的。
—Who is that speaking? 喂,谁呀?
—This is Jane speaking. 是我,简。
(2) this、these 常指即将讲或做的事;that、those 常指已讲或已做的事。例如:
What I want to say is this: No pains, no gains. 我要说的是:没有付出就没有回报。
I had a fever yesterday. That's why I was absent from school. 我昨天发烧了,所以没来学校。
(3) that 可以代替不可数名词,也可代替可数名词的单数,代替可数名词单数时等同于 the one;those 只能替代可数名词复数,此时等同于 those ones 或 the ones。例如:
The windbreaker you bought is cooler than that I bought. 你买的风衣比我买的酷。
The population of China is larger than that of the United States. 中国人口比美国多。
The students in this classroom are more than those in that classroom. 这间教室里的学生比那间教室的学生多。

(二) such 和 same 的用法

such(这/那样的人或物)作代词可单独使用,一般作句子的主语、表语;same(同样的人或物)也是指示代词,在句中作主语、宾语、表语。例如:
Such is my goal. 这是我的目标。
He looks very foolish. In fact he isn't such. 他看上去很傻,事实上并非如此。
The same is the case with me. 我的情况也一样。
We must all say the same. 我们必须都说同样的话。
We are the same. 我们是同样的。

(三) so 的用法

so 用作指示代词时,替代一个句子或短语所表达的事情。
(1) 在 believe、think、expect、suppose、imagine、guess 等词后用 so 代替前文提出的观点,既可用于肯定句也可用于否定句。例如:
—He thinks she is a good girl. 他认为她是个好女孩。
—I don't think so. 我不那样认为。
(2) 用在 hope、I'm afraid 等后面,代替前文提出的观点,此时只能用在肯定句中。例如:
—It is said that there will be a supermarket near my home. 据说我家附近会开一家超市。

—I hope so. 我希望如此。

（3）so 在肯定句中表示与上文相同的情况，分为以下两种情况。

① 当两个主语不同，so 引导句子要用倒装结构。例如：

—I enjoy watching *the Chinese Poetry Conference.* 我喜欢看中国诗词大会。

—So does my daughter. 我女儿也喜欢看。

② 当主语相同，此时不倒装，表示"确实如此"。例如：

—Jack does 100 push-ups every day. 杰克每天做 100 个俯卧撑。

—So he does. 他确实是这样的。

五、不定代词

用来表示非特定对象的代词，叫不定代词。

（一）不定代词的分类

1. 表示数量的不定代词

表示数量的不定代词有 some、any、one、no、none、many、much、few、a few、little、a little、each、every、all、both、either neither、other、another 等。

2. 复合不定代词

复合不定代词由 some、every、any、no 加 one、body、thing 构成，复合不定代词包括：someone、somebody、something、anyone、anybody、anything、no one、nobody、nothing、everyone、everybody、everything、等之间。

一般来说，不定代词在句子中可作主语、宾语、表语或定语。但有些不定代词（如 no 和 every）只能作定语，有些不定代词如 none 以及由 some、any、every 组成的复合不定代词不能作定语。

（二）不定代词的用法

1. all

（1）all 表示"所有，都"，在谈到三个或三个以上的人或物以及在谈到不可数的事物时用 all。all 在句子中可以作主语、宾语、表语、同位语。当 all 作主语指可数名词时，谓语动词用复数形式；当 all 作主语指不可数名词时，谓语动词用单数形式。例如：

All like sports in my family. 我家所有的人都喜欢运动。

All has changed greatly since the launch of reform and opening-up in China. 改革开放以来，中国发生了翻天覆地的变化。

（2）all 作主语时，如果后面有人称代词，必须在 all 和人称代词之间加 of；如果后面是名词，那么它们之间可以加 of，也可以不加 of。例如：

All of us should study hard. 我们都应该努力学习。

All (of) the rooms are booked in the hotel during the holidays. 假期里，这家宾馆所有的房间都被预订了。

（3）all 作同位语时，它的位置并不是固定不变的，它根据谓语动词而定。当谓语动词是 be 时，all 要放在 be 的后面；当谓语动词是行为动词时，all 要放在行为动词的前面；当谓语动词是

由情态动/助动词加行为动词组成时,all 要放在情态动词/助动词与行为动词之间。例如:

We are all dreamers. 我们都是追梦人。

They all like chatting with QQ but WeChat. 他们都喜欢用 QQ 而不是微信聊天。

They are all playing football. 他们都在踢足球。

We must all go to school every day. 我们必须每天都上学。

(4) all 作人称代词宾语的同位语时,all 放在人称代词宾语的后面。例如:

Thank you all. 谢谢你们大家。

I'll invite them all to my party. 我会邀请他们所有人来参加我的派对。

(5) all 的后面加 not 并不是指"所有的都不"的含义,它是不完全否定,是指"并不是所有的都"。例如:

All the people do not like the actress ×××. 并不是所有的人都喜欢演员×××。

① all 可与表示时间的单数名词连用。如:all day、all night、all the morning、all the year 等。而且习惯上不使用 all hour、all the century 的表达方式。

② all 还可与一些特别的单数名词连用。如:all China、all London、all the city、all my life、all the way、all the time、all over the world 等。

③ all 可与 this、that、these、those 连用,放在它们前面,中间可插 of。例如:

All (of) this belongs to me. 所有这一切都属于我。

All (of) these are not right. 所有这些不都对。

④ all 的一些习惯用法。如:all the while、all the way、all alone、all along、all the time、all one's life、all around/round、all at once、all by oneself、all in all 等。

2. both

(1) both 仅指两者"都"。例如:

Both of them are interested in Chinese poetry. 他们俩都对中国古诗感兴趣。

(2) both 作同位语时,其在句中的位置如下。

① 位于行为动词之前。例如:

They both like fishing. 他们两个都喜欢钓鱼。

② 位于系动词如 become、turn、be 等之后。例如:

After the Spring Festival, we become both fatter than before. 春节之后,我们都长胖了。

③ 位于助动词/情态动词与行为动词之间。例如:

We have both kept in touch with each other since we graduated. 我们俩自从毕业以来一直保持联系。

如果助动词/情态动词后面的实义动词省去,则位于助动词/情态动词之前。例如:

—Who can speak English? 谁会说英语?

—We both can. 我们俩(都)会。

—Who has been there? 谁到过那里?

—We both have. 我们俩都去过。

3. some 和 any

(1) some 和 any 都可以表示"一些",既可以用在可数名词之前,也可以用在不可数名词之前。some 常用于肯定句中,any 常用于否定句、疑问句中。例如:

I need some advice on how to improve my English. 我需要一些如何提高自己英语水平的建议。
Do you need any reference books? 你需要一些参考书吗?
I don't have any money on me. 我身上没带钱。

在表示建议、请求、征求对方意见以及邀请的疑问句中,期望得到对方的肯定回答时,用 some 而不是用 any。例如:

Would you like some tea? 你来点茶,好吗?
Can I have some soup? 我能喝点汤吗?

(2) some 和 any 可以与可数名词单数连用,这时 some 表示"一个未指明或未知的人或物",意思是"某一个"; any 表示"无论哪个,任何一个"。例如:

Some person called you yesterday. 昨天有人打电话给你了。
I will remember any word you refer to. 我将会记住你说的每一句话。

(3) some 和 any 还可以在句子中作状语,此时它们为副词。some 表示"大约",相当于 about; 而 any 则表示"稍微,丝毫"。例如:

He can speak some four different languages. 他能讲大约四种不同的语言。
Does your mother feel any better? 你的母亲感觉好点了吗?

(4) "some of"结构,后接可数名词的复数作主语时,谓语动词用复数;后跟不可数名词时,谓语动词用单数。"any of"后跟复数可数名词时,在肯定句中表示"任何一个",谓语动词用单数;若"any of"后跟不可数名词,谓语动词也用单数。例如:

Some of the apples have been rotten. 一些苹果已经烂了。
Some of money is invested. 一部分钱投资了。
Any of the children in the school speaks fluent Chinese. 那个学校任何一个孩子都会讲流利的中文。
Any of milk is out of date. 牛奶全部过期了。

4. each 和 every

(1) each 和 every 都有每个的意思,但 each 强调个体,指两者或两者以上的各自情况; every强调整体,指三者及以上的全体。例如:

I have frostbite on each hand. 我每只手都生了冻疮。
Every student should obey the school rules. 每个学生都应该遵守学校的制度。
Each child will find his own personal road to succeed. 每个孩子都将找到各自的成功之路。
Every contestant must be present. 每位参赛选手必须到场。

(2) each 可以作代词和形容词,在句中可作主语、宾语、定语和同位语,而 every 只能作形容词,不可单独使用,只能作定语。作定语时,each 指两者以上的"每个"; every 指三者以上的"每个"。例如:

Each of the students in my class has a computer. 我们班上每个同学都有一台计算机。(主语)
We each do our best to finish the work. 我们各人都尽力完成工作。(同位语)
He handed a bottle of Fanta to each of us. 他递给我们每个人一瓶芬达。(宾语)
There are famous sayings on every wall in the classroom. 教室的每面墙都有名言。(定语)
There are many camphor trees on each side of the street. 街道的两边都有许多樟树。(定语)

(3) each 没有"反复,重复"之意,every 有"反复,重复"之意。例如:

They came here every(不能用 each) two weeks. 他们每两周来一次。

类似的还有：every year or two(每一二年)、every other (second) day(每隔一天)、every five people(每五人)等。

（4）当前面有 nearly 或 almost 修饰时，通常用 every。例如：

Almost every student attended the lecture. 差不多每个学生都聆听了这个讲座。

（5）each 一般不用于否定结构，表示全否定要用 no one。例如：

No one succeeded in the exam. (不能表达为 Each didn't succeed in the exam.) 这次考试中，没有一个人及格。

表示部分否定用 not everyone。例如：

Not everyone succeeded in the exam. 这次考试不是每个人都及格。

5. both、either 和 neither

（1）either 仅指两者之间的"任一"。

both、either 和 neither 都可以作代词或形容词，表示两者，在句中作主语、宾语、定语。both 意为"两者都"谓语动词用复数；either 意为两者中的任何一个，谓语动词用单数；neither 两者都不，谓语动词用单数；作定语时，either 一般与单数名词连用。例如：

Both of them are experts in medicine. 他们都是医学方面的专家。

You can choose either of the two presents. Either of them is made by hand. 两个礼物，你随便选一个。两个都是手工制作的。

I like neither of the two dishes. Neither of them is delicious. 两个菜我都不喜欢，哪个都不好吃。

（2）either 有"各，每"之意，在与 side、end、bank(岸)等词连用时，either=each。例如：

There are many shops on either side of the street. 街道两边有很多商店。

6. one

one 用来替代前文提到的可数名词，泛指。复数形式为 ones，需带定语；不带定语时用 some。例如：

I don't have a pencil, but I am going to buy one/some. 我没有铅笔，但我打算买一支/几支。

Lily has a red skirt and two blue ones. 李莉有一条红裙子和两条蓝裙子。

7. no 和 none

（1）no 意思是"无"，一般只能作定语，既可以修饰可数名词，也可以修饰不可数名词。例如：

I have no brothers. 我没有兄弟。

In winter there is no water in the pond. 冬天，这个池塘干涸了。

（2）none 表示三个或三个以上的人或物都不，是 all 的反义词，在句中相当于名词。none 作主语时，如果指代的是不可数名词，谓语动词用单数；如果指代的是可数名词，谓语动词单复数都行。例如：

None of the stories is/are true. 没有一个故事是真实的。

None of my time was wasted. 我的时间一点也没浪费。

注：none 与 no one 用法上有区别。no one 只能指人，且多用于口语，谓语动词用单数；而 none 可指人也可指物，谓语动词单复数都可以。例如：

No one believes what he said. 没有一个人相信他所说的话。

None of the money was stolen. 钱没有被偷。

None of his classmates has/have seen him since last year. 去年以来，没有一个同学见过他。

8. other(s)、the other(s) 和 another

other(s)、the other(s) 和 another 的用法如表 3-1 所示。

表 3-1　other(s)、the other(s) 和 another 的用法

用法	单　　数	复　　数	
		作　定　语	作主语或宾语
泛指	another （另外一个，再一个）	other (people)	others
特指	the other （另外那个）	the other (people)	the others

（1）other 指"另外的人和事"，在句中一般用作定语，只能与复数、集合名词等连用。例如：

Some people are dancing and other people are singing. 一些人在跳舞，另一些人在唱歌。（泛指）

（2）在 the other 中，若 other 为代词，the other 指两者中另一个，常用结构：one...+the other...（一个……另一个……），others 是它的复数形式，在句中作主语或宾语；若 other 为形容词，the other 指其他的，后面可以接可数名词和不可数名词；the other+复数名词=the others。例如：

I have two brothers. One is 15 years old, the other is 13 years old. 我有两个弟弟。一个 15 岁，另一个 13 岁。（代词、特指）

Three others and I will play table-tennis this evening. 晚上我将和另外三个人打乒乓球。（泛指）

Don't trust others easily. 不要轻易相信其他的人。（泛指）

The library is on the other side of the street. 图书馆在街道的另一边。（形容词、特指）

（3）another 意为（另一个，又一个），在句中作宾语或定语，只能代替或修饰单数可数名词，前面不用冠词；但当 another 后面有 few 或 two 以上的数字时，则可与复数名词连用。例如：

I don't like the color of the coat, please show me another. 我不喜欢这件衣服的颜色，请给我另外一件。（泛指）

Please give me another cup of tea. 请给我再来一杯茶。（泛指）

I need another three days to finish the work. 我还需要三天完成这项工作。（泛指）

（4）与数字的固定搭配：数词+more；another+数词，表示"再几个"，如：two more、another two。例如：

I would like to ask for two more/another two days' leave. 我想再请两天假。

9. much 和 many

（1）many 和 much 都表示"许多"，在句子中可以作主语、宾语和定语等。many 作代词时，可作主语或宾语，指代可数的人或物；much 作代词时指代不可数事物。例如：

Many of the flowers have withered. 许多花已经凋谢了。

You have a lot of milk but I haven't much. 你有许多牛奶，但我没有多少了。

（2）many a/an+可数名词单数，谓语动词用单数形式，其意义和"many+复数可数名词"一样，都是"许多"的含义。例如：

Many a car was stuck in the road because of the heavy rain. (＝Many cars were stuck in the road...) 因为这场大雨，路上堵了很多车。

10. (a)few 和(a)little

（1）(a) few 和(a) little 均可作代词,作代词时可作主语、宾语。a few、few 指代可数名词的复数,a few 有肯定的意思,强调"有几个",few 强调少,指"几乎没有"。a little、little 指代不可数名词,a little 强调"有少量",little 指"几乎没有"。例如：

A few of them have gone abroad. 他们中有几个出国了。

Very few passed the examination. 很少人通过了这次考试。

We had little rain all summer. 整个夏天几乎没下雨。

—Would you have some rice? 你吃米饭吗？

—Just a little. 来一点点。

（2）作形容词时,用作定语。a few 与 few 修饰可数名词复数,a little 与 little 修饰不可数名词。例如：

My father planted a few jujube trees in the yard. 我父亲在院子里种了几棵枣树。

He makes few friends. 他没交什么朋友。

There is little water in the glass. 杯子里没剩多少水了。

11. 复合不定代词

（1）复合不定代词由 some、any、every、no 和 one、body、thing 等构成,这些不定代词被看作第三人称单数,在句中作主语(作主语时谓语动词用单数)、宾语、表语。例如：

Everything is possible. 一切皆有可能。

I know nothing about her. 我对她不了解。

Money is everything to her. 钱是她的一切。

（2）形容词修饰复合不定代词时,应放在不定代词的后面。例如：

There is something wrong with my telephone. 我手机有点问题。

（3）some-类复合不定代词主要用于肯定句中,any-类复合不定代词主要用于否定句、疑问句和条件句中。当 some-类复合不定代词用于否定句、疑问句和条件句时,往往希望对方给予肯定的答复,表示肯定的意义。当 any-类用于肯定句时表示"任何"之意。例如：

It is difficult for me to solve the questions; I need someone to help me. 我很难解决这些问题,我需要帮助。

Can anyone get in and out of this community? 任何人都能出入这个小区吗？

Please share the happiness with anyone who you love. 请和你爱的任何人分享快乐。

Will you find someone to carry the box for me? 你找个人替我搬箱子,好吗？

（4）复合不定代词(除了与 thing 构成的复合不定代词外)后面都可加 's 构成所有格；当复合不定代词后有 else 时,所有格要加在 else 的后面。例如：

There is someone's bag left in the classroom. 有人把包落在教室里了。

That must be somebody else's coat. 那一定是别人的外套。

六、相互代词

相互代词表示谓语动词所叙述的动作或状态在涉及的各个对象之间是相互存在的。相互代词只有 each other 和 one another 两个。each other 表示两者之间的关系,one another 多表示两者以上相互之间的关系。它们只作动词和介词的宾语。例如：

We should encourage each other. 我们应该互相鼓励。（each other 可用 one another 代替）

The leaders shook hands with one another. 领导们相互握手。

each other 和 one another 也有所有格。例如：

They are familiar with each other's habits. 他们熟悉彼此的习惯。

We should point out one another's shortcomings. 我们应该指出彼此的缺点。

七、疑问代词

疑问代词是用来构成特殊疑问句的代词。常见的疑问代词有 what、which、who、whom、whose 等。

（1）who 一般在句中作主语和表语。口语中 who 可以作动词和介词的宾语。例如：

Who knows Jane's address? 谁知道简的地址？

Who is that man over there? 那边的那位男士是谁？

Who are they waiting for? 他们正在等谁？

（2）whom 只能作宾语。常用于书面语。例如：

Whom is Lily talking with? 莉莉正在和谁谈话？

（3）whose 表示"谁的"，是所有格形式；what 表示"什么"，可指人也可指物，既可表示单数，也可表示复数；which 表示"哪一个"，既可指人也可指物。例如：

Whose umbrella is left in the classroom? 谁的伞落在教室里？

What time is it? 现在几点？

Which of these two children is yours? 这两个孩子哪一个是你的？

Which row are you in? 你坐在哪一排？

注：which 和 what 作定语时指代有所不同。which 是在特定的人或物中进行选择；what 指的是哪一种，不局限于任何一件事情或东西；which 后还可跟 of 短语，表示在介词短语所表示的特定的范围之内选择。例如：

Which magazines do you like best? 你喜欢哪几本杂志？（有一定的范围）

What magazines do you like best? 你喜欢什么样的杂志？（不限制范围）

（4）who、what 都可以作表语，但意思不同。who 主要用于询问别人的姓名和身份；what 仅仅用来询问别人的职业。例如：

Who is the girl in a red coat? 穿着红外套的那个女孩是谁？

What is your sister? 你姐姐是干什么的？

巩 固 练 习

Complete the following sentences by choosing the items marked A, B, C, or D.

1. —Since there is _____ time, we have to take a taxi to the theatre.
   —That's a good idea.

   A. no   B. none   C. a little   D. little

2. The engine in your car works far better than _____.

   A. my car   B. mine car   C. that in mine   D. that in my car's

3. —I feel a bit hungry.

   —Why don't you have _____ bread?

   A. any   B. little   C. some   D. a

4. I want very much to buy a color TV set, but I can't afford _____.

   A. one   B. it   C. that   D. this

5. The students in our class work much harder at English than _____ in their class.

   A. those   B. these   C. that   D. ones

6. That little boy fell off the tree and hurt _____.

   A. him   B. his   C. her   D. himself

7. Is this skirt _____ she likes best?

   A. one   B. that   C. the one   D. which

8. —How many elephants did you see?

   —_____.

   A. None   B. No one   C. Not many ones   D. No many

9. _____ of us knows the reason why winter is colder than summer.

   A. Every one   B. Everyone   C. Someone   D. All

10. Some of the wheat came from Canada. How about _____?

    A. another   B. the other   C. the others   D. the rest

11. There were only _____ people who could get _____ money for the work.

    A. few; many   B. little; many   C. a few; much   D. a little; much

12. You can buy maps at _____ railway station. They all have them.

    A. all   B. every   C. any   D. each

13. —Excuse me, I want to have my watch fixed, but I can't find a repair shop.

    —I know _____. Come on. I'll show you.

    A. that   B. it   C. one   D. some

14. —Which one can I take?

    —You can take _____ of them; I'll keep none.

    A. any   B. both   C. neither   D. all

15. _____ an English-Chinese dictionary.

    A. The students each have   B. The students each has
    C. Each the students has   D. Each of the students have

16. We couldn't eat in a restaurant because _____ of us had _____ money on us.

    A. all; no
    B. any; no
    C. none; any
    D. no one; any

17. By the way, who will teach _____ pop music next term?

    A. us   B. our   C. ours   D. we

18. The English spoken in the United States is only slightly different from _____ spoken in England.

    A. which   B. what   C. that   D. the one

19. —Could you tell me how to get to Victoria Street?
    —Victoria Street? _____ is where the Grand Theatre is.
    A. Such   B. There   C. That   D. his

20. Isn't it amazing how the human body heals _____ after an injury?
    A. himself   B. him   C. itself   D. it

21. It was hard for him to learn English in a family, in which _____ of the parents spoke the language.
    A. none   B. neither   C. both   D. each

22. —I'd like some more cheese.
    —Sorry, there's _____ left.
    A. some   B. none   C. a little   D. few

23. To know more about the British Museum, you can use the Internet or go to the library, or _____.
    A. neither   B. some   C. all   D. both

24. Make sure you've got the passports and tickets and _____ before you leave.
    A. something   B. anything   C. everything   D. nothing

25. Many fast-growing countries are less concerned with protecting _____ against climate change.
    A. one   B. oneself   C. them   D. themselves

26. —Do you want tea or coffee?
    —_____. I really don't mind.
    A. None   B. Neither   C. Either   D. All

27. The manager believes prices will not rise by more than _____ four percent.
    A. any other   B. the other   C. another   D. other

28. —Have you heard the latest news?
    —No, what _____?
    A. is it   B. is there   C. are they   D. are those

29. _____ felt funny watching myself on TV.
    A. One   B. This   C. It   D. That

30. He has made a lot of films, but _____ good ones.
    A. any   B. some   C. few   D. many

31. —There is still a copy of the book in the library. Will you go and borrow _____?
    —No, I'd rather buy _____ in the bookstore.
    A. it; one   B. one; one   C. one; it   D. it; it

32. To save class time, our teacher has _____ students do half of the exercise in class and complete the other half for our homework.
    A. us   B. we   C. our   D. ours

33. The book is of great value. _____ can be enjoyed unless you digest it.
    A. Nothing   B. Something
    C. Everything   D. Anything

34. Little joy can equal _____ of a surprising ending when you read stories.
    A. that   B. those   C. any   D. some
35. One of them hasn't got _____ lessons prepared.
    A. he   B. its   C. one's   D. his
36. Who taught _____ English last term? Was _____ Mr. Smith?
    A. you; it   B. you; he   C. your; it   D. your; that
37. —What do you think of the performance today?
    —Great! _____ but a musical genius could perform so successfully.
    A. All   B. None   C. Anybody   D. Everybody
38. Jim sold most of his things. He has hardly _____ left in the house.
    A. anything   B. everything   C. nothing   D. something
39. —He got his first book published. It turned out to be a bestseller.
    —When was _____ ?
    — _____ was in 2010 when he was still in college.
    A. that; This   B. this; It   C. it; This   D. that; It
40. My father is a farmer, but _____ is yours?
    A. who   B. how   C. which   D. what

第四章 04

数 词

热身训练： 下列句子各有一处错误，请指出并改正。

❶ He served in the army in the 1950s' when he was in his twenties.
❷ The company has two hundred of workers.
❸ David helps his mother with her housework every weekend for about one and a half hour.
❹ Shortly after the accident, dozens police were sent to the spot to keep order.
❺ Peter's jacket looked just the same as Jack's, but it cost two as much as his.
❻ In the summer holiday following my eighteen birthday, I took driving lessons.
❼ During World War Ⅱ, a Jewish lady in her sixty was protected by a local family in Shanghai.
❽ There are three hundreds and sixty-five days in a year.
❾ Several millions students in the country are fighting for their dreams.
❿ Five pounds of pears doesn't cost two dollar.
⓫ The teacher asked us to write a two-thousands-word article.
⓬ It will take one and a half year time to finish the course.
⓭ With the help of the German experts, the factory produced twice many cars in 2020 as the year before.
⓮ They came in by twos or threes.
⓯ My brother lives at Room six on the second floor.

数词是指数目多少或顺序先后的词。数词一般分为基数词和序数词两大类。基数词表示数的大小，序数词表示数的顺序。数词在句中可以作主语、宾语、表语、定语和状语等成分。

一、数词的构成和用法

（一）基数词的构成和用法

在英语中表示数目多少的数词称为基数词。基数词中最基本的就是下面这些，如表 4-1 所示。所有其他数词都可以由这些词构成。

表 4-1 基数词的构成

范 围	特 点	实 例
1~12	无规律	one、two、three、four、five、six、seven、eight、nine、ten、eleven、twelve

续表

范　围	特　点	实　例
13~19	以 teen 结尾	thirteen、fourteen、fifteen、sixteen、seventeen、eighteen、nineteen
20~90	以 ty 结尾	twenty、thirty、forty、fifty、sixty、seventy、eighty、ninety
21~99	十位与个位之间要加连字符"-"	twenty-five、forty-seven、sixty-six、ninety-nine
101~999	百位与十位之间通常用 and	three hundred and twenty-five、five hundred and eighty-six
千及千以上	thousand（千）、million（百万）、billion（十亿）	three hundred and fifty thousand、five hundred、two million three hundred thousand、thirty billion

（1）基数词加 hundred、thousand、million、billion 表示确定数目时不能加-s，如：nine hundred、six thousand、five million、three billion 等。但在表示不确切数目时，要用复数形式，如：hundreds of、thousands of、millions of、billions of、tens of thousands of 等。

（2）基数词的读法，如：100/100 万可用 one hundred/million，或 a hundred/million；但 1000 只能用 one thousand，不能用 a thousand。2746 有 two thousand seven hundred and forty-six 和 twenty-seven hundred and forty-six 两种说法。

（3）dozen 和 score 应注意以下几点。

① dozen 表示一打，十二个；score 表示二十个。

② dozen 表示"一打，十二个"时，与数词连用，不加 s。例如：

We need three dozen boxes. 我们需要三打盒子。

③ dozen 与 several、many、a few 连用时，不加 s。例如：

There are several dozen councillors walking out the meeting in protest. 几十位议员中途愤然退出会议，以示抗议。

④ dozen 表示"大量、许多"时，用 dozens of。例如：

She's got dozens of friends. 她的朋友很多。

⑤ score 表示"二十"时，不加 s，但可以加 of。例如：

There are three score and ten in the village. 这个村子有 70 人。

A score (of) people had to attend the meeting. 有二十人不得不去开会。

⑥ score 表示"很多、大量"时，用 scores of。例如：

Scores of veteran doctors were sent to Shanghai. 许多资深医生被派往上海。

（4）表示"在某个世纪几十年代"用 in+the+"逢十的基数词的复数形式"来表达。如：in the sixties of the 20th century 基数词的复数形式若用阿拉伯数字表示，可直接加 s，也可加 's。如：in the 1990s 或 in the 1990's。

（5）基数词与名词合成的复合形容词作定语，其中的名词用单数。如：a three-month-old baby、a five-year plan、a 7-day holiday、a 30-minute walk、a 10-foot-deep swimming pool。

（6）数词与 another、all 等连用时，一般放在它们的后面；数词与 such、more 等连用时，一般放在它们之前；数词与 last、next、other 等连用时，放在它们之前或之后均可。例如：

Can you have another two apples? 你还能吃两个苹果吗？

Please give me three more books. 请再给我三本书。

His last two (= two last) books are written in Chinese. 他最后的两本书是用中文写的。

（二）序数词的构成和用法

在英语中表示顺序先后的数词称为序数词。最基本的序数词如表 4-2 所示。

表 4-2 序数词的构成

范 围	特 点	实 例
1~19	词尾一般加 th（有几个例外，需牢记）	first、second、third、fourth、fifth、sixth、eighth、ninth、tenth、twelfth、thirteenth、nineteenth
20,30~90	变 y 为 i,再加 eth	twentieth、fortieth、sixtieth、ninetieth
21 以后的多位数	最后一个数用序数词，其余用基数词	twenty-second、thirty-fifth、one hundred and tenth

1. 序数词的缩写

序数词的缩写形式,由阿拉伯数字加序数词最后两个字母构成,如：first—1st；second—2nd；third—3rd；eightieth—80th 等。

2. 序数词前冠词的用法

（1）序数词前有物主代词或有其他修饰语时不用冠词。例如：

His first six years of childhood was spent with his grandparents. 他 6 岁前和祖父母一起过的。

Dr. Black's third child is a wunderkind of American literary history. 布莱克博士的第三个孩子是美国文学史上的一位神童。

（2）明确指明先后顺序或一系列事物按一定规律排列时,序数词前用定冠词 the。例如：

I returned to my hometown on the first year of the 21st century. 21 世纪的第一个年头,我回了家乡。

This is the third time that I have been in Beijing. 这是我第三次来北京。

（3）序数词修饰名词时,前面加 the 表示顺序,加 a/an 表示"再一,又一"。例如：

The pears are delicious. He'd like to have a third one because the second one is rather too small. 这梨子太美味了。他都想吃第三个了,因为第二个太小了。

She devoted all her time to thinking up and making new things and wanted to be a second Edison. 她把全部时间投入思考和创造发明中,她想成为第二个爱迪生。

（4）序数词还可作副词用,此时不用任何冠词。例如：

First, I am short of money; second, I haven't enough time. 首先我缺少钱,其次我没有足够的时间。

It was a sunny day when we first met. 我们初次见面是在一个阳光明媚的日子。

二、数词的功能

（1）数词作主语。例如：

Two and two makes four. 二加二等于四。

The second is yours. 第二个是你的。

> 注：在书面表达中,什么时候用阿拉伯数字,什么时候用英文数词,并没有特别的规定,但 one 到 ten 一般用英文数词,较大的数常用阿拉伯数字来表示。

（2）数词作宾语。例如：

I know three of them. 我认识其中三个。（动词的宾语）

Please give me the second. 请给我第二个。（动词的宾语）

The city has a population of nine million. 这个城市有 900 万人口。（介词的宾语）

The little girl cut the apple in two and left the small part for herself. 这个小女孩把苹果切成两半，把小块留给自己。（介词的宾语）

（3）数词作表语。例如：

Her father is sixty-three. 她父亲 63 岁。

（4）数词作定语。例如：

It would be necessary to move 2000 people from their villages. 有必要将这 2000 人迁移出他们的村子。

As the significant juncture of the 40th anniversary, we should surmount all obstacles to carry the reform further to its ultimate triumph. 以庆祝改革开放四十周年为契机，逢山开路，遇水架桥，将改革进行到底。

（5）数词作同位语。例如：

Who is the man, the first in the front row? 前排第一个人是谁？

Let us three finish the work. 让我们三个人完成这工作吧。

（6）数词作状语。数词也可充当副词，在句子中作状语。例如：

Riding two on a bicycle is not allowed here. 这里骑自行车不允许带人。

Think first, then act. 先想清楚再行动。

> 注：应尽量避免在句首使用阿拉伯数字。例如：
> Twenty-five people, including 15 children, were killed in the three-day hostage crisis. 包括 15 名儿童在内，共有 25 人在这次历时三天的人质危机中丧生。

三、常用数的表示法

（一）分数表达法

（1）分数由基数词和序数词合成，分子用基数词，分母用序数词。分子大于 1 时，分母的序数词要用复数形式，如：$\frac{1}{7}$—one/a seventh、$\frac{2}{5}$—two fifths（或者 two-fifths）、$3\frac{2}{3}$—three and two thirds。$\frac{1}{2}$ 可表述为 one/a half、$\frac{1}{4}$ 可表达为 one/a quarter。

（2）分子与分母之间加 in，分子在前，分母在后，分子分母都用基数词，如：$\frac{1}{10}$—one in ten、$\frac{2}{3}$— two in three、$\frac{4}{5}$—four in five。

（3）分子与分母之间加 out of，分子在前，分母在后，分子分母都用基数词，如：$\frac{1}{8}$—one out of eight、$\frac{4}{5}$—four out of five、$\frac{5}{6}$—five out of six。

(二) 小数表达法

在英语小数中,小数点读 point;零读 o 或 zero;小数点前按基数词读,小数点后则须将数字依次读出,如:0.15 读作 zero point one five、26.42 读作 twenty-six point four two。

(三) 百分数表达法

(1) 百分数由"基数词+百分号(%)"表示,百分号(%)读作 percent(=per cent),无复数形式,如:18%读作 18 percent。

> **注:** ① 分数和百分数后面不能直接跟名词或代词,而应是"分数或百分数 of+冠词+名词(或 of+代词)",其谓语动词与 of 后面的名词在人称和数上保持一致。例如:
> Two-thirds of the money was spent on notebooks. 三分之二的钱用在买笔记簿上。
> About seventy percent(70%)of the earth's surface is covered by water. 地球表面大约 70%的面积被水覆盖。
> ② percent 作为形容词时,可直接跟所修饰的名词,如:10% increase(百分之十的增长)。

(2) 百分比、折价、度数的读法分别如下。

① 百分比

21%读作 twenty-one per cent(注意 per cent = percent. 但不可加-s)。

0.5%读作 point five per cent。

32.4%读作 thirty-two point four per cent。

② 折价

两折读作 eighty percent discount。

九五折读作 five percent discount。

③ 度数

-20℃ 读作 twenty degrees below zero Celsius 或 minus twenty degrees Centigrade。

76℉ 读作 seventy-six degrees Fahrenheit。

29℃ 读作 twenty-nine degrees Centigrade。

(3) 面积、体积、液量、重量的读法分别如下。

① 面积:15×6 feet 读作 fifteen by six feet(fifteen feet by six)。

② 体积:5″×8″×2″读作 five inches by eight by two。

③ 液量:2 gal. 7 qt. 9 pt. 读作 two gallons seven quarts nine pints。

④ 重量:54 kilos 读作 fifty-four kilograms。

(四) 倍数的表示法

(1) 倍数用在形容词原级比较的第一个 as 前面,即倍数+as+形容词/副词原级+as...。例如:

This room is twice as big as that one. 这个房间是那个房间的两倍大。

The table is three times as long as that one. 这张桌子是那张桌子的三倍长。

(2) 倍数用在比较级前,即倍数+形容词/副词的比较级+than。例如:

Line AB is three times longer than line CD. 线段 AB 是线段 CD 的三倍长。

This tree is twice higher than that one. 这棵树是那棵树的两倍高。

(3) 倍数用在表示度量的名词前。即倍数+the+度量名词（width、length、size、level 等）+of。例如：

The earth is 49 times the size of the moon. 地球是月球的 49 倍大。

The reservoir is five times the size of that one. 这个水库是那个水库的五倍大。

(4) by+倍数放在比较级后，即 more+名词+than...+by+倍数。例如：

We produced more computers in 2020 than those in 2019 by twice. 我们 2020 年生产的计算机是 2019 年的两倍。

She makes more money every month than I do by twice. 她每个月赚的钱比我多一倍。

(5) 倍数放在两个比较对象中间，即名词+of+比较对象 A+倍数+that of+比较对象 B。例如：

The size of the new room is three times that of that room. 这个房间是那个的三倍大。

The size of the newly broadened square is four times that of the previous one. 新扩建的广场为以前的四倍大。

(6) 倍数+what 引导的从句中。例如：

The length of the railway is nine times what it was ten years ago. 铁路的长度是十年前的九倍。

Output is now six times what it was before 2000. 现在的产量是 2000 年以前的六倍。

（五）大约数表示法

(1) 用 ten、dozen、score、hundred、thousand、million 等数词的复数加 of 短语来表示几十、几百、成千上万、几百万等大约数概念。例如：

I bought dozens of pencils last year. 去年我买了几十支铅笔。

Hundreds of police are sent to help the people in the flood. 几百名警察被派去帮助洪灾中的人们。

(2) 用 more than、over、above、beyond、or more 等来表示"多于，超过"。例如：

Our school has a history of more than seventy years. 我校有 70 多年的历史。

He has lived in Jiujiang over two years. 他在九江已经住了两年多时间。

(3) 用 less than、under、below、or less、almost、nearly、up to 等来表示"少于，接近"。例如：

How can you finish your homework in less than half an hour? 你怎么能在半小时内完成你的作业呢？

There's nothing below 5 yuan. 没有五元以下的东西。

(4) 用 or、or so、about、around、some、more or less 等，表示"大约，左右"。例如：

The doctor spent five or six hours performing the operation. 那医生花了五六个小时做这个手术。

It's an hour's journey, more or less. 大约有一个钟头的路程。

(5) 表示两数之间可用 from... to... 或 between... and... 等词。例如：

Office hours are from 9 a.m. to 5 p.m. 办公时间从上午 9 点到下午 5 点。

He is a man between sixty and seventy. 他的年龄在六十岁到七十岁之间。

（六）时刻表示法

(1) 表示整点，用基数词加 o'clock 构成，o'clock 也可省略，介词用 at。如：7:00 读作 seven o'clock（或 seven）。例如：

He often gets up at six (o'clock). 他经常 6:00 起床。

(2) 表示"几点过几分",用 past,但分数必须在半小时以内(包括半小时),如:

6:05 读作 five past six(或 six five)。

6:15 读作 fifteen past six(或 a quarter past six 或 six fifteen)。

6:30 读作 half past six (或 six thirty)。

(3) 表示"几点差几分",用介词 to,但分数必须在半小时以上(不包括半小时),如:

6:40 读作 twenty to seven(或 six forty)。

6:45 读作 fifteen to seven (或 a quarter to seven 或 six forty-five)。

6:55 读作 five to seven(或 six fifty-five)。

(七) 编号表示法

(1) 基数词和序数词都可以表示事物的编号。着重编号,用"名词+基数词";着重顺序,用"序数词+名词",如:Lesson Five=the fifth lesson(第五课)、Chapter Three=the third chapter(第三章)。

(2) 国王、王后等的头衔通常用罗马数字表示。例如:

Charles V(查理五世)读作 Charles the Fifth;Elizabeth Ⅱ(伊丽莎白二世)读作 Elizabeth the Second。

(3) 电话号码 Tel. No. 789-79369 或 telephone number 789-79369 读作 telephone number seven eight nine seven nine three six nine。

(4) 其他号码:

Room 102(102 房间)读作 room one zero two;

Bus (No.) 102(102 路车)读作 bus number one O two;

Page 126(第 126 页)读作 page one hundred and twenty-six 或 page one two six。

(八) 年、月、日表示法

(1) 用基数词表示年份,先读前一位或两位数,再读后两位数。例如:

315B.C.(公元前 315 年)读作 three fifteen B.C. 或 three hundred and fifteen B.C.。

576A.D. (或 A.D. 576)(公元 576 年)读作 five seventy-six A.D. (A.D. 在不会误解情况下可省略)。

1998 年读作 nineteen ninety-eight;1900 年读作 nineteen hundred。

1906 年读作 nineteen hundred and six;2002 年读作 two thousand and two。

(2) 表示年代、世纪的英语读法如下。

1990s 或 1990's(20 世纪 90 年代)读作 the nineties of the 20th century。

21st century(21 世纪)读作 twenty-first century。

巩 固 练 习

Complete the following sentences by choosing the items marked A, B, C, or D.

1. The number of people invited _____ fifty, but a number of them _____ absent for different reasons.

    A. were; was   B. was; was   C. was; were   D. were; were

2. You're always wasting things, bad boy! You've got broken two _____ pencils this term.
   A. scores   B. scores of   C. dozen   D. dozens
3. Staying in a hotel costs _____ renting a room in a dormitory for a week.
   A. twice so much as
   B. twice as much as
   C. as much as twice
   D. so much as twice
4. Please turn to Page _____ and take a look at the picture on it.
   A. the eightieth   B. Eightieth   C. Eighties   D. Eighty
5. We gave away _____ books to the library last year.
   A. six thousands
   B. six thousand
   C. six thousands of
   D. six thousand of
6. The length of this rope is _____ that one.
   A. three times the length of
   B. three times larger
   C. as three times long as
   D. the third time as
7. _____ visitors came to take photos of Lushan Mountain during the vacation.
   A. Thousand   B. Thousand of   C. Thousands   D. Thousands of
8. It took me _____ to finish the work.
   A. one and a half hours
   B. one and a half hour
   C. an hour and a half hours
   D. one and half hour
9. It's 10:15. We can say a _____ past ten.
   A. quarter   B. half   C. pound   D. kilo
10. _____ ago, this country was covered by thick forest.
    A. Several millions years
    B. Several million of years
    C. Tens of thousands of years
    D. Ten thousands years.
11. _____ of the trees in the garden are apple trees.
    A. Two third   B. Two thirds   C. Second third   D. Second thirds
12. The hero of the story is an artist in his _____.
    A. thirties   B. thirty   C. thirty's   D. thirtieth
13. How to read 85646 in English?
    A. Eighty-five thousands, six hundreds and forty-six.
    B. Eighty-five thousand, six hundred and forty-six.
    C. Fifty-eight thousand, six hundred and forty-six.
    D. Eighty-five thousands, six hundred and forty-six.
14. The boy students in this school are nearly _____ as the girl students to say they intend to get a college degree in business.
    A. as likely twice
    B. twice as likely
    C. as twice likely
    D. likely as twice
15. Are there seats for us _____?
    A. the third   B. three   C. third   D. the three
16. It seems to me _____ that our plan is not feasible.
    A. in first   B. in the first   C. in a first place   D. in the first place

17. —How many presidents were there before Abraham Lincoln?

　　— _____ , so he was _____ president.

　　A. Fifteen; the sixteenth　　　　　　B. Fifteen; sixteenth

　　C. Fifteenth; sixteen　　　　　　　　D. Fifteenth; the sixteen

18. The living-room is twenty-four square meters, _____ the bedroom.

　　A. twice the size of　　　　　　　　B. two times of

　　C. the twice size of　　　　　　　　D. twice as much

19. The Himalayas is over _____ than the Rocky Mountains.

　　A. twice tall　　　B. tall twice　　　C. twice taller　　　D. twice tallest

20. They have to write two _____ compositions every month.

　　A. three-thousand-words　　　　　　B. three-thousand-word

　　C. three-thousands-word　　　　　　D. three thousand words

21. The price of the oil-painting has reached one million dollars, _____ it was yesterday.

　　A. twice as higher　　　　　　　　　B. twice higher than

　　C. twice as higher as　　　　　　　　D. twice as higher than

22. There are more than thirty and less than forty people present, or in another word, there are _____ people present.

　　A. thirty or less　　　　　　　　　　B. more thirty less forty

　　C. thirty odd　　　　　　　　　　　D. thirty and forty

23. The newly constructed highway is said to be _____.

　　A. in thirty miles long　　　　　　　B. length thirty miles

　　C. about thirty miles long　　　　　　D. thirty mile long

24. A library with five thousand books _____ to the nation as a gift.

　　A. is offered　　　B. has offered　　　C. are offered　　　D. have offered

25. She gave _____ to her brother.

　　A. half cake　　　B. the half's cake　　C. half of cake　　　D. half the cake

26. —What's the date today?

　　— _____ .

　　A. It's Friday　　B. It's hot　　　　C. It's July 3rd　　　D. It's a holiday

27. Over _____ of the money _____ used for the food.

　　A. three-fifth; is　　B. three-fifth; are　　C. three-fifths; is　　D. three-fifths; are

28. After the new technique was introduced, the factory produced _____ cars in 2020 as the year before.

　　A. as twice as many　　B. as many twice　　C. twice as many　　D. twice many as

29. There are _____ people in Dale's family. They live on the _____ floor.

　　A. five; nine　　　B. fifth; nine　　　C. five; ninth　　　D. fifth; ninth

30. Two _____ died of cold last winter.

　　A. hundreds old people　　　　　　B. hundred old people

　　C. hundreds old peoples　　　　　　D. hundred old peoples

第五章 05

形容词和副词

热身训练： 下列句子各有一处错误，请指出并改正。

1. The teachers here are kind and helpfully.
2. I won the race. I felt very proudly of myself.
3. A few minutes late, the instructor asked me to stop the car.
4. The fish tastes well, why not have a try?
5. The workers warm welcomed us at their offices.
6. Nearly five years before, and with the help of our father, my sister and I planted some cherry tomatoes（圣女果）in our back garden.
7. Mom said, "How nice to see you again! Dad and I were terrible worried.
8. My uncles immediate jumped up and shot their arrows at the bird.
9. Still, your happiness makes him happily too.
10. He is in more health now than he was last year.
11. This is quite far the mostly expensive bicycle in the shop.
12. I was so encouraged that I ran faster and fast till I caught up with all the other runners.
13. I was so much nervous that I could hardly tell which direction was left.
14. China is much more bigger than the United State.
15. The more money you make the most you spend.

　　形容词用于修饰名词、代词，表示人或事物的性质、特点或所处的状态，在句子中用作表语、定语和补足语。副词用于修饰动词、形容词、副词、介词短语或整个句子，在句子中用作状语。

一、形容词

（一）形容词的类别

1. 简单形容词和复合形容词

按照形容词的结构，可以分为简单形容词和复合形容词。

(1) 简单形容词,如:delicious、lively、desperate 等。
(2) 复合形容词是指由几个词共同组成并起到形容词作用的词。主要有以下几类。
① 数词+名词(单数),如:one-child、five-year 等。
② 数词+名词(单数)+形容词,如:four-year-old、80-meter-long 等。
③ 形容词/数词+名词+-ed,如:good-tempered、warm-hearted、one-eyed、three-legged 等。
④ 形容词/副词+动词的-ing 形式,如:good-looking、ordinary-looking、far-reaching 等。
⑤ 形容词/副词+动词的-ed 形式,如:wide-spread、so-called、newly-built 等。
⑥ 名词+动词的-ed 形式,如:man-made、ice-covered、state-owned 等。
⑦ 名词+动词的-ing 形式,如:life-saving、peace-loving、time-consuming 等。
⑧ 形容词+(普通)名词,如:full-time、high-class、deep-sea 等。
⑨ 形容词/副词+形容词,如:wide-awake、hardly-conscious、all-round 等。
⑩ 名词+形容词,如:ice-cold、duty-free 等。

2. 中心形容词、定语形容词和表语形容词

按照形容词的句法功能,可以分为中心形容词、定语形容词和表语形容词。

(1) 中心形容词。大多数形容词既可作定语,又可作表语,还可作宾语补足语,这类形容词叫中心形容词。例如:

The table is brown. 这桌子是棕色的。

He has a brown table. 他有一张棕色的桌子。

They painted the table brown. 他们把桌子漆成棕色的。

(2) 定语形容词。这类形容词只能作定语,修饰名词。常见的有:wooden、inner、outer、elder、certain、leading、late、upper、lower、latter、former、foremost、principal、woolen、golden、mere、very、total、sole、silken 等。例如:

It is a wooden pencil-box.(√)这是个木头做的笔盒。The pencil-box is wooden.(×)

Her left hand is in the pocket.(√)她的左手在口袋里。The hand in the pocket is left.(×)

(3) 表语形容词。这类形容词通常只作表语,它们一般以字母 a 开头。常见的有:aware、asleep、ashamed、afraid、ahead、alike、alone、alive、adrift 等。例如:

The two sisters are very much alike. 姐妹俩非常相像。

His mother is afraid that they won't come. 他的母亲担心他们都不会来。

下列形容词一般也只充当表语:ill、unwell、drunk、glad、sure、fond、unable、well、eager、bound、content、accustomed、ready、present 等。例如:

He was ill after the party. 宴会之后,他生病了。

I am glad you can come. 我很高兴你能来。

3. 形容词的主动意义和被动意义

(1) 通常由动词转化而来的-ing 形容词具有主动意义,而由动词转化而来的-ed 形容词则具有被动意义,如表 5-1 所示。

表 5-1　主动意义与被动意义(1)

主　动　意　义	被　动　意　义
an interesting experiment	an interested audience

续表

主 动 意 义	被 动 意 义
a charming girl	a charmed girl
encouraging news	an encouraged boy
a tiring work	a tired housewife
a pleasing voice	a pleased look
an exciting speech	excited children

（2）以 ful、ive、ant、ous、some 等结尾的形容词往往表示主动，以 able、ible 等结尾的形容词往往表示被动，如表 5-2 所示。

表 5-2　主动意义与被动意义（2）

主 动 意 义	被 动 意 义	主 动 意 义	被 动 意 义
respectful	respectable	tolerant	tolerable
imaginative	imaginable	troublesome	troubled
delightful	delighted	desirous	desirable

（二）形容词的作用和位置

（1）形容词作定语，说明被修饰的名词的性质、特征等，一般位于被修饰的名词前，如：disappointing news、a beautiful rose。

（2）形容词修饰不定代词（something、anything、everything、nothing、everyone、anybody 等）时，要放在其后，作后置定语。例如：

He will tell me something important. 他将告诉我一些很重要的事。

Is there anything wrong with your watch? 你的手表有什么问题吗？

（3）名词前有形容词的最高级或 all、every、only、the few 等词修饰时，少数以 a 开头的表语形容词（如 awake、asleep 等）及以 -able、-ible 结尾的形容词，放在名词之后，作后置定语。例如：

I have tried all means imaginable. 所有能想到的办法，我都试过了。

He is one of the greatest persons alive. 他是当今世界最伟大的人之一。

（4）形容词作表语，说明主语的性质或特征。例如：

Books and friends should be few but good. 书和朋友应该少而精。

To my surprise, the driver is still alive after the traffic accident. 令我惊讶的是，车祸后司机还活着。

（5）形容词作宾语补足语，说明宾语的性质、状态或特征。例如：

She made her dad very unhappy. 她让她父亲很不高兴。

Many students find Chinese idioms hard to learn. 许多学生发现汉语成语很难学。

（6）形容词作状语，表示伴随状况、原因、结果等。例如：

The little match girl kept sitting at the street corner, cold and hungry. 卖火柴的小女孩一直坐在角落，又冷又饿。

Angry at the girl oversleeping, Mr. Green went down to wake her up. 格林先生对那女孩睡过

头很生气,于是下楼去叫醒她。

(7) 形容词的名词用法。形容词加冠词,相当于一个名词,泛指一类人或事物。"the+形容词"构成的名词,作主语指一类人时,谓语动词用复数;指事物或某一概念时,谓语动词用单数。例如:

The wise look to the wise for advice. 智者向智者寻求建议。

The beautiful is not always the good. 美丽的并不总是美好的。

(8) 多个形容词作定语。有两个或两个以上的形容词修饰名词时,与被修饰的名词关系越密切的越靠近名词,越疏远的越远离名词。常用的顺序为:限定词(如 these、those 等)+数量(序数词、基数词)+描述性形容词(如 clever、heavy 等)+大小、长短、高低等形容词(如 small、long、short 等)+年龄、温度、新旧(young、hot、new、old)+颜色(如 red、black 等)+产地(如 Chinese、American 等)+材料(如 wood、gold 等)+用途(如 writing、medical 等)+被修饰的词(desk、building 等)。为了便于记忆,可以试试如下两个顺口溜:好美小高状其新,颜色国料用途亲;美小圆旧黄,法国木书房。例如:

a beautiful little red flower 一朵美丽的小红花

a beautiful short new red Chinese woolen sweater 一件崭新的漂亮的中式短款红色羊毛衫

a charming small oblong red wooden box 一个迷人的长方形红色小木盒

(三) 几种特殊情况

(1) 一些形容词作定语既可前置也可后置,且意义变化不变,如:on Monday next 或 next Monday(下周一)、the only solution possible 或 the only possible solution(唯一可能解决的办法)等。

(2) 一些作前置定语和后置定语意义不同的形容词,常见的有:absent、adopted、concerned、present、proper、elect、involved、responsible、used、opposite、responsible 等,如:the present members(现在的成员)、the members present(当时在场的成员)、the responsible man(可依赖的人)、the man responsible(应负责的人)、an involved story(复杂的故事)、the people involved(牵连到的人)、the concerned parents(心情焦虑的家长)、the parents concerned(有关家长)等。

(3) 一些形容词作定语与作表语含义不同,如:the present president(现任总统)、ill news(坏消息)等。例如:

The president was present. 总统出席了。

He was ill. 他生病了。

(4) 形容词与副词连用修饰单数名词时,放在被修饰的名词之前。例如:

That's too small a room for you. 那间房子对你来说太小了。

How clever a baby he is! 他是多么聪明的孩子啊!

(5) 几组容易混淆的形容词,如表 5-3 所示。

表 5-3　易混淆形容词

形容词	释　　意	形容词	释　　意
historic	历史的	historical	有历史意义的
alone	独自的	lonely	孤独的,寂寞的

续表

形容词	释意	形容词	释意
healthy	健康的	healthful	有益于健康的
sensitive	敏感的	sensible	明智的
economic	经济上的	economical	节俭的
industrial	工业的	industrious	勤劳的
dead	死的	deadly	致命的,不共戴天的
alive	活着的	living	活着的,健在的
deathly	死一般的	dead	死的,死亡的

二、副词

(一) 副词的构成

1. 以 ly 结尾的副词

大多数副词以形容词直接加 ly 构成。这些副词主要表示方式,用于描述"如何地、怎样地"。以 le 结尾的形容词需去掉 e,加 y。以 y 结尾的形容词把 y 改为 i,再加 ly。以 c 结尾的形容词直接加 ally,如:

real—really　　　　　helpful—helpfully　　　　　true—truly
gentle—gently　　　　busy—busily　　　　　　　easy—easily
automatic—automatically　　academic—academically

注:有些以 ly 结尾的词是形容词,而不是副词。例如:lovely、friendly、weekly、lively、timely、lonely 等。

2. 与形容词同形的副词

常见与形容词同形的副词如下:

fast *adj.* 快的; *adv.* 快地　　　　　　firm *adj.* 稳固的; *adv.* 稳固地
hard *adj.* 硬的,艰苦的; *adv.* 努力地　　high *adj.* 高的; *adv.* 高高地
inside *adj.* 内部的; *adv.* 在里面　　　　just *adj.* 正义的; *adv.* 正好
late *adj.* 晚的,迟的; *adv.* 迟,晚　　　long *adj.* 长的; *adv.* 长时间地

3. 其他情况

两种形式的副词含义完全不同,举例如下:

hard(努力地)—hardly(几乎不)　　　　near(接近〈地〉)—nearly(几乎)
high(高高地)—highly(高度地)　　　　most(最,很,十分)—mostly(主要地)
late(晚,迟,不久以后)—lately(近来,最近)　tight(紧紧地)—tightly(坚固地)

有些以 ly 结尾的词既可作名词,也可作形容词,还可作副词。例如:
hourly *n.* 小时工; *adj.* 每小时的,每小时一次的; *adv.* 每小时一次,随时
daily *n.* 日报; *adj.* 每日的,日常的; *adv.* 每日
biweekly *n.* 半月刊; *adj.* 双周的; *adv.* 两周一次地

weekly *n.* 周刊,周报;*adj.* 一周一次的;*adv.* 一周一次地
bimonthly *n.* 双月刊;*adj.* 两月一次的;*adv.* 两月一次地
monthly *n.* 月刊;*adj.* 每月一次的;*adv.* 每月一次地
yearly *n.* 年刊;*adj.* 一年一次的;*adv.* 一年一次地

(二) 副词的分类

副词修饰动词、形容词、其他副词、全句或名词词组及介词短语。副词一般可分为以下几类。

(1) 时间副词,如:now、often、usually、always、already、before、early、late、finally、eventually、immediately、recently、shortly、soon、today、yesterday 等。例如:
Soon they will go to visit the Lushan Mountain. 不久,他们将去庐山参观。

(2) 地点副词,如:here、there、everywhere、in、out、above、below、up、down、upstairs、downstairs、anywhere、everywhere、elsewhere 等。例如:
I think she is in. 我认为她在里面。

(3) 程度副词,如:very、much、still、so、almost、awfully、completely、greatly、terribly、hardly、nearly、partly、scarcely、entirely、thoroughly、considerably、tremendously、absolutely、little 等。例如:
The doggies were so lovely that they were sold in no time. 这些小狗很可爱,很快就卖掉了。

(4) 方式副词,如:well、hard、slowly、fast、coldly、bravely、cruelly、kindly、quietly、hurriedly、warmly、seriously、gladly、wisely、stupidly、calmly、pleasantly 等。例如:
How hard they study! 他们学习多努力啊!

(5) 疑问副词,如:when、where、why、how 等。例如:
When did the Sydney-to-Melbourne ultra marathon start? 悉尼至墨尔本的超级马拉松是从什么时候开始举行的?

(6) 关系副词,如:when、where、why 等。例如:
I knew the reason why he came late. 我知道他为什么来晚了。

(7) 连接副词,如:where、why、when、how 等。例如:
That's why they are called the Winter Olympics. 这就是他们被称为冬季奥运会的原因。

(8) 解释性副词,如:namely、for example、i.e.、e.g. 等。例如:
Hot drinks, i. e. tea and coffee, are charged for separately. 热饮料,即茶和咖啡,是分开收费的。

(9) 频度副词,如:always、constantly、frequently、never、often、seldom、sometimes、usually、regularly、occasionally、hardly 等。例如:
Buses run frequently between the city and the airport. 公交汽车频繁地来往于市区与机场之间。

(10) 观点副词,如:fortunately、undoubtedly、probably、personally、frankly、luckily、obviously、hopefully、definitely、unfortunately、evidently、politically、commercially 等。例如:
Personally speaking, I've always preferred Hunan cuisine. 就我个人来讲,我总是偏爱湘菜。

(三) 副词在句中的位置

副词在句中的位置比较灵活,往往要根据这些词所表示的意义和所起的作用而定。一般来说,副词要放在最靠近其修饰的词语旁边,以便能立刻辨别它所修饰的对象。

（1）时间副词、地点副词和一些方式副词一般放在句末。如果在句中同时出现,顺序为方式副词+地点副词+时间副词。例如:

The boy read quietly over there all afternoon. 这男孩整个下午都在那静静地看书。

He told it to me angrily at school yesterday. 他昨天在学校的时候,生气地告诉我那件事。

（2）程度副词(almost、nearly、rather、fairly 等,但 enough 除外)一般放在被修饰的形容词、副词或动词前。例如:

I quite agree with you. 我完全同意你的看法。

The boy nearly fell into the river. 那男孩差点掉进河里。

（3）表示方式的副词,多放在动词的后面。例如:

The lecturer spoke very clearly so that we could hear every word. 演讲者讲得很清楚,以便我们能听到每个字。

They looked into the case carefully. 他们仔细地调查了这个案子。

（4）频率副词(always、never、often、seldom 等)一般放在行为动词前,助动词、系动词、情态动词后。例如:

She does not often take part in such social activities. 她不经常参加这种社交活动。

He has never been to Lushan Mountain. 他从没去过庐山。

（5）修饰名词的副词通常放在名词的后面,但 quite 位于名词的前面。例如:

I like the atmosphere here. 我喜欢这里的气氛。

Our music teacher is quite a character. 我们的音乐老师很有个性。

（6）副词修饰形容词或另一副词时,通常放在所修饰的词前面,但 enough 则要放在所修饰词的后面。例如:

Qingming Festival is a very important traditional festival in China. 清明节在中国是一个非常重要的传统节日。

He speaks Chinese quite fluently. 他汉语说得很流利。

You are old enough to do this. 你已经长大了,可以这样做了。

（四）副词的作用

副词在句中主要作状语,有时也可以作表语、定语和补足语。

1. 作状语

（1）修饰动词,通常放在实义动词后面。例如:

The man ran fast. 那人跑得很快。

（2）修饰形容词,通常放在形容词的前面。例如:

She looks very beautiful. 她很漂亮。

（3）修饰副词,通常放在副词的前面。例如:

Don't drive so fast! 别开那么快!

（4）修饰介词短语,通常放在介词短语前面。例如:

The basketball player must be well past thirty. 那个篮球运动员一定已经三十多岁了。

（5）修饰整个句子,通常放句子前面,用逗号隔开。例如:

Fortunately, I was in time for the interview. 幸运的是,我及时赶上了面试。

2. 作表语、定语和补足语

副句在句中还可以作表语、定语和补足语。例如：
Time is up. Let's start. 时间到了，咱们开始吧。
The building there looks very grand. 那里的建筑看起来很宏伟。
I went to see Jim only to find him out. 我去看吉姆却发现他不在家。

三、形容词和副词的形式

英语中的形容词和副词常有三种形式用于表达事物的等级差别，分别是原级、比较级和最高级。

（一）形容词和副词的原级

(1) 表示被比较双方在某一方面相等或相同时，用以下几种结构。
① as+*adj.*/*adv.*+as。例如：
He speaks English as fluently as you. 他说英语和你说英语一样流利。
② as+much+不可数名词+as。例如：
I have as much money as Helen. 我的钱和海伦的一样多。
③ as+many+可数名词复数+as。例如：
There are as many seats in this hall as in that hall. 这个大厅的座位和那个大厅的一样多。
④ … the same… as。例如：
He has the same intelligent a student as his sister. 他有一个和他妹妹一样聪明的学生。
(2) 表示被比较双方在某一方面不相等或不相同时，用结构"not as/so+*adj.*/*adv.*+as"，意思为"……和……不一样，不如……，不及……"。例如：
His coat is not so (as) new as mine. 他的外套没有我的外套新。
English is not so difficult a subject as Chinese. 英语不像汉语那么难。

（二）形容词和副词的比较级、最高级

大多数形容词和副词有比较级和最高级的变化，即原级、比较级和最高级，用于表示事物的等级差别。原级即形容词的原形，比较级和最高级有规则变化和不规则变化两种。

1. 比较级、最高级的构成

(1) 规则变化：单音节词和少数双音节词，词尾加 -er 和 -est 来分别构成比较级和最高级，如表 5-4 所示。

表 5-4 比较级、最高级的构成（规则变化）

构　成　法	原级	比较级	最高级
一般单音节词，末尾加 er、est	strong	stronger	strongest
	great	greater	greatest
以不发音的 e 结尾的单音节词和少数以 le 结尾的双音节词只加 r、st	nice	nicer	nicest
	late	later	latest
	able	abler	ablest

续表

构 成 法	原级	比较级	最高级
以一个辅音字母结尾的闭音节单音节词,双写结尾的辅音字母,再加 er、est	thin	thinner	thinnest
	hot	hotter	hottest
以辅音字母+y 结尾的词,变 y 为 i,再加 er、est	angry	angrier	angriest
	busy	busier	busiest
其他双音节词或多音节词,在前面加 more、most 来分别构成比较级和最高级	enthusiastic	more enthusiastic	most enthusiastic
	beautiful	more beautiful	most beautiful

(2) 不规则变化如表 5-5 所示。

表 5-5　比较级、最高级的构成(不规则变化)

原　　级	比　较　级	最　高　级
good、well	better	best
bad、badly、ill	worse	worst
many、much	more	most
little	less	least
old	older/elder	oldest/eldest
far	farther/further	farthest/furthest

注:older/oldest(比较老/最老的),elder/eldest(年龄比较大的/最大的);farther/farthest(距离比较远的/最远的),further/furthest(引申意义:更进一步的,更深一层的/最深层的)。

2. 比较级的用法

(1) 两者相比时,用"比较级+than"结构来表示一方在某方面超过另一方。比较级可以用 rather、much、still、even、far、any、a lot、a little、a great deal、by far、a bit 等词修饰。例如:

Actions speak louder than words. 行动胜于雄辩。

He works much harder than before. 他比以前工作努力多了。

(2) "the+比较级+of the two+名词",表示"两个中较……的"。例如:

The taller of the two girls is my sister. 两个女孩中,个子较高的是我妹妹。

The older of the two books is wang Lin's. 两本书中,较旧的那本是王林的。

(3) "the+比较级,the+比较级",意为"越……越……"。例如:

The more difficult the problem is, the more careful we should be. 问题越难,我们就应该越小心。

The harder one works, the more progress he will make. 学习越努力,进步就越大。

(4) "比较级+and+比较级",意为"越来越……"。例如:

My English is improving. It is getting better and better. 我的英语在进步,越来越好了。

The car is cheaper and cheaper. 汽车越来越便宜。

(5) "not+比较级"含义是"不比……怎么样";而"no+比较级"含义是"与……一样不……"。例如:

Peter is not wiser than Tom. 皮特没有汤姆聪明。

Peter is no wiser than Tom (=Peter is as foolish as Tom.) 皮特和汤姆一样笨。

This book is not more interesting than that one. 这本书不如那本书有趣。

This book is no more interesting than that one. 这本书和那本书一样没有趣味。

3. 最高级的用法

（1）当三个或三个以上的人或事物进行比较时，需用最高级。基本形式为：the+形容词或副词最高级+(名词)+表示范围的短语或从句。形容词最高级一般加定冠词the，副词最高级前可不加冠词。最高级可被序数词(first 除外)以及 much、by far、nearly、almost、by no means、not really、not quite、nothing like 等修饰。例如：

The apple is the biggest one on the tree. 这是这棵树上最大的苹果。

Liu Xiang runs (the) fastest among his teammates. 刘翔是他的队友中跑得最快的。

The Yellow River is the second longest river in China. 黄河是中国第二长河。

Among these cities, Suzhou is by far the most beautiful. 在这些城市中，苏州是最美丽的。

（2）否定词(not, never)+比较级，其含义等同于最高级。例如：

I have never heard a more interesting story. 我从未听过比这更有意思的故事了。

I can't agree more. 我完全同意。

（3）比较级+than+any other+单数名词，其含义等同于最高级。例如：

He is more diligent than any other student in the class. 他比班上任一个学生都勤奋。

He is more active than any other student in our class. 他是我们班上最活跃的学生。

（4）比较级+than+anyone/anything else，其含义等同于最高级。例如：

Tom did more work than anyone else. 汤姆做的工作比任何人都多。

（5）比较级+than+any of the others，其含义等同于最高级。例如：

The cake is nicer than any of the others. 这块蛋糕比其他任何一块都好吃。

The flower is more beautiful than any of the others. 这朵花比其他的花都好看。

（6）no、nobody、nothing 等含有否定意义的词+比较级，其含义等同于最高级。例如：

I like nothing better than reading. 我最喜欢的是读书。

（7）最高级结构中冠词的使用。

副词的最高级前常省去定冠词。形容词的最高级前加定冠词，表示最高级含义；有时不加定冠词，表示"非常"的意思，没有比较的含义。例如：

Helen works (the) hardest of all. 海伦工作最努力。

It's the most difficult task that I have ever dealt with. 这是我处理过的最困难的任务。

It's a most difficult task for me. 对于我来说，这是一项非常困难的任务。

4. 几组词语的用法区别

1）any other+名词与 any+名词

（1）两种相同的事物在同一范围内进行比较时，than 后的名词用单数或复数均可，但要加 any other 之类的词。例如：

He is cleverer than any other student in his class. 他比他班上其他任何学生都聪明。

Steel is more useful than any other metal. 钢比其他任何金属都更有用。

This building is taller than any other building in the city.

This building is taller than the other buildings in the city.

This building is taller than the rest of the buildings in the city

This building is the tallest of the buildings in the city.

这座大楼比该市其他大楼都要高。

（2）两种相同事物在不同范围内进行比较,只能用 any,不能用 any other。例如：

The fish in this lake is more delicious than any fish in the ocean. 这个湖里的鱼比海洋中的任何鱼都鲜美可口。

2）no more than+数词与 not more than+数词

no more than 的含义等同于 only,意为"不过,仅仅",表示"少"的意思；not more than 的含义等同于 at most,意为"最多,至多",有"也许不到"的意思,应注意它们所表示的确切含义。例如：

I have no more than 10 dollars in my pocket. 我口袋里只有 10 美元。

I have not more than 10 dollars in my pocket. 我口袋里不超过 10 美元。

3）no more... than 与 not more... than

no more... than 所连接的两个人或物,都含有与所用形容词相反的意义,意为"同……一样不",如：no more clever than 的含义等同于 as dull as（同……一样笨）。not more... than 所连接的人或物,都含有所用形容词所表示的意义,只是程度前者不如后者。例如：

She is no more careful than he is. 她同他一样都不细心。

She is not more careful than he is. 她不比他更细心。

4）no less than+数词和 not less than+数词

no less than 的含义等同于 as many as,意为"有……之多",表示"多"的意思；not less than 的含义等同于 at least,意为"至少",表示"不少于""也许不止"的意思。例如：

I have learnt no less than seventy new words this week. 我这个星期竟然学了 70 个生词。

I can learn not less than sixty new words this week. 我这个星期至少能学 60 个生词。

5）more than+主语+can+谓语

这种结构表示的是否定意义,意为"非……所能,……不能"。例如：

That is more than I can tell you. 那是我不能告诉你的。

The beauty of the city is more than I can describe. 这座城市的美非我所能描述。

6）the same... as 与 the same... that

the same... as 表示"相似,相同",指两个东西是同种类的,但不是同一物；the same... that 表示"同一的",指同一个人或物。例如：

This pen is the same as mine. 这支笔同我的那支笔相似。（两支笔）

This is the same pen that I lost. 这正是我丢失的那支笔。（一支笔）

巩 固 练 习

Complete the following sentences by choosing the items marked A, B, C, or D.

1. _____ to take this adventure course will certainly learn a lot of useful skills.

    A. Brave enough students   B. Enough brave students

    C. Students brave enough   D. Students enough brave

2. Allen had to call a taxi because the box was _____ to carry all the way home.

   A. much too heavy
   B. too much heavy
   C. heavy too much
   D. too heavy much

3. The elderly need special care in winter, as they are _____ to the sudden change of weather.

   A. sensitive   B. sensible   C. flexible   D. positive

4. There are two buildings, _____ stands nearly a hundred feet high.

   A. the larger
   B. the larger of them
   C. the larger one that
   D. the larger of which

5. There's _____ cooking oil left in the house. Would you go to the corner store and get _____.

   A. little; some
   B. little; any
   C. a little; some
   D. a littler; any

6. In _____ Chinese culture, marriage decisions were often made by parents for their children.

   A. traditional   B. historic   C. remote   D. initial

7. I must be getting fat. I can _____ do my trousers up.

   A. fairly   B. hardly   C. nearly   D. seldom

8. —Is your headache getting _____?
   —No, it's worse.

   A. better   B. bad   C. less   D. well

9. Do you enjoy listening to records? I find records are often _____ or better than an actual performance.

   A. as good as   B. as good   C. good   D. good as

10. They have produced _____ they did last year.

    A. twice more grain as
    B. twice as much grain as
    C. twice as many grain as
    D. as twice many grain as

11. The lecture was so _____ that all the people in the hall were _____.

    A. moving; exciting
    B. moving; excited
    C. moved; excited
    D. moved; excited

12. There is _____ to hold the water.

    A. nothing big enough
    B. nothing enough big
    C. big enough nothing
    D. enough big nothing

13. Qingdao is _____ beautiful city in summer.

    A. most   B. a most   C. the most   D. much

14. How did it take _____ time in building the house with _____ workers?

    A. less; fewer
    B. fewer; less
    C. the fewest; the least
    D. a little; a bit of

15. My _____ sister who works in the bank is two years _____ than I.

    A. younger; older
    B. older; elder
    C. elder; elder
    D. elder; older

16. _____ it is to have a picnic by the sea!

   A. What a great pleasure   B. What great pleasure
   C. How a great pleasure   D. How great pleasure

17. We must leave now, _____ we'll be late for work.

   A. so   B. otherwise   C. then   D. and

18. The guide told us that he would organize some businessmen abroad _____ next week.

   A. some time   B. sometime   C. some times D. sometimes

19. What a wonder! They've finished _____ 30% of the task within one week.

   A. no more than   B. no less than   C. not more than   D. much less than

20. I've got _____ work to do on a _____ cold day.

   A. much too; much too   B. too much; too much
   C. too much; much too   D. much too; too much

21. —Is he _____ better today?
   —Of course.

   A. much   B. a bit   C. any   D. even

22. She failed many times, but that just made her _____ determined.

   A. no longer   B. all the more   C. above all D. no more

23. The best time to go to Australia is _____ autumn.

   A. later   B. latest   C. late   D. last

24. This is _____ bridge ever built in China.

   A. longest   B. the longer   C. the longest   D. a long

25. He knows little of mathematics, and _____ of chemistry.

   A. even more   B. still less   C. no less   D. still more

26. This couple have strange habits. He'd like to sleep with the lamp burning and his wife with the window _____.

   A. wide open   B. widely open   C. wide opened   D. widely opened

27. On the bank of the river stands a _____ castle.

   A. old big British   B. British big old   C. big British old   D. big old British

28. _____ the search engine just gave me some brief introductions rather than the whole content of the book to read.

   A. Luckily   B. Mostly   C. Funnily   D. Disappointedly

29. The United States, Britain, New Zealand and so on are _____ countries.

   A. speaking-English   B. English-speaking
   C. spoken-English   D. English-spoken

30. Which do you like _____, English, Chinese or French?

   A. better   B. well   C. best   D. worse

31. —Is the bus stop far from here?
   —It's a quarter's walk, _____.

   A. more and more   B. and so on
   C. all together   D. more or less

32. Bob ran the 100 meters in 9.81 seconds, and I have not seen _____ this year.
    A. the best   B. better   C. the most   D. more
33. The students are _____ young people between the age of sixteen and twenty.
    A. most   B. almost   C. mostly   D. at most
34. The horse is getting old and can't run _____ it did.
    A. as faster as   B. so fast than
    C. so fast as   D. as fast as
35. I'd been expecting _____ letters the whole morning, but there weren't _____ for me.
    A. some; any   B. many; a few
    C. some; one   D. a few; none
36. The pianos in the other shop will be _____, but _____.
    A. cheaper; not as better   B. more cheaper; not as better
    C. cheaper; not as good   D. more cheap; not as good
37. —Excuse me, is this Mr. Brown's office?
    —I'm sorry, but Mr. Brown _____ works here. He left about three weeks ago.
    A. not now   B. no more   C. not still   D. no longer
38. We decided not to climb the mountains because it was raining _____.
    A. badly   B. hardly   C. strongly   D. heavily
39. The experiment was _____ easier than we had expected.
    A. more   B. much more   C. much   D. more much
40. _____ terrible weather we've been having these days!
    A. How a   B. What a   C. How   D. What

第六章 06

介 词

热身训练： 下列句子各有一处错误，请指出并改正。

① If we could show concern to others on need, the world would be a better place to live in.
② Could you share your experiences for us?
③ It was a relief and I came to a sudden stop just in the middle on the road.
④ But on today, at this special time, I just want to tell you loudly.
⑤ If you hear the alarm, stand in line at the door and wait your teacher to lead you outside.
⑥ My uncle says that he never dreams becoming rich in a short period of time.
⑦ While they chatted, my father would lift my sister and me up to sit in the top of the fridge.
⑧ On the front door stood a five-year-old boy from across the street.
⑨ They have also bought for some gardening tools.
⑩ Still I was unwilling to play the games for them sometimes.
⑪ Firstly, a friend is someone you can share your secrets.
⑫ At the end of our trip, I told my father that I planned to return for every two years.
⑬ I realize of how fast time flies.
⑭ Therefore, we have more time with after-school activities.
⑮ Now I am leaving home to college.

介词又称前置词，是一种虚词。介词通常用于名词、代词以及相当于名词的其他词语之前，表示其后词语与句子其他成分之间的关系。介词在句中不能单独作句子成分，必须与名词或代词或相当于名词的其他词类、短语或从句构成介词词组，才能在句中作状语、后置定语、表语、补语等。介词搭配能力很强，可与其他词类搭配构成成千上万个固定词组。

一、介词的分类

（1）简单介词：由一个单词构成的介词。它也可能由形容词、副词、名词、连词等转变而来。常用的有：at、in、over、on、near、up、by、besides、with、after、since、between、from、round、under 等。

（2）合成介词：由两个单词组合而成的介词。常用的有：within、into、inside、outside、

throughout、upon、without、alongside 等。

（3）二重介词：由两个简单介词重叠在一起构成的介词。常用的有：from behind、from under、from beyond、from among、under after、except for、but for 等。

（4）分词介词：由现在分词演变而来。常用的有：including、concerning、regarding、excepting、considering、respecting、following 等。

（5）短语介词：由两个或两个以上的单词构成的短语，其作用就相当于一个介词。常用的有：according to、because of、in spite of、owing to、ahead of、along with、due to、away from、except for、up to 等。

二、介词短语的构成及其句法功能

（一）介词短语的构成

介词短语是由介词加宾语构成。介词宾语可以是名词、代词、动名词、名词性从句、介词短语、(疑问词)+不定式等。例如：

I'm sorry I haven't any money with me. 对不起，我身上没带钱。

The heavy rain prevented us from starting early. 大雨耽误了我们早点出发。

Since then we haven't heard from each other. 从那以后我们再也没有彼此的消息了。

From under the table ran out a black and white cat. 从桌子底下跑出一只黑白相间的猫。

They had no choice but to wait. 他们别无选择，只好等待。

We failed to agree on when to go on a picnic. 我们未能就什么时候去野餐达成一致意见。

The students sit here and there by twos and threes, reading or just taking a rest. 学生三三两两地坐在各处，看书或休息。

He is really an excellent graduate except that he doesn't have enough experience. 他真的是一个优秀的毕业生，只是他没有足够的经验。

In the passage of time, we have seen and experienced a resilient and dynamic China. 在飞逝的时光里，我们看到的、感悟到的中国，是一个坚韧不拔、欣欣向荣的中国。

（二）介词短语的句法功能

介词短语在句中可以用作定语、状语、表语、宾语补足语等，有时也能充当主语。

（1）介词短语作定语，通常位于所修饰的名词或代词之后。例如：

The woman in the kitchen is his wife. 厨房里的女人是他的妻子。

Festivals and celebrations of all kinds have been held everywhere since ancient times. 自古以来，各地都有各种各样的节日和庆祝活动。

（2）介词短语作状语，表示时间、地点、原因、目的、比较、方式等。例如：

We went to the bar for a drink. 我们去酒吧喝一杯。

Unlike most actors, Harry is a rather shy man. 与大部分演员不同，哈里是个相当害羞的人。

Let's go out for a walk along the river. 我们沿河边散散步吧。

At the historical convergence of the Two Centenary Goals, we have set out on a new journey of building a modern socialist country in all respects. "两个一百年"奋斗目标历史交汇，我们开启了全面建设社会主义现代化国家新征程。

The Communist Party of China have made spectacular, epoch-making achievements over the past century. 中国共产党在过去的一个世纪里，取得了惊人的、划时代的成就。

（3）介词短语作表语，位于连系动词之后，对主语进行说明、补充。例如：

The wounded soldier is out of danger. 受伤的士兵脱离了危险。

Mr. Smith is still in bed. 史密斯先生还在床上。

（4）介词短语作宾语补足语，和前面的宾语一起构成复合宾语。例如：

We found her in tears. 我们发现她哭了。

Do you think of him as an honest boy? 你认为他是个诚实的男孩吗？

（5）介词短语作主语补足语。用作宾语补足语的介词短语，在相应的被动语态中则为主语补足语。例如：

He was regarded as a hero. 他被视为英雄。

Only athletes who have reached the agreed standard for their event will be admitted as competitors. 只有达到规定标准的运动员才被允许参加比赛。

三、介词与其他词类的搭配

介词的搭配能力很强，一些常用的介词，能与不同的词搭配，形成固定的用法。

（1）动词+介词，如：look into、insist on、begin with、meet with、die of、object to、lead to、date from、listen to、wait on、play with 等。例如：

Police are looking into the disappearance of two children. 警察正在调查两个孩子的失踪。

（2）形容词+介词，如：be worthy of、be ashamed for、be absent from、be afraid of、be nervous about、be good at、be busy with、be full of、be famous for、be aware of 等。例如：

Peter's suggestion is worthy of being considered. 彼得的建议值得考虑。

General Secretary Xi Jinping is well aware of the changes in the international situation and the trend of the Times. 习近平总书记把握世界变局，洞察时代风云。

The prosperity and stability of Hong Kong and Macao is always close to the heart of the motherland. 祖国一直牵挂着香港、澳门的繁荣与稳定。

（3）名词+介词，如：key to、access to、attention to、devotion to、delay in、congratulation on、application for、love for、emphasis on 等。例如：

Knowledge is a treasure, but practice is the key to it. 知识是宝库，实践是开启宝库的钥匙。

（4）介词+名词，如：across the country、at one's request、in all probability、in excitement、on one's guard（警惕、小心地）等。例如：

The hearts of the people across the country are linked to each other. 全国人民心连心。

四、介词的省略

一般来说介词是不可省略的，但在一些特殊表达或固定搭配中，有些介词是可以省略的。

（1）"for+若干时间或距离"里的 for 在口语中通常会被省略。例如：

He has already waited (for) a whole afternoon. 他已经等了整整一个下午了。

He walked (for) twelve miles. 他走了十二英里。

（2）"of+度量名词"的结构作表语时,其中 of 经常被省略(这种结构一般用于表示大小、年龄、形状、颜色、价格等)。例如：

When I was (of) your age, I didn't have enough money to receive further education. 当我和你一般大时,我没有足够的钱去接受继续教育。

(Of) What size is your hat? 你的帽子多大?

（3）对等连词连接两个相同介词短语时,第二个介词常被省略。例如：

You may go by plane or (by) train. 你可以乘飞机或坐火车去。

We raise many sheep, both for wool and (for) mutton. 我们养了许多羊,既产羊毛又出羊肉。

（4）动名词前介词常被省略。例如：

She has no difficulty (in) learning French. 她学法语很轻松。

Mary was busy (in) preparing for the final exam. 玛丽正忙于期末考试。

五、常用介词

（一）表示方位、地理位置的介词

常用此类介词有：at、in、on、to、off、above、below、over、under、beneath、across、through、beyond、past、out of、around、inside、outside 等。

（1）at、in 表示"在……地点"时,at 一般指较小的地点,而 in 则表示宽大的地点。例如：

She is waiting for you at the station. 她在车站等你。

She arrived in Beijing. 她到了北京。

（2）in、on、at、off 在方位名词前的区别：in 表示在范围之内; to 表示在范围之外; on 表示有边缘衔接; off 表示"与(海岸等)有一定距离,离……不远"。例如：

Guangdong lies in the south of China. 广东省位于中国的南部。（范围之内）

Guangdong lies to the south of Jiangxi. 广东省位于江西南部。（范围之外）

Russia lies on the north of China. 俄罗斯位于中国的北边。（接壤）

The island lies off the coast of China. 这个岛位于中国沿海。（相隔一定距离）

（3）between、among 表示"在……之间"。between 一般指两者之间,其宾语往往是表示两者的名词或代词,也可用于两者以上之间,但仍侧重于每两者之间的关系,常用结构"between A, B and C"。among 一般用于三者或三者以上之间。例如：

There was a fight between the two men. 那两个人发生了一场搏斗。

Switzerland lies between France, Germany, Austria and Italy. 瑞士位于法国、德国、奥地利和意大利之间。

They hid themselves among the trees. 他们躲在树丛间。

（4）in, on 表"在……之上"。in 和 on 可以用于描写两个物体的接触情况。on 表示在一个平面上,侧重于表面接触,而 in 表示在……内,侧重于接触的深度。

① 若打击某人的脸、眼、嘴、胸、腹等较软的部位时,用介词 in；若打击头、额、耳、颈、肩、腿等较硬的部位时,用介词 on。例如：

I patted him on the shoulder when I saw him. 我看见他时拍了拍他的肩膀。

The mother hit the boy in the face angrily. 母亲生气地打了这男孩的脸。

② 若某物是植物本身固有的,如生长出来的枝、叶、花、果等,用介词 on；但若在树上,不

是植物本身的,而是附着物,则用介词 in,意指枝叶遮掩其中。例如:

There are many oranges on the tree. 这棵树上有许多橘子。

There is a bird singing in the tree. 一只鸟儿在树上唱歌。

③ 若表示在墙的表面有某种东西,如地图、字画等,用介词 on;若表示在墙体里面,则用介词 in。例如:

There is a Chinese map on the wall. 墙上挂了幅中国地图。

There is a little hole in the wall. 墙上有一个小洞。

(5) over、under、above、below 的区别:over 和 above 一般表示在"……之上";under 和 below 表示"在……之下"。over 表示"在……正上方",强调垂直;under 表示一种直接的、垂直的下方;over、under 互为反义词;而 above 与 below 表示一般的"高于"与"低于",不一定垂直;above 与 below 互为反义词。例如:

They held a large umbrella over her. 他们给她撑起一把大伞。

The sun has sunk below the horizon. 太阳落到地平线以下了。

(6) across、through、over 的区别:across 表示"穿过,横穿,横过",表示动作是在物体表面进行的,强调从一端到另一端;through 表示"透过,穿过",表示动作是在空间内进行的,强调从物体内部穿过。over 表示"(部分或全部覆盖)在……上面",强调方向性,从一侧到另一侧,表示翻转、穿过(街道,开阔的空间等)。例如:

When walking across the street, we must be careful. 过马路时,我们必须小心。

Finally, they walked through the forest. 他们最后穿过了森林。

The car skidded off the road and rolled over and over. 汽车滑出公路,翻滚了好几次。

(二) 表示时间的介词

表示时间的介词有 at、on、in、during、over、for、within、throughout、till、until、after、since、from... to 等。

(1) at、in、on 表示"时间"用法区别如下。

① at 指某个时间点,一般表示具体的时刻。如:at day break、at noon、at night、at dawn;也可以表示较短暂的一段时间,可指某个节日或一年中标志大事的日子。如:at the beginning、at Christmas。

② in 用于较长的时间,如年、月、周、季节、一天的某个时段等。如:in the morning、in these days、in 1992、in the 1990s、in summer 等。

③ on 用于表示具体的日子或一个特定的时间。如:on Monday、on March 2th、on this occasion、on National Day;也用于表示特定的上午、下午、晚上。如:on the morning/afternoon/evening of March 2nd、on Monday morning、on the eve of victory、on a sunny morning 等。

(2) in、after、later 表示"在……之后"用法区别如下。

① "in+一段时间"表示以说话时为起点,一段时间之后,与一般将来时间连用。例如:

The doctor will be with you in five minutes. 医生五分钟后就到。

He will graduate from Peking University in five months. 还有五个月,他就从北京大学毕业了。

② "after+时间段"表示"在……之后",与过去时连用;"after+时间点"表示"在……之后",与各种时态连用。例如:

My father received my letter after 4 days. 四天后,我父亲收到了我的信。

My father will be back after 4 o'clock. 我父亲四点后回来。

③ "时间段+later"表示某一具体时间或某一具体事件算起，一段时间后。例如：

Mr. Liu graduated in 2014。Six years later he became the manager of the company. 刘先生2014年毕业，六年后成为公司的经理了。

（3）for、from、since 的用法区别如下。

① "for+时间段的名词词组"，表示行为或状态持续了多久。

② "from+时间点的名词词组"，表示以此时间或状态等为起始点，强调开始时间，但并不强调时间的持续性。

③ "since+时间点的名词词组"，表示以此时间为起始点，并且表示某个行为或者状态从起始点开始到说话的时刻一直持续不断，所以与延续性动词的现在完成时连用。例如：

I'm going to travel for one week. 我打算旅行一个星期。

My daughter began to learn singing from the age of five. 我女儿从五岁开始学唱歌。

I lost my keys and I have been worried since then. 我把钥匙弄丢了，从那以后我一直很担心。

> **注**：当时间名词前有 this、that、last、next、some、every 等词限定时，通常不用任何介词。如：this week、last year、every day 等。

（三）表示工具、手段、方式的介词

1. by、in、on 表示方式

（1）by+交通工具的名词，表示"乘，坐"。名词须用单数，其前面不加冠词，如：by bike、by taxi、by plane、by ship/boat、by train 等。

（2）by+交通有关的名词，表示"通过，由……途径"，此时表示交通方式，不涉及交通工具，名词前不带冠词，如：by sea、by water、by air 等。

（3）"in/on+冠词/物主代词/指示代词+交通工具"，表示"乘，坐"，如：in a spaceship、in this plane、on a train、on my bike、on a bus 等。

> **注**：步行、骑马、骑骆驼等用 on，如：on foot、on a horse、on the camel 等。在表示交通工具名词前，若有具体时刻修饰时，介词 by、on 均可。如：by/on the 8：00 train。

2. with、by、in 表示行为的工具、手段或方式

（1）with+冠词/物主代词+有形的工具/身体某些器官，表示"用……"。例如：

My little sister is cutting the tree with a knife. 我的妹妹正在用小刀砍树。

We can see with our eyes, and listen with our ears. 我们可以用眼睛看，用耳朵听。

（2）by+方式手段或无形的工具，如：by phone、by express、by hand、by WeChat 等。

（3）in+语言/材料，如：in English、in pencil、in red ink 等。

（四）表示原因的介词

（1）because of 意为"因为，由于"，通常作状语，位于句首或句末。例如：

Because of my bad leg, I couldn't walk so fast as the others. 因为我的腿不好，我不能像其他人走得那么快。

（2）due to 意为"由于，因……造成"，通常作表语。例如：

The failure is due to your negligence. 失败是由于你的疏忽。

（3）thanks to 意为"幸亏、由于"，多用于句首。例如：

Thanks to your help, we did it. 多亏你的帮助，我们成功了！

六、常考介词

（一）beyond

（1）表示位置，意为"在……的那边，在……以外，在更远处"。例如：

The sea is beyond that mountain. 大海在那座山的那边。

These students came from beyond the seas. 这些学生来自海外。

（2）表示时间，意为"过了，比……晚，超过"。例如：

His parents arrived beyond nine o'clock. 他的父母九点多就到了。

We never see beyond the present. 我们从没超越现在。

（3）表示范围、水平、限度、能力等，意为"为……所不及，超出……的范围"。例如：

They succeeded beyond our hopes. 他们的成功超出了我们的希望。

The young man is living beyond his income. 这个年轻人的生活消费超过了他的收入。

（4）用于否定或疑问句，表示"除……外"。例如：

We know nothing beyond what you tell us. 除了你告诉的以外，其他我们什么都不知道。

What could we do beyond waiting? 除了等待，我们还能做什么？

（二）against

（1）表示"反对；违背"，与 for 意思相反。若表示"强烈反对"时，用副词 strongly 修饰。例如：

We are all against her idea. 我们都反对她的想法。

We are all strongly against her idea. 我们都强烈反对她的想法。

（2）表示位置，意为"逆，顶着；靠着，倚靠；碰着"。例如：

We must not drive against the traffic. 我们不能违规开车。

The guy stood with his back against the big tree. 那个家伙背靠着大树站着。

The cold rain beat against the window. 冰冷的雨水打在窗户上。

（3）表示"预期；以备；为……准备"。例如：

They are all taking medicine against the cold. 他们都在吃药以防感冒。

Some animals store food against the winter. 有些动物储存食物以抵御冬天。

（4）against 做介词后面接动词时，要用动名词。例如：

I'm against doing anything till the police arrive. 我反对在警察到来之前做任何事。

She is against seeing him. 她不想见他。

（三）of

（1）of+名词，表示名词所有格，意为"……的"。如：the window of the room 等。

（2）of+抽象名词等同于形容词，如：of fame 等同于 famed 等。

（3）of+great+抽象名词等同于 very+形容词，如：of great help 等同于 very helpful 等。

(4) of+no+抽象名词等同于 not+形容词,如:of no use 等同于 not useful 等。

注:常见的抽象名词有 help、value、importance、interest、use 等。

(四) but

介词 but 意为"除……外;除了",除了可与 no、nobody、nothing、none、who 等词连用外,后面还可接不定式。但接不定式有两种情况:but 前面有实义动词 do 的某种形式时,but 后面的 to 要省略;but 前面无实义动词 do 的某种形式时,but 后面的 to 不能省略,即"前有 do 后省 to,前无 do 后加 to"。例如:

Nobody knew her but me. 除了我,没人认识她。

Mr. Wang did nothing but play basketball in the afternoon. 下午,王先生除了打篮球什么也没做。

Mr. Wang had no choice but to play basketball in the afternoon. 下午,王先生别无选择,只有打篮球。

另外,can (or could) but 意为"只得,只能",can (or could) not but 意为"不得不,忍不住",cannot (or couldn't) choose but 意为"不得不,只好,必须",cannot (or couldn't) help but 意为"不得不,不能不",这些短语后面接动词原形。例如:

The old lady can but know a few words. 这位老太太只会说几句话。

I cannot but tell my mom the truth. 我只能告诉妈妈真相。

He could not choose but give up smoking. 他只好戒烟。

She could not help but be sorry. 她情不自禁地感到抱歉。

(五) with

(1) 表示人与人之间协同的关系,意为"和……一起,跟……在一起,同……"。例如:

Please go with your mother. 请和你妈妈一起去。

I have been friends with Mr. Ye for five years since we worked with each other, and I have never quarreled with him. 我和叶先生自从共事以来已经是五年的朋友了,我从没和他吵过架。

(2) 表示从属关系,意为"带来"或"在……身边,带有"。例如:

Do you have little money with you? 你身上没带一点钱吗?

China is a country with a long history. 中国是一个拥有悠久历史的国家。

(3) 表示原因或理由,意为"因为,由于"。例如:

The little boy is down with high fever. 这个小男孩发高烧了。

The little girl jumped with joy. 小女孩高兴得跳了起来。

(4) 表示用某种工具或手段,意为"用,用……工具"。例如:

Don't write the letter with a pencil. 不要用铅笔写信。

My mother cut the pear with a sharp knife. 母亲用锋利的小刀切梨。

(5) 表示时间关系,意为"与……同时,随着"。例如:

The big ship is sailing with the wind. 那艘大船随风航行。

With these words, his father went out. 父亲说完话就出去了。

(6) 表示让步,意为"虽……,尽管……"。例如:

With all his money and fame, the famous star feels lonely. 这位著名的明星虽然名利双收,却感到孤独。

With good friends, the girl is not happy. 虽然这个女孩和好朋友在一起,但是不开心。

（7）with 的复合结构,即"with+宾语+宾补"。with 的宾补可以是形容词、副词、不定式、现在分词、过去分词、介词短语等。例如:

Don't speak with your mouth full. 嘴里塞满食物的时候不要说话。

This guy went out with the light on. 这家伙出去了,灯还亮着。

I can't go out with all these clothes to wash. 我不能把这些衣服全部带出去洗。

With the boy leading the way, we found her house easily. 在男孩的带领下,我们很轻松地找到了她的家。

With different techniques used, different results can be obtained. 使用不同的技术,可以得到不同的结果。

She said good-bye with tears in her eyes. 她含泪告别。

巩 固 练 习

Complete the following sentences by choosing the items marked A, B, C, or D.

1. Holmes managed to come up _____ some practical solutions to increasing sales.
   A. with   B. against   C. for   D. from

2. The train leaves at 6:00 p.m. So I have to be at the station _____ 5:40 p.m. at the latest.
   A. until   B. after   C. by   D. around

3. I'm sorry it's _____ my power to make a final decision on the project.
   A. over   B. above   C. off   D. beyond

4. In the preface _____ my book, I thanked all the people who had been of help to me.
   A. to   B. in   C. with   D. of

5. Their rudeness, greed and cruelty were _____ comparison.
   A. beyond   B. on   C. in   D. at

6. You can't wear a blue jacket _____ that shirt. It'll look terrible.
   A. on   B. above   C. up   D. over

7. I only wanted to get shelter _____ the snow, to get myself covered and warm.
   A. of   B. in   C. at   D. from

8. In order to change attitudes _____ employing women, the government is bringing in new laws.
   A. about   B. of   C. towards   D. on

9. The sarcastic remark is typical _____ his attitude.
   A. about   B. of   C. in   D. with

10. This type of car is superior _____ the old one in many aspects.
    A. to   B. over   C. than   D. with

11. The accident is reported to have occurred _____ the first Sunday in February.
    A. at   B. on   C. in   D. to

12. This small suitcase is perfect _____ weekend trips.
    A. at   B. for   C. in   D. on

13. John became a football coach in Sealion Middle School _____ the beginning of March.
    A. on   B. for   C. with   D. at
14. I'd like to buy a house—modern, comfortable, and _____ in a quiet neighborhood.
    A. in all   B. above all   C. after all   D. at all
15. The survival of civilization as we know it is _____ threat.
    A. within   B. under   C. towards   D. upon
16. Things fall to the ground _____ go up into the air because of gravity.
    A. instead of B. than   C. rather than   D. in place of
17. The cobra crawled out _____ the table.
    A. from behind   B. from across
    C. from within   D. from under
18. What else could you do but _____ nothing about it?
    A. pretend to know   B. to pretend know
    C. pretend knowing   D. to pretend to know
19. Mr. Wang went to Nanjing _____ October, 2019 and came back home _____ the morning of November 5th.
    A. at; in   B. on; at   C. in; on   D. by; from
20. Old buildings that are _____ repair should be blown up.
    A. in   B. under   C. beyond   D. out of
21. Children are very curious _____.
    A. by nature   B. on purpose   C. in person   D. at heart
22. The kind of work a person does determines _____ a great extent the kind of life he lives.
    A. to   B. in   C. on   D. with
23. My uncle lives _____ 105 Huanghe Street. His room is _____ the fifth floor.
    A. at; on   B. to; at   C. on; in   D. of; to
24. Tim is independent _____ his parents.
    A. with   B. of   C. on   D. from
25. He is running _____ the wind towards the east of the station _____ Tom running _____ the right.
    A. down; and; on   B. against; with; on
    C. for; with; in   D. with; while; to
26. Between 2014 and 2020, the number of overseas visitors expanded _____ 27%.
    A. in   B. for   C. by   D. to
27. I'm not in the mood _____ going to the party.
    A. of   B. to   C. on   D. for
28. In Hangzhou Mr. Green was so struck _____ the beauty of nature that he stayed _____ another night.
    A. at; on   B. with; at   C. for; in   D. by; for
29. The trees _____ front of the house are _____ the charge of Old Li.
    A. in; in   B. at; in   C. in; by   D. from; in

30. A lot of these children have been deprived _____ a normal home life.

    A. from   B. of   C. for   D. with

31. The old man died _____ cold _____ a cold night.

    A. from; at   B. of; in   C. of; on   D. for; during

32. The speech which he made _____ the project has bothered me greatly.

    A. be concerned   B. concerned   C. being concerned D. concerning

33. Does John know any other foreign languages _____ French?

    A. except   B. but   C. besides   D. beside

34. The bus, travelling _____ sixty miles an hour, just missed the man and ran into an office window.

    A. at   B. in   C. for   D. on

35. The dog seemed suspicious _____ everybody.

    A. to   B. at   C. of   D. on

36. The number of our products was increased _____ almost 10% in this spring.

    A. at   B. with   C. for   D. by

37. The animal has a brain which is nearest _____.

    A. in man's size   B. in size to man
    C. in size to man's   D. to the size in man

38. What he said just now had little to do with the question _____ discussion.

    A. on   B. in   C. under   D. at

39. I will carry out my plan _____ the consequences.

    A. in case of   B. because of   C. regardless of   D. prior to

40. We only know she is a journalist _____ *The Observer*.

    A. with   B. of   C. in   D. to

第七章

连 词

热身训练： 下列句子各有一处错误,请指出并改正。

❶ Study hard, or you'll make great progress.
❷ Mike doesn't like maths and physics.
❸ She doesn't like running and she likes climbing very much.
❹ Hans was about to go out until the phone rang.
❺ We won't give up as though we should fail ten times.
❻ Jack was very tired if he played tennis all afternoon.
❼ It's been a week after we left your family and we are now back home.
❽ Ken was about to say about it while someone interrupted him.
❾ When time passed, things seemed to get worse.
❿ Because she was ill, so she had to ask for leave.
⓫ Though he is old, but he continued to learn.
⓬ He walked about as he had lost something.
⓭ You study too hard that you're sure to pass the exam.
⓮ Our country as well as many other countries love peace.
⓯ For Mike went late, he didn't catch the last bus.

用来连接词、短语、从句与句子的词称为连词。连词是一种虚词,在句中不重读,不能独立担任句子成分。根据其在句中所起的作用,连词可分为并列连词和从属连词两类。

一、并列连词

连接具有并列关系的词、短语或句子的连词称为并列连词。根据其意义,它又可分为表示联合、转折、选择和因果四种关系的连词。

（一）表示联合关系的并列连词

表示联合关系的并列连词有：and、both... and、neither... nor、not only... but also、as well as、and as well、but as well。例如：

This year, the Chinese people have forged ahead in great strides and achieved historic changes. 这是中国人民昂首阔步、勇往直前,创造历史之变的一年。

After 14 years, the Olympic cauldron has been lit once again in Beijing, making the city the world's first to host both the Summer and Winter Olympic Games. 时隔14年,奥林匹克圣火再次在北京燃起,北京成为全球首个"双奥之城"。

Gage has practice as well as theories. 盖奇既有理论,又有实践。

Neither I nor Gage has been to Shanghai. 我没去过上海,盖奇也没去过。

(二) 表示语义转折和对比的并列连词

表示转折关系的并列连词有:but、yet、however、nevertheless、not that... but (that)等。例如:
I am sorry, but I won't be able to come to see you tomorrow. 很抱歉,我明天不能来看你。
Amy is willing, yet unable. 艾米心有余而力不足。
Gill studied hard, however, he failed the exam. 吉尔很努力地学习,但考试还是没及格。
Sarah has long hair, while her younger sister has short hair. 萨拉留长发而她妹妹留短发。
Tom is very generous while Katy is mean. 汤姆非常大方,而凯蒂却小气。

(三) 表示选择关系的并列连词

表示选择关系的并列连词有:or、or else、either...or、rather than、otherwise等。例如:
Seize the chance, or else you'll regret it. 抓住机会,否则你会后悔的。(or else 常置于祈使句的后面)
You can either go to the library or stay in the dormitory. 你可以去图书馆,或者待在寝室。
Benge rather than I is responsible for the project. 应该对项目负责的是本奇而不是我。

(四) 表示因果关系的并列连词

表示因果关系的并列连词有:so、for、thus、therefore、then、hence、accordingly、in that case、consequently 等。例如:
It is summer, for the cicadas are singing. 是夏天了,因为蝉叫了。
It's too late, so I won't go out. 太晚了,因此我就不出去了。
He didn't obey the rules of the company, thus/therefore/consequently/accordingly/hence/then he had to leave. 他没遵守公司的规定,因此只好离开公司。

(五) and 的用法

并列连词 and 的基本含义是表示"增补",但它还可表示两个或两个以上的并列成分之间存在的因果、条件、对比、顺序、让步等关系。

(1) 表示增补。例如:
Bertha has long hair and she often wears sunglasses. 伯莎留长发,而且常戴墨镜。
The CPC's 100-year achievements provide a source of motivation and its 100-year experience a wellspring of inspiration. 中国共产党的百年成就使人振奋,百年经验给人启迪。

（2）表示因果。例如：

Sound is carried by air, and without air there can be no sound. 声音靠空气传播，因此没有空气也就没有声音。

I was uncomfortable, and I went to sleep earlier last night. 我不舒服，所以昨晚我提前睡觉了。

（3）表示条件。例如：

Go straight on and you will see the Hongqi Cinema. 一直朝前走，你就会看到红旗电影院。

Work hard and you'll make greater achievements. 努力学习，你会有更大的成就。

（4）表示顺序。例如：

She turned off the light and went out of the room. 她关了灯，走出了房间。

I pressed a button and the game came out. 我按动按钮，游戏随即出现。

（5）表示对比。例如：

This play is interesting and that one is boring. 这出戏剧很有趣，那出戏剧则相当无聊。

Mary likes playing the piano and Sarah is fond of singing. 玛丽喜欢弹钢琴，萨拉喜欢唱歌。

（6）表示让步。例如：

Charlotte tried hard and (yet) he failed to get the project. 夏洛特努力尝试了，却没能得到这个项目。

It was raining heavily and they were still working at a construction site. 尽管雨下得很大，他们还在工地上干活。

（7）表示解释或评论。例如：

There's one thing you must realize and that is you are incapable of making the decision. 有一件事你必须清楚，那就是你没能力做这个决定。（表解释）

You gave him a piece of your mind, and a very good thing too. 你把你的想法告诉了他，这是件好事。（表评论）

（8）表示反复、渐渐（连接两个相同的词）。例如：

The weather is getting colder and colder. 天越来越冷了。

They talked and talked till the sun set. 他们谈啊谈啊，直到太阳落山。

二、从属连词

用来连接主句和从句的连词称为从属连词。从属连词可分为两类：引导名词性从句的从属连词和引导状语从句的从属连词。

（一）引导名词性从句的从属连词

引导名词性从句的从属连词有 that、whether 和 if，这些连词在从句中不充当任何成分。例如：

We know (that) light travels faster than sound. 我们知道光速比声速快。

I wonder if you could pay it in cash. 我想知道你是否能用现金付款。

The news that we came first in the National Basic Skill Competition was very exciting. 我们在全国基础技能大赛中位列第一，这消息令人十分振奋。

（二）引导状语从句的从属连词

（1）引导时间状语从句的从属连词：when、while、as、after、before、since、till/until、once、as soon as、the moment/instant (that)、no sooner... than、hardly/barely/scarcely... when、every time (that)、just as、immediately 等。例如：

Once you begin, you must persist in the end. 一旦开了头，你就要坚持到最后。

When it is sunny, we go for a picnic outside. 天晴时，我们外出野餐。

I had hardly cleaned my car when it began to rain. 我刚洗车就开始下雨了。

They will keep silent every time the boss enters the meeting room. 每当老板走进会议室时，他们就会保持安静。

（2）引导原因状语从句的从属连词：as、because、since、now (that)、seeing (that) 等。例如：

Ken didn't go to work because he was sick. 肯因为生病没去上班。

Since I'll be away, I'd like to reschedule the meeting. 既然我要离开，我想重新安排会议的时间。

How do you fill your day now that you've retired? 现在你退休了，怎么打发你的日子？

（3）引导地点状语从句的从属连词：where、wherever 等。例如：

Where there is life, there is hope. 活着就有希望。

Wherever the teacher led, the students followed. 老师引向哪里，学生就跟到哪里。

（4）引导条件状语从句的从属连词：if、unless、as/so long as、in case、if only、suppose/suppose(that)、given (that)、provided/providing (that)、on condition(that) 等。例如：

Unless I'm mistaken, she was back at work yesterday. 我没记错的话，她是昨天回来上班的。

You'll miss the last train if you don't hurry. 如果你不快点，你会错过最后一趟火车。

Suppose/Supposing I had seventy-two changes, my dream would come true. 要是我会七十二变，我的愿望就会实现了。

You can fly to London this evening provided/providing (that) you don't mind changing planes in Paris. 要是你不介意在巴黎转机的话，今天晚上你就可以飞往伦敦。

（5）引导目的状语从句的从属连词：that、so that、in order that、in case、lest、for fear that 等。例如：

Sarah took medicine on time in order that she might recover soon. 为了早日康复，萨拉按时吃药。

We spoke quietly for fear that we should wake the guard. 我们悄悄说话以免惊醒警卫。

（6）引导结果状语从句的从属连词：so、so that、so... that/such... that、that 等。例如：

Everyone gave a hand, so that the work was completed in advance. 每个人都帮了忙，结果工作提前完成了。

It was very cold, so that the stream had frozen. 天气很冷，小河的水结冰了。

Miss Zhou is so good a teacher that we all respect her. 周老师是个好老师，我们都尊敬她。

（7）引导让步状语从句的从属连词：though/although、as、while、even if/even though、however、whatever、whoever、no matter how/what/which、whether... or 等。例如：

While I admit that there are problems, I don't agree that they can't be solved. 尽管我承认有问题存在，但我不同意这些问题不能解决。

Even if we fail 100 times, we are not able to give up. 即使我们失败 100 次，我们也不会放弃。
Though he is old, he still learns a lot. 虽然他老了，可他仍然学习。
Strange as it may seem, I'm looking forward to the exam. 尽管有点奇怪，但我在盼望这场考试。

（8）引导方式状语从句的从属连词：as、as if/as though、the way 等。例如：

I gently walked, as I gently came. 轻轻地我走了，正如我轻轻地来。
Mike speaks German as if he were a German. 迈克讲起德语来就像他是德国人似的。
Mike doesn't speak the way you do. 迈克不像你这样讲话。

（9）引导比较状语从句的从属连词：as、than、the... the...等。例如：

He is more outgoing than before. 他比以前更开朗。
His grandfather is as white as a sheet. 他爷爷面无血色。
The harder you work, the luckier you are. 越努力，越幸运。

三、部分连词的用法比较

（一）when 和 while

when 和 while 两个词都可以表示"当……时"，用于引导时间状语从句。when 引导的时间状语从句的谓语动词既可以是延续性的，也可以是终止性的。while 引导的时间状语从句的谓语动词只能是延续性的。例如：

He was watching TV when mother came in. 妈妈进来时，他正在看电视。
Mother came in when/while he was playing computer games. 他在玩电脑游戏时，妈妈走了进来。
Strike while the iron is hot. 趁热打铁。

除此之外，when 还可以译作"这时"，while 可表对比，有"然而"之意。例如：

They were playing basketball outside when it grew dark. 他们在外面打篮球，这时天都黑了。
He is good at English while his elder brother is good at Chinese. 他擅长英语，而他哥哥擅长语文。

（二）though 和 as

though 和 as 两个词都可表示"虽然"，引导让步状语从句。though 引导的从句可用正常语序，也可用倒装语序；as 引导的从句一定要用倒装语序，即把从句中的表语、状语或谓词动词放在 as 之前。例如：

Though the exam is difficult, she'll pass it.
Difficult as/though the exam is, she'll pass it.
尽管这个考试很难，她还是会通过的。
Fast as/though you drive, you can't arrive in Guangzhou before dark.
Though you drive fast, you can't arrive in Guangzhou before dark.
尽管你开得快，你也不能在天黑前到广州。
Tired as/though he felt, he couldn't stop working. (Though he felt tired...)
尽管他觉得累了，却没法停止工作。

(三) because、as、since 和 for

because、as、since 和 for 四个词都可以表示"因为"的意思，但在具体使用时仍有区别。

（1） for 是并列连词，语气最弱，对前面分句加以解释或表示推断的原因。引导的分句一般置于句末，分句前要用逗号。例如：

You must have come back last night, for your shirt is changed. 你昨晚一定回来过，因为你换了衬衫。

（2） because 表示产生某结果的直接原因，语气最强，引导的从句置于句首或句末。放在句首时通常用逗号。例如：

The sports meeting is postponed because it is rainy. 因为下雨，运动会推迟了。

Because it rained, we went to the restaurant by taxi. 因为下雨，我们乘出租车去餐厅。

（3） as 表示原因时，语气不如 because 强，可译为"因为，由于"，引导的从句常置于句首。

As Sarah was in a good mood, we asked her to play with us. 由于萨拉心情好，我们叫她和我们一起玩了。

（4） since 可译为"既然"，往往表示一些显而易见的原因。语气不如 because 强，引导的从句常置于句首。例如：

Since you don't want to go with us, you'll go by yourself. 既然你不想跟我们一起去，你就自己去吧。

巩固练习

Complete the following sentences by choosing the items marked A, B, C, or D.

1. _____ it was early, she turned off the TV and went to bed.
   A. Because   B. Though   C. Since   D. As

2. Which skirt is cheaper, the white one _____ the pink one?
   A. and   B. or   C. but   D. so

3. Some of the studies show the results are very good, _____ others do not.
   A. while   B. so   C. for   D. or

4. You may go _____ you tidy the classroom.
   A. before   B. because   C. as soon as   D. after

5. I like summer _____ I can have a lot of fruit.
   A. but   B. if   C. though   D. because

6. _____ Tom _____ Sarah has come to see me. I don't know when they will come.
   A. Neither; nor   B. Not only; but also
   C. Both; and   D. Either; or

7. Tom stays at home these days. You may come _____ today _____ tomorrow.
   A. both; and   B. either; or
   C. not only; but also   D. neither; nor

8. My grandfather is old _____ strong.
   A. and   B. or   C. but   D. so

9. We'll go back to the playground _____ the rain stops.
   A. but   B. because   C. as soon as   D. and
10. _____ the teacher went into the classroom, the students were talking about the film.
   A. When   B. After   C. While   D. Before
11. I didn't get up _____ father came back from the office.
   A. when   B. because   C. while   D. until
12. The plane flew so high _____ it looked very tiny.
   A. that   B. why   C. whether   D. that if
13. You'd better put on more clothes, _____ it's very cold outside.
   A. for   B. and   C. because of   D. or
14. Ring me up _____ you come to my office.
   A. before   B. as   C. though   D. than
15. Please speak aloud _____ I can hear a little better.
   A. though   B. as   C. such that   D. so that
16. I don't know _____ or not we'll have an English exam tomorrow.
   A. whether   B. when   C. if   D. that if
17. Please take care of the children _____ I am out.
   A. though   B. while   C. that   D. so that
18. You must do _____ I told you.
   A. after   B. before   C. where   D. as
19. I had hardly finished cleaning the house _____ John arrived.
   A. while   B. when   C. as   D. since
20. We'll go to visit the Palace Museum _____ it rains tomorrow.
   A. since   B. as soon as   C. unless   D. when
21. _____ he is old, he can walk very fast.
   A. If   B. Although   C. Since   D. Because
22. Class Two is _____ large _____ Class One.
   A. so; that   B. so; as   C. such; that   D. as; as
23. You must get up early tomorrow, _____ I will go there alone.
   A. or   B. and   C. yet   D. for
24. I don't like him; I'd rather _____ in than _____ to play with him.
   A. to play; to go   B. stay; to go   C. go play; go   D. stay; go
25. He is not a basketball player _____.
   A. but also plays the piano   B. but a famous pianist
   C. but play the piano as well   D. but the pianist
26. It was raining hard, _____, the peasants went on with their work.
   A. however   B. and   C. but   D. although
27. Do you know _____ Lily is getting on well with her classmates?
   A. what   B. which   C. that   D. how

28. _____ Tom _____ Mary are free. You can play with them.
    A. Both; and   B. Not only; but also
    C. Neither; nor   D. Either; or
29. _____ we're all here, we can work out a solution.
    A. Because   B. Though   C. Since   D. For
30. The child is clever _____ healthy.
    A. as soon as   B. as good as   C. as well as   D. as tall as
31. Can you name three countries _____ Chinese is used as one of their languages?
    A. that   B. which   C. where   D. there
32. Plenty of others have advised me to stop, _____ I tried to take another upward step.
    A. at every time   B. every time   C. in every time   D. on every time
33. This is an old clock that is not only very handsome but _____.
    A. also it tells time accurately   B. also accurate
    C. it accurately tells time also   D. it too tells time accurately
34. Some people like coffee, _____ others don't.
    A. so   B. whereas   C. accordingly D. and
35. Mr. Smith comes from Australia, but he worked in China for five years. So you can talk with him _____.
    A. neither in English nor Chinese   B. not in Chinese but in English
    C. just in English not in Chinese   D. either in Chinese or in English
36. The coach was not on good terms with any of the players, _____ team morale was rather low.
    A. however   B. hence   C. otherwise   D. yet
37. She got in touch with her family _____ she received the letter.
    A. as   B. soon   C. immediately D. at once
38. _____ I closed my eyes, I fell asleep.
    A. once   B. while   C. if   D. the moment
39. I'll keep his address _____ I need it.
    A. in case   B. in order that   C. so that   D. when
40. The mother don't let the boy touch the knife _____ he might cut himself.
    A. for fear   B. so as that   C. in order that   D. that

第八章 08

动词概说

热身训练： 下列句子各有一处错误，请指出并改正。

❶ See is to believe.

❷ It is correct give up smoking.

❸ He wanted to going to the park.

❹ I find it interesting for study computer.

❺ I came here see you.

❻ We turned the lights off in order not waste electricity.

❼ My job is help the patients.

❽ Be a student, I must study hard.

❾ He remained to study the sea animals.

❿ Look the girl.

⓫ To play with fire is dangerous.

⓬ While to read the novel, he nodded from time to time.

⓭ There is a swim pool in our school.

⓮ Her job is to teach.

⓯ He finished to read the book.

一、动词的分类

根据意义及句法功能，动词可分为实义动词、连系动词、助动词和情态动词四类。

（1）实义动词：表示行为动作，具有完整的词义，能独立作谓语。实义动词又可分为及物动词和不及物动词两类，如：speak、read、listen、write、play、study、run、walk、watch、happen、learn、go、get、run 等。

（2）连系动词：本身有意义，但不能独立作谓语，必须和表语一起构成谓语，说明主语的性质、状态、特征或身份等，如：be、remain、look、smell、become、turn、keep、feel 等。

（3）助动词：本身无词义，帮助主要动词构成否定、疑问句式或构成时态、语态、语气等。主要有 be、do、have、will、shall 等。

（4）情态动词：本身有一定的词义，表示说话人的语气或情绪、态度，不可单独作谓语，必须和实义动词或系动词一起构成谓语。主要有 can、could、may、might、must、have to、will、would、shall、should 等。

二、动词的变化形式

动词的变化形式如表 8-1 所示。

表 8-1 动词的变化形式

形 式	规 则 变 化	例 句
一般现在时第三人称单数	一般情况在动词后直接加 s	look—looks；work—works
	以 o、s、x、sh、ch 结尾的动词,后加 es	catch—catches；go—goes
	以辅音字母加 y 结尾的动词,变 y 为 i,再加 es	study—studies；try—tries
现在分词	一般情况在动词后直接加 ing	read—reading；go—going
	以 ee、oe、ye 结尾的动词,直接加 ing	see—seeing；toe—toeing
	以不发音字母 e 结尾的动词,先去掉 e,再加 ing	love—loving；write—writing
	以重读闭音节结尾,词尾只有一个辅音字母的动词,先双写辅音字母,再加 ing	cut—cutting；put—putting
	少数以 ie 结尾的动词,先变 ie 为 y 再加 ing	die—dying；lie—lying
过去式和过去分词	一般情况在动词后直接加 ed	ask—asked；help—helped
	以不发音字母 e 结尾的动词,只加 d	like—liked；live—lived
	以辅音字母加 y 结尾的动词,变 y 为 i,再加 ed	cry—cried；study—studied
	以重读闭音节结尾,词尾只有一个辅音字母的动词,先双写辅音字母,再加 ed	stop—stopped；plan—planned

三、动词的限定形式和非限定形式

（一）动词的限定形式

限定动词也叫谓语动词,在句中充当谓语。它的形式受主语的限制,有人称、数的变化,还有时态、语态和语气的变化。例如：

Linda speaks fluent Chinese. 琳达说一口流利的中文。

I was reading a book when he came. 他来的时候,我正在看书。

The cars are made in Germany. 这些汽车是德国制造的。

（二）动词的非限定形式

非限定动词,也称非谓语动词。在句中不能单独充当谓语（但可以和情态动词或助动词一起充当谓语）,它们不受主语的限定,没有人称和数的变化,具有名词、形容词和副词的特征,在句中可以充当主语、宾语、表语、定语、状语、补足语等。非限定动词保留了动词的部分特征,有时态和语态的变化,也可以接宾语、表语、状语等,构成非限定动词短语,在逻辑意义上也有其动作的执行者或承受者,即非限定动词的逻辑主语。

英语非限定动词有三种基本形式:不定式、动名词、分词(现在分词和过去分词)(详细讲解见第十二～十四章)。

四、实义动词

实义动词分为及物动词和不及物动词

(一)及物动词

及物动词本身意思不完整,后面必须接宾语意思才完整。及物动词可接名词、代词、数词、不定式、V-ing 以及从句作宾语。及物动词可以分为以下三类。

(1) 单宾语动词。即接一个宾语的动词,如:accept、discover、enjoy、forget、borrow、buy、catch、invent、found、like、find、forget、receive、see、say、show、make、tell 等。例如:

He discovered a new land. 他发现了一片空地。

He accepted my apology in the end. 最后他接受了我的道歉。

We celebrated the centenary of the Communist Party of China(CPC) in 2021. 我们在 2021 年庆祝中国共产党成立 100 周年。

(2) 双宾语动词。即后面接间接宾语(指人)和直接宾语(指物)的动词,如:give、buy、pay、hand、read、return、sell 等。例如:

I will return him the novels tomorrow afternoon. 我明天下午要把小说还给他。

Tom gave me some books yesterday. 汤姆昨天给了我一些书。

Mr. Zhang teaches us German. 张老师教我们德语。

(3) 复合宾语动词。即后接宾语和宾补的动词,如:believe、find、hear、keep、make、see、elect、call 等。例如:

We elected Liu Hua our monitor. 我们选了刘华做我们的班长。

I'd like this matter handled in this way. 我希望这件事以这种方式处理。

We saw many people boating on the lake. 我们看到很多人在湖面上划船。

You should call me brother. 你应该叫我哥哥。

通常跟复合宾语的动词主要有以下四类。

① 常接名词作宾补的动词有:appoint、call、crown、consider、count、elect、find、leave、make、name、nominate、promote、think 等。例如:

We call him Jones. 我们叫他琼斯。

They appointed him chairman. 他们选他为主席。

② 常接形容词作宾补的动词有:find、consider、get、keep、leave、like、make、think、want、wish 等。例如:

We left the door open. 我们让这个门开着。

They found him honest. 他们发现他很诚实。

③ 常接不定式作宾补的动词有:advise、allow、ask、cause、compel、enable、encourage、expect、feel、forbid、force、have、hear、help、instruct、invite、let、make、need、notice、order、persuade、see、urge、watch、warn 等。例如:

I don't allow him to play outside at night. 我不允许他晚上去外面玩。
Let us all work together for a shared future! 让我们为共同的未来而努力！
④ 常接分词作宾补的动词有：feel、find、get、have（使得）、hear、keep、look at、notice、observe、see、watch 等。例如：
We often hear this song sung in the street. 我们常常在街上听到这首歌。
I saw a thief stealing his wallet yesterday. 昨天我看见小偷偷他钱包。

（二）不及物动词

不及物动词本身意思已经很完整，无须接宾语。常见的不及物动词有：ache、appear、arise、arrive、belong、care、come、cough、go、happen、laugh、lie、listen、live、look、occur、rise、sit、smile 等。例如：
The sun rises in the east. 太阳从东边升起。
The rain stopped when he got out of the car. 他下车时雨停了。
What happened the day before yesterday? 前天发生了什么事？

（三）兼作及物和不及物动词的词

兼作及物和不及物动词的词有：beat（*vi.* 跳动, *vt.* 敲、打）、grow（*vi.* 生长, *vt.* 种植）、play（*vi.* 玩耍, *vt.* 打〈牌、球〉、演奏）、smell（*vi.* 发出〈气味〉, *vt.* 嗅）、ring（*vi.* 〈电话、铃〉响, *vt.* 打电话）、speak（*vi.* 讲话, *vt.* 说〈语言〉）、hang（*vi.* 悬挂, *vt.* 绞死）、operate（*vi.* 动手术, *vt.* 操作）、lift（*vi.* 消散, *vt.* 移动, 提起）等。例如：
We saw the woods when the clouds lifted. 当云升起来时，我们看见了树林。
He lifted his glass and broke it. 他拿起他的杯子摔了。
He shot a hare. 他射中了一只兔子。
He shot at the rabbit, but it ran away. 他向兔子射击，但它却跑掉了。
The house will not stand much rain. 这座房子是经不起大雨的。
She stood by the window reading English. 她站在窗边读英语。

五、连系动词

连系动词（即系动词）用于说明主语的状态、性质、特征或身份。表语通常由名词、形容词、或相当于名词/形容词的词或短语等充当，说明主语是什么或怎么样。
根据其意义，系动词大致可分为以下四类。

（一）感觉类系动词

感觉类系动词是与五种感觉器官相关的动词。常见的有：look、feel、smell、taste、sound 等。例如：
She looks much older in her black dress. 她穿黑衣服看起来老很多。
The music sounds charming. 这音乐听起来很迷人。
This kind of clothes feels very soft. 这种衣服摸起来很柔软。

（二）状态类系动词

状态类系动词表示主语具有某种性质、特征或处于某种状态。常见的有：be、appear、seem 等。例如：

The captain is a clement man. 船长是一个宽厚的人。

He is very satisfied with my work. 他对我的工作非常满意。

She appears/seems to be very unfriendly to us. 她似乎对我们很不友好。

It appears/seems that her team will win. 她的队似乎会赢。

（三）变化类系动词

变化类系动词表示主语从一种状态变化成另一种状态。常见的有：become、turn、grow、go、come、fall、get 等。例如：

Her face becomes red. 她的脸变红了。

Put the vegetables into the fridge, or they will go bad in such hot weather. 把蔬菜放到冰箱里，否则在这么热的天气下会变坏的。

He grew ricn within a short time. 没多长时间，他就富了。

（四）持续类系动词

持续类系动词表示主语持续某种状态。常见的有：remain、keep、stay、lie、continue 等。例如：

The animals will remain loyal to humans if treated well. 如果动物得到善待，它们会保持对人类的忠诚。

The book lay open on the bookshelf. 这本书摊开在书架上。

（五）系动词的固定搭配

常见的系动词固定搭配有：go hungry、go mad、go hard、go wrong、fall ill/sick、fall asleep、fall flat、come true、come short、come loose、keep fit/healthy、go red/white/blue、fall short of、come right、keep quiet 等。

六、短语动词

由两个或两个以上的单词（以动词为中心词）构成的短语，称为短语动词。短语动词分为以下七类。

（一）动词+介词

这类短语动词相当于及物动词，其后需加宾语。常见的有：abide by、account for、act on、aim at、allow for、allow of、amount to、apply for、believe in、break into、call for、care about、come across、complain of/about、conform to、consent to、deal with、live through、stand for 等。例如：

My father didn't care about my feelings at all. 我爸爸一点都不考虑我的感受。

We have lived through landmark events in the history of our Party and our county. 我们经历了

党和国家历史上具有里程碑意义的大事。

（二）不及物动词+副词

这类短语动词相当于不及物动词，其后不加宾语。常见的有：break down、break out、break up、come up、come off、die away、drop out、fade away、fall apart、fall behind、fall off、fight back、give in、give up、hang around、look out、shout out、stay up、watch out、turn up、run out 等。例如：

The girl fell behind after she came back. 女孩回来之后，就落后了。
Many of the town's dropouts hang around. 这个镇上很多脱离社会传统的人到处闲逛。

（三）及物动词+副词

这类短语动词相当于及物动词，其后需加宾语。常见的有：add up、break out、bring about、bring in、bring up、call off、carry out、drive forward、find out、give away、pull down、point out、set up、switch on、switch off、take on、take over、take off、throw away、turn down、wipe out 等。例如：

The policeman found out the thief. 这个警察找出了小偷。
Xi Jinping's diplomatic thinking generates the intellectual strength that drives the times forward. 习近平外交思想彰显着推动时代的思想伟力。

（四）动词+副词+介词

这类短语动词相当于及物动词，其后需加宾语。常见的有：come up with、cut down on、do away with、get along with、get down to、go in for、keep away from、run out of、watch out for、look forward to、look down upon 等。例如：

The teacher looks forward to traveling around the world. 这位老师期待环游世界。
They did away with the law. 他们废除了这项律法。

（五）动词+名词

这类短语动词相当于不及物动词，其后不加宾语。常见的有：catch fire、hold one's tougue、lose courage、lose heart、lose weight、lose interest、make sense、make a bet 等。例如：

The girl finally lost weight. 这个女孩最终减肥成功。
She was standing too close to the fireplace and her dress caught fire. 她站得太靠近壁炉，衣服着火了。

（六）动词+名词+介词

这类短语动词相当于及物动词，其后需加宾语。常见的有：catch sight of、get rid of、make progress in、make sense of、make use of、make room for、make way for、take advantage of 等。例如：

The student took advantage of every minute to study. 这位学生利用每一分钟学习。
She caught sight of a car in the distance. 她一眼瞥见了远处的汽车。

（七）动词+介词+名词

这类短语动词分为带宾语类和不带宾语类两种情况。

（1）带宾语类的短语动词有：bring... to an end、bring... under control、have... in mind、 keep... in mind、keep... in touch、bear... in mind、put... into practice 等。例如：

Please keep the thing in mind. 请把这件事情记在心上。

The trial was swiftly brought to an end. 审判很快结束了。

（2）不带宾语类的短语动词有：put on weight、keep in touch、burst into tears、go to pieces、come into use、come into power、stand on ceremony、come to life 等。例如：

The new teaching building will come into use soon. 这栋新的教学大楼很快就会投入使用。

He has put on a lot of weight since he gave up smoking. 他戒烟后体重增加了许多。

巩固练习

Complete the following sentences by choosing the items marked A, B, C, or D.

1. It may take a few weeks for your application to be _____.
   A. possessed B. processed C. produced D. persuaded

2. Jess was sad and her friend helped her _____ the first awful weeks after her husband died.
   A. break through B. break down C. get through D. get rid of

3. The responsibility of an artist is to create artworks to _____ people's needs for enjoyment.
   A. result in B. serve for C. work at D. cater to

4. There are many online shopping payment methods in China, and you can choose, when the order is _____, cash, POS or checks, to pay for the goods.
   A. deposited B. delivered C. deduced D. defined

5. When I said that someone didn't work hard in our class, I was not _____ you.
   A. picking out B. referring to C. taking out D. sticking to

6. The recent cold weather has prevented residents from going out, which may _____ the decline in customer flows at the shopping mall.
   A. make up B. account for C. apply for D. take up

7. Thousands of products _____ from crude oil are now in daily use.
   A. to make B. made C. making D. be made

8. —What do you think of the jacket and the hat I wear today?
   —I don't think this jacket _____ you and that your hat _____ this jacket perfectly.
   A. suits; fits B. meets; fits C. matches; suits D. fits; matches

9. Don't be _____ by products promising to make you lose weight quickly.
   A. taken off B. taken out C. taken away D. taken in

10. Experts suggest that young parents _____ some time to communicate with their children instead of spending much time playing games on the phone.
    A. set aside B. put away C. make up D. account for

11. The TV *Dwelling Narrowness*（蜗居）is really fantastic. The show has succeeded in _____ much to the audience, which has contributed to its success.
    A. touching on B. diving in C. getting across D. going about

12. Californians and New Englanders speak the same language and _____ by the same federal laws.

    A. stand   B. conform   C. abide   D. sustain

13. Our son doesn't know what to _____ at the university; he can't make up his mind about his future.

    A. take in   B. take up   C. take over   D. take after

14. A lorry _____ Jane's cat and sped away.

    A. ran over   B. ran into   C. ran through   D. ran down

15. When he realized the police had spotted him, the man _____ the exit as quickly as possible.

    A. made off   B. made for   C. made out   D. made up

16. Frequently single parent children _____ some of the functions that the absent adult in the house would have served.

    A. take off   B. take after   C. take in   D. take on

17. The car _____ halfway for no reason.

    A. broke   B. broke down   C. broke up   D. broke out

18. Having decided to rent a flat, we _____ contacting all the accommodation agencies in the city.

    A. set about   B. set down   C. set out   D. set up

19. The student was just about to _____ the question, when suddenly he found the answer.

    A. arrive at   B. submit to   C. work out   D. give up

20. It is not easy to learn English well, but if you _____ , you will succeed in the end.

    A. hang up   B. hang about   C. hang on   D. hang onto

21. A well-written composition _____ good choice of words and clear organization among other things.

    A. calls on   B. calls for   C. calls up   D. calls off

22. The manager needs an assistant that he can _____ to take care of problems in his absence.

    A. count on   B. count in   C. count up   D. count out

23. There are other problems which I don't propose to _____ at the moment.

    A. go into   B. go around   C. go for   D. go up

24. The sports meeting, originally due to be held last Friday, was finally _____ because of the bad weather.

    A. set off   B. broken off   C. worn off   D. called off

25. When a fire _____ at the National Exhibition in London, at least ten priceless paintings were completely destroyed.

    A. broke off   B. broke out   C. broke down   D. broke up

26. If you suspect that the illness might be serious you should not _____ going to the doctor.

    A. put off   B. hold back   C. put aside   D. hold up

27. Jerey told me not to _____ the news.
    A. tell out   B. show   C. let out   D. talk about
28. Her face _____ pale(苍白) when she heard the bad news.
    A. got   B. is   C. turned   D. was
29. We all _____ Lance to be German, but in fact he was Swiss.
    A. thought   B. consider   C. believed   D. supposed
30. Medicine tastes _____ but it cures discases.
    A. bitter   B. badly   C. bitterly   D. well
31. It often rains and the crops _____ fast.
    A. get   B. turn   C. grow   D. become
32. —How are you _____ now?
    —Much better, thank you.
    A. getting   B. feeling   C. making   D. turning
33. No one enjoys _____ at.
    A. laughing   B. to laugh   C. being laughed   D. to be laughed
34. You must do something to prevent your house _____.
    A. to be broken in   B. from being broken in
    C. to break in   D. from breaking in
35. —Where is my passport? I remember _____ it here.
    —You shouldn't have left it here. Remember _____ it with you all the time.
    A. to put; to take   B. putting; taking C. putting; to take D. to put; taking
36. His room needs _____, so he must have it _____.
    A. painting; painted   B. painted; painting
    C. painting; painting   D. painted; painted
37. The young trees we planted last week require _____ with great care.
    A. looking after   B. to look after   C. to be looked after   D. taken good care of
38. Only _____ English doesn't mean _____ the language.
    A. to learn; to learn   B. learning; learning
    C. learning about; learn   D. learning about; learning
39. She returned home only to find the door open and something _____.
    A. missed   B. to be missing   C. missing   D. to be missed
40. She decided to devote herself _____ the problem of old age.
    A. to study   B. studying   C. to studying   D. study

第九章

动词的时和体

热身训练： 下列句子各有一处错误，请指出并改正。

1. My sister saw a lovely dolly when we are shopping the other day.
2. The first time I decide to leave home was when I was upon graduation in high school.
3. We have sometimes accidents on this road, but no accidents have been occurred since last year.
4. He just come back from America last week.
5. The whole class divided into four groups.
6. Some of us often went to school without breakfast; some like to have snacks; some others are particular about food; and still some eat or drink too much.
7. Reading books not only interests you but also benefits you, for reading was always just for fun.
8. As a result, I was tired out and feel unhappy.
9. The sky is full of sunshine, so does my life.
10. On April 16th, we went sightseeing that we have long expected.
11. I believe many people already read this kind of news in newspapers or magazines.
12. I didn't hear what you said; I read a scary novel.
13. We were very sorry to lose the oldest thing we have.
14. Li Ming is a doctor who have been living in Shanghai since he was born.
15. However, if we stress cooperation too much, there would be no progress.

  动词的时(Tense)是表示不同时间的动词形式。"时"和"时间"既有联系，又有区别。"时间"(Time)是一个普通概念，无论什么人都有"过去""现在""将来"的时间概念，然而表达这种时间概念的语言手段却因语言的不同而异。在法语动词中用"过去时""现在时"和"将来时"分别表示过去、现在、将来的时间概念；而英语动词自"古英语"(Old English)以来就只有"现在时"和"过去时"，而没有"将来时"，即英语并没有发展出一种独特的表示"将来"的动词形式——"将来时"。在现代英语中，能用以表示"将来"的语法形式多种多样，但没有一种能称为专职的"将来时"。

  动词的体(Aspect)表示动作或过程在一定时间内处于何种状态的动词形式。英语动词有四种体：一般体(Simple Aspect)、进行体(Progressive Aspect)、完成体(Perfective Aspect)和完成进行体(Perfective Progressive Aspect)，如表9-1所示。有的参考书中也称进行时和完成时。

表 9-1　动词的时和体

体（Aspect）\时（Tense）	一般体（Simple）	进行体（Progressive）	完成体（Perfective）	完成进行体（Perfective Progressive）
现在时（Present）	do/does	am/is/are doing	have/has done	have/has been doing
过去时（Past）	did	was/were doing	had done	had been doing

动词的"时"与"体"相结合，可以衍生出限定词的八种时、体形式。具体如下（以主动词 work 为例）。

（1）一般现在时（Simple Present）：She works as a teacher.

（2）一般过去时（Simple Past）：She worked very hard last year.

（3）现在进行体（Present Progressive）：She is working in a school now.

（4）过去进行体（Past Progressive）：She was working as a volunteer this time yesterday.

（5）现在完成体（Present Perfective）：She has worked here for two years.

（6）过去完成体（Past Perfective）：When you came to the office, she had worked for two hours.

（7）现在完成进行体（Present Perfective Progressive）：She has been working for a long time.

（8）过去完成进行体（Past Perfective Progressive）：By 10 o'clock she had been working for two hours.

一、一般现在时

（1）表示经常性、习惯性的动作或存在的状态。常与频度副词 often、usually、sometimes、every day/week/year 等连用。例如：

I often take a walk in the park. 我经常在公园里散步。

We always care for each other and help each other. 我们总是相互关心，相互帮助。

The only way for the world to emerge from the pandemic is by working together. 世界摆脱疫情的唯一途径就是共同努力。

（2）表示客观事实、真理。例如：

The sun rises in the east and sets in the west. 太阳东升西落。

The earth is round, not flat. 地球是圆的，不是平的。

The earth moves round the sun once a year. 地球每年绕太阳运转一次。

（3）表示希望、承认、建议等意义的动词。例如：

I suggest you (should) be more careful. 我建议你要更加小心点。

I admit we are wrong. 我承认我们错了。

We hope that all the sons and daughters of the Chinese nation will join forces to create a brighter future for our nation. 期盼全体中华儿女携手向前，共创中华民族美好未来。

I salute all your great efforts, and extend to you best wishes for the New Year. 我向你们所有的努力致敬，并向你们致以新年的良好祝愿。

（4）用在比赛、剧情介绍、演示说明、新闻标题、图片说明中。例如：

John throws the ball to Jack and Jack catches it. He jumps and casts it into the basket. 约翰把

球扔给杰克。杰克接过球,跳起来把球投进篮里。

He sits down, shivers a little. Clock inside strikes eight. 他坐了下来,微微有些颤抖,里面钟敲响了八点。

Watch me. I mix the four kinds of liquid in the tube. 看着我,我把四种液体在试管中掺在一起。

Labour Cuts Deals With Investors《削减劳力,应对投资者》

(5) 在时间、条件状语从句中表示将来的动作。例如:

If it doesn't rain tomorrow, I will go hiking in the open air. 如果明天不下雨,我会去户外远足。

I'll tell her the good news when she comes back. 等她回来的时候,我把这个好消息告诉她。

(6) 表示按计划或安排将要发生的动作。这种用法只限于 start、begin、leave、go、come、arrive、return、take place 等动词。例如:

What time does the train arrive in Beijing? 火车什么时候到达北京?

The sports meeting starts at nine tomorrow. 明天运动会 9 点开始。

二、一般过去时

(1) 表示在过去某个时间所发生的动作或所处的状态。常与 yesterday、last week、in+年份、just now、a moment ago、the other day 等表示过去的时间状语连用。例如:

In 2021, elephants in Yunnan Province trudged north and came home. 2021 年云南大象北上回归。

We spared no effort to present a great Games to the world in February 2022. 2022 年 2 月,我们竭诚为世界奉献了一届奥运盛会。

On July 1st, we solemnly celebrated the 100th anniversary of the founding of the Communist Party of China (CPC). 七月一日,我们隆重庆祝了中国共产党成立 100 周年。

(2) 表示在过去一段时间内的经常性或习惯性动作。例如:

We often played together when we were children. 我们小时候常在一起玩。

Mike went to the library every day when he was in college. 迈克读大学时,每天都去图书馆。

Bill always got up too late. 比尔总是很晚起床。

注:表示过去经常发生的动作还可用 used to 和 would。例如:

He used to swim a lot, but he doesn't now. 他过去经常游泳,但现在不游了。

Whenever we were in trouble, our father would help us. 每当我们遇到困难,我们的父亲都会帮助我们。

(3) 表示主语过去的特征或性格。例如:

At that time she was very good at English. 那时,她英语学得很好。

He was a gentle man as a young man. 他年轻的时候是个绅士。

When he was in middle school, he looked like a superstar. 他在中学时就像个大明星。

(4) 用在时间、条件状语从句中表示过去将来时间。例如:

He said he would wait until they came back. 他说他会一直等到他们回来。

He told me that he would go out if I didn't come. 他告诉我如果我不来的话他就会出门。

It was reported that the teacher would help the little boy if he was left alone. 据报道如果这个小男孩被抛弃时,这位老师会帮助他。

(5) 一般过去时有时可以表示现在,仅限于 want、hope、wonder、think、intend 等几个动词,使语气更委婉。例如:

I wondered if you could help me. 不知你能不能帮我一下忙。

有时用一般过去时也是时态一致的需要。例如:

I didn't know he was here. 我不知道他在这里。

> 注:① 表示一系列的动作时,尽管有先后,都用一般过去时,最后两个动词之间用 and 连接。例如:
>
> He opened the door, rushed out and then disappeared. 他打开门,冲了出去,然后就消失了。
>
> ② 注意在语境中理解"我刚才/原来还不……"。例如:
>
> Your address again? I didn't quite catch it. 请再说一次你的地址好吗?我刚才没听清楚。

三、现在进行体

(一) 现在进行体的一般用法

(1) 表示现在(指说话人说话时)正在发生的事情。例如:

The world is turning its eyes to China, and China is ready. 世界期待中国,中国做好了准备。

Our numerous dream-chasers are keeping up their good work. 我们无数的追梦者都在继续努力。

We are making confident strides on the path toward the great rejuvenation of the Chinese nation. 我们正昂首阔步行进在实现中华民族伟大复兴的道路上。

(2) 表示长期的或重复性的动作,说话时动作未必正在进行。例如:

She is learning to play the violin under Mr. Smith. 她目前跟着史密斯先生学小提琴。

Members of China's foreign service are studying and implementing at greater depth Xi Jinping Thought on Diplomacy. 中国外交战线学习贯彻习近平外交思想正在不断引向深入。

(二) 现在进行体的特殊用法

(1) 现在进行体表暂时的情况。现在进行体可用来表示不会长期发生的动作或情况,或被认为在短期内正在进行的动作或存在的状况。例如:

——What's your son doing these days? 你儿子最近在干什么?

——He's studying English at Durham University. 他现在在达勒姆大学学习英语。

① 这种情况不一定在说话时发生。例如:

Don't take that ladder away. Your grandfather's using it. 别把梯子拿走,你祖父在用呢。

She's at her best when she's making big decisions. 她在做重大决定时处于最佳状态。

② 暂时发生的事情(也可以是在说话时正在进行着的事情)。例如:

The river is flowing very fast after last night's rain. 昨夜下过雨后,河水流速很快。

③ 现在进行体也可以用来表示当前的动向。例如:

Houses are costing more these days. 如今房价越来越贵了。

People are becoming less tolerant of smoking these days. 现在人们对吸烟越来越不能容忍了。

（2）现在进行体表示已经确定或安排好的将来的活动。意为"意图、打算、安排"，常用于人。常用词为 come、go、start、arrive、leave、stay 等。例如：

Mr John is arriving tonight. 约翰先生今晚到达。

I'm leaving next week. 我下周就要离开。

I'm leaving for Shanghai next week. 我下周要去上海。

（3）表示短促动作的动词（如 jump、knock、beat、pick、skip 等）的进行体，表达动作的重复。例如：

The children are jumping over there. 孩子们在那边跳。

Her heart is beating fast. 她的心脏跳得很快。

（4）某些表示希望或想法的动词（如 hope、wonder、want 等）的进行体，表示委婉客气。例如：

I'm wondering whether you can help us now. 我不知道你现在能否帮我们一个忙。

I'm hoping that he will succeed. 我希望他成功。

（三）现在进行体与一般现在时的区别

（1）现在进行体强调目前正在进行的动作，而一般现在时强调经常性或习惯性的动作。例如：

I'm reading a book now. 我在看一本书。（目前正在干的事情）

I read books in my spare time. 我有空时会看书。（经常性的行为）

（2）现在进行体强调现阶段一直在进行的动作，而一般现在时只表动作的重复，而不表示动作的持续。例如：

What are you doing these days? 这几天你在干什么？

They learn New Concept English in after-school class. 他们在课外辅导班学新概念英语。

（四）四类动词不用进行体

英语中有四类动词一般不用进行体（即不用现在进行体和过去进行体）。

（1）表心理状态、情感的动词，如 love、hate、like、care、respect、please、prefer、know 等，若用进行时则词义改变。

（2）表存在、状态的动词，如 appear、exist、lie、remain、stand、seem 等。

（3）表感觉的动词，如 see、hear、feel、smell、sound、taste 等。

（4）表意识性的动词，如 accept、allow、admit、decide、end、refuse、permit、promise 等。

四、过去进行体

（一）过去进行体的一般用法

（1）表示在过去某一时间正在进行的动作，此时句中往往有表示过去的时间状语，如：then、at that time、this time、last night、yesterday 等。

I was answering the phone when my parents got home. 我父母到家时，我正在接电话。

He was surfing on the Internet this time yesterday. 昨天这个时候他正在上网。

At that time she was writing a novel. 那个时候她正在写小说。

（2）描述在过去的同一时间进行的几个动作，通常用 while 连接。例如：

I was studying at college while my sister was teaching at the university. 我姐姐在大学教书时，我在上大学。

She was reading while her mother was cooking. 妈妈在做饭时她在读书。

The man was repairing the bike while his wife was cleaning the room at that time. 那位男士在修理自行车的时候，他的妻子在打扫房间。

（3）表示在过去某一段时间内一直持续进行的动作。例如：

They were expecting you yesterday, but you didn't turn up. 他们昨天一直期待你的出现，但你却没有露面。

The parents were looking for their lost kid last night. 这对父母昨晚一直在寻找他们丢失的孩子。

（二）过去进行体的特殊用法

（1）表示临时性。即表示在过去短期内正在进行的动作或存在的临时情况，这种情况通常不会长期持续。例如：

It was raining at 6 o'clock this morning. 今早六点钟正在下雨。

It happened while I was living in Paris last year. 这件事发生于去年我住在巴黎的时候。

（2）表示计划。即表示在过去安排好的计划或活动。这类用法在没有明确上下文的情况下，通常会和表示将来时间的状语连用。例如：

He said that his sister was getting married next May. 他说他妹妹明年五月结婚。

用 arrive、come、go、leave、take off 等动词的进行体描写行程安排，也通常含有将来意义。例如：

He said he was leaving for home in a day or two. 他说他一两天之内就动身回家了。

（3）表示委婉语气。动词 hope、wonder 等过去进行体常用来表示提出要求，语气比一般现在时要委婉。例如：

I was wondering if you had two single rooms. 不知道你们是否有两个单人间。

I was hoping you would give me some advice. 我希望你给我出点主意。

（4）表示重复。过去进行体有时可以与 always、constantly、continually、forever 等表示动作屡次发生的副词连用，强调动作的不断重复。例如：

The couples were always quarrelling. 这对夫妻老是吵架。

She was forever complaining. 她总是抱怨。

注：现在进行体也有类似用法，不同的是过去进行体是表示过去不断重复的动作，而现在进行体是表示现在不断重复的动作。

（三）过去进行体与一般过去时的区别。

（1）过去进行体强调在过去某时刻正在进行的动作，而一般过去时表示完成的动作。例如：

He was writing his paper last night. 他昨晚在写论文。

He wrote his paper last night. 他昨晚写了论文。

（2）表示过去的状态、感觉及心理活动的静态动词（如 be、like、love、hate、fear、own、hear、see、know、want、notice）可用于一般过去时，但通常不用于过去进行时。例如：

My sister hated it when I spoke with my mouth full of food. 我姐姐讨厌我嘴里含着食物说话。

（3）一般过去时与 always、constantly、forever、continually 等连用，表示"过去经常性、习惯性的动作"；而过去进行体与 always、constantly、forever、continually 等连用，表示动作的重复，常具有感情色彩。

My mom always got up at five. 我妈妈过去总是五点起床。

The mother was always thinking of his children. 这位妈妈总是想着孩子们。

（4）有时过去进行体可以用来替换一般过去时，但一般过去时表示主语的行为是经过认真思考的；而过去进行体表示一种较随便或没有进行仔细思考的行为。

I thought that she would agree with us. 我原以为她会同意我们的意见的。

I was thinking of persuading him to follow my advice. 我想说服他接受我们的建议。

五、现在完成体

（一）现在完成体用法

（1）现在完成体用来表示已经发生或已经完成的动作对现在造成影响或后果。也就是说，动作或状态发生在过去但它的影响现在还存在，强调的是现在。例如：

He has just run a nucleic acid test. 他刚做过核酸检测。

The director has nearly made forty films. 这个导演拍了将近40部电影。

Xi Jinping's diplomatic thinking has achieved a high degree of unity of historical mission and trend of the Times, national spirit and internationalism, Chinese style and world sentiment. 习近平外交思想实现了历史使命与时代潮流的高度统一，民族精神与国际主义的高度统一，中国气派与世界情怀的高度统一。

（2）现在完成体可以用来表示发生在过去某一时刻的且持续到现在的动作（用行为动词表示）或状态（be 动词表示），常与 for（+时间段）、since（+时间点或过去时的句子）连用，谓语动词必须是延续性动词。例如：

The man has lived here since 2008. 自从2008年以来，这个男士一直住在这儿。

> **注**：for 和 since 的用法如下。
> ① for+时间段，译为：……时间。
> ② since+过去一个时间点，译为：自从……以来。
> ③ since+时间段+ago，译为：自从……以来。
> ④ since+从句（过去时），译为：自从……以来。
> ⑤ It is+时间段+since+从句（过去时），译为：自从……以来。
> 瞬间动词（buy、die、join、lose 等）与 for 或 since 引导的时间段连用时，要改成延续性动词。变化如下：come/arrive/reach/get to—be in、go out—be out、finish—be over、open—be open、die—be dead、buy—have、fall ill—be ill、come back—be back、put on—be on/wear、worry—be worried、catch a cold—have a cold、get up—be up。

(二) 与现在完成体连用的时间状语

现在完成体是一个与过去和现在都有关系的时态。因此,具有这样时间特点的状语都可以与现在完成体连用。

(1) 与表示一段时间的状语连用,如"for+时间段""since+时间点"。例如:

The teacher has lived in this city for more than 40 years. 这位老师在这个城市已生活了40多年。

The engineer has worked in this factory since 2011. 这位工程师从2011年起就在这工厂工作。

(2) 与表示不具体的过去时间状语连用,如 already、never、ever、just 等。例如:

I've just found this library book. 我刚刚找到这本图书馆的书。

General Secretary Xi Jinping has already put forth a Global Development Initiative. 习近平总书记郑重提出了全球发展倡议。

(3) 与表示包含过去和现在的一整段时间的状语连用,如 lately、recently、in the past few years、these few years、these days、up to now、so far 等。例如:

How have your parents been recently? 你的父母近来状况如何?

The famous writer has written two new books in the past two years. 那位著名的作家在过去两年里写了两本新书。

Have you seen her uncle these days? 这些天你看见她的叔叔了吗?

The Greens have visited a lot of places in Australia so far. 迄今为止,格林一家已经参观了澳大利亚的许多地方。

> **注**:现在完成体不能与单纯表示过去的时间状语连用,如 yesterday、last week/year/month、three days/years/weeks ago、in+年份等。

(三) 现在完成体与一般过去时区别

(1) 侧重点不同。现在完成体和一般过去时所表示的动作都发生在过去,但它们所强调的重点不同。现在完成体侧重于对现在的影响;而一般过去时侧重于某一动作发生在过去某个时间或某段时间,即现在完成体侧重于现在的结果,而一般过去时侧重于动作发生的时间。例如:

I have seen the film. 我看过这部电影。

I saw the film three days ago. 三天前我看了这部电影。

Mr. Green has bought a new computer. 格林先生买了一台新计算机。

Mr. Green bought a new computer yesterday. 格林先生昨天买了一台新计算机。

(2) 时间状语不同。现在完成体常与 already、yet、just、ever、never、before 等副词以及"for+段时间""since+过去时间/从句"等时间状语连用;而一般过去时则常与时间段+ago、just now、yesterday、last week 等表示过去的时间状语连用。例如:

She has lived here since six years ago. 她自六年前以来就一直住在这里了。

She lived here six years ago. 六年前她住在这里。

The boy has been in the League for three years. 男孩入团已经三年了。

Tom wrote a letter to his girlfriend last night. 昨晚汤姆给他的女朋友写了一封信。

六、过去完成体

（一）过去完成体的用法

（1）表示过去某一时间之前就已发生或完成的动作，即"过去的过去"。通常与 by、before 等连用。例如：
We had learned 10,000 words by the end of last week. 到上周末，我们已经学了10000个单词。
The bus had left before we reached the station. 在我们到达车站之前，公交车已经走了。
The sports meeting had begun when we got to school. 我们到学校时，运动会已经开始了。

（2）表示从过去的某一时间开始，一直延续到过去另一时间的动作或状态，常和 for、since 构成的时间状语连用。
The man had been at the bus stop for 20 minutes when a bus finally came. 当公共汽车来的时候，那人在车站已等了20分钟。
He had worked in the factory for five years before he moved here. 他搬到这里之前，已经在那家工厂工作了五年。

（3）表示某一动作或状态在过去某时间开始，一直延续到另一过去时间，而且动作尚未结束，仍然有继续下去的可能。
By the end of last year, he had worked in the factory for twenty years. 到去年年底为止，他已经在这个工厂工作了20年了。

（4）过去完成体需要与一个表示过去的时间状语连用，它不能离开过去时间而独立存在。此时多与 already、yet、still、just、before、never 等时间副词及 by、before、until 等引导的短语或从句连用。
Before she came to China, Mary had taught English in a middle school for about five years. 玛丽来中国之前，就已经在一所中学教了五年英语了。
Jim had collected more than 300 Chinese stamps by the time he was ten. 吉姆在他十岁的时候就已经收集了300多张中国邮票了。
I had finished reading the novel by eight o'clock last night. 到昨晚八点钟，我已经读完了这本小说。
The workers had planted six hundred trees before last Wednesday. 上周三之前，工人们已经种了600棵树。

（二）过去完成体与一般过去时的区别

虽然这两者都表示过去发生的动作或存在的状态，但在使用时应注意以下几点。
（1）时间状语不同：过去完成体在时间上强调"过去的过去"；而一般过去时只强调过去某一特定的时间。例如：
They had arrived at the train station by ten yesterday. 他们昨天十点之前已经到了火车站。
They arrived at the train station at ten yesterday. 他们昨天十点钟到达火车站。
（2）在过去时间状语没有明确时，谓语动词动作发生的时间先后须依据上下文来判断：先发生的用过去完成时，后发生的则用一般过去时。例如：

Her whole family were pleased with her, too. She had just won the first place in the composition competition. 她整个家族都为她高兴,因为她刚刚获得了作文大赛第一名。

(3) 当两个或两个以上接连发生的动作用 and 或 but 连接时,按时间顺序,只需用一般过去时来代替过去完成体即可;另外,在 before、after、as soon as 引导的从句中,由于这些连词本身已经表示出时间的先后,因此也可以用一般过去时代替过去完成体。例如:

He entered the room, turned on the light and read an evening paper. 他进入了房间,打开了灯,然后读了一份晚间报纸。

Grace (had) called her before I left the office. 在我离开办公室之前,格蕾丝已经打电话给她了。

(三) 过去完成体与现在完成体的区别

现在完成体表示的动作发生在过去,但侧重对现在产生的结果造成的影响,与现在有关,其结构为"助动词 have/has+过去分词";过去完成体则是一个相对的时态,它所表示的动作不仅发生在过去,更强调"过去的过去",只有和过去某动作相比较时,才用到它。例如:

The girl has learned 1000 English words so far. 到目前为止,这个女孩已经学会了 1000 个英语单词。

The girl had learned 1000 English words till then. 到那时为止,这个女孩已经学会了 1000 个英语单词。

七、现在完成进行体

现在完成进行体表示动作从过去某一时间开始,一直延续到现在,可能还要继续下去。

(一) 现在完成进行体的用法

(1) 强调动作还未结束,还要继续下去。例如:

I've been reading this book for two hours, but I haven't finished it. 这本书我已读了两个小时了,但我还没读完。

I've been working with her for 10 years. 我和她一起工作 10 年了。

(2) 强调动作的持续性或带感情色彩。例如:

We have been waiting for you for half an hour. 我们一直等你半小时了。

She has always been doing like that. 她一贯是那样做的。

(3) 现在完成进行体也可表示从过去某个时间到现在这个时间段内反复发生的事情。

They've been seeing quite a lot of each other recently. 最近他们经常见面。

He has been saying that for years. 他这话已经说了好几年了。

(二) 现在完成体和现在完成进行体的区别

(1) 现在完成体和现在完成进行体都表示动作从过去开始,但现在完成体强调动作的结束,而现在完成进行体则强调动作持续的过程。例如:

The workers have been widening the road. 工人们一直在加宽马路。

They have widened the road. 他们把马路加宽了。

（2）现在完成进行体更强调动作的延续性,它是现在完成体的强调形式。例如：

The old man has been living here for ten years. 老人一直住在这儿,已经十年了。

The old man has lived here for ten years. 老人在这儿已经住了十年了。

（3）在不用时间状语的情况下,现在完成进行体表示动作仍在进行；而现在完成体则表示动作已结束。例如：

The students have been preparing for the test. 学生们一直在为考试做准备。

The students have prepared for the test. 学生们为考试做了准备。

（4）在表示反复发生的动作时,现在完成体强调动作的次数；而现在完成进行体则强调动作的持续的过程。例如：

—How many times have you visited China this month? 这个月你去了中国多少次呢？

—I have visited China twice this month. 我这个月去了两次。

—How long have you been touring China? 你在中国旅行了多长时间？

—I have been touring China for two months. 我在中国已经旅行了两个月。

（5）有些表示状态、感情、感觉的动词如：have、exist、like、hate、hear、know、sound 等动词不能用于现在完成进行体,但可用于现在完成体。例如：

They've known each other since 1980. 自从 1980 年起他们就相互认识了。

She has had the necklace for 30 years. 她保存这项链有 30 年了。

八、过去完成进行体

过去完成进行体表示动作在过去某一时间开始,一直延续到另一过去时间。同过去完成体一样,过去完成进行体也必须以过去时间为前提。

（1）表示过去某一时间之前一直进行的动作。例如：

I had been looking for the cat for days before I found it. 这只猫我找了好多天才找着。

She had been cleaning the office, so we had to wait outside. 她一直在打扫办公室,所以我们不得不在外面等着。

（2）表示反复的动作。例如：

She had been losing things last year. 她去年常丢东西。

He had been mentioning your job to me before you came here. 你来这儿之前,他多次向我提到你的工作。

（3）过去完成进行体还常用于间接引语中。例如：

His father asked what he had been eating. 他爸爸问他一直在吃什么。

I asked where they had been staying all those days. 我问他们那些天是一直待在哪儿的。

（4）过去完成进行体之后也可接具有"突然"之意的 when 引导的从句。例如：

I had only been cooking a few minutes when he came in. 我刚做了几分钟饭他就进来了。

I had been sleeping when my friend called me. 我正在睡觉,此时我的朋友打电话来了。

九、将来时间表示法

（一）一般将来时间表示法

（1）will/shall+动词原形,表将来。shall 用于第一人称,常被 will 所代替。will 可用于各人称。例如：

They will fly to beijng for a meeting this Saturday. 他们周六坐飞机去北京开会。

I shall/will go home with my parents after school. 放学后我会和父母一起回家。

This year will be an important one for global developments, with both crises and opportunities. 今年，是世界变局纵深发展、危机并存的重要年份。

（2）be going to do，表示将来。具体含义如下。

① 表示主语的意图，即将做某事。例如：

My mother is going to travel next week. 我妈妈打算下周去旅行。

What are you going to do tomorrow? 明天打算做什么呢？

② 表示计划、安排的事情。例如：

The board of directors are going to held a meeting this Friday. 董事会准备周五召开会议。

The play is going to be produced next month. 这场戏下月开拍。

③ 表示已有迹象表明即将发生的事情。例如：

I'm not feeling well, and I'm going to fall ill. 我感觉身体不太好，可能要生病了。

Look at the clouds, there is going to be a storm. 看那些云，暴风雨快来了。

（3）be to do 表将来，指按计划或正式安排将要做的事。例如：

We are to discuss the experiment next Saturday. 我们下星期六将讨论这个实验。

The first task is to set up a communications system. 首要任务是架设通信设备。

（4）be about to do，意为"马上做某事"。例如：

He is about to leave for the United State. 他马上要去美国。

Hurry up, the train is about to leave. 快，火车就要开了。

注：① be about to do 不能与 tomorrow、next week 等表示明确将来时的时间状语连用。

② be to do 和 be going to do 的区别在于：be to do 表示客观安排或受人指示而做某事；而 be going to do 表示主观的打算或计划。例如：

I am to play basketball tomorrow afternoon. 明天下午我要去打篮球。

I'm going to swim tomorrow afternoon. 我准备明天下午去游泳。

（5）be doing 结构：有些动词的现在进行体可以表示将来的动作。这些动词有：go、come、fly、leave、start、begin、finish、end、arrive 等。例如：

She is leaving for Beijing tomorrow. 她明天要去北京。

The class is beginning. 马上上课了。

注：be going to 和 will 的用法虽然都表示将来发生的动作或情况，一般情况下能互换。但它们用法的区别如下。

（1）be going to 主要用于以下情况。

① 表示事先经过考虑、计划要做的事情。例如：

What are you going to do today? 今天你们打算做什么？

Dad and I are going to watch a film this afternoon. 我和爸爸打算今天下午去看电影。

I'm going to play the piano. 我打算弹钢琴。

She's going to visit the aged in the nursing room. 她打算去敬老院看望老人。

② 表示根据目前某种迹象判断，某事非常有可能发生。例如：
Look! There come the dark clouds. It is going to rain. 瞧！乌云密集，要下雨了。
I am afraid I am going to have a fever. 恐怕我要发烧了。
（2）will 主要用于以下几个方面。
① 表示单纯的未来"将要"，通用各个人称。例如：
They will go to visit the factory tomorrow. 明天他们将去工厂参观。
I'll come with Wang Bing, Liu Tao and Yang Ling. 我将和王兵、刘涛、杨玲一起来。
China will keep forging ahead hand in hand with fellow developing countries toward a shared future. 中国永远和广大发展中国家同呼吸、共命运，心手相连，团结奋进。
② 表示不以人的意志为转移、自然发展的未来之事。例如：
Today is Sunday. Tomorrow will be Monday. 今天是星期日。明天是星期一。
He will be forty years old this time next year. 明年这个时候他就四十岁了。

（二）过去将来时间表示法

（1）would+动词原形：过去将来时间表示法常用于宾语从句和间接引语中。例如：
I didn't know if she would come. 我不知道她是否会来。
She told us that she would not go with us, if it snowed. 她告诉我们，如果下雪，她就不和我们一起去了。
（2）was/were going to do：可用来表示按计划或安排即将发生的事。例如：
She said she was going to set off at once. 她说她将立即出发。
I was told that he was going to join in the army. 有人告诉我他准备参军。
此结构还可表示根据当时情况判断有可能但不一定会发生的事。例如：
It seemed as if it was going to rain. 看来好像要下雨。
（3）was/were about to do：表示过去将要发生的事情。例如：
He was about to speak, but she raised a finger to her lips. 他正要说话，但她举手捂唇示范。
I couldn't go to Mary's birthday party as I was about to go to hospital.
我不能参加玛丽的生日派对，因为我要去医院。
（4）was/were to do：可以表示曾在过去预计将要发生并且发生了的事，或者表示过去无法预见的结果，常用在间接引语和宾语从句。例如：
Little did they know they were to be reunited five years later. 他们当时几乎都不知道五年后会重聚。

（三）将来进行体表示法

将来进行体的结构为主语+will be doing，其含义如下。
（1）表示将来某一时间正在进行的动作。例如：
Hurry up! The leader will be arriving at any minute! 快！领导就要来了！
A space vehicle will be circling Jupiter in three years' time. 航天器 3 年后将绕木星飞行。

（2）表示按计划或安排要发生的动作。例如：

The girl will be taking her holidays soon. 这个女孩不久要去度假了。

We shall be going to Pairs next week. 下周我们要去巴黎。

We'll be spending the winter in Guangzhou. 我们将在广州过冬。

Professor Chen will be giving a lecture on Etruscan pottery tomorrow. 陈教授明天作关于伊特拉斯坎陶器的讲座。

（3）表示委婉语气。例如：

When will you be paying back the money? 这钱你什么时候还呢？（委婉地商量）

When will you be seeing me? 你什么时候会见我？（委婉地询问如下属对上司）

Will you be joining us for the party? 你会和我们一起聚会吗？（表将来）

Won't you be coming with us? 你会和我们一起去吗？（表将来）

（四）将来完成体表示法

将来完成体的表示方法为主语+will have+过去分词,其含义如下。

（1）表示到将来某个时间为止势必会完成或预计要完成的动作。例如：

When we get there, the teacher will have gone to work. 我们到那里时,老师已经上班去了。

I expect you will have changed your mind by next week. 我想下周你就改变主意了。

I will have lived here for 6 years by next year. 到明年,我就在这里住六年了。

（2）表示某种状况将一直持续到说话人所提及的某一将来时间。例如：

They will have been married a year on March 25th. 到3月25日他们俩结婚就满一年了。

By this time next week, I will have been working for this factory for 24 years. 到下星期此刻,我就为该工厂工作24年了。

十、时态的呼应

时态的呼应也称为时态的一致,是指在复合句中,某些从句(主要是宾语从句等名词性从句)的时态常受主句时态的影响,因此要注意主从句两部分时态的呼应。

（1）主句是现在时态,从句可以用任何所需要的时态。例如：

He says his son is/was/will be a teacher. 他说他儿子是（过去是/将来要做）一位教师。

（2）主句是过去时态,从句的时态要注意下列几点。

① 从句与主句动作同时发生,从句须用一般过去时或过去进行体。例如：

I thought he worked hard. 我认为他工作努力。

He told me his son was reading books. 他告诉我他儿子正在看书。

② 从句动作发生在主句动作之后,从句须用过去将来体。例如：

He said he would post the letter. 他说他将要邮寄这封信。

They did not know when they would go to Beijing. 他们不知道什么时候去北京。

③ 从句动作发生在主句动作之前,从句须用过去完成体。例如：

He said he had posted the letter. 他说他已经把信邮寄出去了。

They asked me whether I had been there before. 他们问我以前是否去过那里。

但是，如果从句有具体的过去时间状语，尽管从句动作发生在主句动作之前，有时仍用一般过去时。例如：

She told me her grand father died in 2016. 她告诉我她爷爷是2016年去世的。

They said they checked everything yesterday. 他们说昨天他们全部检查过了。

另外，从句说的是一般真理或客观事实，即使主句用过去时态，从句仍用一般现在时。例如：

The teacher told the pupils that the earth is round. 老师告诉学生们地球是圆的。

Somebody told me you are a doctor. 有人告诉我你是个医生。

除了宾语从句外，其他名词性从句一般也要遵守这种时态呼应的规律。而状语从句和定语从句则是根据本身意思的需要选用适当的时态。例如：

He saw the boy whose mother is our teacher. 他见过这个男孩，这个男孩的妈妈是我们的老师。

It was not so cold yesterday as it is today. 昨天没有今天这样冷。

巩固练习

Complete the following sentences by choosing the items marked A, B, C, or D.

1. Hello, I _____ you _____ in America. How long have you been here?
   A. don't know; were
   B. hadn't known; are
   C. haven't known; are
   D. didn't know; were

2. My brother _____ while he _____ his bike and hurt himself.
   A. fell; was riding
   B. fell; were riding
   C. had fallen; rode
   D. had fallen; was riding

3. The students _____ busily when Miss Green went to get a book she _____ in the office.
   A. had written; left
   B. were writing; has left
   C. had written; had left
   D. were writing; had left

4. —We haven't heard from Jim for a long time.
   —What do you suppose _____ to him?
   A. was happening
   B. to happen
   C. has happened
   D. having happened

5. We _____ half an hour for the bus, but it has not come yet.
   A. have waited
   B. are waiting
   C. had been waiting
   D. have been waiting

6. When Jack arrived, he learned Mary _____ for almost an hour.
   A. had gone
   B. had set off
   C. had left
   D. had been away

7. —Was he studying for an examination?
   —Yes, he's _____ it next week.
   A. doing
   B. to take
   C. making
   D. to give

8. —Are there going to be many people at your party today?
   —We hope that _____ .
   A. there will be B. there are going
   C. there are D. there going to be

9. The harder I _____ , the greater progress I'll make.
   A. will study B. study
   C. studied D. have been studied

10. The bus _____ at 6 a.m. in the morning.
    A. will leave B. is leaving C. leaves D. left

11. The little boy _____ his heart out because he _____ his toy bear and believed he wasn't ever going to find it.
    A. had cried; lost B. cried; had lost
    C. has cried; has lost D. cries; has lost

12. The price _____ , but he doubts whether it will remain so.
    A. went down B. will go down C. has gone down D. was going down

13. The last time I _____ Jane, she _____ cotton in the fields.
    A. had seen; was picking B. saw; picked
    C. had seen; picked D. saw; was picking

14. Old McDonald gave up smoking for a while, but soon _____ to his old ways.
    A. returned B. returns C. was returning D. had returned

15. —You're drinking too much.
    —Only at home. No one _____ me but you.
    A. is seeing B. had seen C. sees D. saw

16. They asked me to have a drink with them. I said that it was at least ten years since I _____ a good drink.
    A. had enjoyed B. was enjoying C. enjoyed D. had been enjoying

17. Hello, I _____ you _____ in London. How long have you been here?
    A. don't known; were B. hadn't known; are
    C. haven't known; are D. didn't know; were

18. What _____ now? Why are there so many people?
    A. is doing B. is to be done C. is being done D. is to do

19. By the time the boy was five, he _____ three languages.
    A. learned B. had learned C. was learning D. would learn

20. When the chairman entered the hall, all the listeners _____ .
    A. had seated B. were seated C. seated D. were seating

21. _____ you _____ the 6:30 news on the radio?
    A. Have; listen to B. Were; listening to
    C. Did; listen to D. Had; listened to

22. He _____ to work there though he didn't like to.
    A. wanted B. was wanted C. was wanting D. had wanted

23. He _____ anyone the minute he _____ they needed help.
    A. would help; saw   B. helped; saw   C. will help; sees   D. helps; sees
24. I waited for him half an hour, but he never _____.
    A. turned in   B. turned down   C. turned off   D. turned up
25. Many a player who had been highly thought of has _____ from the tennis scene.
    A. disposed   B. disappeared   C. discouraged   D. discarded
26. There was a knock at the door. It was the second time someone _____ me that evening.
    A. had interrupted   B. would have interrupted
    C. to have interrupted   D. to interrupt
27. Until then, his family _____ from him for six months.
    A. didn't hear   B. hasn't been hearing
    C. hasn't heard   D. hadn't heard
28. We _____ to start our own business, but we never had enough money.
    A. have hope   B. would hope   C. had hoped   D. should hope
29. By the end of April, Peter _____ here for three months.
    A. will have stayed   B. will stay   C. stays   D. has stayed
30. My train arrives in New York at eight o'clock tonight. The plane I would like to take from there _____ by then.
    A. would leave   B. will have left   C. has left   D. had left
31. The school board listened quietly as John read the demands that his followers _____ for.
    A. be demonstrating   B. Demonstrate
    C. had been demonstrating   D. have demonstrated
32. Every since Picasso's paintings went on exhibit, there _____ large crowds at the museum every day.
    A. have been   B. has been   C. is   D. are being
33. John is a good friend of mine. He _____ to see me from time to time.
    A. came   B. will come   C. comes   D. has come
34. If she doesn't tell him the truth now, he'll simply keep on asking her until she _____.
    A. does   B. has done   C. will do   D. would do
35. It is reported that Uruguay understands and _____ China on human rights issues.
    A. grants   B. changes   C. abandons   D. backs
36. The city of Montreal _____ over 70 square miles.
    A. covers   B. that covers   C. covering   D. is covered
37. The company _____ a rise in salary for ages, but nothing has happened yet.
    A. is promised   B. has been promising
    C. is promising   D. promised
38. After searching for half an hour, she realized that her glasses _____ on the table all the time.
    A. were lain   B. had been lain
    C. have been lying   D. had been lying

39. The conference _____ a full week by the time it ends.
   A. must have lasted   B. will have lasted
   C. would last   D. has lasted
40. By the time you get to New York, I _____ for London.
   A. would be leaving   B. am leaving
   C. have already left   D. shall have left

第十章

被动语态

热身训练: 下列句子各有一处错误,请指出并改正。

① The boy was made cry by his sister.
② The strange was let to go.
③ My coat is washed easily.
④ Her forehead is felt hot. I'm afraid she is ill.
⑤ Eggs won't be kept long in summer.
⑥ Who was the book written?
⑦ English is not easy to be learnt.
⑧ The traffic accident was happened yesterday.
⑨ This desk needs to mend.
⑩ The People's Republic of China was found on October 1st, 1949.
⑪ Wet clothes are often hanged up near a fire in rainy weather.
⑫ Newly-born babies are taken good care in hospital.
⑬ The price has been risen.
⑭ Please seat.
⑮ I'll come after the meeting if time is permitted.

英语有两种语态:主动语态和被动语态。主动语态表示主语是谓语动作的执行者;被动语态表示主语是谓语动作的承受者。其结构为 be+过去分词。例如:
Columbus discovered America in the 15th century. 15 世纪,哥伦布发现了美洲。
America was discovered by Columbus in the 15th century. 美洲是哥伦布在 15 世纪发现的。

一、被动语态的各种时态形式

(1) 一般现在时被动语态的形式:主语+am/is/are+过去分词+其他成分。例如:
Culture is made by the people. 文化是人们创造的。
These bookcases are designed for children. 这些书架是为孩子们设计的。

(2) 一般过去时被动语态的形式:主语+was/were+过去分词+其他成分。例如:
The letter was written in Chinese. 这封信是用中文写的。

The emergency supplies reserve was officially launched early this month. 应急物资储备已于本月初正式启动。

（3）一般将来时间被动语态的形式：主语+will be+过去分词+其他成分。例如：

Your job will be kept open for your return. 你的工作将保留到你回来。

When will the program be finished? 这个项目什么时候完成？

（4）现在进行体的被动语态形式：主语+am/is/am+being+过去分词+其他成分。例如：

A new bridge is being built here. 一座新的桥梁正在这里修建。

Because my car is being repaired, I have to go to work by bus. 因为我的车正在修理，所以我不得不坐公交车上班。

（5）过去进行体的被动语态形式：主语+was/were+being+过去分词+其他成分。例如：

The hall was being built two years ago. I'm not sure if it is completed. 这个大厅两年前正在修建，我不清楚完工了没有。

The road was being widened when I passed by the place. 当我经过那个地方时，道路正在加宽。

（6）现在完成体的被动语态形式：主语+have/has been+过去分词+其他成分。例如：

He has been sent to work in Guangzhou. 他已经被派往广州工作了。

Has the sports meeting been put off until next week? 运动会已经推迟到下周了吗？

（7）过去完成体的被动语态形式：主语+had been+过去分词+其他成分。例如：

The building had been broken into before the police came. 警察来之前已经有人强行进过这座房子。

A new school had been built when I got there. 我到那儿时，一所新的学校已经建好了。

（8）情态动词的被动语态形式：主语+情态动词+be+过去分词+其他成分。例如：

Her temperature should be taken four times a day. 她的体温应该一天量四次。

If heated, water can be turned into vapour. 如果受热，水会变成蒸汽。

二、被动语态的用法

（1）不知道或者不必说出动作的执行者。例如：

How is this word spelled? 这个单词怎么拼写？

The book was published in 2021. 这本书是2021年出版的。

（2）强调动作的承受者。例如：

A new hospital will be opened in our town. 我们城镇将开办一所新的医院。

The South-North Water Diversion is known as a project of the century. 南水北调是世纪工程。

（3）当动作的执行者是泛指时。例如：

The man is suspected of robbing the shop. 有人怀疑是这个男子抢劫了商店。

（4）表示委婉或礼貌，避免提及动作的执行者。例如：

The boys have been told many times not to make noises. 多次告知这些男孩不要吵闹。

I was given 10 minutes to decide whether I should accept the offer. 给了我10分钟时间考虑是否接受这份工作。

（5）句法修饰的需要。例如：

The lecture will be made by Tom, who is a young musician from England. 这个报告将由汤姆

来做,他是一位年轻的英国音乐家。

The well-known person got on a bus and was recognized by people immediately. 这位名人上了公交车,很快就被人们认出来了。

(6) 有些动词习惯上常用被动语态。例如:

He was born in this city. 他出生在这个城市。

It is reported that he is a professor from Australia. 据报道,他是来自澳大利亚的一位教授。

三、主动语态变被动语态

(1) 含有单个宾语的主动句(主语+谓语动词+宾语)变被动语态时,应把主动句的宾语变为被动句的主语,将谓语改为被动形式。如果需要说明动作的发出者,则需加上"by+主动句的主语(人称代词宾格)"。例如:

The famous professor gave a lecture in English.

→A lecture was given (by the famous professor) in English.

那位著名的教授用英语作了一次报告。

(2) 含有双宾语的主动句(主语+谓语动词+间接宾语+直接宾语)变被动语态:当直接宾语是名词或代词时,可将间接宾语和直接宾语中的任意一个变为被动的主语,另一个则保持不动。但是,当直接宾语变为主语时,间接宾语前要加上介词 to 或 for。例如:

The teacher gave me some good advice on the pronunciation.

→I was given some good advice on the pronunciation.

→Some good advice was given to me on the pronunciation.

老师给我提了一些关于发音方面的好建议。

(3) 含有复合宾语的主动句(主语+谓语动词+宾语+宾语补足语)变被动语态时,应把主动句的宾语变为被动句的主语,宾补保持不动,成为主语补足语,简称主补。例如:

We call him Li Min. →He is called Li Min. 我们叫他李民。

They painted the room yellow. →The room was painted yellow. 他们把房间刷成了黄色。

注:① 感官动词和使役动词后接动词原形作宾补,变为被动语态时,需要在动词原形前加上省略的不定式符号"to",即 be seen/heard/found/observed/noticed/made to do sth。例如:

She was seen to enter the meeting room just now. 刚才有人看见她进入了会议室。

② 含有动词短语(作谓语)的主动句:谓语为及物动词短语的主动句方可变为被动语态。例如:

These children are taken good care of. 他们把这些孩子照顾得非常好。

The good chance should be made full use of. 我们应该充分利用这次好机会。

③ 短语动词用于被动语态时,把它们看作一个整体变成被动结构,其后的介词和副词不可丢掉。例如:be taken care of、be dealt with、be put forward、be done away with 等。

四、主动形式表示被动意义

(1) 说明主语的性质、特征的动词,一般用主动形式表达被动意义,如:lock、open、read、sell、teach、wash、write 等。例如:

The clothes wash well. 这些衣服耐洗。

The baked cake doesn't cut easily. 这个烤好的蛋糕不容易切。

（2）表示感官的连系动词，用主动形式表达被动意义，如 smell、feel、taste、sound 等。例如：

This piece of melody sounds good. 这段曲子听起来不错。

Hamburgers taste delicious. 汉堡包尝起来很美味。

（3）某些动词后用动名词的主动形式表达被动意义，如 need、want、require、worth 等。例如：

The bus needs repairing. 这辆公交车需要修理。

His hair wants cutting. 他的头发该理了。

> 注：常见的被动形式表示主动意义的词组，如 be seated（坐着，就座）、be hidden（躲藏）、be lost（迷路）、be drunk（喝醉）、be dressed（穿着）等。

五、不可用被动语态的情况

（1）有些及物动词或短语动词不能用于被动语态，如 belong to、last、have、own、suit、fine、cost、suffer、hold、fit 等。例如：

The newly built hospital holds 3,000 beds. 新建的医院有 3000 个床位。

They have a beautiful villa. 他们有一幢漂亮的别墅。

（2）系动词没有被动语态。如 taste、look、feel、sound、smell 等只有主动语态。例如：

The fish tastes good. 这鱼尝起来很好吃。

These flowers smell fantastic. 这些花闻起来很香。

（3）有些及物动词做不及物动词用，特别是动词后面加副词 well、easily 等词，主动语态含有被动含义。例如：

The article reads smoothly. 这篇文章读起来很流畅。

The apartment here sells well. 这里的公寓卖得好。

（4）need 表示需要时，后面常接 doing 表被动，意义相当于 to be done。类似词还有 require、deserve、bear 等。例如：

The clothes need washing. 衣服要洗。

The table requires mopping. 餐桌需要擦了。

（5）在 too... to... 及 enough to... 结构中有时表示被动意义。例如：

The problem is too difficult to solve. 这个问题很难解决。

The stone is not light enough to carry. 石头太重搬不动。

These boxes are not strong enough to use as a platform. 这些箱子不够牢固，不能用作站台。

巩 固 练 习

Complete the following sentences by choosing the items marked A, B, C, or D.

1. He arrived in Beijing, where he _____ his friend.

   A. was met by   B. was met   C. was meeting   D. met by

2. The war _____ in 1949.
   A. was broken out　　　　　　　　　　B. had been broken out
   C. has broken out　　　　　　　　　　D. broke out
3. The mistakes in the exercises will _____ the teacher.
   A. cross　　　B. be crossing　　　C. be crossed by　　　D. cross by
4. My sister and I have _____ her birthday party.
   A. been invited　　B. been invited for　　C. invited to　　D. been invited to
5. This kind of glasses manufactured by experienced craftsmen _____ comfortably.
   A. is worn　　　B. wears　　　C. wearing　　　D. are worn
6. The meeting _____.
   A. is put off　　B. is to put off　　C. is to be put off　　D. puts off
7. Mary realized she _____.
   A. was making fun of　　　　　　　B. was made fun
   C. was being made fun of　　　　　D. was being made fun
8. _____ to say a thing in that way.
   A. It is considers wrong　　　　　　B. It is considered wrong
   C. It is considered it's wrong　　　　D. It is considering wrong
9. He ordered that the books _____ suddenly.
   A. would be printed　　　　　　　　B. would print
   C. be printed　　　　　　　　　　　D. print
10. The story _____ in China.
    A. was taken place　　　　　　　　B. was happened
    C. took place　　　　　　　　　　D. has been taken place
11. The building _____ my parents.
    A. is belong to　　　　　　　　　　B. belong to
    C. belongs to　　　　　　　　　　　D. is belonged to
12. He _____ by his teacher.
    A. happened to see　　　　　　　　B. was happened to see
    C. happened to be seen　　　　　　D. was happened to be seen
13. The new hall is the tallest building in this town. _____ from here?
    A. Can it see　　B. Can it be seen　　C. Can it seen　　D. Can see
14. When we got to the airport, we found that the plane _____.
    A. had already taken off　　　　　　B. already took off
    C. was already taking off　　　　　　D. was already taken off
15. Some of the houses in my hometown _____.
    A. have now been rebuilding　　　　B. are now rebuilding
    C. are now being rebuilt　　　　　　D. are rebuilt now
16. If city noises _____ from increasing, people _____ shout to be heard even at dinner.
    A. are not kept; will have to　　　　B. are not kept; have
    C. do not keep; will have to　　　　D. do not keep; have to

17. The fifth generation computers, with artificial intelligence, _____ and perfected now.

    A. developed   B. have developed

    C. are being developed   D. will have been developed

18. —_____ the sports meet might be put off.

    — Yes, it all depends on the weather.

    A. I've been told   B. I've told   C. I'm told   D. I told

19. I need one more stamp before my collection _____.

    A. has completed   B. completes

    C. has been completed   D. is completed

20. Rain forests _____ and burned at such a speed that they will disappear in the near future.

    A. cut   B. are cut   C. are being cut   D. had been cut

21. The new suspension bridge _____ by the end of last year.

    A. has been designed   B. had been designed

    C. was designed   D. would be designed

22. When a pencil is partly in a glass of water, it looks as if it _____.

    A. breaks   B. has broken

    C. was broken   D. had been broken

23. That car _____ over 60 dollars.

    A. had costed   B. costed   C. is costed   D. cost

24. —Look! Everything here is under construction.

    —What's the pretty small house that _____ for?

    A. is being built   B. has been built   C. is built   D. is building

25. — Do you like the material?

    —Yes, it _____ very soft.

    A. is feeling   B. felt   C. feels   D. is felt

26. It is difficult for a foreigner _____ Chinese.

    A. write   B. to write   C. to be written   D. written

27. I have no more letters _____, thank you.

    A. to type   B. typing   C. to be typed   D. typed

28. Take care! Don't drop the ink on your shirt, for it _____ easily.

    A. won't wash out   B. won't be washed out

    C. isn't washed out   D. isn't washing out

29. Nobody noticed the thief slip into the house because the lights happened to _____.

    A. be put up   B. give in   C. be turned on   D. go out

30. —What do you think of the book?

    —Oh, excellent. It's worth _____ a second time.

    A. to read   B. to be read   C. reading   D. being read

31. The rabbit was lucky that it just missed _____.

    A. catching   B. to be caught   C. being caught   D. to catch

32. This page needed _____ again.
    A. being checked   B. checked
    C. to check   D. to be checked
33. _____ many times, the boy still didn't know how to do the exercises.
    A. Having taught   B. Having been taught
    C. taught   D. Teaching
34. A speech _____ in the school hall next week.
    A. given   B. will be given   C. has been given   D. give
35. His new book _____ next month.
    A. will be published   B. is publishing
    C. is being published   D. has been published
36. —Mum, can I go to the zoo with Jack?
    —When your homework _____, you can.
    A. is done   B. was done   C. does   D. did
37. Kids should not _____ to drive in China.
    A. allow   B. be allow   C. be allowed   D. allowed.
38. Seeing him rush into the room with tears in his eyes, I asked him what _____.
    A. would happen B. had happened   C. happened   D. was happened.
39. The book *Business the Speed of Thought* _____ in 1999.
    A. writes   B. is written   C. wrote   D. was written.
40. Trees and flowers _____ every year to make our country more beautiful.
    A. is planted   B. was planted   C. are planted   D. were planted.

第十一章

助动词和情态动词

热身训练： 下列句子各有一处错误，请指出并改正。

❶ Collecting stamps are one of my hobbies.
❷ If you must smoking, you could at least go to the smoking area.
❸ We should do everything we can protect the environment.
❹ He may also to leave for America.
❺ Walking is a good exercise. You say you want to get more exercise. You can walk to and from work instead of taking the bus.
❻ When I was a child, I can watch TV whenever I wanted to.
❼ Children needs to learn how to get along with other people, how to spend their time wisely, and how to depend on themselves.
❽ We must found ways to protect our environment.
❾ —Please don't tell anybody.
　—No, I will. I promise.
❿ I left school as soon as I can and started to work.
⓫ —Catherine, I have cleaned the room for you.
　—Thanks. You need have done it. I could manage it myself.
⓬ I have lost one of my gloves. I must have drop it somewhere.
⓭ When I lived with my roommates in the university, we will often talk into the night.
⓮ Almost all of the students in our class speaks English well.
⓯ With the development of economy, more and more people in China will able to afford their private cars.

一、助动词

协助主要动词构成谓语的词称为助动词，也称为辅助动词。助动词具有语法意义，表示时态、语态、语气、否定式、疑问式等。助动词一般没有词义，不可单独作谓语。常见助动词有be、have、do。有时shall、will、should、would 等也能起助动词的作用。

（一）助动词 be 的用法

（1）be+现在分词构成进行时态。例如：
They are discussing how to solve the problem. 他们正在讨论怎样解决这个问题。

China has been improving people's livelihood in recent years. 中国近几年一直在改善民生问题。

（2）be+过去分词,构成被动语态。例如：

The Olympic Games are held every four years. 奥运会每四年举办一次。

The sick boy has been sent to hospital. 生病的男孩已经被送往医院。

（3）be+动词不定式具有以下含义。

① 表示未来的安排或计划,相当于一种将来时间的表达法（接近 be going to do）。例如：

Who is to question her? 谁将向她提问？

Professor Li was to give a report on the history of the Party the next day. 李教授定于次日做一场关于党史的报告。

② 表示可能性（接近 can 或 may）。例如：

The girl was nowhere to be found. 哪儿也找不到那女孩。

Such blue and white porcelain is to be found in the Palace Museum. 这样的青花瓷在故宫博物院里能找到。

③ 表示责任、义务、需求或规定（接近 should）。例如：

You are to report this to the police, they will help you. 这件事你应该报警,警察会帮你。

No one is to leave the room without permission. 没有准许谁也不得离开房间。

④ 表示想要做的事（接近 want to,多用于条件句中）。例如：

If you are to be trusted, you must be honest. 如果你想获得信任,你就必须诚实。

A new fridge must be very good if it is to compete with the many already in the market. 一款新冰箱要想与市场上已有的许多冰箱竞争,必须做到质量上乘。

⑤ 表示相约、商定。例如：

We are to set off to call on the old people in the nursing home at 6 tomorrow morning. 我们明天早晨6点出发,去探望敬老院的老人。

（二）助动词 have 的用法

（1）have+过去分词构成完成时态。例如：

She has left for Vancouver. 她已经去了温哥华。

Poor Jim has just failed the exam. 可怜的吉姆刚考试挂科了。

（2）have+been+现在分词构成完成进行时。例如：

You have been chatting online for more than two hours. 你已经在网上聊了两个多小时了。

My teacher has been teaching for 30 years. 我老师已经教了30年书了。

（3）have+been+过去分词,构成完成式被动语态。例如：

All means have been used to get her to change her mind. 为了转变她的想法,所有的办法都用过了。

Large numbers of trees have been planted to stop the soil erosion. 为阻止泥土流失,已经大量种树。

（4）构成不定式、动名词和分词的完成式。例如：

He pretended to have known it already. 他假装已经知道这事了。

He regretted having been so careless while taking the exam. 他很后悔考试时那么粗心。

Having finished university, Xu Le went abroad for further study. 徐乐读完大学后,便出国深造去了。

(三) 助动词 do 的用法

(1) 构成否定句和疑问句。例如:

Does your mother always ask you to do so? 你妈妈总是让你这么做吗?

He did not come to help us though he had promised. 虽然他答应会帮我们的,但他没来。

(2) 用来代替前面出现的动词,避免重复或表示对比。例如:

I think China is the safest place during the pandemic, and so does he. 我觉得在疫情期间中国最安全,他也认为如此。

He spent as much time watching videos as he did studying. 他看视频的时间和学习的时间一样多。

(3) do+动词原形,加强动词语气。例如:

Do come to my birthday party. 你一定来参加我的生日宴会。

She does want to have a try. 她的确想试一试。

(4) 用于倒装句。例如:

Never did I think of such a terrible result. 我从未想过会有这么糟糕的结果。

To few people does such an opportunity occur. 很少有人能有这样的机遇。

(四) 助动词 shall、will 的用法

(1) shall/will+动词原形,表示将来某个时间要发生的动作或存在的状态。例如:

I shall/will not come if it rains tomorrow. 如果明天下雨我就不来。

Next Tuesday will be their golden wedding anniversary. 下周二是他们的金婚纪念日。

> 注:一般情况下,shall 用于第一人称。如果 shall 用于第二、第三人称,就失去助动词的意义,就变为情态动词。例如:
> Lucy shall leave. 露西必须离开。(shall 有命令的意味。)
> Lucy will leave. 露西会离开。(will+动词原形,表示将来发生的动作。)

(2) should/would+动词原形,表示从过去某一时间来看将要发生的动作。例如:

I asked her yesterday what I should do next week. 我昨天问她我下周该干什么。

He didn't tell me whether he would agree with my plan. 他没告诉我他是否同意我的计划。

注:shall、will(should、would)也可用作情态动词,具体用法见"情态动词"部分。

二、情态动词

情态动词表示说话人对某一动作或状态的态度,如可能、义务、必要、推测等。情态动词有其自身的词义,但无人称和数的变化,不能单独作谓语,必须和动词原形连用。英语的情态动词主要有 can、could、may、might、shall、should、will、would、must、ought to、have to、need、dare、used to 等。

（一）can 的用法

（1）表示能力。例如：

Can you finish the task all by yourself? 你能独自完成这项任务吗？

No one can succeed without any effort. 没有人不经努力就可以成功。

（2）表示可能性或推测。在肯定陈述句中表示某事发生的可能性；在否定句或疑问句中表示说话者的猜测。例如：

He can be the only right one. 他有可能是唯一正确的人。

Where can she have hidden? 她会藏在哪里了呢？

That can't be Mr. White. He flew to America yesterday. 那不可能是怀特先生。他昨天坐飞机去了美国的。

（3）表示请求或许可，在口语中代替 may。例如：

Can I do it tomorrow? 我明天做可以吗？

You can have a break if you've finished your homework. 如果你做完了家庭作业，可以休息一下。

（4）表示惊讶、怀疑、不相信等态度，常用于疑问句、否定句。例如：

How can you do the football pool? 你怎么能去赌球？

How can he take drugs? What a sunny boy he used to be! 他怎么会吸毒？他曾经是多么阳光的一个孩子！

（5）表示偶尔发生的情况。例如：

Tom can be very naughty. 汤姆有时很顽皮。

It can be very cold in spring in the south. 南方的春天有时很冷。

（6）含有 can 的一些固定结构。

① cannot... too/over...表示"再怎么……也不过分""越……越好"。例如：

One cannot be too careful when driving. 开车时越小心越好。

This point cannot be over emphasized. 这一点无论怎样强调也不过分。

② cannot (help) but+动词原形表示"不得不……"，与"have to"同义。例如：

She can't but wait until her parents come. 她只好等到她父母来。

I always can't help but wonder, how do they spin so fast for so long without getting dizzy? 我总是不由地去想：他们是怎样才能转得这么快这么久而又不眩晕的？

③ cannot help+动名词，表示"禁不住……，忍不住……"。例如：

Hearing that they've got the champion, they couldn't help jumping. 听到获得了冠军，他们忍不住跳了起来。

（二）could 的用法

（1）用于 can 的过去式，表示过去的能力。例如：

Nobody could solve that problem then. 当时没人能够解决那个问题。

（2）表示可能性或猜测。could 可以表示过去的可能性，也可以表示现在的可能性，程度比 can 要弱。例如：

The telephone is ringing. Who could it be? 电话铃响了，可能是谁打来的呢？

It was said that the film could be adapted from a true story. 据说那部电影可能是改编自一个真实的故事。

（3）表示请求或建议，语气比 can 婉转。常用于"Could I...?""Could you...?"等句型。例如：

Could I use your bicycle? 我能用一下你的自行车吗？

Could you please speak a little more slowly? 你能说慢点吗？

（4）表示惊异、怀疑、不相信等态度。此用法同 can，常用于否定句、疑问句，表示现在的情况，语气委婉。例如：

How could you be so stingy? 你怎么会这么小气啊？

Could he be the murderer? 他真的是凶手吗？

（三）be able to 的用法

（1）表示具体的能力，与 can 的用法相近。例如：

Are you able to swim?（=Can you swim?）你会游泳吗？

He wasn't able to/couldn't understand what she said. 他不能理解她所说的意思。

（2）be able to 有更多的时态形式，can 只有一般现在时和一般过去时。例如：

Will he be able to arrive on time? 他明天能准时到吗？

I'm sorry I haven't been able to call back in time. 很抱歉我没能及时回电。

（3）be able to 与 can 的区别在于：be able to 表示经过一番努力，成功地做成了某事，与 manage to do sth./succeed in doing sth. 意思相近；而 can 表示客观上有某种能力，不表示实施该能力后的结果。例如：

He was able to leave Europe before the war broke out. 战争爆发之前他才得以离开欧洲。

Cathy could read Greek and Latin at the age of 7. 凯西七岁时就能读希腊文和拉丁文了。

（4）be able to 可用在 may/might、want 等动词之后。例如：

He might be able to fix the lock. 他可以修那把锁。

I want (my daughter) to be able to live happily. 我希望（我的女儿）能快乐地生活。

（四）may 的用法

（1）表示请求或许可。例如：

May I leave my luggage here? 我可以把行李放这儿吗？

You may take whatever you like. 喜欢什么你可以拿什么。

（2）表示可能性或猜测。不用于问句中，表示的可能性比 can 小。例如：

Tina may know his address. 蒂娜可能知道他的住址。

He may come to help us very soon. 或许他很快就会来帮助我们了。

（3）表示祝愿。例如：

May happiness and health be with you forever! 愿健康和快乐与你常伴！

May our people live in peace and harmony! 愿人民安居乐业！

（五）might 的用法

（1）表示征求对方意见。用于现在或将来，语气比 may 更委婉。例如：

I wonder if I might ask you a favor. 不知能否请您帮个忙？

Might I have a look at your camera? 我可以看看你的照相机吗？

（2）表示许可，此时指过去的许可。例如：

He said that I might ask others for help if necessary. 他说如果有必要我可以向他人求助。

The boy was wondering if he might play computer games. 男孩想知道他能否玩电脑游戏。

（3）表示猜测。可以指对过去的猜测，也可以指对现在的猜测，比 may 的可能性小，不用于疑问句。例如：

He might be waiting for us at the station. 他可能在车站等我们。

She told me she might have left for Tokyo. 她可能去东京了。

This might be the pen Tom has been looking for. 这可能是汤姆一直在找的钢笔。

（4）表示责备、不满或建议。例如：

She might at least tell me the truth. 她至少可以跟我说实话啊。

You might have done it yourself. 你本来可以自己做的。

You might perhaps make sure he is in before you go to his home. 去他家前你最好确认一下他在家。

（5）may、might 在一些固定结构中的用法如下。

① may well do 可译作"有理由……，理所当然……"。例如：

She may well say so. 她大可这么说。

He may well be proud of his son. 他完全有理由为他的儿子骄傲。

② may/might as well do 可译作"不妨……，倒不如……"，用于提出建议。例如：

You may as well ask him. 你不妨问问他。

There is nothing to do, so I may/might as well go to sleep. 既然没什么事可做，我还是去睡觉好了。

（六）must 的用法

（1）表示必要性。must 表示"一定要，必须"之意，一般指现在或将来的情况，强调说话人的主观语气。其否定形式 mustn't 表示禁止。例如：

We must dismantle not build walls, and we must remain true to openness and oppose isolation. 我们要拆墙而不要筑墙，要开放而不要隔绝。

Pets mustn't be taken in. 禁止带宠物入内。

（2）表示"应该"。这种用法多用来建议别人做某事。例如：

You really must go to the Picasso exhibition. It's fantastic. 你真应该去看看毕加索画展，真是太棒了。

The cost must be taken in consideration. 应该把成本考虑在内。

（3）表示推测。常译为"一定，肯定"，指有把握、有根据的推测。而且此用法只能用于肯定句。在否定句中要换成 can't，译为"不可能"。例如：

You have worked hard all day. You must be tired. 你工作一天了，一定累了。

It can't be Lucy. She is having a class now. 那不可能是露西，她现在正在上课。

（4）表示说话人对主语发出的动作或行为不满或愤怒，可译为"偏要，偏偏"。例如：

Why must she be so mean to others? 她为什么非得对别人这么刻薄？

Just as I was going to bed, the doorbell must ring. 正当我准备去睡觉时,偏偏门铃响了。

（5）表示强调。此用法常在口语中出现,表示说话者的坚定的态度。例如:

I must confess, what I said hurt her deeply. 我得承认,我的话伤她好深。

I must say, it gave me quite a shock. 不得不说,这使我很震惊。

> 注: must 可表示过去情况,主要用在宾语从句或间接引语中。例如:
> I felt I must go to the bank and get some money. 我觉得必须去银行取点钱。
> Mum said we must help each other. 妈妈说:"我们必须互相帮助。"

（6）must 与 have to 的区别。must 更强调说话者的主观意愿,have to 强调客观上的必要性,常译为"不得不";have to 有多种时态形式,而 must 一般只用于一般现在时;have to 的否定形式为 not have to,表示"不必";而 must 的否定 mustn't 意为"不许,禁止";把含 have to 的句子变成否定或疑问句时,要加上相应的助动词。例如:

I must call the police and inform about the crime. 我必须报警并告知犯罪情况。

She had to pass an examination before she could get her promotion. 她必须通过一次考试才能得到晋升。

Do you have to get there before 8 o'clock? 你一定要8点之前到那儿吗?

He doesn't have to cook three times a day. 他没有必要一天做三次饭。

（七）dare 的用法

（1）dare 表示"敢……",无人称、数的变化,通常用于否定句、疑问句和条件状语从句中。dare 的否定形式为 dare not/daren't。例如:

Tone dare not say what he thinks. 托恩不敢说出自己的想法。

Dare he tell his parents the exam result? 他敢把考试结果告诉父母吗?

You will be punished if you dare break the school rules. 如果你敢违反校规,就会受到处罚。

（2）I dare say（或 I daresay）是一个习语,意为"我想……,我认为……",而不是"我敢说……"的意思,且只用于第一人称单数和现在时。例如:

I dare say we'll be late. 我想我们会迟到的。

He will keep his word, I dare say. 我觉得他不会食言的。

（3）dare 也可以作为行为动词使用,这时 dare 有人称、数的变化,后跟动词不定式 to do。其否定式、疑问式应通过助动词 do 构成。例如:

She dares to swim across the river. 她敢游过这条河流。

He didn't dare to admit his fault. 他不敢承认他的错误。

（八）need 的用法

（1）need 表示"需要,有义务做……",无人称、数的变化,通常用于否定句、疑问句和条件句中。例如:

That's all settled. It needn't be talked about. 那事已完全解决了,不必谈了。

Why need he set off today? 为什么他今天要出发?

I wonder if I need take an umbrella with me. 我不知是否需要带上雨伞。

由 need 构成的一般疑问句,其肯定回答用 must,否定回答用 needn't。例如:

—Need I tell him about his disease? 我有必要向他告知病情吗?
—Yes, you must./No, you needn't. 是的,必须告诉他。/不,没必要。

(2) need 作行为动词,这时 need 有人称、数的变化,后接名词/代词/动名词/不定式。例如:

You don't need to be so worried. 你不必如此担心。

The room needs airing. 房间需要通风。

need doing 结构中,动名词是主动形式表示被动的意义,可以与 need to be done 转换。例如:

This plant needs watering/ to be watered twice a week. 这株植物一周需要浇两次水。

(九) shall 的用法

(1) 表示征求对方的意见。主要用于主语为第一、第三人称的疑问句中。例如:
Shall we have the discussion after school? 我们放学后讨论好吗?
Shall the letter be sent over to you at once? 那封信要马上给你送过去吗?

(2) 表示警告或承诺等。用于主语是第二、第三人称的陈述句中,表示说话人给对方的警告、许诺、命令、禁止、威胁等。例如:

You shall have my answer tomorrow. 你明天就会得到我的答复。(允诺)

You shall not touch anything in this room. 你不得动房间里的任何东西。(命令)

He shall be fined if he parks the car in a wrong place. 如果他把车停错地方,会挨罚的。(警告)

You shall not have it, it's mine. 你不能拿走,这是我的。(禁止)

(3) 表示必要性或义务。用于主语是第三人称的陈述句,表示条约、命令、义务或规定等,常译为"应,必须"。shall 的否定形式为 shall not/shan't。例如:

Each competitor shall wear a number. 每个参赛选手必须佩戴号码。

Party members shall pay dues. 党员必须交党费。

The new regulations shall take effect on January 1st. 新章程将于元月一日起生效。

(十) should 和 ought to 的用法

(1) 表示"应该",两者常可换用,但 ought to 语气更强烈。例如:

She ought to/should work harder. 她应该更努力地工作。

He ought to be punished, oughtn't he? 他应该受到惩罚,是不是?

In a volatile world, we should stay cool-headed and not be affected by any distractions. 在一个动荡的世界里,我们应该保持冷静,不受任何干扰。

(2) 表示推测。表示说话者根据一定的依据进行推测,常译为"按道理说应该"。例如:

The professor ought to/should be in the lab by now. 教授现在应该在实验室了。

There oughtn't to be any difficulty in finding your lost book. 找到你丢失的书应该是没有任何困难的。

(3) 表示说话人的愤怒、失望、惊奇等情感。例如:

Why should I go? 为什么是我去?(不满)

I am sorry that he should be so stubborn. 我很遗憾,他居然如此固执。(失望)

It's strange that a top student should fail. 很奇怪,一个尖子生竟然不及格。(惊奇)

（十一）will 和 would 的用法

（1）表示意愿。通常 will 表示现在的意愿；would 表示过去的情况，也可以表示现在的意愿，但语气比 will 更委婉。例如：

I will offer you any information you need. 我愿为你提供你需要的任何信息。

Tony will have his own way. 托尼总是一意孤行。

He would marry her even if his parents objected. 纵然他父母反对，他也会和她结婚的。

（2）表示请求、邀请。主要用于第二人称作主语的疑问句中，用 won't you 加强邀请的语气，would 比 will 更客气、委婉。例如：

Will/Would you accept this invitation? 你愿意接受这份邀请吗？

Won't you go and play ping-pong with us? 不和我们一起去打乒乓球吗？

（3）表示习惯性动作或一种自然倾向。will 用于现在，would 表示过去，带有主观性，常译为"总是"。例如：

A drowning man will catch at a straw. 〈谚〉溺水的人连一根稻草也要抓。/病急乱投医。

Man will die without air. 没有空气，人注定会死亡。

She would sit for hours doing nothing. 她总是一坐几个小时，什么事也不做。

（4）表示推测、可能性。例如：

He will be the person you are looking for. 他可能就是你在找的人。

It would be about twelve when he left the office. 他离开办公室时大约是十二点钟。

（十二）used to 的用法

used to 表示"过去常常"，没有人称和数的变化，可以与表示过去的时间状语连用。其否定形式为 usedn't to 或 didn't use to。一般疑问句用"Did... use to...?"结构，或将 used 提到主语之前构成。例如：

I used to get up very early in the morning. 我原来早上起得很早。

She usedn't/didn't use to drive to work. 她以前不开车上班。

Used you to/Did you use to be friends? 你们以前是朋友吗？

> 注：used to 和 would 的区别在于二者都表示过去的习惯，但 used to 可以指动作或状态，强调现在已经不存在或不发生；would 仅指动作，而且不说明现在的情况如何。这动作现在可能继续发生，也可能不发生了。例如：
> He used to live in Jiujiang. 他过去住在九江。（现在不住了）
> We would go swimming in the river every summer. 以前每到夏天我们都要去河里游泳。（现在可能还去，也可能不去了）

（十三）had better 的用法

had better do sth. 表示建议、劝告等，意思是"最好……"，否定形式为 had better not do sth. 意思是"最好不……"。例如：

We had better set off early. 我们最好早点出发。

You'd better not speak ill of others. 你最好不要说别人的坏话。

What had we better do next? 下一步我们最好该怎么做？

（十四）would/had rather 的用法

（1）would/had rather+动词原形/从句,表示"宁愿……"。接从句时,从句谓语用虚拟语气。例如：

I'd rather stay at home. 我宁愿待在家里

I'd rather he hadn't won the first prize. 我倒希望他没有拿一等奖。

I would rather they left earlier. 我宁愿他们早点走。

（2）如果在两者中进行取舍,表示"宁愿……而不愿……,与其……宁可……"的意思时,则可用 would rather...than...或 would...rather than...的句型。例如：

She'd rather die than lose the children. 她宁可死也不愿失去孩子们。

The children would walk there rather than take a bus. 孩子们宁愿步行去那里,而不愿乘公共汽车。

三、情态动词+have done 的用法

（一）must have done

must have done 表示对过去发生的事情的推测,只用于肯定句。常译为"一定……,必定……"。例如：

He must have gone to bed, for the light is out. 灯都熄了,他一定睡觉了。

She must have had an accident, or she would have been here. 她一定是出事了,否则该到了。

（二）can/could have done

（1）表示对过去情况的推测、怀疑或不确定,一般用于否定句和疑问句中。否定句 can't/couldn't have done 译为"不可能",表示很有把握的猜测；疑问句常译为"难道……,可能……?"。但 could 的语气较 can 弱。例如：

He can't/couldn't have finished the work so soon. 这项工作他不可能完成得这样快。

Mary can't/couldn't have stolen your money. She has gone home. 玛丽不可能偷你的钱,她回家去了。

There is nowhere to find them. Where can they have gone? 到处都找不到他们,他们可能去了什么地方呢?

Could he have heard the news? 难道他已经听说过这消息了?

（2）could have done 还可以表示对过去情况委婉的责备或抱怨,意思是本来能够做某事而没有做。此时用于肯定句中。例如：

You could have come earlier. 你本可以早点来的。

He could have passed the exam, but he was careless. 本来他能够通过考试,但是他粗心了。

（三）may/might have done

（1）may/might have done 表示对已经发生的事情或存在的状态不太肯定的推测,意为"可

能已经,或许已经",might 的语气比 may 弱。例如:

George hasn't arrived yet. He may/might have got lost. 乔治还没到,他可能迷路了。

They may/might not have known the news beforehand. 他们事先可能不知道这消息。

(2) might have done 还可以表示过去可能发生但实际没有发生的事,含有委婉的责备或遗憾的意思,常译为"本来可以……,本该……"等。例如:

You might have told me earlier. 你本可以早点(把消息)告诉我的。

You might have done this better. 你本可以做得更好。

(四) should/ought to have done

(1) 表示对过去情况的推测,译为"应该已经……"。例如:

Mary should/ought to have finished reading the book. 玛丽应该读完了那本书。

They should/ought to have arrived in Beijing now. 他们现在应该到了北京。

(2) 表示过去本应该做某事但没做,其否定形式表示过去不该做某事却做了。这种句式含有责备或不满之意。而且 ought to 语气比 should 强。例如:

It was an easy test and he should/ought to have passed, but he failed. 那个测试很容易,他本来应该通过的,却没有通过。

You shouldn't/oughtn't to have offended him. 你不该冒犯他的。

(五) needn't have done

needn't have done 表示过去做了某事,但没有做的必要,可译为"本不需要……"。例如:

It is so near, we needn't have taken a taxi. 这么近,我们本没必要坐出租车的。

It was just a general survey of people's livelihood, you needn't have been so nervous. 那只是个普通的民生情况调查,你本没有必要那么紧张的。

四、情态动词+be doing 的用法

情态动词+be doing 的结构表示对现在和将来正在进行的行为的推测,译为"或许正在,应当正在,想必正在,准是"。例如:

They must be discussing the project in the office. 他们肯定正在办公室里讨论那个项目。

We may be cycling at 4 p.m. tomorrow. 明天下午 4 点我们可能在骑自行车。

What class can she be having now? 她现在可能在上什么课呢?

She might not be going shopping. 她现在可能没去逛街。

五、情态动词+have been doing 的用法

情态动词+have been doing 结构表示对过去某一时间内一直进行的动作的推测,译为"应当一直在……,想必一直在……"。例如:

They are so tired. They must have been training all day. 他们太累了,肯定是训练了一整天。

She might have been waiting for you when you phoned her. 你给她打电话时,她可能已经在等你了。

巩固练习

Complete the following sentences by choosing the items marked A, B, C, or D.

1. I _____ you a valuable present for your birthday, but I was short of money.
   A. would have liked to give   B. liked to give
   C. have liked to give   D. would like to give

2. —Wasn't it Professor Wang who spoke to you just now?
   —_____.
   A. No, he didn't   B. No, he wasn't
   C. Yes, it was   D. Yes, he did

3. He _____ the 9:20 train because he didn't leave home till 9:25.
   A. can reach   B. could catch
   C. may not catch   D. couldn't have caught

4. They must have finished the work by the end of last month, _____?
   A. mustn't they   B. haven't they
   C. hadn't they   D. didn't they

5. This pen looks like mine, yet it isn't. whose _____ it be?
   A. must   B. may   C. would   D. can

6. You _____ lead a horse to the water, but you _____ not make it drink.
   A. may; can   B. can; may   C. will; may   D. can; might

7. —Shall I tell John about the bad news?
   —No, you _____. I think that will make him sad.
   A. needn't   B. wouldn't   C. shouldn't   D. mustn't

8. Henry _____ have kept his words. I wonder why he changed his mind.
   A. must   B. should   C. would   D. need

9. The thief _____ in from the kitchen window as the door was closed.
   A. may climb   B. must have climbed
   C. could have climbed   D. should have climbed

10. —Why hasn't the speaker turned up?
    —He _____ the flight. I'll find it out at once.
    A. must have missed   B. might have missed
    C. would have missed   D. could have missed

11. _____ you continue in your efforts and achieve new and greater successes.
    A. Would   B. Will   C. May   D. Should

12. —Would you be here to attend the English party this evening?
    —Yes, we _____.
    A. shall   B. would   C. will   D. must

13. Our house is on the top of the hill, so in summer the wind _____ be pretty cold.
    A. must   B. can   C. ought to   D. need

14. You _____ to town to see the film yesterday. It will be on TV tonight.

   A. needn't go   B. had better not go

   C. should not go   D. needn't have gone

15. —I'm told that John had another car accident this morning.

   — I believe not. He _____ so careless.

   A. shouldn't have been   B. wouldn't have been

   C. couldn't have been   D. mustn't have been

16. With all the work on hand, he _____ to the cinema last night.

   A. mustn't go   B. should have gone

   C. could not go   D. couldn't have gone

17. Eve was late for class again. She _____ earlier.

   A. should get up   B. must get up

   C. need to get up   D. should have got up

18. If I hadn't stood under the ladder to catch you when you fell, you _____ now.

   A. won't smile   B. couldn't have smiled

   C. wouldn't be smiling   D. didn't smile

19. What _____ would happen if the director knew you felt that way?

   A. will you suppose   B. you suppose

   C. do you suppose   D. you would suppose

20. Everyone _____ make mistakes. But what is important is that we _____ profit from making mistakes.

   A. can; will   B. will; must

   C. will; should   D. should; will

21. We came early and had to wait two hours before the ceremony began. We _____.

   A. need not hurry   B. needn't have hurried

   C. should not hurry   D. can't have hurried

22. His bottle is nearly empty; you two _____ a lot.

   A. must have drunk   B. ought to drink

   C. must drink   D. could have drunk

23. She can speak quite fluent English. She _____.

   A. must been in the USA for some time

   B. must have been in the USA for some time

   C. should have been in the USA for some time

   D. May be in the USA for some time

24. You should bear in mind that he is not so strong as he _____.

   A. was used to be   B. used to be   C. was used to   D. use to

25. —We didn't see him at the exhibition yesterday.

   —He _____ it.

   A. mustn't visit   B. can't have visited

   C. should have gone to see   D. may see

26. Mary _____ my letter, otherwise she would have replied before now.
    A. should have received   B. has received
    C. couldn't have received   D. might have received

27. Mr. Wang _____ be in Nanjing now, he went to Beijing only this morning.
    A. mustn't   B. may not   C. can't   D. needn't

28. —Who is the girl standing over there?
    — Well, if you _____ know, her name is Mabel.
    A. may   B. can   C. must   D. shall

29. I _____ like to make a suggestion.
    A. could   B. would   C. must   D. might

30. I can't find the recorder in the room. It _____ by somebody.
    A. may have been taken away   B may leave
    C. may take away   D. must have taken away

31. —Must I stay at home, Mum?
    —No, you _____ .
    A. needn't   B. mustn't   C. don't   D. may not

32. You need to find a good guide, _____ ?
    A. need you   B. should you   C. don't you   D. needn't you

33. —There is a lot of smoke coming out of the teaching building there.
    —Really? It _____ be a fire, most probably.
    A. can   B. ought to   C. may   D. must

34. —Where _____ my umbrella?
    —Somebody _____ it away by mistake.
    A. is; must have taken   B. is; must take
    C. have been; must take   D. is; takes

35. The room is in a terrible mess; it _____ cleaned.
    A. mustn't have been   B. shouldn't have been
    C. can't have been   D. wouldn't have been

36. It's said that there are plenty of hotels in that town. There _____ be any difficulty for you to find somewhere to stay.
    A. wouldn't   B. mustn't   C. shouldn't   D. needn't

37. We ought to help each other in our work, _____ ?
    A. oughtn't we   B. should we
    C. shouldn't we   D. ought to we

38. —Is there any flight to Tokyo today?
    — I think there _____ , for the weather is too bad.
    A. mustn't be   B. mightn't be C. needn't be   D. can't be

39. We _____ the letter yesterday, but it didn't arrive.
    A. must receive   B. ought to receive
    C. must have received   D. ought to have received

40. It was playing computer games that cost the boy a lot of time that he _____ doing his lessons.

    A. might have spent   B. ought to have spent

    C. must have spent   D. could have spent

41. —Could I call you by your first name?

    —Yes, you _____.

    A. will   B. could   C. may   D. might

42. To make our city more beautiful, rubbish _____ into the river.

    A. needn't be thrown   B. mustn't be thrown

    C. can't throw   D. may not throw

43. —Shall I go and buy more fruit for the party?

    —No, I have already bought 3 baskets. That _____ be enough.

    A. can   B. ought to

    C. may   D. might

44. I _____ pay Tom a visit, but I am not sure whether I will have time this Sunday.

    A. should   B. might   C. would   D. could

45. An Englishman who _____ not speak Italian was once traveling in Italy.

    A. must   B. could   C. may   D. might

46. It has been announced that candidates _____ remain in their seats until all the papers have been collected.

    A. can   B. will   C. may   D. shall

47. Always the old lady _____ sit for hours doing nothing at all.

    A. was used to   B. would   C. used to   D. should

48. There used to be a small school, _____?

    A. was there   B. wasn't it   C. usedn't there   D. usedn't it

49. Bob said he was going to join our club but he didn't. He _____ his mind.

    A. can't have changed   B. wouldn't have changed

    C. must have changed   D. shouldn't have changed

50. I'm surprised that he _____ in the match.

    A. should fail   B. should have failed

    C. would have failed   D. may have failed

第十二章

动词不定式

热身训练： 下列句子各有一处错误，请指出并改正。

1. I'd like to staying there for half a year, visiting places of interest and practicing my English as well.
2. In short, I will try my best to help making the Games a success.
3. When summer comes, they will invite their students pick the apples!
4. I don't know whether you happen to hear, but I am going to study in England this September.
5. The news reporters hurried to the airport, only to tell the film stars had left.
6. I would love to go to the party last night but I had to work extra hours to finish a report.
7. My family considers to buy a house.
8. As a result of my laziness, I failed finishing my homework in time.
9. The purpose of the scheme is not to help the employers but provide work for young people.
10. We are not allowed playing outdoors with some other children.

一、动词不定式的特征

动词不定式具有以下特征。

（1）及物动词的不定式可以接宾语。例如：

It's necessary to learn two foreign languages. 掌握两门外语很有必要。

Mr. Green promised to buy his daughter a birthday gift. 格林先生答应给他的女儿买一件生日礼物。

（2）可以被状语修饰。例如：

He told me to drive carefully and slowly at night. 他告诉我夜晚开车要小心、速度要慢。

（3）没有人称和数的变化。例如：

He seems to know nothing about the factory. 对于这家工厂的情况他似乎一点都不了解。

I/We/They want to go hiking tomorrow. 我/我们/他们想明天去远足。

（4）其否定形式是在不定式符号 to 前面加 not。例如：

I decided not to work in this school any more. 我决定不再在这所学校工作了。

（5）不定式有自己的逻辑主语，常用 for 或 of 引出。例如：

It is very important for the patient to keep happy every day. 对于病人而言，每天保持心情愉

快是非常重要的。

It is careless of you to leave things about. 你太粗心了,把东西到处乱扔。

> 注:部分形容词后面接 for 和 of 的区别。一般情况下用 for 引导,但前面的形容词可以修饰人、表示称赞和责备时,则使用 of。如:good、kind、clever、nice、bold、honest、polite、careful、brave、right、unselfish、wise wrong、bad、rude、stupid、silly、cruel、care-less、foolish、naughty、lazy、selfish、impolite 等。例如:
> It is stupid of you to refuse her. 你拒绝她是很愚蠢的。
> It is kind of you to say that. 你那样说话真是太友好了。
> It is cruel of him to kill the dog. 他把那只狗杀死,太残忍了。
> 在这种句型中,不定式的逻辑主语名词或代词可以转换为句子的主语。例如:
> He is cruel to kill the dog. 他把那只狗杀死,太残忍了。
> 但是"It is+形容词+for+名词/代词+不定式"句型不可进行这种转换。例如:
> It is not necessary for us to go to hospital. (√) 我们没有必要去医院。
> We are not necessary to go to the hospital. (×)

二、不定式的时式与语态

不定式有一般式、进行式、完成式、完成进行式四种,还有主动和被动两种语态,如表12-1所示。

表 12-1 不定式的时式与语态

时　式	语　态	
	主动语态	被动语态
一般式	to give	to be given
进行式	to be giving	—
完成式	to have given	to have been given
完成进行式	to have been giving	—

(一) 不定式的一般式

不定式的一般式表示的动作与谓语动词的动作同时发生或在其后发生。例如:

The patient seems to be surprised! 这病人似乎很吃惊!

To catch the train, we'd better take a taxi. 为了赶上火车,我们最好乘出租车。

(二) 不定式的进行式

不定式的进行式表示动作正在进行,这一动作可以和谓语动词的动作同时发生,有时也可表示将来意义。例如:

The children seem to be getting along quite well. 孩子们似乎相处得很融洽。

The thief pretended to be waiting for someone. 那小偷装着在等人。

The old man seems to be sleeping. 那位老人似乎在睡觉。
You are lucky to be going by plane. 你挺幸运的,能乘飞机走。

(三) 不定式的完成式

不定式的完成式表示的动作通常发生在谓语动词的动作之前,特别强调动作已经完成。例如:

He is said to have worked in London. 据说他在伦敦工作过。
She is said to have been poor. 据说她曾经很穷。

(四) 不定式的完成进行式

不定式的完成进行式表示的动作在谓语动词的动作之前就已经发生,并一直进行着。例如:

The old woman is said to have been learning how to use a smartphone. 据说那老太太一直在学习如何使用智能手机。
It's a great pleasure to have been working with Mr. Smith. 同史密斯先生在一起工作是一件乐事。

(五) 不定式的被动形式

当动词不定式的逻辑主语是不定式动作的承受者时,不定式一般需用被动形式。不定式的被动形式只有一般式和完成式两种。

(1) 一般式(to be done)。一般式的被动形式表示一个被动的动作与谓语动词的动作同时发生,或在它之后发生。例如:

The couple wish to be loved and respected by all. 这对夫妻希望受到大家的爱戴和尊重。
All the work needs to be finished next week. 所有的工作需要下周完成。
The next thing to be done is (to) welcome our guests. 下一步要做的是迎接客人。

(2) 完成式(to have been done)。完成式的被动形式表示一个被动的动作发生在谓语动词的动作之前。例如:

She felt a bit annoyed to have been asked such a question. 被问到这样的问题,她感到有点儿生气了。
The window is likely to have been broken by the naughty boy. 窗户可能是被这个调皮的男孩打碎了。

三、不定式的句法功能

不定式具有名词、形容词和副词的特征,因此在句中可充当主语、宾语、表语、定语、状语、宾语补足语等成分。

(一) 作主语

(1) 不定式作主语表示泛指。例如:
To study hard is necessary. 努力学习是有必要的。

To realize the great rejuvenation of the Chinese nation will be no easy task like a walk in the park. 中华民族伟大复兴,绝不是轻轻松松就能实现的。

（2）为了避免头重脚轻,常用 it 作形式主语。例如：

When you do not use your phone, it is necessary for you to lock it. 当你不使用手机时,你最好锁屏。

It calls for hard work to succeed. 成功需要付出艰辛的努力。

It is important (for us) to study hard. 对我们来说,努力学习很重要。

（二）作表语

不定式作表语表示主语的职业、职责、性质或解释主语的内容等。例如：

The old man's job is to take care of the flowers in the garden. 这个老人的工作是照看花园里的花。

He seems to be very unhappy these days. 他这几天似乎不开心。

His wish is to write a good book for students. 他的愿望是为学生们写一本好书。

（三）作动词（短语）的宾语

Have you decided to meet your friends this afternoon? 你是否决定下午和朋友见面？

I am upset in what to do and how to do it. 我不知道该做什么、该怎样做。

> 注：常跟不定式作宾语的动词有：afford、agree、aim、apply、ask、attempt、beg、bother、care、choose、claim、consent、decide、demand、determine、expect、fail、hope、intend、learn、manage、need、offer、plan、prepare、pretend、promise、refuse、seek、threaten、volunteer、want、wish 等。例如：
> He can't afford to offend his boss. 他得罪不起老板。
> I've long expected to meet my teacher. 我一直盼望着见到我的老师。
> Didn't she promise to wake him up? 她不是答应叫醒他吗？

当不定式作宾语,后面带有宾语补足语时,要用 it 作形式宾语,真正宾语后置。例如：

We thought it a great honor to be invited to your party. 能被邀请参加你的聚会是我们的荣幸。

Grace found it hard to achieve the goal her parents set for her. 格蕾丝发现很难实现父母给他制定的目标。

This has made it necessary for us to apply for a new passport. 这使得我们有必要申请一份新的护照。

（四）作宾语补足语

常接不定式作宾语补足语的动词有：advise、allow、ask、beg、cause、command、compel、encourage、expect、force、get、instruct、intend、invite、order、permit、persuade、prefer、press、remind、request、tell、trouble、urge、want、warn、wish 等。例如：

I asked him to show me the new mobile phone. 我让他把新手机给我看看。

He doesn't want her to attend the school. 他不想让她上学。

We ought to ask the students to think critically. 我们应要求学生辩证地思考问题。

有的动词,如感知动词(see/watch/hear/observe 等)、使役动词(have/make/let 等),则需要用不带 to 的不定式作宾语补足语。

These photos made me think of my college. 这些照片使我想起了我的大学。

He saw his child enter the school. 他看见他的孩子进了学校。

(五) 作定语

(1) 不定式在句中作定语,置于被修饰的名词或代词后面,常表示未发生的动作。例如:

The disease shows a tendency to improve. 这种疾病有好转的倾向。

I would like something to drink. 我想要一些喝的东西。

There are some plates to wash. 有些盘子要洗。

Have you got anything to be posted? 你有什么要邮寄的吗?

He has a lot of work to do today. 今天他有许多工作要做。

常跟不定式作定语的名词有:ability、agreement、ambition、anxiety、attempt、campaign、claim、chance、decision、determination、eagerness、effort、inclination、intention、impatience、movement、need、obligation、opportunity、plan、pressure、promise、readiness、reason、reluctance、right、tendency、time、way、willingness、wish 等。

一些词组如 the first、the second、the last、the best、the only thing 等,后面也常跟不定式作定语。例如:

The girl is always the first to answer questions. 这个女生总是第一个回答问题。

The next bus to arrive is from Paris. 下一趟到站的公共汽车来自巴黎。

(2) 不定式作定语,有时与其前面被修饰的名词逻辑上有动宾关系。如果不定式是不及物动词或所修饰的名词是不定式的地点、工具等,不定式后面须有相应的介词。例如:

Give me a pen to write with. 给我一支笔写字。

I need some paper to write a letter on. 我需要一些纸写一封信。

Is he a man to depend on? 他是一个可以依靠的人吗?

当句子主语或说话人是动词不定式中动作的发出者时,动词不定式用主动形式;当句子主语或说话人不是动词不定式动作的发出者时,动词不定式用被动式。例如:

He is the first athlete to finish the line. 他是第一个到达终点线的运动员。

Mr. Green preferred to be given heavier work to do. 格林先生宁愿被分配干更重的活。

(3) 由 only、last、next、序数词或形容词最高级修饰的名词常用不定式作定语。例如:

He is the only one to get here. 他是唯一一个到达这里的人。

This is the fittest juice for you to drink. 这是最适合你喝的饮料。

He was always the last person to arrive. 他总是最后一个到。

It's the worst time to go for an outing. 现在是出去游玩最糟糕的时间。

(六) 作状语

不定式作状语时,可以表示目的、结果、条件、原因等。

(1) 作目的状语。作目的状语的不定式位于句末时,不定式前不能有逗号;作目的状语的不定式前可加上 in order 或者 so as 来加强说话语气。in order to do 可放于句首,而 so as to do 不能放于句首。例如:

I went to Italy to learn Italian. 我去意大利是为了学习意大利语。

The young man put on his glasses in order to/so as to see the object more clearly. 这位年轻人戴上眼镜，以便看得更清楚一些。

In order to ensure that everyone leads a better life, we must never rest on what we have achieved, and there is still a long way to go. 让大家过上更好的生活，我们不能满足于眼前的成绩，我们还有很长的路要走。

（2）作结果状语。不定式可以表示出乎意料的结果，常见结构为 only to do。例如：

He came back home happily, only to find his room broken into. 他开心地回到家，却发现有人闯入了他的房间。

I hurried to the butcher's only to find it had been closed. 我匆忙地赶到肉店却发现它关门了。

（3）作条件状语。动词不定式用作条件状语，可扩展成 if 引导的条件状语从句。例如：

I should be very happy to be of service to you. 我很高兴为您服务。

To turn to the right, you could find a bookstore. 向右拐，你就会发现一家书店。

（4）作原因状语。不定式常跟在一些表示喜、怒、哀、乐等情感的形容词或动词-ed 形式后面，说明产生这种情绪的原因。例如：

They are proud to be members of the team. 作为这个团队的一员，他们感到很自豪。

He was disappointed to have failed in the interview. 他对这一次面试的失败感到很失望。

I'm sorry to have made this mistake. 我犯了这个错误，很抱歉。

四、不定式的特殊用法

不定式的特殊用法主要有以下三类。

（一）不带 to 的不定式

（1）当不定式充当一些感知动词以及使役动词的宾语补足语时一般不带 to。这类词有：hear、watch、perceive、feel、observe、listen to、see、look at、make、let、have 等。例如：

The nurse let me go to see my friend in hospital. 护士让我去看住院的朋友。

Will you please make your brother come to my office? 你能让你哥哥来我办公室吗？

I will have my son write an article about love. 我想要我儿子写一篇关于爱的短文。

（2）在 than、would/had sooner... than、would/had rather... than 等习惯用法中一般不带 to。例如：

The children could do nothing else than admit their mistakes. 孩子们除了认错外，别无选择。

I would rather walk than drive a car in such fine weather. 这么好的天气，我情愿步行也不开汽车。

I had no sooner arrived home than the bell rang. 我一到家铃就响起来了。

（3）当句子的主语部分含有实义动词 do 时，充当表语的不定式常可省略 to。例如：

The only thing he has to do is press the button. 他唯一要做的只是按一下电钮。

All we do is fish and hunt. 我们所有要做的就是钓鱼和打猎。

What the plan does is ensure a fair match. 该计划所做的就是确保公平的比赛。

（4）充当 help 的宾语或宾语补足语的不定式可带 to,也可不带 to。例如：
They helped (to) mend the roof. 他们帮忙修屋顶。
Their criticisms help us (to) improve our service work. 他们的批评有助于我们改善服务工作。
The fine weather will help the farmers (to) get the harvest in. 好天气有助于农民收割庄稼。

（二）"疑问词+不定式"结构

不定式前面可加上 where、how、what、which、whether、when、whom 等疑问词,这种结构可作主语、宾语、表语和同位语等。例如：
I don't know when to do the work. 我不知道什么时候做那工作。
He wondered what to do next. 他不知道接下去该做什么。
The question is how to cultivate these only children. 问题是如何教育这些独生子女。
I had no idea which article to read first. 我不知道先读哪一篇文章。
Where to borrow this sum of money is not known. 从哪里去借这笔钱还不得而知。

（三）"介词+关系代词+不定式"结构

"介词+关系代词+不定式"这种结构一般充当名词的定语,作用类似于定语从句。例如：
He had no excuse on which to delay his decision. 他没有借口来拖延他的决定。
He also had another pencil with which to write. 他还有另外一支铅笔来写字。
It was a good day on which to have outings. 这是一个可以进行短途游玩的好日子。
We moved to the suburb so that the children would have a garden in which to play. 我们搬到郊区,好让孩子们有个花园,可以在里面玩。

巩 固 练 习

Complete the following sentences by choosing the items marked A,B,C,or D.

1. I am sorry _____ written you a letter at the time.
   A. to have not   B. to not have   C. not to have   D. not having

2. Will you lend him a magazine _____?
   A. to be read   B. for reading   C. to read   D. he read

3. He could do nothing but _____ for the bus _____.
   A. wait, to come   B. wait; come   C. waiting; coming   D. waited; came

4. Robert is said _____ abroad, but I don't know what country he studied in.
   A. to have studied   B. to study
   C. to be studying   D. to have been studying

5. I don't know whether you happen _____, but I am going to study in the USA this September.
   A. to be heard   B. to be hearing   C. to hear   D. to have heard

6. The news reporters hurried to the airport, only _____ the film stars had left.
   A. to tell   B. to be told   C. telling   D. told

7. You were silly not _____ your car.
   A. to lock   B. to have locked   C. locking   D. having locked
8. A number of paintings in the castle are believed _____ in a fire.
   A. being destroyed   B. having been destroyed
   C. to be destroyed   D. to have been destroyed
9. The meeting _____ next week is sure to be a great success.
   A. to take place   B. to be taken place
   C. to have taken place   D. being taken place
10. This company was the first _____ portable radios as well as cassette tape recorders in the world.
    A. producing   B. to produce   C. having produced   D. produced
11. The purpose of new technology is to make life easier, _____ it more difficult.
    A. not making   B. not make   C. not to make   D. nor to make
12. Helen had to shout _____ above the sound of the music.
    A. making herself hear   B. to make herself hear
    C. making herself heard   D. to make herself heard
13. The teacher asked us _____ much noise.
    A. don't make   B. not make   C. not making   D. not to make
14. An army spokesman stressed that all the soldiers had been ordered _____ clear warnings before firing any shots.
    A. to issue   B. being issued   C. to have issued   D. to be issued
15. I'd rather have a room of my own, however small it is, than _____ a room with someone else.
    A. to share   B. to have shared C. share   D. sharing
16. The bank is reported in the local newspaper _____ in broad daylight yesterday.
    A. robbed   B. to have been robbed
    C. being robbed   D. having been robbed
17. It is a problem that doesn't need _____ right now.
    A. to solve   B. solving   C. being solved   D. to be solving
18. There's a man at the reception desk who seems very angry and I think he means _____ trouble.
    A. making   B. to make   C. to have made   D. having made
19. I lost my way in complete darkness and, _____ matters worse, it began to rain.
    A. made   B. having made   C. making   D. to make
20. At _____ time does the salesgirl get up late in the morning, though she is always too busy _____ a good rest.
    A. no; to take   B. no; taking   C. any; to take   D. one; taking
21. —Are you a student?
    —No, but I used _____ .
    A. to be   B. to was   C. to do   D. to be a

22. Who will you get _____ the project for us?
    A. design   B. to design   C. designed   D. designing
23. It is said in Australia there is more land than the government know _____.
    A. it what to do with   B. what to do it with
    C. what to do with it   D. to do what with it
24. We are not allowed _____ outdoors with some other children.
    A. playing   B. to be playing
    C. to play   D. be playing
25. —Where should I _____ my application?
    —The personnel office is the place _____.
    A. send; to send it   B. send for; to send it to
    C. send for; for sending it   D. send; to send it to
26. I've worked with children before, so I know what _____ in my new job.
    A. expected   B. to expect   C. expects   D. to be expecting
27. I feel it is your husband who _____ for the spoiled child.
    A. is to blame   B. is going to blame   C. is to be blamed   D. should blame
28. Can you imagine the questions I had _____ our teacher?
    A. asked   B. to ask   C. asking   D. ask
29. —Will you have anybody _____ the flowers?
    —Yes, I'll have the flowers _____.
    A. plant; planted   B. to plant; planted
    C. plant; to be planted   D. to plant; plant
30. They are looking forward with hope _____ from you soon.
    A. to hearing   B. of hearing   C. hearing   D. to hear

第十三章

动 名 词

热身训练： 下列句子各有一处错误，请指出并改正。

① Now I really enjoy study because I'm growing old and know what I want.
② They've been spending a lot of time sing in karaoke bars.
③ As a kid, I loved to watch cartoons, but no matter how many times I asked to watching them, my parents would not let me.
④ She isn't good at talk but she gets on well with other people.
⑤ He kept to put off writing to his parents.
⑥ We can choose between staying at home and take a trip.
⑦ I showed them I was independent by wear strange clothes.
⑧ My grandpa said last winter they earned quite a lot by sell the fish.
⑨ My favorite picture at the party is of my coach and me enjoy the biscuits with happy laughter!
⑩ I have often dreamed of talk face to face with my Mom.

一、动名词的时式和语态

动名词有动词和名词的特征，有一般式、完成式和否定式三种形式，有主动语态和被动语态两种语态，如表 13-1 所示。

表 13-1　动名词的时式和语态

时　式	语　态	
	主动语态	被动语态
一般式	doing	being done
完成式	having done	having been done
否定式	not doing	not being done

（一）动名词的一般式

动名词的一般式可以表示没有时间先后的动作，也可以表示发生在谓语动词之前或之后的动作。例如：

I wish you would stop talking. 希望你不要再讲了。

We suggest giving them help without pay. 我们建议无偿帮助他们。

I don't remember her once sending me a message. 我不记得她曾经给我发过信息。

（二）动名词的完成式

动名词的完成式表示的动作通常发生在谓语动词所表示的动作之前，特别强调动作已经完成。例如：

He hated himself for not having studied hard. 他恨自己之前没有努力学习。

I did not deny having told him a white lie. 我不否认对他说过一个善意的谎言。

（三）动名词的被动式

如果动名词动作的逻辑主语为动名词动作的承受者，该动名词就要用被动式。

（1）动名词被动式的一般式所表示的动作可以在谓语动词之前、同时或之后发生。例如：
No one likes being laughed at. 谁也不喜欢受人嘲笑。

The children enjoy being praised. 孩子们喜欢受表扬。

（2）动名词被动式的完成式表示动作发生在句子谓语动词所表示的动作之前。例如：

I appreciate having been given the opportunity to study abroad two years ago. 我很感激两年前得到一次出国留学的机会。

The safe showed no signs of having been touched. 保险箱没有被人动过的痕迹。

（四）动名词的否定形式

动名词的否定形式是在动名词之前加 not。例如：

I'm sorry for not being present at the sports meeting on time. 我很抱歉没能按时参加运动会。

She was unhappy for not having been invited to the wedding. 她未被邀请参加婚礼，很不高兴。

（五）动名词的复合结构

当动名词的逻辑主语与句子的主语不一致时，要在动名词之前加上自己的逻辑主语，即物主代词、名词所有格或人称代词宾格、名词，构成动名词的复合结构。

（1）动名词的复合结构作主语时，其逻辑主语只能用形容词性物主代词或名词所有格。例如：

His coming to help encouraged all of us. 他来帮忙鼓舞了我们大家。

Grace's being ill made her mother upset. 格蕾丝病了，这使她妈妈很不安。

（2）如果动名词复合结构作宾语，其逻辑主语可以用物主代词、名词所有格或人称代词宾格、名词。例如：

Would you mind my/me using your computer? 你介意我用一下你的计算机吗？

The father insisted on his son's/his son going abroad. 爸爸坚决要求儿子出国。

All these conditions tend to increase the probability of a teenager/a teenager's committing a criminal act. 所有这些条件往往会增加青少年犯罪的可能性。

二、动名词的基本用法

动名词具有名词的特征,在句中可以作主语、宾语、表语、同位语和定语。同时,动名词仍保留着动词的一些特征,可以接自己的宾语和状语。

(1) 动名词作主语。例如:

Smoking does a lot of harm to one's health. 吸烟对人体非常有害。

Getting mad at others means other people are getting control of my emotions! 如果我生别人的气,就意味着我的情绪被别人控制了。

(2) 动名词作表语。例如:

My hobby is playing the guitar. 我的爱好是弹吉他。

His favorite pastime is surfing the Internet. 他最喜欢的消遣方式是上网。

(3) 动名词作宾语。

动名词作宾语有以下两类。

① 作谓语动词的宾语。例如:

He has finished writing the paper. 他已经写完了这篇论文。

Would you mind passing me the salad? 把沙拉递给我好吗?

My father tried several times to give up smoking, but failed. 我父亲尝试戒烟好几次,但是都没有成功。

② 作介词的宾语。动名词作介词宾语主要出现在带有介词的动词词组后面。例如:

He thinks of going to visit his friends. 他想去拜访他的朋友。

We have set out on a new journey of building a modern socialist country in all respects. 我们开启了全面建设社会主义现代化国家新征程。

Members of the People's Liberation Army and Armed Police devoted themselves to building a strong military and protecting our country. 人民解放军和武装警察矢志强军、保家卫国。

(4) 动名词作同位语。例如:

He enjoys his part-time job, working as a secretary to the manager. 他喜欢他现在的兼职——就是担任经理的秘书。

My interest, teaching some pupils, takes up much of my spare time. 我的兴趣——教小学生,占用了我大量的业余时间。

(5) 动名词作定语:动名词作定语主要放在被修饰的名词前面,表示所修饰名词的用途或性能。例如:a sleeping car = a car which is used for sleeping、a dancing hall = a hall which is used for dancing、a swimming pool = a pool which is used for swimming、a fishing rod = a rod which is used for fishing 等。

三、动名词和现在分词的区别

动名词是名词性质,一方面保留着动词的某些特征,具有动词的某些变化形式;另一方面动名词在句中的用法及功能与名词相同,在句中可以作主语、宾语、表语、同位语、定语。而现在分词相当于形容词、副词,在句中可以作定语、表语、状语。两者都可以作表语和定语。

1. 动名词和现在分词作表语的区别

(1) 作表语的动名词与主语指的是同一件事,此时系动词相当于"是",主语和表语的位置可以互换,语法和意思不变。例如:

My hobby is swimming. 可改为 Swimming is my hobby.

(2) 现在分词作表语主要用于说明主语的性质,不能与主语互换位置。例如:

The game is uninteresting. 不可改为 Uninteresting is the game.

2. 动名词和现在分词作定语的区别

(1) 动名词修饰名词时主要表示该名词的用途,如:a swimming suit、a washing machine、a smoking room、a waiting room、an opening speech、working hours 等。

(2) 现在分词修饰名词时,表示名词的动作,名词是现在分词的逻辑主语,如:a swimming boy(= a boy who is swimming)、running water(= water that runs)、a sleeping baby(= a baby who is sleeping)、a walking man(= a man who is walking) 等。

四、动名词和不定式的区别

1. 不定式和动名词作主语的区别

(1) 动名词作主语,通常表示抽象动作,而不定式作主语多用来表示具体动作。例如:

Talking loudly is prohibited here. 这里禁止大声喧哗。

Hating others people is like burning your own house to get rid of a rat. 憎恨别人,就像为了赶走一只老鼠而把自己的房子烧掉。

To know everything is to know nothing. 什么都懂就是什么都不懂。

It is bad for you to smoke so much. 抽这么多烟对你的身体很不好。

(2) 动名词作主语时,通常用于表示一件已知的事或经验;不定式短语通常用来表示一件未完成的事或目的。例如:

To get there by bike will take us an hour. 骑自行车到那里需要一个小时。

Telling lies is wrong. 撒谎是错误的。

Driving a car during the rush hour is tiring. 在高峰时间开车很累人。

(3) 不定式作主语,一般用 it 作形式主语,把作主语的不定式短语后置。例如:

It took me only thirty minutes to finish the work. 我只花了三十分钟就完成了这项工作。

It is impossible for us to master English in a short time. 我们不可能在很短的时间内掌握英语。

2. 不定式、动名词作表语的区别

(1) 不定式作表语,一般表示具体动作,特别是表示将来的动作。例如:

The question is how to raise money. 问题是如何筹集资金。

What I would suggest is to insist on. 我的建议是继续坚持下去。

(2) 动名词作表语,表示抽象的一般性的行为。例如:

Our work is serving customers. 我们的工作是为服务顾客。

Her hobby is jogging. 她的爱好是跑步。

3. 不定式和动名词作宾语的区别

英语中大多数动词既可跟不定式，也可跟动名词作宾语。但有些动词有一定要求。

（1）有些动词只能用不定式作宾语。这类动词有：decide、learn、regret、choose、hesitate、profess、begin、expect、omit、appear、determine、manage、cease、hate、pretend、ask、need、agree、desire、love、claim、hope、promise、beg、fail、plan、bother、forget、prefer、care、happen、prepare、start、undertake、want、consent、intend、refuse、afford、demand、long、arrange、destine、mean、swear、volunteer、wish、bear、endeavor、offer、decide、learn、contrive、incline、propose、seek 等。

（2）有些动词只能用动名词作宾语，这类动词有。consider、detest、fancy、favor、mind、repent、imagine、postpone、risk、figure、miss、resent、finish、pardon、resist、forgive、permit、resume、appreciate、confess、endure、avoid、contemplate、enjoy、bear、defer、envy、can't help、delay、escape、acknowledge、cease、mention、admit、tolerate、dislike、advocate、complete、can't stand、deny、excuse、involve、practise、suggest、hate、prevent、save、keep、quit、stand、loathe 等。

（3）有些动词用动名词和用不定式作宾语的意义完全不同。例如：

① mean to do sth. 打算做某事　　　　　　mean doing sth. 意味着……
② try to do sth. 努力、企图做某事　　　　try doing sth. 尝试去做某事
③ propose to do sth. 打算要做某事　　　 propose doing sth. 建议做某事
④ remember to do sth. 记住去做某事　　　remember doing sth. 记得做过某事
⑤ go on to do sth. 继而去做某事　　　　　go on doing sth. 继续做某事
⑥ stop to do sth. 停止……去做　　　　　 stop doing sth. 停止正在做的事
⑦ forget to do sth. 忘记要去做某事　　　 forget doing sth. 忘记做过某事
⑧ want/need/require/deserve/demand 等词+动名词/不定式被动语态，表示被动意义。例如：

Your hair wants cutting/to be cut. 你的头发需要修剪了。

These young seedlings will require looking/to be looked after carefully for a long time. 这些幼苗需要长时间的精心照管。

巩 固 练 习

Complete the following sentences by choosing the items marked A, B, C, or D.

1. I know it isn't important but I can't help _____ about it.
   A. thinking　　　　B. to think　　　　C. think　　　　D. but to think
2. I don't mind _____ the decision as long as it is not too late.
   A. you delay to make　　　　　　　　B. your delaying to make
   C. you to delay making　　　　　　　D. your delaying making
3. The man confessed to _____ a lie to the manager of the company.
   A. be told　　　　B. having told　　　　C. being told　　　　D. have told
4. I don't mind _____ by bus, but I hate _____ in queues.
   A. to travel; standing　　　　　　　　B. traveled; standing
   C. traveling; to stand　　　　　　　　D. traveling; to standing

5. It's worth considering what makes "convenience" foods so popular, and _____ better ones of your own.
    A. introduces   B. to introduce   C. introducing   D. introduced
6. I hear they've promoted Tom, but he didn't mention _____ when we talked on the phone.
    A. to promote   B. having been promoted
    C. having promoted   D. to be promoted
7. "Goodbye, then." she said, without even _____ from her book.
    A. looking down   B. looking up   C. looking away   D. looking on
8. It is difficult to imagine his _____ the decision without any consideration.
    A. accept   B. accepting   C. to accept   D. accepted
9. —I did it again. I slept until noon.
   —_____ through the alarm seems to be your biggest problem.
    A. To sleep   B. To be asleep   C. Asleep   D. Sleeping
10. There is no _____ still in this life; one must either advance or fall behind.
    A. to stand   B. having stood   C. stand   D. standing
11. I don't allow _____ in my office and I don't allow my family _____ at all.
    A. smoking; to smoke   B. to smoke; to smoke
    C. smoking; smoking   D. to smoke; smoking
12. No one enjoys _____ at.
    A. laughing   B. to laugh   C. being laughed   D. to be laughed
13. You must do something to prevent your house _____.
    A. to be broken in   B. from being broken in
    C. to break in   D. from breaking in
14. After finishing his homework he went on _____ a letter to his parents.
    A. write   B. writing   C. wrote   D. to write
15. The young trees we planted last week require _____ with great care.
    A. looking after   B. to look after   C. to be looked after   D. taken good care of
16. Remember _____ the newspaper when you have finished it.
    A. putting back   B. put back   C. to put back   D. be put back
17. He was afraid _____ for being late.
    A. of seeing   B. of being seen   C. to be seen   D. to have seen
18. I'd like to suggest _____ the meeting till next week.
    A. to put off   B. putting off   C. put off   D. to be put off
19. The thief drove as fast as he could to escape _____ by the police.
    A. to be caught   B. be caught   C. being caught   D. catching
20. I searched for my wallet and it wasn't there. At first, I thought I _____ it at home. Then I remembered _____ it out to pay for the taxi.
    A. must have left; to take   B. may leave; taking
    C. might leave; to take   D. could have left; taking

21. The sentence needs _____.
    A. improve   B. a improvement   C. improving   D. improved
22. If he succeeded _____ a job, his children wouldn't be suffering from hunger now.
    A. to find   B. to look for   C. in finding   D. in looking for
23. _____ his mother, the baby could not help _____.
    A. To see; to laugh   B. Seeing; to laugh
    C. Seeing; laughing   D. To see; laughing
24. She returned home only to find the door open and something _____.
    A. missed   B. to be missing   C. missing   D. to be missed
25. —Where is my passport? I remember _____ it here.
    —You shouldn't have left it here. Remember _____ it with you all the time.
    A. to put; to take   B. putting; taking
    C. putting; to take   D. to put; taking

第十四章

分　　词

热身训练： 下列句子各有一处错误，请指出并改正。

① Everyone was silent, wait to see who would be called upon to read his or her paragraph aloud.
② He would ask who we were and pretend not to knowing us.
③ The position of the classroom with its view made me felt like I was dreaming.
④ One evening at sunset, we sat by the fire, have our barbecue.
⑤ I'm looking forward to hear from you soon.
⑥ Have tea in the late afternoon provides a bridge between lunch and dinner, which might not be served until 8 o'clock at night.
⑦ With the help of Kate, a roommate of mine, I've soon got used to live without my parents around.
⑧ Felt hungry, we built a fire by the lake and barbecued the fish. It was delicious.
⑨ The man did as told and slept really well, wake up before the alarm went off.
⑩ I just want to thank you for helping me becoming a different person.
⑪ After hear your sad stories, he will say some words that are nice and warm.
⑫ We could hear the sound of the rain and our footsteps mixing with our laughter.
⑬ He agreed to reading my story and give me some advice on how to write like a real writer.
⑭ Even the heavy rain in the morning could not prevent us go.
⑮ When our six children were young, suppertime was always being interrupted by neighborhood children ring the bell.

英语中的分词有两种：现在分词和过去分词。现在分词表主动、进行意义；过去分词表被动、完成意义。

一、现在分词

现在分词既有形容词、副词的特征，也保留动词的部分特征，可以带宾语（及物动词）、表语（连系动词）和状语，构成现在分词短语。现在分词或现在分词短语在句中可以作定语、表语、补足语和状语。例如：

I found him drinking my coffee. 我发现他在喝我的咖啡。

Being ill, he didn't go to school yesterday. 由于生病,他昨天没有上学。

The girl sitting behind me is our monitor. 坐在我后面的女孩是我们的班长。

现在分词有一般式、完成式两种时式,有主动、被动两种语态,如表 14-1 所示。

表 14-1　现在分词的时式和语态(以及物动词 write 和不及物动词 go 为例)

时式	主动语态	被动语态	时式	主动语态	被动语态
一般式	writing	being written	一般式	going	无
完成式	having written	having been written	完成式	having gone	无

(一) 现在分词的基本用法

1. 作定语

现在分词作定语时,其动作应和谓语动词同时发生,常常起定语从句的作用。单个的分词作前置定语,分词短语常作后置定语。如:a sleeping baby(=a baby who is sleeping)、developing countries(=countries which are developing)、a barking dog、the rising sun、the setting sun、the coming year、falling leaves、attacking players、leading comrades、failing sight、the hard-working people 等。例如:

She has many friends living in Singapore. 她有很多居住在新加坡的朋友。

That is a really exciting experience. 那确实是一次令人激动的经历。

The building being built now is a library. 正在建造的那座楼是图书馆。

China is developing rapidly with each passing day. 中国发展日新月异。

> 注:如果现在分词的动作发生在谓语动作之前,则不可用现在分词作定语,而要用定语从句。
> 例如:
> 你认识刚才吸烟的那个人吗?
> Do you know the man smoking just now? (×)
> Do you know the man who smoked just now? (√)
> 已经到达的客人正在园子里闲谈。
> The guests having arrived are having a chat in the garden. (×)
> The guests who have arrived are having a chat in the garden. (√)

2. 作表语

现在分词作表语往往表示主语的性质、特征。例如:

The music is much pleasing to the ear. 这音乐听起来很悦耳。

The dinner looks inviting. 晚餐看上去很吸引人。

What Simon said is a bit embarrassing. 西蒙刚说的话有点令人尴尬。

The flowers look even more charming after the rain. 雨后的花儿格外迷人。

3. 作补足语

现在分词可以作宾语和主语的补足语。

(1) 宾语补足语:现在分词及其短语可以用在感官动词(如 see、observe、notice、watch、hear、smell、listen to、look at、feel 等)以及使役动词(如 set、have、make、get、leave、keep 等)的宾

语后面作宾语补足语。例如：

I found Mabel lying on the grass. 我发现梅布尔躺在草地上。

Sorry, I have kept you waiting a long time. 对不起,我让你久等了。

The joke set everybody laughing. 这笑话使大家都笑了。

Don't have children doing their homework all the time. 别让孩子们一直做作业。

（2）主语补足语。上述结构如使用被动语态,现在分词即作主语补足语。例如：

Mabel was found lying on the grass. 梅布尔被发现躺在草地上。

The child was heard crying in the next room. 有人听到孩子在隔壁哭。

He was caught doing evil. 他做坏事被当场抓住。

Children should be kept using their mind. 应该让孩子们自己动脑筋。

> **注**：有些感官动词后面,既可接现在分词也可接不带 to 的不定式作宾语补足语。两者的区别在于前者表示动作正在进行；后者侧重动作的完成,强调的是动作的全过程。例如：
> —Did you hear the door bell ringing? 你听见门铃响了吗?
> —Yes, I did. I heard it ring three times. 是的,我听见了。我听见门铃响三次。
> I saw her crossing the street. 我看见她正在过街。
> I saw Mond cross the street. 我看见蒙德过了街。

4. 作状语

现在分词作状语可以表示时间、原因、条件、结果、让步和伴随情况等意义。一般用逗号和其他成分隔开,通常相当于一个状语从句。现在分词短语作状语时,其逻辑主语要和句子的主语保持一致。

（1）现在分词作状语表示时间（可用 when、while、until、after 等连词引出）,相当于时间状语从句。例如：

Passing by the house, Iris saw a girl playing the piano. 艾瑞斯路过那所房子时,看见一个女孩在弹钢琴。

We must maintain strategic focus and determination, and attain to "the broad and great while addressing the delicate minute". 我们要保持战略定力和耐心,做到"宽而精、细而精"。

Chatting with each other, we enjoyed our dinner. 我们边吃边聊。

When arriving at the station, John found that his friend had left. 到达车站时,约翰发现他的朋友已经走了。

（2）现在分词作状语表示原因,相当于原因状语从句。例如：

Knowing English well, he translated the article without much difficulty. 他的英语水平很高,没费多大劲就翻译了这篇文章。

Believing in my secretary, I left her an important job to do. 由于信任我的秘书,我把一项重要的工作交给她去做。

Not knowing Russian, Ira couldn't understand the film. 因不懂俄语,艾拉看不懂这部电影。

（3）现在分词作状语表示条件,相当于 if、unless 等引导的条件状语从句。例如：

Staying in the seashore for a time, you will feel fresh. 如果你在海边待上一段时间,你会感觉神清气爽。

Working hard, you will succeed. 努力工作，你就会成功。

Opening the window, you will see the garden below. 打开窗户，你就能看见下面的花园。

（4）现在分词作状语表示结果，前面有时加 thus、thereby、hence 等副词，相当于并列句。例如：

She got home, finding the door locked. 她回到家发现门锁着。

He escaped, not being seen by anyone. 他逃走了，没有被任何人看见。

His car was caught in a traffic jam, thus causing the delay. 他遇到了交通堵塞，因而耽搁了时间。

The old scientist died, leaving the project unfinished. 那位老科学家去世了，留下这个项目没有完成。

（5）现在分词作状语表示让步，相当于 though、even if 等引导的让步状语从句。例如：

Not having found the wallet, he still had some money with him. 他虽然没有找到钱包，但身上还有一些钱。

Although knowing all this, they made me pay for the damage. 虽然他们了解所有的情况，但还是要我赔偿损失。

Even if coming by taxi, I will arrive in at least 45 minutes. 即使乘出租车来，我至少也要45分钟以后才能到。

（6）现在分词作状语表示伴随情况等。现在分词表示行为方式、伴随情况或补充说明时，常置于句末，相当于一个并列句。例如：

Angel walked down the hill, singing softly to himself. 安吉尔朝山下走去，轻轻地唱着歌。

There was a big bright moon hanging in the sky, giving off a magic glow. 一轮明月挂在天空，向大地发出神奇的光芒。

Looking beyond the horizon, we have worked to steer the world in the right direction amid turbulence and changes. 坚持登高望远，我们为动荡变革世界引领正确方向。

People in disaster-stricken areas stood together rebuilding their homes. 受灾群众守望相助重建家园。

注：现在分词作状语时，其逻辑主语就是句子的主语。当句子的主语不是现在分词的逻辑主语时，就要改为从句表达。例如：

她看书的时候，电话铃响了。

While reading the book, the telephone rang. （×）

While she was reading the book, the telephone rang. （√）

（7）现在分词作评注性状语。有些分词短语往往作为句子的独立成分来修饰全句，表明说话者的态度、观点等，这种状语称为评注性状语。例如：

Frankly speaking, I don't like the picture. 坦率地说，我不喜欢这幅画。

Generally speaking, Chinese prefer tea to coffee. 一般来说，茶和咖啡相比，中国人更爱喝茶。

Judging from the appearance, he must be a strong man. 从外表上看，他肯定很强壮。

Considering everything, it is worth trying. 通盘考虑，这值得一试。

它们的逻辑主语可以和句子的主语不一致,这种结构已经成为固定的用法。常见的评注性状语有:generally speaking、frankly speaking、strictly speaking、broadly speaking、roughly speaking、narrowly speaking、judging from...、talking of...、concerning...、setting aside...、coming to...、allowing for...、considering(that)...、supposing(that)...、taking all into consideration、considering everything 等。

(8) 现在分词作状语修饰形容词。有少数现在分词常放在某些形容词前面,起副词的作用,意思是"极"或"非常",表示其程度或状态。例如:

It was freezing/biting cold that day. 那天刺骨的寒冷。

The weather has been burning/steaming hot this week. 这一周天气极热。

(二) 现在分词的一般式、完成式和被动式

1. 现在分词的一般式

现在分词所表示的动作与谓语动词的动作(几乎)同时发生或之后发生,现在分词用一般式。例如:

We saw a ship coming slowly towards us. 我们看见一艘船朝我们慢慢驶来。

Walking along the road, he found a stray dog. 他在走路的时候,发现了一只流浪狗。

The students sitting in the classroom are having an examination. 坐在教室里的学生正在考试。

2. 现在分词的完成式

如果现在分词的动作发生在谓语动词的动作之前,现在分词需用完成式,即 having+done。例如:

Having lived there for many years, Bloor knew the place well. 布卢尔在那里住了许多年,所以他很了解那个地方。

Having finished the course, we had an exam. 这门课程结束后,我们进行了一次考试。

Having worked in the countryside himself, he knows precisely what poverty feels like. 他自己在农村工作过,对贫困有着切身的感受。

Not having heard from her son for a long time, the mother worried a great deal. 好长时间没有收到儿子的来信,妈妈非常担心。

3. 现在分词的被动式

现在分词的被动式表示其逻辑主语是分词动作的承受者,且这一被动动作正在发生。具体形式为:being+done。例如:

The problem being discussed is very important. 正在讨论的那个问题非常重要。

The meeting being held now is about the fight against COVID-19. 正在召开的会议是关于新冠病毒疫情防控的。

The house being built will be finished next year. 那座正在建造的房子将于明年完工。

4. 现在分词的完成被动式

现在分词的完成被动式所表示的动作具有完成和被动的双重性。具体形式为:having+been+done。例如:

Having been given a wrong number, I couldn't ring him. 因为给我的是一个错误的号码,所以我没法给他打电话。

Having been invited to speak, I started making preparations. 收到发言的邀请,我就开始做准备。

Having been praised too much, he became conceited. 由于得到了过多的夸奖,他变得骄傲了。

Not having been given enough money, they could not carry out the experiment. 由于没有得到足够的资金,他们无法进行实验。

二、过去分词

过去分词表示已经完成的动作或被动意义。过去分词既有形容词、副词的特征,也有动词的特征,可接状语。

(一) 过去分词的基本用法

及物动词的过去分词表示被动和完成的意义;不及物动词的过去分词只表示完成,不表示被动。

1. 作定语

单个过去分词一般放在被修饰的名词前作前置定语(修饰代词时后置),过去分词短语通常作后置定语,相当于定语从句。如:spoken language、finished article、cooked food、untold sufferings、newly laid eggs、a lost child、a satisfied smile、the lost time 等。例如:

The excited people rushed into the building. 激动的人们冲进大楼。

The novel written by Simon is very popular. 西蒙写的那本小说很受欢迎。

下列短语中的过去分词不表被动,只表完成:boiled water、faded flowers、a retired teacher、departed friends、the fallen leaves、the changed situation、a returned overseas Chinese 等。

2. 作表语

过去分词作表语往往表示主语所处的状态。例如:

He looked worried. 他看上去忧心忡忡。

They are satisfied with their present job. 他们对目前的工作很满意。

The shop has remained closed for a week. 这家商店关门一周了。

He seemed very delighted at the idea. 听了这个主意他似乎很高兴。

常用作表语的过去分词有:astonished、broken、bored、confused、disappointed、discouraged、excited、gone、interested、known、lost、pleased、puzzled、satisfied、surprised、tired、touched、worried 等。

> 注:不要把作表语的过去分词误认为谓语动词的被动语态。作表语的过去分词表示状态,被动语态中的过去分词表示动作。例如:
> All the doors are locked. 所有的门都是锁着的。
> All the doors were locked by the guard. 所有的门都被卫兵锁上了。

3. 作补足语

过去分词可以作宾语和主语的补足语。

(1) 宾语补足语。过去分词及其短语可以用在感官动词、心理状态的动词(如 see、observe、notice、watch、hear、smell、feel、listen to、look at、think、consider 等)以及使役动词(如 set、

have、make、get、leave、keep 等)的宾语后面作宾语补足语(句子宾语是其逻辑宾语,即分词动作的承受者)。例如:

The traveler found himself lost in the valley. 那游客发现自己在山谷中迷路了。

She saw the thief (being) caught by the policeman. 她看到小偷被警察抓住了。

He still could not make himself understood in English. 他仍然不能用英语把事情讲清楚。

If you want to get yourself respected, you should respect others first. 如果你想让别人尊重你,你应该先尊重别人。

(2)主语补足语。上述结构如使用被动语态,过去分词即作主语补足语。例如:

The boy was found lost and couldn't find his way back. 有人发现这个男孩迷路了,找不到回去的路。

The path was seen covered with leaves. 这条小路落满了树叶。

This song is often heard sung everywhere. 大街小巷,都能听见人们唱这首歌。

4. 作状语

过去分词在句中作状语时,相当于一个状语从句,可以用来表示时间、原因、方式、条件、结果、目的、让步等含义。过去分词短语作状语时,其逻辑宾语要和句子的主语保持一致。

(1)过去分词作状语表示时间,相当于时间状语从句。例如:

The security guard stood at the entrance until (he was) told to come in. 警卫员一直站在入口处,直到被叫才进来。

Metals expand when heated and contract when cooled. 金属热胀冷缩。

Confronted by various acts of infringements and bullying, we have stayed unflinching and fought back resolutely. 面对各种侵权欺压行为,我们坚定不移并坚决反击。

(2)过去分词作状语表示原因,相当于原因状语从句。例如:

Greatly encouraged, we made up our mind to go on with the training. 因为受到了很大的鼓舞,我们决心继续训练下去。

The child learns fast, well brought up by his parents. 因父母教育得好,这孩子学得很快。

The over 1.4 billion Chinese people, filled with an even stronger sense of self-confidence and self-reliance, have unleashed a mighty force for building China into a modern socialist country. 14亿多的中国人民更加自信自强,迸发出建设社会主义现代化国家的磅礴伟力。

(3)过去分词作状语表示条件,相当于 if、unless 等引导的条件状语从句。例如:

Given more time, we could do it much better. 如果多给点时间,我们会做得更好些。

Punished, they will not cooperate. 要是受到惩罚,他们就不合作了。

United we stand, divided we fall. 〈谚〉团结则存,分裂则亡。

(4)过去分词作状语表示让步,相当于 though、even if 等引导的让步状语从句。例如:

Considered as a building material, wood is not very strong. 尽管木材被认为是一种建筑材料,但强度不大。

Locked in Canada, she didn't lose heart. 虽然被扣押在加拿大,但她并没有灰心。

Provided with COVID-19 vacines, the country has not fought against COVID-19 well. 尽管给那个国家提供了新冠病毒疫苗,但是他们的防疫工作还是没做好。

（5）过去分词作状语表示伴随情况，相当于一个并列句。例如：

Mabel left the station, dissatisfied. 梅布尔失望地离开了车站。

The pop star hurried up to her car, followed by her fans. 明星匆忙地走向自己的轿车，后面跟着她的粉丝。

The old man came out of the hospital, supported by the volunteers. 老人在志愿者的搀扶下出了医院。

（二）"have+名词+过去分词"结构

"have+名词+过去分词"结构中的过去分词作宾语补足语，表示被动含义。

（1）表示让人（自己/别人）做某事。等同于 get sth. done。例如：

I'll have/get the dead branch cut. 我要把那枯枝砍掉。

I am going to have/get the letter mailed. 我打算邮寄这封信。

You must have/get your air conditioner repaired. 你一定要把空调修好。

（2）表示遭遇或经历某事。此时 have 不能用 get 替代。例如：

I had my wallet stolen on the bus. 我的钱包在公交车上被偷了。

Jack had his leg broken on his way home. 杰克在回家的路上把腿弄折了。

Lucy had her cap blown off. 露西的帽子被风吹掉了。

Sarah had her house damaged in the storm. 萨拉的房屋在暴风雨中毁坏了。

三、分词的独立结构

分词作状语时，其逻辑主语与句子的主语应该一致；如果不一致，分词就有自己的逻辑主语。逻辑主语通常由名词或代词主格充当，置于分词之前，即名词或代词+分词。这种结构称为分词独立主格结构。在意义上相当于状语从句，表示时间、原因、条件、方式或伴随状况（伴随情况时替换为并列句）等。

（1）名词/代词+现在分词。例如：

Weather permitting, we'll go to the zoo tomorrow. 如果天气允许，我们明天去动物园。

There being no bus, we had to go home on foot. 因为没有公共汽车，我们不得不步行回家。

She lay against the wall, the sun shining upon her face. 她倚靠着墙，太阳照在她的脸上。

The little girl ran away, her hand waving in the air. 小女孩跑开了，手在空中挥舞着。

（2）名词/代词+过去分词。例如：

My shoes removed, I entered the room. 脱掉鞋子后，我走进了房间。

The table set, they began to dine. 桌子摆好以后，他们开始吃饭。

All the tickets sold out, we went back home disappointedly. 所有的票都卖完了，我们沮丧地回家了。

He stood still, his whole attention fixed upon the famous picture. 他一动不动地站着，全神贯注地看着那幅名画。

四、现在分词和过去分词的区别

现在分词和过去分词的区别主要表现在"时间"和"语态"两个方面。

（1）一般说来，现在分词表示正在进行的动作；过去分词表示已经完成的动作。例如：

the rising sun(正在升起的太阳)   the risen sun(升起了的太阳)

falling flowers(正在飘落的花)   fallen flowers(已落下的花)

boiling water(正在沸腾的水)   cold boiled water(凉开水或烧开过的水)

developing countries(发展中国家)   developed countries(发达国家)

（2）现在分词表示主动，所修饰的人或物是分词动作的执行者；过去分词则表示被动，所修饰的人或物是分词动作的承受者。试比较：

an exciting speech(激动人心的报告)   excited audiences(激动的观众)

the surprising news(令人吃惊的消息)   the surprised boy(受了惊吓的男孩)

a moving story(感人的故事)   moved students(受感动的学生)

a tiring journey(累人的旅行)   tired players(疲惫的运动员)

She heard someone closing the door. 她听见有人在关门。

She heard the door closed. 她听见门被关上了。

Tom came into the room following his father. 汤姆跟着他爸爸进了房间。

She came into the room supported by her daughter. 她在女儿的搀扶下进了房间。

五、现在分词和动名词的区别

现在分词具有形容词和副词性质，动名词具有名词性质，两者都可以作定语和表语，但意义完全不同。

1. 作定语的区别

现在分词作定语时，与被修饰的词有逻辑上的主谓关系，表示动作正在进行；动名词作定语时，则表示被修饰的词的性质、用途等，两者不存在逻辑上的主谓关系，没有时间性，如：a sleeping boy (= a boy who is sleeping)、a sleeping bag (= a bag for sleeping)、a singing bird、a singing competition、running water、a running track、the walking people、a walking stick、the swimming ducks、a swimming pool 等。

2. 作表语的区别

现在分词作表语时，表示主语的性质、特征，说明主语怎么样；动名词作表语时，表示主语的内容，说明主语是什么。例如：

His job is very interesting. 他的工作很有趣味。

Her mother's job is looking after the children. 她母亲的工作就是照看孩子。

My hobby is playing the piano. 我的爱好是弹钢琴。

The news is encouraging. 这条消息令人鼓舞。

巩固练习

Complete the following sentences by choosing the items marked A, B, C, or D.

1. To learn English well, we should find opportunities to hear English _____ as much as we can.
   A. speak　　　B. speaking　　　C. spoken　　　D. to speak

2. Almost all English prepositions when _____ into Chinese look like verbs.
   A. turning　　　B. being turned　　　C. to be turned　　　D. turned

3. You must follow the directions exactly and if you become _____, you must take the time to go back again and reread them.
   A. confuse　　　B. confusing　　　C. confused　　　D. to confuse

4. _____ to reach them on the phone, we sent an email instead.
   A. Fail　　　B. Failed　　　C. To fail　　　D. Having failed

5. The living room is clean and tidy, with a dining table already _____ for a meal to be cooked.
   A. laid　　　B. laying　　　C. to lay　　　D. being

6. —Look over there.
   —There's a very long, winding path _____ up to the house.
   A. leading　　　B. leads　　　C. led　　　D. to lead

7. He was busy writing a story, only _____ once in a while to smoke a cigarette.
   A. to stop　　　B. stopping　　　C. to have stopped　　　D. having stopped

8. The lady walked around the shops, _____ an eye out for bargains.
   A. keep　　　B. kept　　　C. keeping　　　D. to keep

9. Dina, _____ for months to find a job as a waitress, finally took a position at a local advertising agency.
   A. struggling　　　B. struggled　　　C. having struggled　　　D. to struggle

10. He had a wonderful childhood, _____ with his mother to all corners of the world.
    A. travel　　　B. to travel　　　C. traveled　　　D. traveling

11. I'm calling to enquire about the position _____ in yesterday's *China Daily*.
    A. advertised　　　B. to be advertised　　　C. advertising　　　D. having advertised

12. —Is there anything you want from town?
    —I'm going to get _____.
    A. these letters mail
    B. to mail these letters
    C. mailed
    D. these letters mailed

13. _____ not to miss the flight at 15:20, the manager set out for the airport in a hurry.
    A. Reminding
    B. Reminded
    C. Remind
    D. Having reminded

14. The next thing he saw was smoke _____ from behind the house.
    A. rose　　　B. rising　　　C. to rise　　　D. risen

15. I smell something _____ in the kitchen.
    A. burning   B. burnt   C. being burnt   D. to be burnt
16. A small plane crashed into a hillside five miles east of the city, _____ all four people onboard.
    A. killed   B. killing   C. kills   D. to kill
17. Where do you think the railroad _____ in the south of the city leads to?
    A. lying   B. lies   C. being laid   D. being lying
18. —Good morning. Can I help you?
    —I'd like to have this package _____, madam.
    A. to be weighed B. weighed   C. to weigh   D. be weighed
19. The news shocked the public, _____ to great concern about students' safety at school.
    A. having led   B. led   C. leading   D. to lead
20. _____ that she was going off to sleep, I asked if she'd like that little doll on her bed.
    A. Seeing   B. To see   C. See   D. Seen
21. Mrs. White showed her students some old maps _____ from the library.
    A. to borrow   B. to be borrowed
    C. borrowed   D. borrowing
22. In Australia, the Asians make their influence _____ in businesses large and small.
    A. feel   B. felt   C. to be felt   D. feeling
23. _____ many times, he finally understood it.
    A. Told   B. Telling
    C. Having told   D. Having been told
24. Lucy has a great sense of humor and always keeps her colleagues _____ with her stories.
    A. amused   B. amusing   C. to amuse   D. to be amused
25. Without sunlight _____ the earth surface, it would be so cold that life could not exist on the earth.
    A. to warm   B. warms   C. warmed   D. warming
26. _____ the right kind of training, these teenage soccer players may one day grow into international stars.
    A. Giving   B. Having given C. To give   D. Given
27. It rained heavily in the south, _____ serious flooding in several provinces.
    A. caused   B. having caused
    C. causing   D. to cause
28. _____ the city center, we saw a stone of about 10 meters in height.
    A. Approaching   B. Approached
    C. To approach   D. To be approached
29. _____ in this way, the situation doesn't seem so disappointing.
    A. Looking at   B. Looked at   C. To be looked at   D. To look at
30. The lawyer listened with full attention, _____ to miss any point.
    A. not trying   B. trying not   C. to try not   D. not to try

31. The traffic rule says young children under the age of four and _____ less than 40 pounds must be in a child safety seat.

    A. being weighed   B. to weigh   C. weighed   D. weighing

32. Listen! Do you hear someone _____ for help?

    A. calling   B. call   C. to call   D. called

33. Lots of rescue workers were working around the clock, _____ supplies to the flooded area.

    A. sending   B. to send   C. having sent   D. to have sent

34. Sarah pretended to be cheerful, _____ nothing about the argument.

    A. says   B. said   C. to say   D. saying

35. _____ from the top of the tower, the south foot of the mountain is a sea of trees.

    A. Seen   B. Seeing   C. Having seen   D. To see

36. There is a great deal of evidence _____ that music activities engage different parts of the brain.

    A. indicate   B. indicating   C. to indicate   D. to be indicating

37. Now that we've discussed our problem, are people happy with the decisions _____ ?

    A. taking   B. take   C. taken   D. to take

38. With the government's aid, those _____ by the earthquake have moved to the new settlements.

    A. affect   B. affecting   C. affected   D. were affected

39. _____ at my classmates' faces, I read the same excitement in their eyes.

    A. Looking   B. Look   C. To look   D. Looked

40. Though _____ to see us, the professor gave us a warm welcome.

    A. surprising   B. was surprised   C. surprised   D. being surprised

第十五章

虚拟语气

热身训练： 下列句子，各有一处错误，请指出并改正。

❶ Some classmates suggest we can go to places of interest nearby.
❷ Her parents wish she can do better next time.
❸ Was I you, I would go with him to the party.
❹ If he had spent more time practicing speaking English before, he will be able to speak it much better now.
❺ As usual, he put on a show as though his trip has been a great success.
❻ If only I know how to operate an computer as you do.
❼ Your advice that she would wait till next week is reasonable.
❽ It is time that the government takes measures to protect the rare birds and animals.
❾ As for the English examination, I would have gone to the concert last Sunday.
❿ He was very busy yesterday, otherwise he would come to the meeting.
⓫ I wish I am back home; I do not like this place.
⓬ I can't stand him. He always talks as though he knows everything.
⓭ We would rather our daughter stays at home with us, but it is her choice, and she is not a child any longer.
⓮ If he has caught the morning train, he would not have been late for the meeting.
⓯ If Mr. Dewey has been present, he would have offered any possible assistance to the people there.

一、语气的分类

在英语中，动词一般有三种不同的语气，用于表达说话者对事情的看法或态度。不同的语气可以用动词的不同形式来表示。

（1）陈述语气：一般用来讲述事实。例如：
He went to the supermarket yesterday. 他昨天去了超市。
The situation could still be remedied. 事情还有挽回的余地。

（2）祈使语气：主要用于祈使句，表示请求、劝告、命令等。例如：
Please keep the classroom clean. 请保持教室干净。

Don't forget to E-mail me. 别忘了发邮件给我。

（3）虚拟语气：用于表示说话人所说的话不是事实，而是想象、假设或打算、愿望等。例如：

If I had met him last night, I would have told him the truth. 如果我昨晚见到他，我就会告诉他这个事实。

He wishes his parents would show him a little more sympathy. 他多希望父母能再体谅他一点。

二、虚拟语气在条件状语从句中的应用

条件状语从句分为真实条件句和虚拟条件句。真实条件句所表示的假设是真的或可能发生的，条件句和主句都用陈述语气。例如：

If I have free time, I'll help you with your English. 如果我有空，我就会帮助你学习英语。

而虚拟条件句所表示的假设是无法实现或实现的可能性不大的情况。其谓语动词的主要形式如表 15-1 所示。

表 15-1　虚拟语气谓语动词的主要形式

种　　类	if 条件句	主　句　结　构
与现在事实相反	过去式(be,常用 were)	would/should/could/might+动词原形
与过去事实相反	had+过去分词	would/should/could/might+have+过去分词
与将来事实相反	过去式(be,常用 were) should+动词原形 were to+动词原形	would/should/could/might+动词原形

1. 虚拟条件句的用法

（1）与现在事实相反的假设。例如：

If I knew her address, I would go to meet her at once. 假如我知道她的地址，我就会立马去见她。

If Kate were a boy, she would join the army. 如果凯特是男孩，她会去参军。

（2）与过去事实相反的假设。例如：

Kate might have missed the show if you had not given her a lift in your car. 要不是你让凯特搭车的话，她可能就错过了这场演出。

If she hadn't taken your advice, she might have been hurt. 假如她没听你的建议，也许她就受伤了。

（3）与将来事实相反的假设。例如：

If I had enough time, I would be a volunteer. 假使我有足够的时间，我会去做一名志愿者。

If the sun were to rise in the west tomorrow, I would trust you. 如果明天太阳从西边出来，我就相信你。

2. 虚拟条件句的省略与倒装

如果虚拟条件状语从句中含有 were、had、should,那么可以把它们提到句首,将句首的 if 省略,构成倒装句式:Were/Had/Should+主语+其他部分。例如:

Were my father here, everything would be all right. 如果我父亲在这儿,一切都会好的。

Had I had time, I would have run round that lake again. 如果我有时间,我就再绕湖跑一圈了。

Should it rain tomorrow, we would have to cancel the important show. 如果明天下雨,我们就得取消这个重要的演出。

3. 含蓄条件句

有时虚拟条件句中,表示假设的 if 条件句不出现,而通过介词(短语)或其他方式引出,这种句子称为含蓄条件句。常见的介词(短语)有 with、without、but for、but that、under、otherwise、or、in that case 等。例如:

But for a knee injury, he would play Romeo on stage instead of lying in bed now. 如果不是膝盖受伤,他就在舞台上演罗密欧了,而不是像现在这样躺在床上。

Without your help, I couldn't have made such great progress in English last term. 若没有你的帮助,上学期我的英语就不会取得这么大的进步。

Tom took my advice; otherwise he would have lost the chance. 汤姆采纳了我的建议,不然他就失去这次机会了。

Mike would have helped us but that he was in trouble at that time. 迈克要不是那时候有麻烦,他就会帮助我们的。

In that case we could have finished the work earlier. 如果是那样的话,我们就能更早一点完成工作。

We could have done better under more favourable conditions. 如果条件更优越的话,我们还可以做得更好些。

4. 混合条件句

在非真实条件句中,有时主句与从句的动作发生的时间不一致,主句和从句的谓语动词要依照假设的时间而定。这种句子称为混合条件句或错综时间条件句。

(1) 混合条件句中的条件指过去,而结果指的是现在或将来。例如:

If you had seen the doctor yesterday, you might know what kind of disease you have got now. 要是你昨天去看了医生,你现在就知道自己生了什么病。

If Tom had studied hard last term, he wouldn't be in such trouble now. 假如汤姆上学期认真学习的话,他现在就不会如此麻烦了。

The Greens wouldn't be feeling so tired if they hadn't been walking for a whole day. 假如格林夫妇没有走一整天的路,他们就不会感到这么累的。

(2) 混合条件句中的条件并不指某一确定时间,而结果指的是过去。例如:

If I weren't afraid of snakes, I would have touched it. 如果我不害怕蛇的话,我就触摸它了。

If I were you, I would have taken his advice then. 我要是你,当时就会听取他的建议。

三、虚拟语气的另一种表达形式——(should)+动词原形

英语中有一些词或词组后面的 that 从句也需要用虚拟语气，但虚拟语气的表达形式是 should+动词原形，且 should 常被省略。主要有以下几类。

(1) 表示建议、主张、要求、命令等动词后面的宾语从句。常见的这类动词有：suggest、propose、recommend、move、advise、insist、maintain、hold、urge、ask、request、require、demand、desire、prefer、arrange、order、command。例如：

Sarah suggested that I (should) save some money after receiving my wages. 萨拉建议我在领到工资后存一些钱。

The boss proposed that all the plans (should) be discussed at the meeting. 老板建议在会上讨论所有的计划。

Our teacher insists that we (should) be as attentive as possible when we visit the museum. 我们老师坚持要求我们在参观博物馆时要尽可能地细心观察。

The coach demanded that the players (should) try their best to beat their opponents. 教练要求运动员们尽全力打败对手。

> 注：这类词用于被动语态时，其后面的主语从句也要用虚拟语气，例如：
> It is requested that all members (should) be present at the speech contest. 所有人都被要求出席演讲比赛。
> It is recommended that students (should) develop the habit of reading after school. 建议学生养成课后阅读的习惯。
> 当 suggest 不表示"建议"，而是表示"暗示、表明"；insist 不表示"坚决要求"，而是表示"坚持说"时，其后不用虚拟语气，而用陈述语气。例如：
> Jane's pale face suggested that she was ill. 简脸色苍白表明她生病了。
> Tom insisted that he had done nothing wrong. 汤姆坚持说自己没有做错事。

(2) 与上述动词相关的同位语从句和表语从句。表示建议、主张、要求、命令等动词若以名词形式出现，相关的同位语从句和表语从句中的谓语动词须用相同的虚拟语气句式。例如：

My suggestion is that our disagreement (should) be set aside in this tense situation. 我建议在这种紧张的局势下，我们的分歧应先放到一边。

I'm in favor of his proposal that a new club (should) be set up to satisfy the needs. 我赞成他的提议，应该建立一个新俱乐部，以满足大家的需求。

My advice is that you (should) make adequate preparations. 我的建议是你应该做好充分的准备。

Our only request is that this task (should) be assigned as soon as possible. 我们唯一的要求是应该尽快地分配这项任务。

I second his motion that an emergency conference (should) be held to discuss this problem. 他提议应该举行紧急会议讨论这一问题，我赞成。

(3) 某些形容词后面的主语从句。这类形容词主要表示"要紧，急迫，必须"等意思，如

appropriate、insistent、necessary、imperative、natural、essential、vital、important、urgent、advisable、preferable 等。例如：

It is necessary that those serious problems (should) be solved immediately. 那些严重的问题很有必要立即解决。

It is urgent that they (should) sign the contract before dark. 他们急需在天黑之前签合同。

It is imperative that the representation and voice of developing countries be increased so that the UN could be more balanced in reflecting the interests and wishes of the majority of countries in the world. 要切实提高发展中国家在联合国的代表性和发言权，使联合国更加平衡地反映大多数国家利益和意愿。

(4) it is a pity、it is a shame、it is no wonder、it is strange、it is incredible 等后面的主语从句。此类主语从句也可以用虚拟语气，意为"居然，竟然"，表示说话人的惊讶、失望情感等。例如：

It is a great pity that he should make such a mistake. 真遗憾他竟然犯了这样的错误。

It is a shame that he should be drunk in the street. 他竟然喝醉在大街上，真丢脸。

It seems incredible that their team should have won the contest. 他们队竟然赢得了比赛，真让人难以置信。

注：上述句子也可以用陈述语气，表示只叙述事实，而不带感情色彩。

(5) 以 lest、for fear (that)、in case 等引导的目的状语从句。此类从句谓语动词形式多用 should+动词原形。例如：

They spoke in whispers lest they should be heard. 他们低声耳语，怕被别人听见。

He hid his school report for fear that he should let his parents down. 他把成绩单藏起来，生怕令父母失望。

In case it should rain, I would take an umbrella. 万一下雨，我会带把雨伞的。

注：for fear that 和 in case 引导的从句中的谓语动词也可以用 may(might、can、could 等)+动词原形表示。例如：

We were afraid to tell the truth for fear it might cause trouble. 我们不敢说出事实，怕引起麻烦。

四、虚拟语气在其他结构中的使用

（一）wish、would rather (sooner/prefer)、if only、as if (though) 及 it's (high/about/right) time 后面的从句

wish、would rather (sooner/prefer)、if only、as if (though) 及 it's (high/about/right) time 等词及词组后面的从句常表示与事实相反或难以实现的事情，所以这些从句常用虚拟语气。

(1) 动词 wish 后接的宾语从句中，谓语动词的形式和虚拟条件句中的条件从句的谓语动词形式相似。表示对现在事实的虚拟，从句谓语动词应用过去式(be,常用 were)；表示对过去事实的虚拟，从句谓语动词应用 had+过去分词或 could/would+have+过去分词；表示对将来事实的虚拟，从句谓语动词应用 would (could 及 might)+动词原形。例如：

I wish it were a sunny day today. 我希望今天是个晴天。

I wish I had taken courage like him to fight with the thief that day. 我希望那天我也能像他一样有勇气和小偷搏斗。

注：如果动词 wish 是过去时态，其后的宾语从句的虚拟语气形式不变。例如：
She wished she knew how to operate the machine. 她当时希望知道怎样操作这台机器。

（2）would rather(sooner)等后接的宾语从句中，表示对现在事实和将来事实的虚拟，从句谓语动词应用过去式（be 常用 were）；表示对过去事实的虚拟，从句谓语动词应用 had+过去分词。例如：

I would rather (sooner) she gave up her plan for the time being. 我宁愿她暂时放弃她的计划。

I would sooner (rather) you hadn't given away the secret. 我宁愿你没有把这个秘密泄露出去。

（3）if only 引起的感叹句，与 I wish 表达的意思相近，表示愿望。谓语动词的形式与 wish 后面的宾语从句中谓语动词的形式相同。例如：

If only I were more graceful! 我要是更优雅一点就好了！

If only I hadn't been busy yesterday! 要是我昨天不忙就好了！

（4）even if/though 引导的让步状语从句，有时用虚拟语气，形式同 if 引导的虚拟条件句。例如：

He would go abroad for further study even if his parents objected. 即使父母反对，他也要出国深造。

（5）as if 和 as though 引导的方式状语从句要用虚拟语气，从句谓语动词的形式与 wish 后面的宾语从句中谓语动词的形式相同。例如：

She looks at me in terror as if (though) I were the evil stepmother. 她恐惧地看着我，就好像我是恶毒的后妈。

Pamela talked about Sydney as if (though) she had been there herself. 帕梅拉谈起悉尼就仿佛自己去过那里似的。

注：在 look、seem、taste、smell 等词后面的由 as if (though) 引导的从句中，也可以用陈述语气。例如：
She looks as if she is going to smile. 她好像要笑了。
The meat tastes (smells) as if it has gone bad. 这肉尝（闻）起来像是坏了。

（6）在 it is (high/about) time (that)…句型中，后面的从句要用虚拟语气，其谓语动词常用过去式或 should ＋动词原形，且 should 不可以省略。例如：

It's high time that we held a meeting to discuss the problem. 我们该开会讨论这个问题了。

Global warming could bring disastrous effects to the earth, so it is about time that we should protect the earth. 全球变暖给地球带来灾难性的影响，是时候应该保护地球了。

（二）情态动词 may(might)

情态动词 may(might) 作为一种特殊的虚拟式，它可以用在让步状语从句中，也可以用在独立句中表示祝愿。例如：

However it may be, I shall follow my heart. 无论如何，我都会追随我的本心。

No matter what you may say, I am determined to buy what I need. 不管你怎么说，我还是决定

要买我需要的东西。

May you succeed! 祝你成功！

May there never be another world war! 愿永远不再有世界大战！

（三）"be 型"虚拟语气

在一些感叹句中，用"be 型"虚拟语气，表示祝愿。例如：

Be it so! 但愿如此！

Far be it from me to hurt your feelings! 我决不愿伤害你的感情。

巩 固 练 习

Complete the following sentences by choosing the items marked A, B, C, or D.

1. Were I to do it, I _____ it some other way.
   A. will do   B. were to do
   C. would have done   D. would do

2. Mary is ill today. If she _____, she _____ absent from school.
   A. were not ill; wouldn't be   B. had been ill; wouldn't have been
   C. had been ill; should have been   D. hadn't been ill; could be

3. If they _____ earlier than expected, they _____ here now.
   A. had started; would be   B. started; might be
   C. had started; would have been   D. will start; might have been

4. If I _____ where he lived, I _____ a note to him.
   A. knew; would   B. had known; would have sent
   C. know; would send   D. knew; would have sent

5. She wishes she _____ to the theatre last night.
   A. went   B. would go
   C. had gone   D. were going

6. We wish we _____ what you did when we were at high school.
   A. did   B. should do   C. have done   D. could have done

7. Without your help, we _____ so much.
   A. won't achieve   B. wouldn't have achieved
   C. don't achieve   D. didn't achieve

8. I insisted that he _____ at once.
   A. be gone   B. might go   C. would go   D. go

9. Do you think of Wang Fang's suggestion that he _____ Mr. Li to the party?
   A. will invite   B. invite   C. is invited   D. have invited

10. He asks that he _____ an opportunity to explain why he's refused to go there.
    A. is given   B. must give   C. should give   D. be given

11. My sister advised me that I _____ accept the invitation.
    A. could   B. must   C. should   D. might

12. Tom is very short now. His mother wishes that he _____ be tall when he grows up.
    A. could   B. should   C. would   D. were able to
13. They got up early in order that they _____ they first train.
    A. caught   B. will catch   C. might catch   D. shall catch
14. Read it aloud so that I _____ you clearly.
    A. may hear   B. will hear   C. hear   D. have heard
15. He acts as if he _____ everything in the world.
    A. knew   B. knows   C. has known   D. won't know
16. It is quite natural that my coming late again _____ them very angry.
    A. had made   B. make   C. makes   D. would make
17. Li Ming insisted that he _____ anything at all.
    A. hadn't stolen B. shouldn't steal C. doesn't steal D. steal
18. If only I _____ to the lecture!
    A. listen   B. had listened   C. am listening   D. will listen
19. I'd rather that you _____ home.
    A. went   B. have gone   C. will go   D. had gone
20. It is high time we _____ home.
    A. will go   B. would go   C. have gone   D. went
21. That is a good book. You _____ it yesterday.
    A. could buy   B. should buy
    C. should have bought   D. bought
22. I am sorry that he _____ in such poor health.
    A. are   B. should be   C. were   D. shall be
23. He _____ you more help, even though he was very busy.
    A. may have given   B. might give
    C. might have given   D. may give
24. Without electricity, human life _____ quite different today.
    A. is   B. will be   C. would have been D. would be
25. I didn't see your sister at the meeting. If she _____, she would have met my brother.
    A. has come   B. had come   C. came   D. did come
26. If you _____ that film late last night, you wouldn't be so sleepy.
    A. didn't see   B. haven't seen
    C. wouldn't have seen   D. hadn't seen
27. If you had enough money, what _____?
    A. will you buy   B. would you buy
    C. would you have bought   D. will you have bought
28. Jane would never have gone to the party _____ that Mary would come to see her.
    A. has she known B. had she known C. if she know   D. if she has known
29. Mr. Smith insisted that he _____ the work all.
    A. had done   B. have done   C. did   D. will do

30. Mike's father, as well as his mother, insisted that he _____ home.
    A. stayed　　　B. could stay　　　C. has stayed　　　D. stay

31. I didn't know his telephone number, otherwise I _____ him.
    A. had telephoned　　　B. would telephone
    C. would have telephoned　　　D. telephone

32. His tired face suggested that he _____ really tired after the long walk.
    A. had been　　　B. should be　　　C. be　　　D. was

33. —Would you have called her up had it been possible?
    —Yes, but I _____ busy doing my homework.
    A. was　　　B. were　　　C. had been　　　D. would be

34. How I wish I _____ to repair the watch! I only made it worse.
    A. had tried　　　B. didn't try
    C. have tried　　　D. hadn't tried

35. I did not attend the lecture by Pro. Jackson. I _____ but I _____ all this morning.
    A. would; have washed　　　B. could; have been washing
    C. would have; have been washing　　　D. could have; had washing

36. —Sorry, Joe. I did not mean to...
    —Don't call me "Joe". I am Mr. Parker to you, and _____ you forget it!
    A. do　　　B. don't
    C. did　　　D. didn't

37. The teacher demanded that the exam _____ before eleven.
    A. must finish　　　B. would be finished
    C. be finished　　　D. must be finished

38. We took a taxi to the airport. Otherwise we _____ late.
    A. would be　　　B. would have been
    C. will be　　　D. were

39. If law-breakers _____, the society would be in disorder.
    A. made unpunished　　　B. came unpunished
    C. went unpunished　　　D. not punished

40. If the hurricane had happened during the day-time, _____ more deaths.
    A. it would have been　　　B. it would be
    C. there would be　　　D. there would have been

第十六章

构 词 法

英语中的构词方法主要有合成法、派生法、转换法三种。

一、合成法

合成法(compounding),即由两个或更多的词合成一个词,有的用连字符"-"连接,有的直接连写在一起,还有的由分开的两个词构成。

(1) 合成名词有以下几类。
① 名词+名词,如 credit-card、drugstore、gas-cooker 等。
② 形容词+名词,如 blueprint(蓝图)、civil-rights、deadline 等。
③ 动名词+名词,如 diving-board、drinking-water、frying-pan 等。
④ 现在分词+名词,如 flying-fish、ruling class(统治阶级)、sleeping beauty 等。
⑤ 动词+名词,如 makeshift(权宜之计)、pickpocket(扒手)、worksite 等。
⑥ 介词+名词,如 aftereffect、by-product、overcoat 等。
⑦ 名词+动词,如 daybreak、heartbeat、rainfall 等。
⑧ 名词+动名词,如 sightseeing、weight-lifting、wind-surfing 等。
⑨ 动词+副词,如 breakthrough、look-over(过目)、makeup、takeoff 等。
⑩ 副词+动词,如 by-product、downfall(垮台)、income、out-break 等。
⑪ 其他方式,如 comrade-in-arms(战友)、forget-me-not(勿忘我草)、go-between(中间人)、good-for-nothing(无用之人)、he-goat(公山羊)、mother-in-law(岳母)、passer-by 等。

(2) 合成形容词有以下几种。
① 名词+形容词,如 bullet-proof(防弹的)、homesick、ice-cold 等。
② 形容词+形容词,如 bitter-sweet、deaf-mute、light-blue 等。
③ 现在分词+形容词,如 freezing-cold、steaming-hot、soaking-wet 等。
④ 名词+现在分词,如 heartbreaking、time-consuming 等。
⑤ 名词+过去分词,如 hand-made、heartfelt、state-owned(国营的)等。
⑥ 形容词+现在分词,如 easy-going、good-looking、sweet-smiling 等。
⑦ 形容词+过去分词,如 dry-cleaned、long-dated、new-born 等。
⑧ 副词+现在分词,如 ever-lasting、hard-working、outstanding 等。
⑨ 副词+过去分词,如 newly-built、well-known、so-called(所谓的)等。
⑩ 副词+名词,如 off-budget(预算外的)、off-guard、out-door 等。

⑪ 形容词+名词,如 deep-sea、front-page、high-speed 等。
⑫ 动词+名词,如 break-neck(非常危险的)、cut-rate(打折扣的)等。
⑬ 数词+名词,如 first-class、one-way、ten-minute 等。
⑭ 形容词+名词+ed,如 absent-minded、good-tempered 等。
⑮ 名词+名词+ed,如 brick-headed、iron-willed、paper-backed 等。
⑯ 数词+名词+ed,如 six-storied、one-sided、three-legged 等。
⑰ 动词+副词,如 breakeven(不盈不亏的)、drive-in(开车进去的〈影院〉)、see-through 等。
⑱ 过去分词+副词,如 broken-down、built-in(嵌在墙内的)、cast-off 等。
⑲ 副词+形容词,如 over-anxious、evergreen、oversensitive(过分敏感的)等。
⑳ 其他方式,如 all-out(全力以赴的)、ever-victorious、well-off、happy-go-lucky、life-and-death(殊死的)、out-and-out(彻头彻尾的)、out-of-the-way、up-to-date、word-for-word(逐字逐句的)等。

（3）合成动词有以下几类。
① 名词+动词,如 air-drop、proof-read、sleepwalk、water-ski 等。
② 形容词+动词,如 blacklist(把……列入黑名单)、cross-examine、ill-treat 等。
③ 形容词+名词,如 blackmail(勒索)、double-check、mass-produce 等。
④ 副词+动词,如 backtrack、outdo、outshine(比……优异)、overcome 等。
⑤ 其他方式,如 blow-dry、court martial(军法审判)、dilly-dally(浪费时间)、spin-dry、stir-fry(翻炒)、tittle-tattle(闲聊)、underline、withdraw 等。

二、派生法

派生法是通过在词根上加后缀或前缀来构成新词的一种方法。

(一) 常用前缀的含义及例词

（1）表示否定的前缀如表 16-1 所示。

表 16-1　表示否定含义的前缀及例词

前缀	含义	例　　词
a-	缺乏,不	amoral(非道德性的)、apolitical(不关心政治的)、aseptic(无菌的)
un-		uncommon(非凡的)、unexpected(意外的)、unexploded(未爆炸的)
non-		non-metal(非金属)、nonconductor(非导体)、nonexistence(不存在)
dis-		disclose(揭露)、disobey(不服从)、disorder(混乱、无秩序)
in-		inaccurate(不精确的)、incomplete(不完全的)、infinite(无限的)
im-(在字母 m、p、b 前)	相反的,不	imbalance(不平衡)、immature(不成熟的)、impatient(不耐烦的)
il-		illegal(不合法的)、illogical(不合逻辑的)
ir-		irregular(不规则的)、irresponsible(无责任感的)、irreligious(反宗教的)

（2）表示相反的前缀如表 16-2 所示。

表 16-2　表示相反含义的前缀及例词

前缀	含义	例　词
un-	相反动作的	undo（毁灭）、unpack（取出）、undress（脱衣服）、unwrap（解开）
de-		decode（解码）、defrost（解冻）、devalue（使贬值）、deforest（砍伐森林）
dis-		disconnect（断开）、discolor（褪色）、dishearten（使气馁）

（3）使词义转贬的前缀如表 16-3 所示。

表 16-3　使词义转贬的前缀及例词

前缀	含义	例　词
mis-	错误的	misconduct（行为不正）、mishear（听错）、misinform（误传）、mislead（误导）
mal-	坏的	malfunction（功能障碍）、maltreat（虐待）、malnutrition（营养不良）
pseudo-	假,伪	pseudoscience（伪科学）、pseudo-intellectual（假知识分子）、pseudonym（假名）

（4）表示程度或大小的前缀如表 16-4 所示。

表 16-4　表示程度或大小含义的前缀及例词

前缀	含义	例　词
arch-	首位的	archbishop（大主教）、archenemy（主要敌人）
super-	超级	superpower（超级大国）、supermarket（超级市场）、supersonic（超音速）
out-	超过	outclass（比……等级高）、outgrow（长得比……快）、outlive（比……活得长）
sur-	高于	surcharge（超载）、surplus（过剩,剩余）、surpass（超过）、surtax（附加税）
sub-	在下,次于	subordinate（次要的）、subconscious（下意识的）、subnormal（低于正常的）
over-	过度的	overcharge（要价太高）、overeat（暴食）、overestimate（过高评价）
under-	不够,在下	undercharge（少收价款）、underline（在……下画线）、underestimate（低估）
hyper-	极度	hypertension（高血压）、hyperactive（异常活跃的）、hypercritical（苛求的）
ultra-	超,外	ultrasonic（超声速的）、ultraviolet（紫外线）、ultra-fashionable（超时尚的）
mini-	小、微	minibus（小公共汽车）、minicar（小型汽车）、miniskirt（超短裙）
macro-	比较大的	macrocosm（宏观世界）、macroeconomics（宏观经济学）
micro-	微小的	microcomputer（微型计算机）、microwave（微波）、microscope（显微镜）

（5）表示位置的前缀如表 16-5 所示。

表 16-5　表示位置含义的前缀及例词

前缀	含义	例　词
ante-	在前面	anteroom（前室、接待室）、antenatal（出生前的）
mid-	中	midday（正午）、middle（中间的）、midnight（午夜）
sub-	下面的	subordinate（下级的、次要的）、subway（地铁）
pro-	向前	proceed（前进）、project（突出、伸出）、progress（前进,进展）
inter-	之间的,互相	inter-city（城市间的）、interact（相互作用）、interpersonal（人际的）
trans-	跨越,移	trans-Atlantic（跨大西洋的）、transmit（传输、传递）、translate（翻译）

续表

前缀	含义	例 词
fore-	前	forehead（前额）、foreword（前言）、foreleg（前腿）
extra-	……之外	extracurricular（课外的）、extralarge（特大的）、extraordinary（非同寻常的）
in-	在内，向内	inside（〈在〉内部）、inlet（入口）、include（包括）、invasion（入侵、闯入）
intra-	……之内	intramuscular（肌内的）、introspection（反省）、intrauterine（子宫内）
dia-	横过，穿过	diagram（图解）、dialogue（对话）、diameter（直径）
over-	在……之上	overhead（在头顶上的）、overlook（眺望）、overland（经由陆路的）

（6）表示态度的前缀如表 16-6 所示。

表 16-6　表示态度含义的前缀及例词

前　缀	含义	例　词
co-	共同	coaction（共同行动）、coauthor（合著者）、cooperate（合作）
col-（用在字母 l 前）	共同	collaborate（协作、合作）、collect（收集、聚集）
com-（用在字母 m、b 或 p 前）	共同	compassion（同情）、combine（结合）
cor-（用在字母 r 前）	共同	correlate（相互关联）、correspond（对应、符合）
counter-	反	counterclockwise（逆时针的）、counterculture（反主流文化）
anti-	反对	antifreeze（防冻）、antiwar（反战的）、anti-social（厌恶社交的）
contra-	相反	contradict（反驳）、contra-natural（违反自然的）、controversy（争论）

（7）表示时间和顺序的前缀如表 16-7 所示。

表 16-7　表示时间和顺序含义的前缀及例词

前缀	含义	例　词
fore-	预先，在前	forecast（预测）、foresee（预见）、fore-judge（预断）、forefather（祖先、祖宗）
pre-	在……之前	precede（领先）、preset（预置）、prewar（战前的）、prehistory（史前的）
post-	在……之后	postgraduate（研究生）、postpone（推迟）、postwar（战后的）、postscript（附言）
ex-	前任	ex-wife（前妻）、ex-mayor（前任市长）、ex-president（前任校长）
re-	再，重新	rebuild（重建）、recover（〈使〉痊愈）、redesign（重新设计）、redouble（再加倍）
retro-	向后	retrospect（回顾）、retro-rocket（制动火箭）

（8）表示数字的前缀如表 16-8 所示。

表 16-8　表示数字含义的前缀及例词

前缀	含义	例　词
semi-	半	semiconductor（半导体）、semicircle（半圆）
demi-	半	demigod（半神半人）、demilune（半月，半月形堡垒）
hemi-	半	hemicycle（半圆形）、hemisphere（半球，大脑半球）
uni-	单，一	uniform（〈统一的〉校服）、union（一致）、unity（统一）、unicorn（独角兽）
mono-	单，一	monolayer（单层）、monologue（独白）、monotone（单调〈的〉）

续表

前缀	含义	例　词
bi-、di-	双，二	bicycle(自行车)、bilingual(双语的)、bimonthly(双月刊)
tw-、du-		twice、twin、duad(〈一〉对，双)、dual(二重的)
tri-	三	triangle(三角形)、tricycle(三轮车)、triplane(三翼飞机)
quadr-、quadri-	四	quadrangle(四角形，四边形)、quadrifid(分成四部分的)
tetra-		tetragon(四角形，四边形)、tetrad(四个，四个一组)
quart-		quarter(四等分，四分之一)、quartern(四分之一)、quartet(四人一组)
quint	五	quintet(五重奏乐团，五重奏曲)、quint(五度，五度音)
penta		pentagon(五角形)、pentad(五个，五年，五天)、pentagraph(连续的五个字母)
dec-	十	decade(十，十个合成的一组，十年)、decimal(十进制)
centi-	百，百分之一	centimeter(厘米)、centigrade(百分度的，摄氏温度计的)
kilo-	千	kilogram(千克)、kilometer(千米)、kilowatt(千瓦)
milli-	千分之一	milligram(毫克)、millimeter(毫米)、milliliter(毫升)
poly-	多	poly-technical(多种工艺的，多种科技的)
multi-		multitude(众多)、multipurpose(多用途的)、multiple(多样的)

(9) 转换性前缀如表16-9所示。

表16-9　表示转换性含义的前缀及例词

前缀	含　义	例　词
a-	处……的情况，呈现……的状态	aboard(在船上)、afire(燃烧着)、afloat(浮着，在水上)、ahead(向前〈的〉)、ashore(在岸上)、ablaze(兴奋，激昂)
be-	使，使显得	becalm(使平静)、belittle(使相形之下显得微小)
en-	使，使成为	enlarge(扩大)、enrich(使富有)、enslave(奴役)
em-(在字母p和b前)	使处……状态	embed(嵌入)、embody(体现)、empower(授权)

(10) 其他前缀如表16-10所示。

表16-10　表示其他含义的前缀及例词

前缀	含　义	例　词
ab(s)-	脱离，反常	abnormal(异常的)、abuse(滥用)、abortion(流产)、abstract(提取)
all-	纯的，全部的	all-male(全部男性的)、all-wool(纯羊毛的)、all-sided(全面的)
auto-	自己，自动的	automatic(自动的)、automobile(汽车)、autobiography(自传)
bene-	好，善	beneficent(行善的)、benevolent(仁慈的)
by-	(附属的，次要的)	by-product(副产品)、bypath(小路)、byname(别名，绰号)
chron(o)-	时间的	chronology(年代学)、chronometer(计时器)
cyber-	计算机网络的	cyber-cafe(网吧)、cybercrime(网络犯罪)、cyber-fraud(网络诈骗)
e-	电子的	e-book(电子书籍)、e-business(电子商务)、e-shopping(电子购物)

续表

前缀	含义	例词
e-	出,外	emerge(出现)、emigrate(移居国外)
eco-	生态的	ecology(生态学)、ecocide(生态灭绝)、eco-disaster(生态灾难)
electr(o)-	与电有关的	electrocute(处电刑)、electromagnet(电磁石)
equi-	相等,相同	equal(同等〈的〉)、equivalent(等量物〈的〉)、equidistant(等距的)
ex-	除去,离开,出自	except(除……之外)、exclude(除掉)、expel(开除)、extract(抽出,提取)
extra-	超越,极	extraordinary(非凡的)、extrasensory(超感觉的)
ge(o)-	地球的	geography(地理)、geology(地质学)
homo-	相同,同	homogeneous(同类的)、homosexual(同性恋的)、homotype(同型)
neo-	新的,新近的	neologism(新语)、neo-classical(新古典主义)
photo-	光的,摄影的	photoelectric(光电的)、photocopy(复印件)
physio-	身体的,生物的,自然的	physiotherapy(理疗)、physiology(生理学)、physiolatry(自然崇拜)、physiography(自然地理学)
proto-	最早的,原始的	prototype(原型,样本)、protoplasm(原生质)
psych(o)-	精神的,心理的	psycho-analysis(心理分析)、psychiatry(精神病学)
soci(o)-	社会的	sociology(社会学)、social-economic(社会经济)
sub-	分,再	subarea(分区)、sublet(转租)、subdivide(再分)
sym-	共同,连同	symmetric(对称的)、sympathy(同情)
syn-		synonym(同义词)、synthesis(合成)、synthetic(合成的)
techn(o)-	技术的	technology(工艺学,技术)、technocracy(技术统治论)
tele-	远距离的	telecommunications(电信)、telegram(电报)、telephone(电话)
thermo-	与热有关的	thermometer(温度计)、thermos(热水瓶)、thermostat(自动调温计)
vice-	次,副	vice-consul(副领事)、vice-president(副总统)

(二)常用后缀的含义及例词

(1)表示名词含义的后缀如表16-11所示。

表16-11 表示名词含义的后缀及例词

后缀	含义	例词
-ability、-ibility	表示抽象概念(性质、状态、行为等)	inability(无能)、capability(能力)、availability(有效性)
-age		postage(邮费)、shortage(不足)、breakage(破坏)、voltage(电压)
-al		renewal(更新)、withdrawal(撤回)、removal(除去)、approval(同意)
-ance、-ence		assistance(援助,帮助)、resistance(抵抗)、difference(差别)
-ancy、-ency		brilliancy(光辉灿烂)、efficiency(效率)
-cy		bankruptcy(破产)、privacy(隐私)
-dom		wisdom(智慧)、kingdom(王国)、boredom(厌烦,无趣)

169

续表

后缀	含义	例　　词
-hood	表示抽象概念(性质、状态、行为等)	boyhood(少年)、likelihood(可能性)、neighborhood(邻里关系)
-ion、-tion -sion、-xion		action(作用)、connexion(连接)、expansion(膨胀)、possession(所有,拥有)
-ing		painting、building、understanding、reading(读数)、boxing(拳击)
-ism		socialism(社会主义)、realism(现实主义)、idealism(理想主义)
-ment		amazement(惊讶)、development(发展)、government(政府)
-ness		emptiness(空虚)、happiness(幸福)、hardness(硬度)、kindness(和善)
-ship		friendship、leadership(领导)、ownership(所有制)
-th		growth(生长)、strength(力度)、length(长度)
-ty、-ity		activity(活动性,活跃)、probability(概率)、prosperity(繁荣)
-ure		departure(启程)、mixture(混合物)、pleasure(愉快)、pressure(压力)
-y		modesty(谦逊)、currency(流通,通货)、tendency(趋势)
-er	表示人或物	computer、farmer、thinker(思想家)、worker
-or		director、sailor、tractor
-graphy	表示"……学,学科"	biography(传记文学)、calligraphy(书法)、geography(地理)
-ics		politics(政治〈学〉)、aesthetics(美学)、statistics(统计学)
-nomy		astronomy(天文学)、taxonomy(分类学)
-ology		zoology(动物学)、sociology(社会学)、ecology(生态学)
-aholic	表示人	workaholic(工作狂)、computeraholic(计算机迷)
-ain		captain(船长)、villain(恶棍)
-an		American、Russian、Asian、African
-ant		assistant、applicant(申请人)、inhabitant(居民)、contestant(竞争者)
-ar		scholar(学者)、beggar(乞丐)
-ard		bastard(私生子)、sluggard(懒汉)
-arian		librarian(图书管理员)、vegetarian(素食者)
-ee		employee(受雇者)、interviewee(被面试者)、payee(收款人)
-eer		engineer、mountaineer(登山者)、profiteer(奸商)、pioneer(先驱)
-en		citizen(公民)、netizen(网民)
-ent		resident(居民)、recipient(接受者)
-ess		actress、lioness(母狮子)、princess(公主)、waitress(女服务员)
-ian		Asian、historian(历史学家)、custodian(监护人)、musician(音乐家)
-ist		artist(艺术家)、communist(共产主义者)、scientist(科学家)
-person		layperson(外行,门外汉)、yes-person(唯唯诺诺的人)

(2) 表示形容词含义的后缀如表 16-12 所示。

表 16-12 表示形容词含义的后缀及例词

后缀	含义	例 词
-able、-ible	表示可能性	acceptable(可以接受的)、movable(可移动的)、visible(看得见的)、washable(耐洗的)
-al	表示"……的"	cultural(文化的)、musical(音乐的)、national(国家的)
-ant、-ent		dependent(从属的)、pleasant(令人愉快的)、ignorant(无知的)
-ar、-ary		circular(圆形的)、imaginary(想象中的)、secondary(次要的)
-ed		aged(老化的)、large-sized(大尺寸的)、pointed(尖锐的,尖角的)
-en	表示"……制(质)的"	golden(金〈色〉的)、wooden(木质的)、woolen(羊毛的)
-free	表示"无……；免除……"	interest-free(无息的)、maintenance-free(无须维修的)、nuclear-weapon-free(无核武器的)、toll-free(不交费的)
-ful	表示"充满"	delightful(快乐的)、hopeful(有希望的)、successful(成功的)
-ic、-ical	表示"属于"	economic(经济方面的)、magic(有魔力的)、heroic(英雄的)
-ish	表"稍微有点"	reddish(稍带红色的)、warmish(稍暖的)、blackish(稍黑的)
-ish	表"……似的"	foolish(傻的)、childish(幼稚的)、girlish(少女似的,少女的)
-ive	表示性状	creative(创造性的)、effective(积极的)、talkative(健谈的)
-less	表示否定	careless(粗心的)、colourless(无色的)、harmless(无害的)
-like	表示相似	glasslike(玻璃似的)、childlike(孩子般的)、monkeylike(猴子似的)
-ly	表示性状	costly(昂贵的)、friendly(友好的)、manly(有男子汉气概的)
-ory		refractory(难熔的)、compulsory(强制的)、contradictory(矛盾的)
-ous		various(各种的)、numerous(许多的)、glorious(光荣的)
-proof		water-proof(防水的)、bullet-proof(防弹的)
-some		tiresome(使人疲劳的)、troublesome(令人烦恼的)、wholesome(有益的)
-y		hairy(多毛发的)、handy(灵便的)、woody(木质的)

(3) 表示副词含义的后缀如表 16-13 所示。

表 16-13 表示副词含义的后缀及例词

后缀	含义	例 词
-ly	表示方式、程度	automatically(自动地)、perfectly(完美地)、suddenly(突然地)
-ward(s)	表示方向	backward(s)(向后)、eastward(向东)、outwards(向外)
-wise	表示方向、样子	clockwise(顺时针方向)、likewise(同样地)、crabwise(蟹似地)

(4) 表示动词含义的后缀如表 16-14 所示。

表 16-14 表示动词含义的后缀及例词

后缀	含义	例 句
-ate	表示"使……"	separate(分离)、indicate(指明)、operate(操作)
-en		broaden(加宽)、harden(硬化)、lengthen(加长)、ripen(使成熟)
-fy		amplify(放大)、beautify(美化)、identify(认出)、verify(证实)
-ize(-ise)		apologize/apologise(道歉)、realize(实现)、computerize(计算机化)

三、转化法

转化法(conversion)指由一种词性转化为另一种或几种词性。这种构词法主要涉及名词、形容词和动词。

（1）名词转化为动词。由名词转换而成的动词（一般为及物动词）。例如：

butter *n.* 黄油→*v.* 涂黄油　　bottle *n.* 瓶子→*v.* 装瓶　　carpet *n.* 地毯→*v.* 铺地毯
fish *n.* 鱼→*v.* 钓鱼　　　　　floor *n.* 地板→*v.* 铺地板　　group *n.* 种类→*v.* 分类

（2）名词转化为形容词。例如：

back *n.* 背（部）→*adj.* 背后的　　chemical *n.* 化学药品→*adj.* 化学的
Chinese *n.* 中国人→*adj.* 中国人的

（3）形容词转化为动词。例如：

calm *adj.* 平静→*v.* 使平静　　dry *adj.* 干→*v.* 变干
full *adj.* 满→*v.* 装满　　　　lower *adj.* 较低→*v.* 降低

（4）动词转化为名词。例如：

catch *v.* 抓住→*n.* 捕捉物　　cheat *v.* 欺骗→*n.* 骗子　　coach *v.* 辅导→*n.* 教练
cover *v.* 覆盖→*n.* 封面　　　desire *v.* 渴望→*n.* 愿望　　divide *v.* 划分→*n.* 分界

（5）动词转化为形容词。例如：

complete *v.* 使完整→*adj.* 完整的　　cool *v.* 使凉爽→*adj.* 凉的
dirty *v.* 弄脏→*adj.* 脏的　　　　　empty *v.* 倒空→*adj.* 空的

> **注：** 有一些词转化为另一类词时，发音、重音会发生变化。较常见的是一些双音节词，作动词时重音在后，作名词时重音在前。如 record、transfer、abstract、extract、progress、conduct、discount、import、export、object 等。还有一些词通过改变词尾的清浊音来改变词性，有时拼法也跟着改变。例如：
>
> abuse/ə'bjuːs/(*n.*)—abuse/ə'bjuːz/(*v.*)　　advice/əd'vaɪs/(*n.*)—advise/əd'vaɪz/(*v.*)
> belief/bɪ'liːf/(*n.*)—believe/bɪ'liːv/(*v.*)　　excuse/ɪk'skjuːs/(*n.*)—excuse/ɪk'skjuːz/(*v.*)
> grief/griːf/(*n.*)—grieve/griːv/(*v.*)　　　　house/haʊs/(*n.*)—house/haʊz/(*v.*)

四、其他构词法

（一）缩略法

缩略法主要包括首字母缩略词、截成词和混成词三种。

（1）首字母缩略词是由原词中的每个单词的第一个字母组成。例如：BBC(British Broadcasting Corporation,英国广播公司)、CEO(Chief Executive Officer,首席执行官,公司总裁)、CIA(Central Intelligence Agency,中央情报局)、WHO(World Health Organization,世界卫生组织)等。

（2）截成词是指多音节词截去一部分，用剩下的部分代替原有意义。例如：ad(advertisement,广告)、auto(automobile,汽车)、bus(omnibus,公交车)、chute(parachute,降落伞)、dozer(bulldozer,推土机)、exam(examination,考试)等。

（3）混成词是指从两个词中各取一部分，合在一起组成一个新词的构词法。例如：

breakfast and lunch→brunch 早午餐
multi-university→multiversity 综合大学
television broadcast→telecast 电视播送
smoke and fog→smog 烟雾

news broadcast→newscast 新闻广播
net citizen→netizen 网民
teleprinter exchange→telex 电传
transfer resistor→transistor 半导体

（二）逆生法

逆生法（backformation）与派生法恰好相反。派生法是先有词根再加词尾（后缀）构成新词。而逆生法则是先有名词再去掉词尾构成动词。这和一般构词的步骤相反，称为逆生法。例如：

day-dreamer（做白日梦的人）←day-dream（白日梦）
housekeeper（管家）←housekeep（管家）
television（电视）←televise（电视播送）
proof-reading（校对）←proof-read（校对）
editor（编辑）←edit（编辑）
sleep-walker（梦游者）←sleep-walk（梦游）
donation（捐赠）←donate（捐赠）
sightseeing（观光游览）←sightsee（观光游览）

第十七章

句　子

热身训练： 读下列句子各有一处错误，请指出并改正。

① The water in it is so dirty that it smells terribly.
② I appreciate your help very well.
③ Please excuse us for not able to say goodbye to you.
④ It was until midnight that it stopped raining.
⑤ There used to have a church in front of the school.
⑥ She is a brave and honesty girl.
⑦ It is convenient for me to prepare for the exam than before.
⑧ He gave me an order worthy 15 million dollars.
⑨ The ice isn't thick enough for us to skate.
⑩ Is teaching kids English as interested as you expected in college?
⑪ We had guests last night who had not stayed in it ago.
⑫ If you won't want to take a taxi, you can go by bus.
⑬ Our city is a modern city. It set up in the early 1980s.
⑭ Bad habits not come suddenly.
⑮ Following the road and you will find the store.

一、句子的成分

句子是构成篇章、表达思想的基本单位，是按照一定的语法规则，把各种词或短语组合起来表示一个完整概念的语言单位。每个句子由词或短语构成，这些词或短语便是句子成分。句子成分包括主语、谓语、宾语、表语、同位语、定语、状语和补足语等。主语和谓语是句子的主体部分。

（一）主语

主语是一个句子的主体，一般位于句首。在主动语态中，主语是谓语所表示的状态或行为动作的执行者；而在被动语态中，主语通常是谓语所表示动作的承受者。可以充当主语的有名词（短语）、代词、数词、不定式（短语）、动名词（短语）和从句等。例如：

A breeze disturbed the surface of the lake. 微风使湖面泛起涟漪。

Three-fourths of us are fond of playing the piano. 我们中四分之三的人喜欢弹钢琴。

To visit the Potala Palace this summer is very good news to the children. 今年夏天去参观布达拉宫对孩子们来说是一个好消息。

Watching English movies is a good way to learn English. 看英文电影是学英语的一种好方式。

What she said is suspicious. 她说的话令人怀疑。

（二）谓语

谓语用来描述主语的动作或状态,说明主语做什么、是什么或处于什么情况、状态。一般谓语放在主语之后。谓语的中心词是限定动词,在人称和数上必须和主语保持一致,同时还有时态、语态和语气的变化。谓语分为简单谓语和复合谓语。

1. 简单谓语

由单个行为动词或动词词组构成的谓语称为简单谓语。例如：

They flew to Tokyo yesterday. 昨天他们乘飞机去了东京。

Tom took care of the old man a year ago. 汤姆一年前照顾过那位老人。

2. 复合谓语

复合谓语的结构包括以下三种。

（1）情态动词+不定式（省略 to 的），例如：

She can play the Guqin very well. 她古琴弹得很好。

She must have come on foot. 她准是走路来的。

（2）连系动词+表语，例如：

Both of my parents are geologists. 我父母都是地质学者。

It sounds great. 听起来不错。

（3）其他动词+不定式,包括 have to do、be going to do、be about to do、be to do、happen to do、be likely to do 等。例如：

I was about to go out when the telephone rang. 我正要出门,这时电话铃响了。

Dan says he isn't going to make any concession. 丹说他不会作任何让步。

（三）宾语

宾语是谓语动作的承受者,即表示谓语动作、行为的对象,一般放在及物动词或介词的后面。

1. 宾语的形式

宾语可以由名词（短语）、代词、数词、名词化的形容词、动词不定式（短语）、动名词（短语）和从句等来充当。例如：

May I see your driving licence, please? 请让我看一下你的驾照好,吗？

I saw nobody in the workshop this morning. 我今天上午在车间谁都没看到。

Some relief fund will be given to the unemployed. 失业者将会收到救济金。

Please excuse my being absent. 请原谅我的缺席。

I don't know how to solve the problem. 我不知道怎样解决那个问题。

I take back what I said. 我收回我所说的话。

2. 宾语的种类

宾语可以分为单宾语、双宾语(直接宾语、间接宾语)、复合宾语、同源宾语等类型。

(1) 单宾语。多数动词后面接一个宾语。例如：

We love our motherland. 我们热爱祖国。

He covered a distance of 5 miles this morning. 他今天早上走了5英里。

(2) 双宾语。英语中有些动词可以接双宾语，即直接宾语和间接宾语。直接宾语指物，间接宾语指人。可接双宾语的动词主要有：answer、ask、bring、buy、deny、do、fetch、find、get、give、hand、keep、leave、lend、make、offer、owe、pass、pay、promise、read、save、sell、show、take、tell、teach、throw、wish、write 等。例如：

Mr. Brown taught us English last semester. 布朗先生上学期教我们英语。

I played them some classical music. 我给他们演奏了一些古典音乐。

> 注：间接宾语通常位于直接宾语之前，有时为了强调间接宾语，会用"直接宾语+to/for+间接宾语"结构，把间接宾语后置。例如：
>
> Will you fetch my coat for me? 你帮我把大衣拿来好吗？
>
> A wise man gave some good suggestions to the villagers. 一位智者给了村民们一些好的建议。

(3) 同源宾语。少数动词后面能跟一个特定的名词作宾语，这个名词和前面的动词在词根上是相同的或者在意义上是相近的，这样的宾语就称为同源宾语。同源宾语前面可带形容词作定语。常见的能带同源宾语的动词有：lead、live、die、sleep、dream、breathe、smile、laugh、fight、run、sing 等。例如：sleep a sound sleep、dream a terrible dream、die a sudden death、begin a good beginning 等。

(4) 复合宾语。在英语中，有些及物动词接了一个宾语后，句子意思仍不完整，还需要再加上一个词或短语来补充说明其身份、特征、状态或所做的动作，这种"宾语+宾语补足语"结构称为复合宾语。例如：

They appointed the young man leader of the group. 他们任命那年轻人为小组长。

The crosstalk made all of us chortle. 相声逗得我们哈哈大笑。

He thought himself fooled in the bargain. 他认为自己在交易中被愚弄了。

(四) 表语

表语位于系动词之后，用于说明主语的身份、特征、状态等。表语与其前面的系动词一起构成复合谓语。表语可以由名词、代词、形容词、副词、数词、介词短语、动名词、分词、不定式或句子等充当。除系动词 be 之外，常见的能构成系表结构的动词还有：appear、come、become、fall、feel、get、go、grow、keep、look、prove、remain、make、smell、seem、stay、taste、turn 等。连系动词没有被动语态(若用作行为动词则除外)。例如：

When he heard his name mentioned, he was all ears. 他听见有人提到他的名字，就仔细听了。

Fifty? You really don't look it. 五十岁？真是看不出来。

What the old man said sounds reasonable. 老人的话听起来有道理。

I must be off in 5 minutues. 我5分钟之后得走了。

The boy is only five, but he takes care of his disabled father. 那男孩只有 5 岁,但他照顾着身患残疾的爸爸。

Mr. Brown got drunk on only two drinks. 布朗先生只喝了两杯就醉了。

To have knowledge is to know the true from the false, and high things from the low. 求知就是辨别真伪与高下。

The problem is how to find the lost child. 问题是怎样找到走丢的孩子。

That is where the hero worked. 这就是英雄曾经工作过的地方。

(五) 定语

定语在句子中用来修饰名词或代词,常和名词一起构成名词短语。

1. 前置定语

可以充当前置定语的单词有形容词、代词、数词、名词、名词所有格、动名词、现在分词和过去分词等。例如:

The girl has a natural ability for arranging flowers. 那姑娘有插花的天赋。

There is no quality inspection department in this small workshop. 这家小作坊没有质检部门。

If I can get a second chance, I will definitely succeed. 如果再给我一次机会,我一定会成功。

You should keep up with the changing situation. 你应该跟上形势的变化。

I'll treasure the faded photo, for it is the only one I had with my mom. 我会珍藏那褪色的照片,因为这是我和妈妈唯一的一张合影。

> 注:同根的名词与形容词作定语时,意义有所不同。例如:
>
> horror films 恐怖电影片　　　　　　　horrible films 令人感到恐怖的电影片
> a wonder book 一部充满奇事的书　　　a wonderful book 一部奇妙的书
> a stone path 一条石板路　　　　　　　a stony path 一条铺满碎石的路
> gold reserve 黄金储备　　　　　　　　golden sunshine 金色的阳光
> silver coins 银币　　　　　　　　　　silvery hair 银白的头发
> heart trouble 心脏病　　　　　　　　 a hearty welcome 热情的欢迎
> education experts 教育专家(从事教育工作的专家)
> educational films 教育影片(具有教育意义的影片)

2. 后置定语

形容词、副词、介词短语、不定式(短语)、现在分词、过去分词短语、从句等可以充当后置定语。例如:

I think he is the man suitable for preaching the policy. 我认为他是宣讲政策的合适人选。

It's easy to get the news abroad nowadays. 现在很容易得到国外的新闻。

I have a wish to travel around the world. 我有一个愿望——去周游世界。

This is the funniest news found on the Internet. 这是网上最搞笑的新闻。

Those who help others are surely helped. 帮助他人的人也一定会得到帮助。

Anyone touching that wire will get an eclectic shock. 碰到那条电线的人会被电击。

(六) 同位语

同位语是对句子中某一成分作进一步解释、说明,与其前面的名词在语法上处于同等地位的句子成分。名词、代词、数词和从句等可以充当同位语。同位语一般置于它所说明的名词或代词之后,既可以不用标点符号隔开,也可以用逗号、冒号或破折号隔开。同位语也可以由引导词引出,常用引导词有:of、or、such as、namely、that is、that is to say、in other words、for short、for example、especially、chiefly、mostly、in particular、particularly、possibly 等。例如:

Mr. Smith, our math teacher, is very strict with us. 我们的数学老师史密斯先生对我们的要求很严格。

The teachers each have a strong sense of responsibility for teaching the students. 在教育学生方面,每一位老师都有强烈的责任心。

I agree with his point that the anti-poverty project will benefit the poor in this district. 我同意他的观点,扶贫项目将使该地区的贫困人口受益。

(七) 状语

状语是句子的一个重要修饰成分,是谓语部分的一个附加成分。状语用于修饰动词、形容词、副词或整个句子,用来表示时间、地点、原因、方式、程度、目的、结果、条件、让步、频度等情况。通常用作状语的词有副词(短语)、介词短语、不定式、分词(短语)、名词(短语)、从句等。例如:

I haven't seen him recently! 我最近没见过他!

Lights were blazing and men were running here and there. 灯火通明,人们在东奔西跑。

Did his words entirely match his actions? 他言行完全一致吗?

There would be no new China without the Chinese Communist Party. 没有中国共产党就没有新中国。

They continued to walk in spite of the heavy rain. 尽管下着大雨,他们仍然继续向前走。

To get a good view of the countryside, I sat in the front of the bus. 我坐在汽车的前部,以便饱览农村风光。

Mary arrived late only to find the bus gone. 玛丽来晚了,结果发现汽车已经开走了。

Having studied for a whole day, the students were so tired. 学习了一天,学生们都很累。

Frightened, the little boy sat in the corner soundlessly. 因为受到了惊吓,小男孩安静地坐在角落里。

Faced with the situation, what are we supposed to do? 面对这种情形,我们该怎么办?

Come this way! 走这边!

Although they tried hard, they were still eliminated. 尽管他们尽了最大的努力,还是被淘汰了。

(八) 补足语

1. 宾语补足语

有些及物动词加宾语后,要求有一个宾语补足语来补充说明宾语的情况,句子意义才能完整。宾语和宾语补足语在逻辑上有着主谓关系,它们一起构成复合宾语。常用的这类及物动词有:appoint、ask、call、cause、consider、declare、elect、expect、encourage、find、get、have、keep、let、make、notice、see、permit、prove、want、watch 等。例如:

You can't expect me to approve of it. 你别指望我赞成。

I find learning physics well difficult. 我觉得学好物理很难。

可以作宾语补足语的有名词、形容词、副词、介词短语、动词不定式、现在分词(短语)、过去分词(短语)等。例如：

A good friend is someone who makes you happy and relaxed. 好朋友是能让你开心、放松的人。

I saw the kite up and down in the sky. 我看见风筝在天空忽高忽低地飞着。

Keep what I said in your mind. 记住我说的话。

The robber forced us to leave our house. 强盗强迫我们离开屋子。

He could sense danger approaching. 他能感觉到危险正在迫近。

The report about school dropouts set me thinking. 那篇有关辍学儿童的报道使我陷入沉思。

I heard Li Bai's poems reeled off by many children. 我听到许多孩子把李白的诗倒背如流。

I raised my voice to make myself heard. 为使大家都能听见，我提高了音量。

We expect the problem of property management solved in our community. 我们期待小区的物业管理问题得到解决。

2. 主语补足语

含有宾语补足语的句子在变为被动句时，宾语补足语便成了主语补足语。例如：

He was found the right man for the job. 大家发现他是这份工作的合适人选。

He was seen to swim in the river alone. 有人看见他一个人在河里游泳。

The books in the study must be kept in order. 书房里的书必须摆放有序。

The dog was found abandoned by the side of the road. 人们发现狗狗被遗弃在路边。

（九）独立成分

如果在句子中一个词或一个词组和其他的词或词组没有语法上的联系，则称为独立成分。独立成分有三种：感叹语、称呼语和插入语。例如：

Aha! That is it. 啊哈！就是它。

Why! The guy has ruined the whole plan. 哎呀，那家伙坏了全盘计划！

Look out, Peter! The evildoer has got a dagger. 彼得小心！歹徒有匕首。

I can't be there so early, I'm afraid. 恐怕我那么早到不了。

The boy in black, I presume, was not listening. 我想那穿黑衣服的男孩当时没听。

Who do you think is best qualified for the position? 你认为谁最能胜任这个职位？

二、句子的种类

（一）按照结构分类

英语的句子按照结构可分为以下三种。

1. 简单句

简单句是指只有一个完整主谓结构的句子。例如：

An old man came in. 一老头进来了。

An old man came in and sat down on the sofa. 一老头进来了，并坐在了沙发上。

An old man and an old woman came in. 一老头和一老太太进来了。

An old man and an old woman came in and sat on the sofa. 一老头和一老太太进来了,并坐在了沙发上。

2. 并列句

并列句是指具有两个或两个以上完整的主谓结构的句子,且句子之间通常由并列连词或分号连接,用来表达平行、关联、选择、转折、否定、递进等关系。(注意:英语中,通常不用逗号连接两个主谓结构)常见的并列句有以下几种。

(1) 用来连接两个并列概念的连接词有 and、not only... but also...、neither... nor...、as well as 等。and 所连接的前后分句往往表示平行关系、顺接关系、对照关系、先后关系、递进关系,而且前后分句的时态往往保持一致关系,若第一个分句是祈使句,那么第二个分句用将来时。例如:

She likes playing golf and she plays well. 她喜欢打高尔夫而且打得不错。

Hurry up and you will catch the 6 o'clock flight. 快点,你就能赶上六点钟的航班。

as well as 是英语中常用的连接词(并列连词),侧重于前项。例如:

The child is healthy as well as lively. (＝The child is not only healthy but also lively.) 这孩子既健康又活泼。

(2) 表示在两者之间选择一个,常用的连接词有 or、otherwise、either... or... 等。前后分句的时态往往保持一致关系,若第一个分句是祈使句,那么第二个分句用将来时。例如:

You can go to the movies with us or you just stay at home. 你可以跟我们一块儿去看电影或者就待在家里。

Hurry, or you won't make the train. 赶快,不然你赶不上火车。

Shut the window, otherwise it'll get too cold in here. 把窗户关好,否则屋子里就太冷了。

(3) 表明两个概念彼此有矛盾、相反或者转折。常用的连接词有 but、yet、still、however、while 等。前后分句时态要一致。例如:

It isn't that Dave lied exactly, but he did tend to exaggerate. 大卫不见得是真的说谎,但他的确是有意夸大。

It is strange, yet it is true. 那真是怪事,然而却是事实。

He wants to be a singer, while I want to be a teacher. 他想当歌手,而我则想当医生。

She thought I was seeing her, while I was seeing the advertise ment besideher in fact. 她以为我在看她,而实际上我在看她旁边的广告。

whereas others are slandering her. 有些人在保卫祖国,而另一些人却在诋毁她。

His first response was to feel shocked. Later, however, he embraced the hard truth. 他最初的反应是震惊,可是后来他接受了严酷的事实。

Modesty helps one to go forward while/whereas conceit makes one lag behind. 虚心使人进步,而骄傲使人落后。

Wise men seek after truth while/whereas fools despise knowledge. 智者求真理,而愚人贬知识。

(4) 说明原因或理由,用连接词 for,前后分句时态一致。例如:

He has many good friends, for he is an honest and warm-hearted man. 他有许多好朋友,因为他是个诚实而且热心的男子汉。

(5) 表示结果,用连接词 so,前后分句时态一致。例如:

He got up late, so he missed the early bus. 他起床晚了,结果没赶上早班车。

3. 复合句

复合句是指含有一个主句以及一个或几个从句的句子。从句通常由连接词引导。例如：

When I came in, uncle Wang was repairing the old radio. 我进来时，王叔叔正在修那台旧收音机。

I like singers who write their own songs. 我喜欢自己写歌的歌手。

It's true that one can master everything is difficult. 一个人很难能够样样精通，这是真的。

The concerns of the people are what I always care about, and the aspirations of the people are what I always strive for. 民之所忧，我必念之；民之所盼，我必行之。

（二）按照目的分类

英语句子按照使用目的和交际功能分为陈述句、疑问句、祈使句和感叹句。

1. 陈述句

叙述一个事实或观点的句子称为陈述句。陈述句有肯定和否定两种形式，一般用降调，句末用句号。陈述句的语序一般是"主语+谓语部分"。

1）陈述句的肯定形式

陈述句的肯定形式分为两种：一种为正常语序，另一种为倒装语序。例如：

The boy whose father is a doctor does well in biology. 他爸爸是医生的那个男孩生物学得不错。

In front of the outpatient department building stands the statue of Hua Tuo. 门诊部大楼前面树立着华佗的雕像。

2）陈述句的否定形式

（1）如果句子的谓语动词含 be 动词、助动词或情态动词等，其否定形式是在这些动词后加 not。例如：

He is not from a small village in the mountains. 他不是来自大山里的一个小村庄。

You must not leave such a young child alone. 你不能把这么小的孩子单独留下。

I have not seen him since he left this city. 自从他离开这座城市我就没见过他。

（2）如果句子的谓语动词是实义动词，则把句子变成否定形式要在谓语动词之前加 don't、doesn't 及 didn't。例如：

My children don't have any extra curricular classes on weekends. 我孩子周末不上任何课外辅导班。

She doesn't like talking to strangers. 她不喜欢跟陌生人讲话。

My parents didn't ask me about my marks. 我父母没有问我的分数。

> 注：have 在表示"有"的意思时，否定形式有两种：一种是直接在 have 后面加 not，另一种是用助动词 do 构成。例如：
> I haven't any brothers or sisters (=I don't have any brothers or sisters.)
> 我没有兄弟姐妹。

（3）其他否定词，如 no、never、seldom、hardly、nobody 等，也可以构成否定。例如：

I have never been to his new house. 我从未去过他的新房子。

I can hardly believe what the young man said. 我几乎不相信那年轻人的话。

My brother seldom speaks in public. 我兄弟很少在公共场合讲话。

2. 疑问句

疑问句是用来提出疑问的句子，可分为五类：一般疑问句、特殊疑问句、选择疑问句、反义疑问句和修辞性疑问句。

1）一般疑问句

一般疑问句用来询问一件事情或一种情况是否属实，一般用 yes 或 no 来回答，但在口语中也用 yes 和 no 之外的词回答。口语中若无特殊含义，读时句末用升调。例如：

（1）用 yes、no 回答的一般疑问句。例如：

——Is Xiao Ming the son of the man with glasses? 小明是那个戴眼镜的人的儿子吗？

——Yes, he is. 是的，他是。

——Do you think Lily can solve the problem all by herself? 你觉得丽丽能全靠她自己解决这个问题吗？

——No, I don't think so. 不，我认为她不能。

（2）口语中还可以用 yes、no 之外的词回答的一般疑问句。例如有些表示肯定或否定的词也可以回答一般疑问句，如 all right、certain、sure、I think so、sure、of course、sorry、not at all、not、yet、certainly not、I'm afraid not 等。用这些词回答一般表示语气较委婉或答案较肯定。例如：

——Am I hired? 我被录用了吗？

——Sure./Sorry, I'm afraid you don't have enough work experience. 当然。/对不起，恐怕你的工作经验不够。

（3）省略式一般疑问句。在非正式文体中，尤其是在口语中，常用一般疑问句的省略形式。例如：

Got it? 懂了吗？

Need help? 需要帮助吗？

Want some drink? 喝点什么吗？

另外，在英语中，在拒绝邀请时，一般先表示感谢，再讲明原因，而不是直接说 no。例如：

——Could you come to my birthday party at 8 p.m. next Saturday? 下周六晚上 8 点来参加我的生日宴会好吗？

——That's very nice of you, but I'm afraid I have to prepare for the coming exam./I wish I could, but I have to meet a friend of mine at the station that day. 你真是太好了，不过我要准备即将到来的考试。/我想去的，不过那天我要去车站接一个朋友。

在回答带有否定词的一般疑问句时，答语中必须保持"yes+简略肯定句""no+简略否定句"的一致，同时还要注意 yes 译成"不"，no 译成"是"。例如：

——Haven't they been there before? 他们以前没去过那里吗？

——Yes, they have./No, they haven't. 不，他们去过。/是的，他们没去过。

2）特殊疑问句

特殊疑问句是由疑问代词 what、who、whom、whose、which 或疑问副词 when、where、why、how 引导的疑问句。这种疑问句是针对句中某一部分提问，不可用 yes 或 no 作简略回答，且句尾用降调。

（1）普通特殊疑问句。普通特殊疑问句由一般特殊疑问词引导。这种疑问句一般用来询问具体信息。例如：

When will the professor deliver the speech? 教授什么时候演讲？

Who laid these packs of books here? 这几包书是谁放这儿的？

Why didn't you tell me the truth yesterday? 昨天你为什么不告诉我真相？

（2）强调特殊疑问句。通过一定的手段对普通疑问句进行强调，表达愤怒、惊奇等感情色彩的特殊疑问句称为强调特殊疑问句。一般通过三种方式表达。

① 在特殊疑问词后加 ever。可把 ever 直接放在特殊疑问词的词尾，构成一个单词，也可以与特殊疑问词分开写，构成两个单词。例如：

Whatever/What ever does Lucy want to say? 露西到底想说什么？

However/How ever should we solve the air pollution problem? 我们究竟如何解决空气污染问题？

② 在特殊疑问词后加表示惊讶、诅咒的词，常见的这类词有 on earth、in the world、the hell、the devil 等。例如：

What the hell are you talking about? 你们究竟在讨论什么？

How on earth can I get on well with such a man? 我究竟如何才能跟这样一个人相处好呢？

③ 添加副词，即在特殊疑问词后增加 exactly、just、merely 等副词，以表达强烈语气。例如：

When exactly will you come here again? 你究竟什么时候再来这里？

Who merely hasn't got the key to the dormitory? 谁还没有拿到寝室的钥匙？

（3）省略式特殊疑问句。在日常会话中，特殊疑问句常以省略形式出现。例如：

What about an apple? 吃个苹果怎么样？

Who else? 还有谁？

What time? 什么时间？

3）选择疑问句

提供两种（或两种以上）的情况，要求对方从中选择一种的疑问句称为选择疑问句。供选择的两部分用 or 连接。朗读时，or 前的部分用升调，or 后的部分用降调。

选择疑问句有以一般疑问句为基础和以特殊疑问句为基础两种形式。or 连接的两个并列成分可以是宾语、表语、状语、谓语或者是两个句子。例如：

Do you go to school on foot or by bike? 你是走路上学还是骑自行车上学？

Shall I do it or will you do it by yourself? 是我做还是你自己做？

Where are you going, to the classroom or to the library? 你到哪儿去，教室还是图书馆？

Which city do you like better, Beijing or Shenzhen? 你更喜欢哪个城市，北京还是深圳？

How shall we go to Beijing, by air or by high-speed train? 我们怎么去北京，坐飞机还是乘高铁？

选择疑问句一般不用 yes 或 no 来回答，通常是在所提供的备选范围内选择进行回答。有时也要视具体情况灵活处理。通常情况下，用一个完整的陈述句或其简略形式回答选择疑问句，主语和谓语均省略；也可使用一个关键词，如不定代词作简略回答。常用的不定代词有 all（三者或三者以上都）、both（两者都）、either（两者中任意一个）、neither（两者都不）、none（三者或三者以上都不）。在使用时，要根据上下文语境选择合适的不定代词。例如：

—Are you from Jiangxi or Hunan? 你来自江西还是湖南？

—Jiangxi. 江西。

—Shall we watch TV or go to the movies? 我们是看电视还是看电影？

—I prefer to go to the movies. 我想去看电影。

—Which instrument can you play, piano or clarinet? 你能演奏什么乐器,钢琴还是竖笛?

—Both. But I am better at playing the clarinet. 都会。但我竖笛吹得好些。

注：一般疑问句后面加 or not,表示选择,其中也包含不耐烦等感情色彩,回答时可用 yes 或 no. 例如：

—Are you serious or not? 你到底是不是认真的?

—Yes, I am. 是的,我是认真的。

—Are you going shopping or not? 你还去不去买东西了?

—No, I am not. 不,不去了。

4) 反义疑问句

反义疑问句是附加在陈述句后的简短问句(又称附加疑问句),它用来征询对前面陈述内容的意见是肯定还是否定,或者希望证实陈述内容。陈述部分用肯定形式,附加问句用否定形式,反之亦然。朗读时,陈述句部分用降调,附加问句用升调。附加问句的主语及动词形式须与陈述部分一致,且主语为人称代词。例如：

He is the boy you are looking for, isn't he? 他就是你们在找的孩子,对吗?

They haven't been there before, have they? 他们以前没去过那里,对吗?

5) 修辞性疑问句

修辞性疑问句,指形式上是问句、而意义上是陈述句的句子。例如：

Isn't she beautiful? (=She is beautiful.) 她可漂亮了。

What can mean more than life? (=Nothing can mean more than life.) 没有什么比生命更重要。

How can you say such things? 你怎么能说这种话?(即你不能说这种话。)

3. 祈使句

祈使句是表示请求、命令、劝告或建议的句子。朗读时,一般用降调,但为使其听起来比较委婉,可使用升调。祈使句句末用句号或感叹号。祈使句动词无人称和时态的变化。

1) 祈使句的基本结构

(1) 肯定形式：动词原形(be 动词或实义动词)+其他部分。例如：

Be sure to arrive on time. 请务必准时到。

Wear masks in public places, please. 在公共场所请佩戴口罩。

Keep off the grass. 请勿践踏草坪。

(2) 否定形式：Don't+动词原形(be 动词或实义动词)+其他部分。例如：

Don't ever do that again. 不要再做那种事了。

Don't stay up too late. 不要熬夜到太晚。

注：否定形式也可加 never 构成。例如：

Never be half-hearted. 不要三心二意。

2) 祈使句的强调

(1) 为指明向谁提出请求或命令、加强语气或表示感情色彩,而在句首加上主语。例如：

Women and children go to the front, please. 妇女和儿童请到前面去。

You be quiet for a moment. 你安静一会儿。

（2）句首加助动词 do。例如：

Do be honest. 一定要诚实。

Do tell me the reason. 务必告诉我理由。

3）其他形式的祈使句

（1）以 let 开头的祈使句，例如：

Let's have a discussion. 我们讨论一会儿。

Let Tom try a second time. 让汤姆再试一次。

Don't let others disturb the professor. 不要让其他人去打扰教授。

（2）以 no 开始的禁止性祈使句，例如：

No swimming. 禁止游泳。

No photos. 禁止拍照。

No parking. 禁止吸烟。

（3）其他常用表达方式，例如：

Pardon！再说一遍！

Out with it. 有话快说。

Slower！慢点！

This way, please. 请往这边走。

4）祈使句婉转的表达方式

为了使祈使句听起来比较客气婉转，除了用低声调外，还可用下列方法。

（1）加 please。例如：

Show me your passports, please. 请出示护照。

（2）加 will you。例如：

Come and give me a hand, will you? 过来帮帮我，好吗？

（3）please 和 will you 同时运用。例如：

Don't make your mother sad, please, will you? 请不要让你母亲伤心，好吗？

（4）用 would you 则更加客气。例如：

Shut the door, would you? 关上门，行吗？

Don't be late, would you? 别迟到，好吗？

4. 感叹句

感叹句是表示喜、怒、哀、乐、惊叹、赞赏等情感的句子。英语中，一般用 what 或 how 引导感叹句。what 作定语，修饰名词（名词前可以有形容词或冠词）；how 作状语，修饰形容词、副词、或句子。朗读时，感叹句要用降调，句末用感叹号。

（1）由 what 引导的感叹句，结构有以下三种。

① What a/an+（形容词）+单数可数名词+（主语+谓语部分）！例如：

What a great pity you failed the exam! 你没通过考试，真是太遗憾了！

② What+（形容词）+可数名词复数+（主语+谓语部分）！例如：

What ingenious cooks they are! 这些厨师真是心灵手巧！

③ What+（形容词）+不可数名词+（主语+谓语部分）！例如：

What nice music it is! 真美妙的音乐！

（2）由 how 引导的感叹句,结构包括以下两种。

① How+形容词(副词)+主语+谓语！例如：

How surprising it is that you should hide the truth！你竟然在隐瞒真相,真是太令人吃惊了！

How quickly the boy is running！男孩跑得真快！

② How+主语+谓语！例如：

How time flies！时光飞逝！

How I wish to travel around the world！我多么想环游世界啊！

注："what+a/an+形容词+可数名词单数+主语+谓语"这一结构可与"how+形容词+the+可数名词单数+谓语"这一结构相互转换,转换后意义不变。例如：

What a moving story it is！(=How moving the story is！) 多么动人的故事！

What a beautiful dress it is！(=How beautiful the dress is！) 多么漂亮的礼服！

（3）其他形式的感叹句有以下三种。

① 陈述句、疑问句、祈使句表示强烈的感情时,句末使用感叹号,也是一种感叹句。例如：

He is so hard-working！他真勤奋！

Am I surprised to meet you right here！在这里碰到你真是个惊喜！

Stop chatting！不要聊天了！

② 句首有感叹词的句子也是感叹句。例如：

Ah，what splendid clothes！啊,多华丽的衣服啊！

Oh，wise young man！噢,聪明的年轻人！

③ 感叹词或短语。例如：

Hurrah！好哇！　　　　Wonderful！太精彩了！　　　Dear me！哎呀！

My goodness！天哪！　　Good idea！好主意！　　　Thank goodness！谢天谢地！

None of your nonsense！不要胡说了！

三、简单句的基本句型

简单句有五种最基本的句型：主谓结构(S+V)、主谓宾结构(S+V+O)、主系表结构(S+V+P)、主谓双宾结构(S+V+Oi+Od)、主谓宾宾补结构(S+V+O+OC)。

（1）主谓结构(S+V)。这种结构中动词为不及物动词。例如：

The wind is blowing. 风在刮着

The war broke out in 1937. 战争爆发于 1937 年。

注：有些及物动词也可作不及物动词使用。常见的此类动词有 cut、wash、sell、lock、wear、write、read 等。例如：

This kind of cloth washes easily. 这种布料很容易清洗。

This knife cuts well. 这把刀好用。

Your pen writes more smoothly than mine. 你的笔比我的写起来要顺畅些。

（2）主谓宾结构(S+V+O)。这种结构中谓语动词为及物动词,须接宾语。例如：

He never forgives others for their mistakes. 他从不原谅别人的错误。

They enjoy swimming in the river in summer. 他们夏天喜欢在河里游泳。

（3）主系表结构(S+V+P)。这种句型结构主要指谓语动词为连系动词的情况。连系动词本身有一定的词义，但不能独立作谓语，必须与表语一起构成谓语，说明主语是什么或怎么样。例如：

It's getting colder and colder. 天气越来越冷了。

Prices of vegetables are usually up and down according to the weather. 蔬菜价格通常随气候变化而上下波动。

She appears much younger than she really is. 她看上去比实际上年轻。

The apple tastes good and sells well. 这苹果尝起来很甜，很好卖。

Food will easily go bad in such hot weather if it's not kept in the fridge. 在这么热的天，食物不放在冰箱的话很容易坏。

（4）主谓双宾结构(S+V+Oi+Od)。在这种结构中，谓语动词是带有双宾语的及物动词。直接宾语是指物的名词或代词，表示动作给予的对象；间接宾语是表示人的名词或代词，表示动作的接受对象。例如：

She offered me her new book./She offered her new book to me. 她把她的新书让给了我。

He sends her a letter every day./He sends a letter to her every day. 他一天给她写一封信。

（5）主谓宾宾补结构(S+V+O+OC)。在这种结构中，谓语动词是及物动词，其后须接宾语和宾语补足语（又称复合宾语）。例如：

We elected him chairman of the Student Union. 我们选举他为学生会主席。

The students consider this interview very important. 学生们认为这次面试很重要。

Father kept the boy in and doing homework when he is out. 爸爸外出的时候就把男孩关在家里做作业。

You will find him always at work. 你会发现他总是在工作。

They encouraged us not to lose the opportunity to say what we thought of the events. 有人鼓励我们抓住机会说出我们对事件的看法。

We can hear birds singing in the tree. 我们能听见鸟儿在树上唱歌。

You should make your opinion known. 你应该让别人知道你的想法。

巩固练习

Complete the following sentences by choosing the items marked A, B, C, or D.

1. The shocking news made him realize _____ terrible problems they would face.
   A. what   B. why   C. that   D. how

2. The factory used 70 percent of the raw materials, the rest of which _____ saved for other purposes.
   A. is   B. were   C. was   D. are

3. Lucy's beautiful hair reached below her knees and made _____ almost an overcoat for her.
   A. itself   B. her   C. them   D. herself

4. One-third of the country _____ covered with trees and the majority of the citizens _____ black people.
   A. is; are   B. are; is   C. is; is   D. are; are

5. Experiments of this kind _____ in both the U.S. and Europe well before the World War Ⅱ.
   A. have conducted   B. had been conducted
   C. had conducted   D. have been conducted

6. The ability _____ an idea is as important as the idea itself.
   A. to be expressed   B. expressed   C. to express   D. expressing

7. —That must have been a long trip.
   —Yeah, it _____ us a whole week to get there.
   A. takes   B. was taking   C. took   D. has taken

8. As the story _____, the truth about the strange person is slowly discovered.
   A. begins   B. develops   C. ends   D. happens

9. Tsinghua University, _____ in 1911, is home to a great number of outstanding figures.
   A. found   B. to be founded   C. founded   D. founding

10. It's important for the figures _____ regularly.
    A. to be updated   B. to update
    C. to have updated   D. to have been updated

11. The players _____ from the whole country are expected to bring us honor in this summer game.
    A. having selected   B. to select   C. selected   D. selecting

12. Sometimes proper answers are not far to seek _____ food safety problem.
    A. in   B. on   C. to   D. after

13. Do you wake up every morning _____ energetic and ready to start a new day?
    A. feel   B. feeling   C. to feel   D. felt

14. In the near future, more advances in the robot technology _____ by science.
    A. will be made   B. are made   C. will make   D. are making

15. It is the most instructive lecture that I _____ since I came to this school.
    A. attended   B. have attended   C. am attending   D. had attended

16. We feel _____ our duty to make our country a better place.
    A. that   B. this   C. it   D. one

17. In the last few years thousands of films _____ all over the world.
    A. have been produced   B. have produced
    C. are producing   D. are being produced

18. _____ regular exercise is very important. It's never a good idea to exercise too close to bedtime.
    A. As   B. It   C. Unless   D. Although

19. Passengers are permitted _____ only one piece of hand luggage onto the plane.
    A. being carried   B. carrying   C. to be carried   D. to carry

20. _____ into English, the sentence was found to have an entirely different word order.
    A. Translating   B. Having translated
    C. To translate   D. Translated

21. Try _____ she might, Sue couldn't get the window open.
    A. as   B. when   C. since   D. if

22. Planning so far ahead _____ no sense—so many things will have changed by next year.
    A. made   B. has made   C. makes   D. is making

23. Michael put up a picture of Yao Ming beside the bed to keep himself _____ of his own dreams.
    A. remind   B. to remind   C. reminded   D. reminding

24. Look at the pride on Tom's face. He _____ to have been praised by the manager just now.
    A. seemed   B. seems   C. had seemed   D. is seeming

25. She was surprised to find the fridge empty; the children _____ everything!
    A. had been eating   B. have eaten   C. had eaten   D. have been eating

26. The town has narrow streets and small houses _____ are built close to each other.
    A. they   B. where   C. that   D. what

27. Claire had luggage _____ an hour before her plane left.
    A. check   B. checked   C. to check   D. checking

28. _____ all of them are strong candidates, only one will be chosen for the post.
    A. Since   B. As   C. If   D. While

29. More highways have been built in China, _____ it much easier for people to travel from one place to another.
    A. having made   B. made   C. to make   D. making

30. —What a mistake!
    —Yes. I _____ his doing it another way, but without success.
    A. would suggest B. will suggest   C. was suggesting D. had suggested

31. _____ an important role in a new movie, Andy has got a chance to become famous.
    A. Offer   B. To offer   C. Offered   D. Offering

32. Simon made a big bamboo box _____ the little sick bird till it could fly.
    A. keeping   B. kept   C. keep   D. to keep

33. Modern science has given clear evidence _____ smoking can lead to many diseases.
    A. where   B. what   C. that   D. which

34. "Things _____ never come again!" I couldn't help talking to myself.
    A. lost   B. have lost   C. to lose   D. losing

35. Having checked the doors were closed and _____ all the lights were off, the boy left quickly.
    A. why   B. that   C. where   D. when

36. Men of science are trying to find ways _____ disease.
    A. prevent   B. of preventing   C. to prevent   D. B and C

37. Realizing that he hadn't enough money and _____ to borrow from his father, he decided to sell his watch.
    A. wanting not   B. not wanting
    C. not to want   D. not wanted

38. It is foolish of Bob _____ that post.

    A. to not agree to take   B. not to agree taking

    C. to not agree taking   D. not to agree to take

39. If you want _____, you have to get the fund somewhere.

    A. that the job is done   B. to have done the job

    C. the job done   D. the job that is done

40. When one is speaking to foreigners, it is sometimes difficult _____.

    A. understanding oneself   B. for one to understand oneself

    C. to understand oneself   D. to make oneself understood

第十八章

名词性从句

热身训练： 下列句子各有一处错误，请指出并改正。

1. My aunt is the owner of a hotel close to that I live.
2. My friend and I are talking about how to do during the winter holiday.
3. "Every time you eat a sweet, drink green tea." This is that my mother used to tell me.
4. He wonders that he can pass the driving test.
5. This is how I need to improve in the future.
6. That I want to tell you is the deep love and respect I have for my parents.
7. It suddenly occurred to him what he had left his keys in the office.
8. It is by no means clear that the president can do to end the strike.
9. I think important that we learn English well.
10. The news which our team had won pleased everyone.
11. Before a problem can be solved, it must be obvious that the problem itself is.
12. It is still under discussion if the old bus station should be replaced with a modern hotel or not.
13. Anyone breaks the law should be punished.
14. There is a virtue that we lend a helping hand to others.
15. Here is my idea about how a friend is like.

在句子中，具有名词作用的从句称为名词性从句。名词性从句的功能相当于名词词组，在复合句中能担任主语、表语、宾语、同位语、介词宾语等。因此根据它在句中的句法功能，名词性从句又可以分为主语从句、宾语从句、表语从句、同位语从句和宾语补足语从句。例如：

Where the English evening will be held has not yet been announced. 英语晚会将在哪里举行，还没有宣布。

We must never think (that) we are good in everything while others are good in nothing. 我们决不能认为自己什么都好，别人什么都不好。

China is not what it used to be. 中国已不是过去的中国了。

The thought came to him that Mary had probably fallen ill. 他想到玛丽可能生病了。

We made them what they are. 我们使他们有了今天。

一、引导名词性从句的关联词

引导名词性从句的关联词有从属连词、连接代词和连接副词,如表 18-1 所示。

表 18-1　名词性从句的关联词及用法

关联词	简单句	连接词的词义和成分	能 否 省 略
从属连词 that	陈述句	that 无词义,在从句中不作任何成分	引导宾语从句的 that 一般可以省略
从属连词 whether 和 if	一般疑问句	whether 和 if(if 只用在宾语从句中)在从句中不作任何成分,但有词义	不能省略,因为有词义
连接代词 who、whom、what、which、whose	特殊疑问句	who、whom、what、which 在从句中作主语、宾语或表语;what、which 还可以作定语;whose 只能作定语	不能省略,因为它们都保留各自的疑问含义,既起连接作用,又在从句中充当一定的成分
连接副词 when、where、how、why		when、where、how、why 在从句中分别作时间、地点、方式和原因状语	

除以上连词外,还有 wh+ever 类:whoever、whomever、whatever 和 whichever 等

(一) that 与 wh-连接代词和连接副词引导名词性从句的区别

连词 that 没有词义,在从句中不作成分,有时可以省略;而 wh-连词在从句中作成分,且带有疑问意义。例如:

He made the suggestion that they go for a drive. 他建议他们去开车兜风。

What makes the book so special is the creative imagination of the writer. 这本书如此特别的原因是作者的创意。

(二) that 与 whether 引导名词性从句的区别

that 与 whether 都是连词,引导名词性从句时,在从句中只起连接作用,都不担任句子成分,使用时有下列区别。

(1) 动词 doubt 表示"怀疑、不知道"时,肯定句接 whether 引导的宾语从句;否定句 don't doubt 和疑问句 do you doubt 要接 that 引导的从句。例如:

I doubt whether it is true. 我怀疑那是不是真的。

I don't doubt that Mike will come back soon. 我不怀疑迈克不久会回来。(不能用 whether)

Do you doubt that he will win the competition? 你怀疑他会赢得比赛吗?(不能用 whether)

注:doubt 表示强烈的不相信时,在陈述句中可接 that 从句。例如:
I doubt that he will come to the cafe to see me on time. 我不信他会按时到咖啡馆见我。

(2) that 本身无意义,有时可以省略;whether 本身有意义,在句中不可省略。例如:

He said (that) we were too young to understand the matter. 他说我们太年轻,还无法理解这件事。(that 无意义,可以省略)

Whether the project should be carried out is not decided yet. 这项工程是否应该实施还没定

下来。(whether 有意义,不可以省略)

(3) 如果宾语从句表示两种可能性具备其一时,只能用 whether(or not),不可用 that。例如:

I don't know whether Mary will take her parents' advice (or not). 我不知道玛丽是否听从她父母的建议。(不能用 that)

I am not sure whether the news is true. 消息是不是真的我没把握。(不能用 that)

(4) whether 引导的从句几乎能作所有介词的宾语;而 that 引导的从句只能作 except、but、besides 等介词宾语,此时 that 不能省略。例如:

I have no interest in whether he will pass the exam. 我对他能否通过考试不感兴趣。(不能用 that)

Tom is a good boy except that he is naughty sometimes. 汤姆是个好孩子,只是有时有点顽皮。

(三) whether 和 if 的区别

从属连词 if 和 whether 意思相同,都是"是否"的意思,但用法有区别。

(1) whether 比较正式,在口语中人们经常使用 if。另外,if 通常不用来引导主语从句、表语从句和同位语从句。例如:

She asked me if someone had helped me with the housework. 她问我是否有人帮我做了家务。(也可用 whether)

Whether Jackie Chan will come to the party is still not known. 成龙是否来参加宴会还不知道。(主语从句,不可用 if)

(2) whether 后面可以直接跟 or not,而 if 后面不可以直接跟 or not。例如:

I don't care if or not she has kept the promise. (×)

I don't care whether or not she has kept the promise. (√)

I don't care if she has kept the promise or not. (√)(口语中常用)

我不在乎她是否遵守承诺。

(3) whether 引导的宾语从句可以用在介词之后,而 if 不可以。例如:

They were worried about whether we could be independent. 他们担心我们能否独立。

(4) 在动词不定式前面只能用 whether,而不能用 if。例如:

He hasn't decided whether to support the election. 他还没有决定是否支持这次选举。

(5) whether 引导的从句可以放于句首作为全句的宾语从句,这时一般不用 if 代替。例如:

Whether he is a professor or not, I don't know. 他是不是教授,我不知道。

Whether he can pick you up that day, I wonder. 我想知道,他那天是否能接你。

(6) 某些动词,如 discuss 等后面只能接 whether,不能接 if。例如:

We discussed whether we should buy a new car. 我们讨论了是否该买辆新车。

(7) if 还可以引导条件状语从句,所以用 if 会引起误解时,则用 whether 代替。例如:

Let me know whether you can look after yourself. 告诉我你是否能照顾自己。

试用 if 代替 whether,则上句变为:

Let me know if you can look after yourself. 如果你能照顾自己,请告诉我。

用 if 会引起歧义,此时最好不用 if。

(四) what 与 that 的用法区别

在名词性从句中，what 和 that 都可作为关联词。其区别在于：what 在从句中充当某个成分（如主语、宾语或表语），在任何情况下都不能省略；that 本身没有意义，在从句中不充当任何成分，引导宾语从句的 that 往往可以省略。例如：

I think (that) your daughter will like the new toy. 我认为你女儿会喜欢这个新玩具的。

What he said at the meeting astonished everybody present. 他在会上说的话震惊了在场所有人。

> 注：当名词性从句已有疑问词引导时，不可再加 that。例如：
> I don't understand that what he told you just now. (×)
> I don't understand what he told you just now. (√) 我不明白他刚刚跟你说的话。
> 当从属连词 that 引导主语从句、表语从句和同位语从句时，that 不能省略。例如：
> That you don't like him is none of my business. 你不喜欢他，这不关我的事。
> The reason for his absence was that he was ill. 他缺席的原因是他生病了。
> The news that she won the championship spread throughout the motherland. 她夺冠的消息传遍祖国的大街小巷。

(五) wh-ever 引导的名词性从句

wh-ever 引导的名词性从句不含疑问意义，whatever (= anything that)、whoever (= anyone who)、whomever、whichever 表示泛指。例如：

Many experts don't agree that parents give a child whatever he or she wants. 许多专家不赞成父母给孩子他们想要的任何东西。

Whoever comes is welcome. 无论谁来都受欢迎。

Take whichever book you prefer. 你喜欢哪本书就拿哪本书。

We will hire whomever you recommend. 你推荐谁我就雇用谁。

二、名词性从句的种类

(一) 主语从句

在复合句中起主语作用的从句称为主语从句。引导主语从句的关联词有从属连词 that、whether，连接代词 who、what、which、whom、whose、whatever、whoever、whomever、whichever，连接副词 when、where、how、why、however、whenever、wherever 等。

1. 从属连词 that 和 whether 引导的主语从句

从属连词 that 和 whether 在主语从句中的作用只是引导主语从句，它们在从句中不担任成分，不能省略。例如：

Whether we will go camping depends on the weather. 我们是否去野营取决于天气。

That she is a rich woman is known to us. 她是一个很有钱的女子，这一点我们都知道。

2. 由连接代词或连接副词引导的主语从句

(1) 由连接代词 what、which、whose、who、whom、whatever、whoever、whomever、whichever 等

引导的主语从句,连接代词在从句中担任主语、宾语、表语或定语,不能省略。例如:

What the teacher said had a great effect on the children. 老师所说的话对孩子们影响很大。

Which team will win the championship is uncertain. 哪支队会赢得冠军还不确定。

Who was responsible for the accident is not clear yet. 谁对这次事故负责还不清楚。

Whoever leaves the classroom last ought to turn off the lights. (=Anyone who leaves the classroom last) ought to turn off the lights. 无论是谁最后离开教室都应该关灯。

(2) 由连接副词 when、where、how、why 等引导主语从句时,连接副词在从句中担任状语,不能省略。例如:

When they will start has not been decided yet. 他们什么时候出发还没决定。

When and why he came here is not known yet. 他什么时候来这里的以及为什么而来都还不知道。

3. 以 it 作形式主语的主语从句

如果主语从句太长,为避免句子结构头重脚轻,我们可用 it 作形式主语,而把主语从句放在主句谓语部分之后。例如:

It's strange that he didn't go to the concert yesterday. 很奇怪他昨天没去听音乐会。

It is quite clear that he is guilty about what he has done. 很明显他对自己做的事感到内疚。

It is common knowledge that the earth moves around the sun. 地球围绕太阳转,这是常识。

It is a pity that she has made such a mistake. 她犯这样的错误是令人遗憾的事。

It is said that the couple have left the country. 据说那对夫妇已离开了这个国家。

It is reported that the temperature will decline sharply in the near future. 据报道,在不久的将来气温将大幅下降。

It happened that I saw her in the shopping mall yesterday. 昨天我碰巧在购物中心看见她。

It occurred to Jack that he had left his homework at home. 杰克突然想到他把作业落在家里了。

It struck me that Mike had invited me to his anniversary. 我忽然想起迈克邀请我去他的周年庆。

4. 主语从句不可位于句首的四种情况

(1) 含主语从句的复合句是疑问句、感叹句时,主语从句不可提前,只能用 it 作形式主语。例如:

Is it really true that he has resigned from the company? 他真的从公司辞职了吗?

How surprising it was that his team gained the first in the chorus competition! 真令人惊奇,他们队在合唱比赛中得了第一!

(2) It is said(reported,estimated,demanded,suggested 等)that... 结构中的主语从句不可提前。例如:

It's said that the song is very pleasant. 据说这首歌很好听。

It's reported that the freeway will be opened to traffic next month. 据报道那条高速路下个月通车。

(3) It happens(occurs to...)that... 结构中的主语从句不可提前。例如:

It happened that I met Sarah at the concert. 我恰巧在音乐会上遇到了萨拉。

It occurred to her that she had forgotten to take the key away. 她突然想起忘了带走钥匙。

(4) It doesn't matter how(whether or not)... 结构中的主语从句不可提前。例如：

It doesn't matter how he will get along with his classmates. 他怎么和同学相处不重要。

It doesn't matter whether he is willing or not. 他愿不愿意无关紧要。

(二) 宾语从句

在复合句中用作宾语的从句称为宾语从句。宾语从句的位置与陈述句基本结构中的宾语相同。宾语从句可作谓语动词的宾语，也可以作介词和非谓语动词（动词不定式、动名词、分词）和某些形容词的宾语。宾语从句可以由从属连词（that、whether、if）、连接代词（what、who、whose、which）和连接副词（when、where、how、why）等引导。

1. 及物动词后的宾语从句

（1）由从属连词 that、whether、if 引导宾语从句时，这些词只起引导词作用，在句中不作成分。例如：

I wonder whether(if) you are willing to help me. 不知您是否愿意帮个忙。

I want to know whether(if) he has told you the story. 我想知道他是否给你讲了这个故事。

I believe (that) you will take the front-line medical workers as examples and strive to be good doctors that the Party and the people can rely on. 我相信，你们一定会以一线医务工作者为榜样，努力做党和人民信赖的好医生。

（2）由连接代词 what、who、whom、whose、which 引导的宾语从句，连接代词在从句中充当主语、宾语、表语或定语，连接代词在句中不能省略。例如：

The book will show you what the true history was. 这本书会告诉你真实的历史。

Do you know who has taken my umbrella away? 你知道谁拿走了我的雨伞吗？

I forgot whom I lent the book to. 我不记得把书借给谁了。

He doesn't know which storybook his son will choose. 他不知道他儿子会选哪本故事书。

（3）由连接副词 when、where、how、why 等引导，连接副词 when、where、how、why 既有疑问意义，又起连接作用，而且在宾语从句中充当状语，分别表时间、地点、方式、原因，不能省略。例如：

I wonder why she dropped out of college. 我不知道她为什么辍学。

Can you tell me where the nearest supermarket is? 你能告诉我最近的超市在哪儿吗？

He didn't tell me when we should meet again. 他没有告诉我什么时候我们再见面。

Would you please tell me how I can carry out the plan? 请告诉我怎样实施这个计划好吗？

（4）动词+间接宾语+宾语从句。此类动词如：advise、ask、inform、promise、question、remind、show、teach、tell、warn 等，宾语从句前可以有一个间接宾语，这个宾语有的可以省略，有的不能省略。例如：

He has informed me when my book is to be published. 他已经通知我将在什么时候出版我的书。（me 不可省略）

She promised (us) that she would give us a speech. 她答应以后给我们做次演讲。（us 可以省略）

2. 介词和某些形容词之后的宾语从句

（1）介词后的宾语从句。例如：

Mike is a nice employee, except that he is sometimes late for work. 除了上班有时迟到外，迈

克算是个好员工。

The headmaster is pleased with what she has achieved. 校长对她取得的成绩很满意。

It depends on whether the boss will agree to the project or not. 这件事取决于老板是否同意这个项目。

I always think of how I can improve my written English. 我经常思考如何才能提高我的英语写作能力。

（2）某些形容词后的宾语从句。例如：

I'm afraid (that) we can't find a solution to this tricky problem. 恐怕我们找不到这个棘手问题的解决方法。

I am sure that they can swim across the river. 我确信他们能游过河去。

The manager was surprised that he had got no experience of teamwork. 经理惊讶于他没有团队合作的经验。

Mother was very pleased that her son had got promoted in such a short time. 儿子这么短时间就升职了，母亲很高兴。

3. 非谓语动词之后的宾语从句

非谓语动词后可以接宾语从句。例如：

Not knowing what she should do, the little girl began to cry. 小女孩不知道该做什么，就哭起来了。

To understand what the teacher was saying, the students listened carefully. 为了理解老师说的话，学生们很认真地听讲。

4. it 用作形式宾语

正如我们常用 it 作形式主语代替主语从句一样，我们也常将 it 用作形式宾语代替宾语从句，把真正的宾语从句后置，特别是在带有复合宾语的句子中。在这种结构中 that 不可省略。有下列几种情况。

（1）在 believe、consider、declare、estimate、fancy、feel、find、guess、hear、imagine、know、make、prove、reckon、think、understand 等动词接复合宾语（宾语+宾补）时，要用 it 作形式宾语。例如：

We have made it clear that our purpose is to learn knowledge. 我们已经表明了我们的目的是学知识。

She thinks it wrong that he didn't compete in the match. 她认为他不参赛是错误的。

（2）介词短语作宾语补足语时，常用 it 作形式宾语。例如：

Keep it in mind that you will meet them at the station this afternoon. 要记住今天下午去车站接他们。

We took it for granted that 40 miles was not long. 我们想当然地认为40英里路程不长。

（3）在 like、enjoy、love、hate、resent 等表喜、怒、哀、乐的动词后，接宾语从句时，需跟形式宾语 it。例如：

I hate it when we compete with each other for the contract. 我不喜欢我们为这个合同互相竞争。

Mike resents it when someone laughs at him. 迈克讨厌别人嘲笑他。

（4）由动词和介词构成的短语动词后接 that 宾语从句时，要用形式宾语。例如：

We are thinking of it that we'll invest a lot of time in the experiment. 我们正在考虑投入大量时间做实验。

I shall see to it that my baby brother is taken good care of when parents are absent. 父母不在的时候我负责把弟弟照顾好。

5. 特殊类型的宾语从句

当主句中的谓语动词是表示"认为""建议""猜测"等意义的动词,如 think、say、guess、suppose、suggest、say、believe、feel、consider 时,引导宾语从句的连接代词 who、which、what 和连接副词 when、where、how、why,不能按正常语序安排,经常将这类引导词置于句首。例如:

Who do you think the members might choose as their partner in the project? 你认为这个项目大家会选谁做他们的合作伙伴?

Which film do you say I should see this evening? 你觉得今晚我应该看哪部电影?

(三) 表语从句

在复合句中用作表语的从句称为表语从句。表语从句和主语指同一内容,它对主语进行解释、说明,使主语的内容具体化。引导表语从句的词有从属连词(that、whether、as though〈if〉)、连接代词(who、what、which、whom、whose、whatever、whoever、whomever、whichever 等)、连接副词(when、where、why、how、however、whenever、wherever 等)。可以接表语从句的连系动词有 be、look、remain、seem 等。that 引导表语从句时,在口语中,有时可以省略。

(1) 由从属连词 that 和 whether 引导。例如:

The question is whether we should accept their invitation. 问题是我们是否应该接受他们的邀请。

Our decision is that all of us are to start at 6 a. m. tomorrow. 我们决定明天早上六点钟出发。

(2) 由连接代词 who、what、which、whom、whose、whatever、whoever、whomever、whichever 等引导,连接代词在从句中担任某一成分,不能省略。例如:

The problem is who can take over his business. 问题是谁能接管他的生意。

What she wants to know is which skirt she should choose to attend the interview. 她想知道的是她应该选哪条裙子去参加面试。

Realization of a moderately prosperous society in all respects and elimination of extreme poverty is what the CPC has delivered to our people. 实现全面小康、摆脱贫困是中国共产党给人民的交代。

(3) 由连接副词 when、where、how、why 等引导。例如:

That is where my teacher used to teach. 那就是我老师曾经教书的地方。

That is why he didn't seize the chance. 那就是他没有抓住机会的原因。

That's how the house problem is solved. 那就是房子问题的解决方式。

(4) 表语从句还可以由 because、as、as if、as though 引导。例如:

That's because we were in need of money at that time. 这是因为我们那时候需要钱。

It looks as if/though we're going to have trouble with Mr. Jones again. 看来琼斯先生又要找我们麻烦了。

Mary looks as if/though she is afraid of nothing. 玛丽看上去好像什么都不怕。

> 注：主语是 reason 时，表语从句常用 that 引导，不用 because。例如：
> The reason for his absence was that he had a fever. 他没来是因为他发烧了。

（四）同位语从句

在复合句中用作同位语的从句称为同位语从句。它一般跟在抽象名词 fact、idea、news、hope、request、belief、promise、thought、truth、doubt、suggestion、warning、instruction、reason、information、order 等之后，对这些名词进行说明或解释。引导同位语从句的词除连词 that、whether 外，还有连接代词 what、which、who 以及连接副词 how、when、where、why 等。句型 there is no doubt 后用 that，there is doubt 后用 whether。例如：

We all know the fact that smoking is harmful to health. 我们都知道吸烟危害健康这个事实。
There is no doubt that he has a good handwriting. 毫无疑问他写的一手好字。
There is great doubt whether Mike did so or not. 迈克是否这样做了，还很有疑问。
They haven't yet settled the question where they are going to spend their winter vacation. 去哪儿度寒假，这个问题他们还没有决定。

> 注：同位语从句是对名词加以说明的，而定语从句是对名词加以限定的。区分同位语从句和定语从句最简便的方法，就是将"名词+that"结构取出，能在名词和 that 之间加上 be 动词构成一个表语从句的，则是同位语从句，否则是定语从句。例如：
> The suggestion (that) she has put forward is very good. 她提出的建议很好。（定语从句）
> The suggestion that we clean the classroom by turns is very good. 我们轮流打扫教室，这个建议很好。（同位语从句）
> The fact (that) we talked about is important. 我们所谈论的情况很重要。（定语从句）
> The fact that he succeeded in the experiment pleased everybody. 他的实验成功了，这使大家很高兴。（同位语从句）

（五）宾语补足语从句

在复合句中用作宾语补足语的从句称为宾语补足语从句，通常用 what 引导。例如：

The umbrella has made the Englishman what they are. 英国人之所以是英国人，就是因为总带着伞。
The Internet has made the word what it is today. 互联网造就了今天的世界。
We call him what his teacher named him. 我们叫他老师给他取的名字。

三、名词性从句注意事项

（一）名词性从句的语序

尽管许多名词性从句是用 if、whether、what、who、which、how、when 等词引导的，但名词性从句必须使用陈述语序，不能用疑问语序。例如：

When will you leave for Shanghai? Can you tell me?
→Can you tell me when you will leave for Shanghai? 能告诉我你什么时候去上海吗？

（二）时态的一致

在名词性从句中，从句谓语动词与主句谓语动词的时态要保持一致。

（1）在宾语从句中，当主句是一般过去时，宾语从句根据需要使用各种对应的过去时态。如果宾语从句表示的是客观真理，其谓语动词仍用一般现在时。例如：

He asked me whether Mr. Smith had returned home from the trip. 他问我史密斯先生是否旅行归来了。

The teacher said that light travels in a straight line. 老师说光是沿直线运行的。

（2）在主语从句、表语从句和同位语从句中，也要注意从句谓语动词与主句谓语动词的时态一致性。关键要注意动作发生的先后关系。例如：

When he will go to America has not been fixed. 他何时去美国，还没有定下来。

Our village of today is not what it was ten years ago. 今天我们村子已不是十年前的村子。

巩 固 练 习

Complete the following sentences by choosing the items marked A, B, C, or D.

1. _____ we really cared for most of all was science.
   A. That　　　　B. Which　　　　C. What　　　　D. If

2. That's _____ we learn the meaning of the words in our own language.
   A. what　　　　B. that　　　　C. how　　　　D. which

3. _____ food is related to illness is not a new discovery.
   A. what　　　　B. if　　　　C. /　　　　D. that

4. It is not known yet _____ we can take the bus near the bridge when there is a heavy fog.
   A. if　　　　B. whether　　　　C. how far　　　　D. what

5. Everything depends on _____ they will support you.
   A. if　　　　B. which　　　　C. whether　　　　D. that

6. The reason why it was called "the wind's eye" was _____ the slit let in more wind than light.
   A. because　　　　B. which　　　　C. what　　　　D. that

7. That's _____ you've been looking so worried these last few days.
   A. why　　　　B. what　　　　C. that　　　　D. how

8. No one knows _____ suggestion works.
   A. when　　　　B. where　　　　C. how　　　　D. that if

9. The ex-neighbour asked Mr. Medina _____ he had paid for the book.
   A. how long　　　　B. that　　　　C. how far　　　　D. how much

10. Mrs. Brown asked _____ the policeman could help when she was at a loss.
    A. that　　　　B. how　　　　C. if　　　　D. where

11. All Benjamin hoped was _____ people would remember him and say "He led a useful life."
    A. that　　　　B. what　　　　C. when　　　　D. where

12. Many doctors believe _____ hobbies help to make our lives more enjoyable.
    A. if   B. where   C. when   D. that
13. We couldn't imagine _____ he was behaving so strangely.
    A. why   B. if   C. whether   D. how
14. David's wife realized _____ had happened and went very white.
    A. that   B. whether   C. which   D. what
15. The air hostess asked _____ any of the passengers knew anything about the machines.
    A. that   B. if   C. how   D. what
16. _____ is terrible _____ river pollution can become so bad that fish and plants can not live.
    A. That; that B. It; that   C. It; it   D. There; that
17. _____ is most important to me is that I don't have to go to work by ferry.
    A. what   B. that   C. it   D. there
18. Galileo concluded that heavy objects and light objects _____ at the same time.
    A. fell   B. falling   C. fall   D. fallen
19. I wonder _____ he _____ abroad.
    A. if; had gone   B. that; has gone   C. if; has gone   D. that; had gone
20. I don't doubt _____ Li Ping has entered the key university.
    A. if   B. /   C. that   D. where
21. I doubt _____ Shenhua Football Team will gain the third prize.
    A. that   B. /   C. whether   D. what
22. The problem is _____ will tie the bell to the cat.
    A. that   B. who   C. no matter who   D. whoever
23. _____ surprised me most was _____ we met with each other here.
    A. That; that B. It; if   C. It; what   D. What; that
24. Ask him how much _____.
    A. did the suit cost   B. cost the suit
    C. the suit costs   D. the suit costed
25. I did _____ I could _____ others.
    A. that; help   B. what; help
    C. that; to help   D. what; to help
26. _____ do you think _____ is the best student in your class?
    A. Whom; that   B. Who; /
    C. Who; that   D. Whom; /
27. _____ has helped to save the drowning girl is worth praising.
    A. Who   B. Whoever   C. Anyone   D. The one
28. We haven't settled the question of _____ it is necessary for him to study abroad.
    A. if   B. where   C. whether   D. that
29. _____ makes his shop different is that it offers more personal services.
    A. What   B. Who   C. Whatever   D. Whoever

30. Elephants have their own way to tell the shape of an object and _____ it is rough or smooth.

   A. /   B. what   C. how   D. whether

31. We saw several natives advancing towards our party, and one of them came up to us, _____ we gave some bells and glasses.

   A. to which   B. with which
   C. with whom   D. to whom

32. Mary wrote an article on _____ the team had failed to win the game.

   A. why   B. what   C. who   D. that

33. Doris' success lies in the fact _____ she is cooperative and eager to learn from others.

   A. which   B. why   C. when   D. that

34. Some researchers believe that there is no doubt _____ a cure for AIDS will be found.

   A. which   B. whether   C. what   D. that

35. Great changes have taken place in that school. It is no longer _____ it was 20 years ago, _____ it was so poorly equipped.

   A. what; when   B. that; which   C. what; which   D. which; that

36. Danny left word with my secretary _____ he would call again in the afternoon.

   A. who   B. that   C. as   D. which

37. Go and get your coat. It's _____ you left it.

   A. there   B. where there   C. there where   D. where

38. —We haven't heard from Jane a long time.
   —What do you suppose _____ to her?

   A. was happening   B. has happened
   C. to happen   D. having happened

39. Why do you want a new job _____ you've got such a good one already?

   A. that   B. where   C. which   D. when

40. After the war, a new school building was put up _____ there had once been a theatre.

   A. that   B. when   C. which   D. where

第十九章 19

直接引语和间接引语

热身训练: 下列句子各有一处错误,请指出并改正。

❶ Tom said that he is going to Sydney.
❷ The twins said they finished the homework yesterday.
❸ Sarah asked his husband don't smoke in the bathroom.
❹ His parents asked that he was at school.
❺ I asked you when was he going to London.
❻ The teacher told us not laugh at others.
❼ He said to his son, "Not stretch the hand out of the window."
❽ Ann said that her sister was going here with them tonight.
❾ Mary said that she would have an interview tomorrow.
❿ Mother asked what the matter was.
⓫ The biology teacher said that the leaves came out in spring.
⓬ Mike said that he had watched the movie the day ago.
⓭ Tom asked Mike what difference it did made.
⓮ The servant asked there was anything else she could do.
⓯ The teacher asked the students to lift these books to their classroom.

一、直接引语和间接引语的概念

当转述别人的话时,可以引用别人的原话,被直接引用的部分称为直接引语;也可以用自己的话转述别人的意思,被转述的部分称为间接引语。间接引语多数构成宾语从句。直接引语变为间接引语时,时态、语序、人称代词、状语等方面需作必要的调整。例如:

He said to me, "Jane spent the whole day making this bookshelf." 他对我说:"简用了一整天的时间制作这个书架。"

→He told me (that) Jane had spent the whole day making that bookshelf. 他告诉我简花了一整天时间做那个书架。

Mary said, "I am looking forward to the lecture." 玛丽说:"我期待着那场讲座。"

→Mary said that she was looking forward to the lecture. 玛丽说她期待着那场讲座。

二、直接引语和间接引语的转换

（一）时态的变化

（1）直接引语变为间接引语时，谓语动词的规律变化如表 19-1 所示。

表 19-1　间接引语谓语动词的变化

直 接 引 语	间 接 引 语
一般现在时	一般过去时
现在进行体	过去进行体
现在完成体	过去完成体
一般过去时	过去完成体
过去完成体	过去完成体（不变）
一般将来时间	过去将来时间
一般将来进行体	过去将来进行体
一般将来完成体	过去将来完成体

例如：

"She's looking for her dictionary." I said. 我说："她正在找字典。"

→I said (that) she was looking for her dictionary. 我说她在找字典。

I said to them, "Jack will know what you have done for him." 我对他们说："杰克会知道你们为他所做的事情。"

→I told them (that) Jack would know what they had done for him. 我告诉他们杰克会知道他们为他所做的事。

（2）直接引语中的谓语动词为一般过去时，如果与具体的表示过去的时间（如 in 2015、last month 等）连用，在变为间接引语时时态可以不变。例如：

I said to my mother, "I watched the movie in 2016." 我告诉母亲："我 2016 年看了这部电影。"

→I told my mother I watched the movie in 2016. 我告诉母亲我 2016 年看了这部电影。

（3）直接引语表达的意思是客观真理或习惯性、经常性动作时，在变为间接引语时时态不变。例如：

The geography teacher said to us, "The sun rises in the east and sets in the west." 地理老师告诉我们："太阳东升西落。"

→ The geography teacher told us that the sun rises in the east and sets in the west. 地理老师告诉我们太阳东升西落。

"My father always works late at night." Tom said. 汤姆说："我父亲总是工作到深夜。"

→ Tom said that his father always works late at night. 汤姆说他父亲总是工作到深夜。

（4）虚拟过去时如果位于 wish、would rather/sooner 和 It is time… 等之后，在间接引语中保持不变。例如：

She said, "It is time I had an English class." 她说："我该上英语课了。"

→She said it was time she had an English class. 她说她该上英语课了。

"We wish everyone would no longer suffer from poverty and hunger in the world." said the children. 孩子们说："我们希望世界上所有人都不再遭受贫穷和饥饿。"

→The children said they wished everyone would no longer suffer from poverty and hunger in the world. 孩子们说他们希望世上所有人都不再遭受贫穷和饥饿。

（5）如果直接引语中动词所表示的情况仍然存在和进行，其时态在间接引语中可以不变。例如：

"I'm twelve years old." the boy said. "我12岁了。"那个男孩说。

→The boy said that he is twelve years old. 那个男孩说他12岁。（现在还是12岁）

"I work as an air hostess." she told me. "我是一名空乘。"她告诉我。

→She told me that she works as an air hostess. 她告诉我她是空乘。（现在仍是空乘）

（6）直接引语变间接引语，过去完成（进行）时仍为过去完成（进行）时，不需改变。例如：
He said, "The train had left when we arrived." 他说："当我们赶到的时候，火车已经开走了。"

→He said the train had left when they arrived. 他说当他们赶到的时候，火车已经开走了。

（7）直接引语中时间状语从句的谓语，如果是一般过去时或过去进行时，在间接引语中保持不变，而主句的谓语动词可变可不变。例如：

Mike said, "When we lived/were living in Shanghai, we often saw Lin Tao." 迈克说："住在上海的时候，我们经常看见林涛。"

→Mike said that when they lived/were living in Shanghai, they often saw/had seen Lin Tao. 迈克说，他们住在上海时常看见林涛。

（8）直接引语中含有情态动词时，要注意情态动词的不变或多变，如表19-2所示。例如：

表19-2　间接引语情态动词的变化

直接引语中的情态动词	间接引语中的情态动词
can	could
may	might
must	must（表示推测）、had to、would have to
ought to	ought to、should
dare not	dare not、didn't dare to
need not	need not、didn't need to、didn't have to、wouldn't have to

She said, "The crayon must be in the desk." 她说："蜡笔一定在桌子里。"

→She said that the crayon must be in the desk. 她说蜡笔一定在桌子里。

He said, "We must tell the truth." 他说："我们必须说真话。"

→He said that they had to tell the truth. 他说他们必须说真话。

He said, "I dare not sleep with the door open." 他说："我不敢开着门睡觉。"

→He said that he dare not/didn't dare to sleep with the door open. 他说他不敢开着门睡觉。

She said, "You needn't decorate the house now." 她说："你现在没有必要装饰房子。"

→She said I needn't/didn't need to/didn't have to decorate the house then. 她说我那时不必装饰房子。

(二) 人称代词的变化

(1) 人称代词,除引述本人的原话外,通常第一、第二人称需要作相应的变化。例如:
"I've been to Paris." Lily said. "我去过巴黎。"莉莉说。
→Lily said she had been to Paris. 莉莉说她去过巴黎。
"I've heard of your name before." Lily said to me. "我曾听说过你的名字。"莉莉对我说。
→Lily told me that she had heard of my name before. 莉莉告诉我她以前听说过我的名字。

(2) 指示代词 this 和 these 分别变为 that 和 those。例如:
Tom said, "I will buy this air-conditioner tomorrow." 汤姆说:"明天我将买这台空调。"
→Tom said that he would buy that air-conditioner the next day. 汤姆说他第二天将买那台空调。

(三) 时间状语和地点状语的变动

直接引语变为间接引语时,句子中间接引语时间、地点状语的变化如表 19-3 所示。

表 19-3　间接引语时间、地点状语的变化

直 接 引 语	间 接 引 语
today	that day
this morning/afternoon, etc.	that morning/afternoon, etc.
yesterday	the day before, the previous day
the day before yesterday	two days before
tomorrow	the following day/the next day
tonight	that night
the day after tomorrow	two days after/in two days' time
next week/month, etc.	the next week/month, etc. the following week/month, etc.
last week/month, etc.	the week/month before, etc. the previous week/month, etc.
now	then
two/three days/weeks/months ago	two/three days/weeks/months before
here	there
this place	that place
these places	those places

例如:"I'll wait for you this evening, Tom." he said. "晚上我会等你的,汤姆。"他说。
→He told Tom (that) he would wait for him that evening. 他告诉汤姆晚上他会等他。
He said, "The shopping mall was completed half a year ago." 他说:"购物中心半年前就竣工了。"
→He said the shopping mall had been completed half a year before. 他说购物中心在半年前

就竣工了。

另外，在句子的意义不会引起误解的情况下，状语有时也可以不变。例如：
"I'll come to see you here again today." Sarah said. "我今天还要来这看你。"萨拉说。
→Sarah said (that) she'd come to see me here again today. 萨拉说她今天还要来这儿看我。

（四）引导语和语序

1. 直接引语为陈述句

当直接引语为陈述句时，间接引语用 that 引导，此时 that 无意义，可以省略。例如：
She said, "I work as a teacher here." 她说："我是这里的老师。"
→She said(that) she works as a teacher there. 她说她是那里的老师。

2. 直接引语为疑问句

当直接引语是疑问句时，除了在人称、时态和状语等方面作相应的变动外，还要注意以下两点。

（1）特殊疑问句的疑问词要保留，用作间接引语的引导词；原来的疑问句语序改为陈述句语序。例如：
The girl was wondering, "How does the AI work?" 那个女孩正在好奇："人工智能是怎样工作的。"
→The girl was wondering how the AI worked. 那个女孩对人工智能是怎样工作的感到好奇。
"Why do you come to the meeting so late?" He asked me. "为什么你到会这么晚？"他问我。
→He asked me why I came to the meeting so late. 他问我，我为什么这么晚到会。

（2）一般、选择疑问句则在间接引语前加 whether 或 if，疑问句语序改为陈述句语序。例如：
"Is there anything wrong, sir?" asked the policeman. 警察问道："出什么事情了吗，先生？"
→The policeman asked the man whether/if there was something wrong. 警察问那个男人是否出了什么事。
I asked him, "Will you take a bus or a train?" 我问他："你将坐巴士还是坐火车？"
→I asked him whether he would take a bus or a train. 我问他是坐巴士还是坐火车。

（五）祈使句、感叹句的变化

1. 直接引语为祈使句

当直接引语为祈使句时，主句中的谓语动词在变动时，往往根据直接引语中的口气换用 ask、invite、advise、warn、tell、order 等动词，而直接引语中的谓语动词则变成动词不定式。如果原来的直接引语是祈使句否定式（don't、never），改为动词不定式否定式。

肯定式为 sb.+tell/ask… sb.+to do sth.。

否定式为 sb.+tell/ask… sb.+not/never to do sth.。

例如：
"Please explain why you're absent from the meeting," the boss said to him. "请解释一下你为什么缺席会议，"老板对他说。
→The boss asked him to explain why he was absent from the meeting. 老板要他解释一下为什

么没来开会。

Her mother said to her, "Don't bring the stray cat home." 她母亲对她说:"不要把流浪猫带回家。"

→Her mother told her not to take the stray cat home. 她母亲叫她不要把流浪猫带到家里来。

2. 直接引语为感叹句

在引述感叹句时,一般有下列两种方式。

(1) 保留引导词 how 或 what,或者改为陈述句(以 that 为引导词)。例如:

"What a lovely cat!" he said.

→He remarked what a lovely cat it was. 或 He remarked that it was a lovely cat. 他说这只小猫好可爱。

"How wonderful the contest is!" she said.

→She said how wonderful the contest was. 或 She said that the contest was wonderful. 她说这个比赛棒极了。

(2) 可以根据句子的原意进行改写,使之变为具有相同含义的陈述句。例如:

"Hello!" he said to me.

→He greeted me. 他向我打招呼。

"Have a good time!" she said.

→She wished me a happy journey. 她祝我旅途愉快。

巩 固 练 习

Complete the following sentences by choosing the items marked A, B, C, or D.

1. "Why don't you quit that job?" he said.
   →He _____ .
   A. asked why didn't I quit that job   B. advised me to quit that job
   C. suggested that I quitted that job   D. asked why I don't quit that job

2. "Which do you prefer?" she asked.
   →She asked me _____ .
   A. which I preferred   B. which do I prefer
   C. which did I prefer   D. I prefer which

3. She suggested that they _____ to Shanghai by train.
   A. go   B. went   C. would go   D. was going

4. My teacher always told me that failure _____ the mother of success.
   A. was   B. had been   C. is   D. were

5. I'd like to know _____ Chinese.
   A. when he began to learn   B. when did he begin to learn
   C. when did he begin learning   D. for how long he began to learn

6. "How marvelous the performance is!" she said.
   →She said _____ .
   A. how marvelous was the performance

B. how marvelous the performance had been

C. how marvelous the performance is

D. how marvelous the performance was

7. He told me he _____ the Party in 1985.

　A. had joined　　　　　　　　　　B. joined in

　C. joined　　　　　　　　　　　　D. had joined in

8. John asked me _____ to visit his uncle's farm with him.

　A. how would I like　　　　　　　B. if or not would I like

　C. whether I would like　　　　　D. which I would like

9. I don't know _____.

　A. the reason why can be　　　　B. why the reason may be

　C. what the reason can be　　　 D. what the reason may be

10. What did he say?

　→I don't know what _____.

　A. did he say　　B. he said　　C. he has said　　D. he says

11. The teacher asked her, "Does the sun rise in the east?"

　→The teacher asked her _____ the sun _____ in the east.

　A. if; rise　　B. whether did; rise　　C. whether; rose　　D. if; rises

12. Jack said to her, "Where do you spend your holidays?"

　→Jack asked her where _____ holidays.

　A. she spend her　　B. you spend your　　C. she spent her　　D. you spent your

13. She asked, "Whose house will he break into next time?"

　→She asked whose house _____ break into _____.

　A. will he; next time　　　　　　B. he would; the next time

　C. he will; next time　　　　　　D. would he; the next time

14. Can you make sure _____?

　A. that he will come here today　　B. when he will come here today

　C. will he come here today　　　　D. whether will he come here today

15. He said, "Mr Black, introduce yourself to them, please."

　→He _____ Mr Black _____ to them.

　A. asked; to introduce yourself　　B. ordered; introduce himself

　C. told; introduce yourself　　　　D. asked; to introduce himself

16. The mother said, "Be friendly to others, son."

　→The mother _____ friendly to others.

　A. asked her son be　　　　　　　 B. told her son to be

　C. told her son be　　　　　　　　D. ordered her son to be

17. The man said to me, "Please send for a doctor now!"

　→The man _____ me _____ for a doctor _____.

　A. ordered; to send; then　　　　B. told; send; now

　C. asked; to send; then　　　　　D. asked; send; now

18. She said that she _____ there for a long time.
    A. has lived   B. was living   C. lived   D. had lived
19. The mother said, "Doctor, please save my son."
    →The mother _____ son.
    A. asked doctor save my
    B. told the doctor to save her
    C. told doctor save my
    D. asked the doctor to save her
20. The captain said, "Take hold of this end, man!"
    →The captain _____ the soldier _____ hold of _____ end.
    A. asked; to take; that
    B. asked; take; this
    C. ordered; to take; that
    D. ordered; take; this
21. "_____?" she asked her son.
    A. Where you have been
    B. Where you went
    C. Where had you been
    D. Where have you been
22. He asked me _____ my home was.
    A. what   B. when   C. which   D. where
23. Please tell me _____ these books you like best.
    A. what   B. what of   C. which   D. which of
24. She told me that her mother _____ for several days.
    A. has been ill   B. had been ill   C. is ill   D. was ill
25. Tom told me that he _____.
    A. will help me with my geography
    B. will help me for my geography
    C. would help me with my geography
    D. would help me for my geography
26. The students said, "We have finished cleaning our classroom."
    →The students said _____ cleaning _____ classroom.
    A. they had finished; their
    B. they finished; their
    C. they have finished; their
    D. we had finished; our
27. The children said, "We had a football match today."
    →The children said _____ a football match _____.
    A. they had; today
    B. we had had; that day
    C. we had; today
    D. they had had; that day
28. The boy said, "I don't like dancing."
    →The boy said _____ like dancing.
    A. I don't   B. that he didn't   C. I didn't   D. he doesn't
29. The teacher said to us, "Light travels much faster than sound."
    →The teacher said to us that light _____ much faster than sound.
    A. will travel   B. traveled   C. travels   D. was traveling
30. He didn't tell me _____ or go home.
    A. whether to wait
    B. if to wait
    C. to wait
    D. if that she shout to wait

第二十章

定 语 从 句

热身训练： 下列句子各有一处错误，请指出并改正。

❶ The watch which I bought it last year was stolen.
❷ The people with who I work are all friendly.
❸ Have you ever been to the factory where your grandfather once worked there?
❹ The chairman of the meeting, that spoke first, sat on my right.
❺ There are some people whom faces you can never forget.
❻ This is the new bicycle which I spent five hundred dollars.
❼ The words to whom we should pay attention are written on the blackboard.
❽ This is the mountain village where I visited last year.
❾ At the moment I travel into Nottingham every day to the shop as I work.
❿ They also had a small pond which they raised fish.
⓫ Henry Royce did not like his car, that ran badly and often broke down.
⓬ It is reported in the newspapers, talks between the two countries are making progress.
⓭ The children, all of who had played the whole day long, were worn out.
⓮ The course attracts 20 students per year, of which up to half will be from overseas.
⓯ There, Katina will introduce me to some of her friends, one of who has been to China several times.

在句子中用来修饰名词、代词或修饰整个主句并起定语作用的从句称为定语从句。定语从句又称形容词性从句。被定语从句所修饰的词、短语或句子通常称为先行项。定语从句一般跟在先行项之后，由关系代词或关系副词引导。定语从句分为限制性定语从句和非限制性定语从句两种。

一、限制性定语从句与非限制性定语从句的区别

根据定语从句和主句的疏密关系，分为限制性定语从句和非限制性定语从句。其区别如表20-1所示。

表 20-1　限制性定语从句和非限制性定语从句的区别

种类	意义	形式	译法	关系代/副词
限制性定语从句	起限定作用,若省略,原句意义不完整	紧接先行项后,无逗号	常译为先行项的定语	有时可省略
非限制性定语从句	起附加说明作用,若省略,原句意义仍然清楚	有逗号与主句隔开	常译为另一并列分句	不可用 that,不可省略

例如:

This is the book which/that I borrowed from Sandy last week. 这是我上周从桑迪那儿借来的书。

The book, which I borrowed from Sandy last week, is very interesting. 这本书很有趣,它是我上个月从桑迪那儿借的。

Sarah, who is serious and responsible to us, becomes our classroom teacher this term. 萨拉本学期担任我们的班主任,她对我们认真负责。

The teacher who/that taught us oral English last term is from Pakistan. 上学期教我们英语口语的老师来自巴基斯坦。

The Memorial Hall of the Victims in Nanjing Massacre by Japanese Invaders which/that they visited yesterday was built in 1985. 他们昨天去参观的侵华日军南京大屠杀遇难同胞纪念馆建于 1985 年。

二、关系代词

(一) 常见关系代词

常见关系代词及其用法如表 20-2 所示。

表 20-2　常见关系代词及其用法

指代功能 在从句中的成分	用于限制性从句或非限制性从句		只用于限制性从句
	指代人	指代物	指代人或物
主语	who	which	that
宾语	whom	which	that
定语	whose (=of whom)	whose (=of which)	—

引导定语从句的关系代词在从句中可作主语、宾语和定语等。具体用法如下。

1. who、whom、that 指代人

(1) that/who 在定语从句中作主语,不可以省略。例如:

Yesterday, I met the girl that/who lives next door. 昨天我碰到了那个住在隔壁的女孩。

The teacher will praise the students who/that perform well. 老师会表扬那些表现好的学生。

(2) that/who/whom 在定语从句中作宾语,可以省略。例如:

Sam married the girl that/who/whom he always wanted to marry. 山姆娶到了他一直想要娶的女孩。

She liked the workmates whom/who she shares a flat with. 她喜欢与她合租公寓的同事。

（3）介词+whom，当定语从句中的介词放在关系代词前，指代人的关系代词就只能用whom作宾语，且不可省略。例如：

I know the girl (that/who/whom) my teacher is talking with.

→I know the girl with whom my teacher is talking. 我认识我老师正在与之交谈的那个女孩。

（4）who/whom在非限制性定语从句中指代人时，不可用that代替，不可省略。例如：

Mr. Black, who gave a talk several days ago, will come again. 布莱克先生还会再来，他前几天作过一场演讲。

Chinese scientist Yuan Longping, who is the father of hybrid rice, has made great contributions to solving the problem of food shortage in the world. 中国科学家袁隆平是杂交水稻之父，为解决世界粮食短缺的问题做出了极大的贡献。

My uncle has come back from Beijing, whom I haven't met for a long time. 我舅舅从北京回来了，我好久没见到他了。

2. which、that 指代事物

（1）that/which在定语从句中作主语时，不可省略。例如：

I bought the pen that/which was the most expensive in the store. 我买了店里最贵的那支笔。

（2）that/which在定语从句中作宾语，可以省略。例如：

To be frank, I don't like the movie (which/that) you recommended to me yesterday. 说实话，我不喜欢你昨天推荐给我的那部影片。

（3）介词+which，当定语从句中的介词放在关系代词前，指代事物的关系代词就只能用which作宾语，且不可省略。例如：

The pen (that/which) I paid 150 yuan for was lost.

→The pen for which I paid 150 yuan was lost. 我花了150元买的钢笔丢了。

Give me a piece of paper on which I can write the phone number. 给我一张可以在上面写电话号码的纸。

（4）which在非限制性定语从句中，指代事物或主句整个句子，不可用that代替，不可省略，引导的定语从句不可放句首。例如：

Yesterday I bought a coat, which cost me more than 500 yuan. 我昨天买了件外套，花了我500多元。

The film *Changjin Lake*, which was made in 2020, tells us a moving history of resisting U.S. aggression and aiding Korea. 2020年拍的电影《长津湖》给我们讲述了一段可歌可泣的抗美援朝的历史故事。

He seems not to have understood what I meant, which greatly upsets me. 他似乎没明白我的意思，这使我心烦。

3. whose 指代人或物

whose是形容词性的关系代词，在定语从句中作定语，后面必须加名词。

（1）whose指代人。例如：

I know the girl whose mother is our teacher. 我认识那个女孩，她妈妈是我们老师。

注：whose mother在定语从句中作主语，相当于the girl's mother。例如：

I know the girl whose mother we all respect. 我认识那个女孩，她妈妈受到我们所有人的尊重。

（2）whose 指代事物。例如：

I have a pen whose cap is purple. 我有一支笔盖是紫色的笔。

The pen whose cap I have lost was given by my father. 这支被我弄丢了笔盖的笔是我爸爸送的。

He lives in the house whose window opens to the south. 他住在窗户朝南的房子里。

（3）介词+whose+名词结构，例如：

He was the man from whose room the thief had stolen the watch（whose room the thief had stolen the watch from）. 他就是被小偷从其房间偷走了手表的那个人。

> 注：在限制性定语从句中，先行词前面不能用指示代词（如 this）或物主代词（如 his）所修饰。
> 例如：
> That lady who is smiling at me is my mother.（×）
> The lady who is smiling at me is my mother.（√）正对着我微笑的女士是我妈妈。

（二）特殊的关系代词 as 和 but

1. as 在定语从句中作主语或宾语

（1）在限制性定语从句中，如果 as 在定语从句中作宾语，不可省略。常用在 the same… as、such… as 等结构中。例如：

I have the same book as you have. 我有一本和你一样的书。

This is the same machine as I used yesterday. 这台机器跟我昨天用过的那台一样。

I never heard such information as he told. 我从未听过他说的那样的消息。

A clever man rarely talks about such things as he doesn't understand. 聪明人很少谈论他不懂的事情。

> 注："the same… as"和"the same… that"两者的区分。the same… as 表示"和……一样"；the same… that 表示"同一"，例如：
> This is the same watch as I left in the classroom. 这块表和我落在教室里的那块表一样。
> That is the same watch that I lost. 那就是我掉了的那块表。

（2）在非限制性定语从句中，as 指代整个主句，在从句中作主语或宾语，意为"正如/就像……的"，所引导的定语从句可放句首、句中或句尾，和主句之间用逗号隔开，如表 20-3 所示。

表 20-3　as 在非限制性定语从句中的应用

as 作宾语	as 作主语
as we all know（正如我们所知道的）	as is known to all（正如大家都知道的）
as they had expected（正如他们所预料的）	as is said above（正如上面所说的）
as anybody can see（正如人人都看到的）	as has been pointed out（正如已经指出的）
as we have imagined（正如我们想象的）	as is often the case（情况常常如此）

例如：

As we all know, he studies very hard. 如我们所知道的那样（众所周知），他学习很努力。

As is known to all, he is the best student in our class. 正如大家都知道的那样（众所周知），他是我们班里最好的学生。

> 注：which 和 as 指代整个主句的区别如下。
> ① as 引导的定语从句放句首、句尾都可以，which 引导的只能放句尾，不能放句首。
> ② as 有"正如/就像……的"的含义，which 没有。例如：
> We won the game, as our teacher expected. 我们赢了比赛,正如我们老师预料的那样。
> We won the game, which made us excited. 我们赢了比赛,这使我们很兴奋。

2. but 在从句中作主语或宾语

but 在定语从句中作关系代词，引导限制性定语从句，可作主语或宾语，but 表否定含义，即表示 who/whom/that... not 的意思。例如：

There is no fortress in the world but we can break. 世界上没有我们攻不破的堡垒。

There are few people but have their own secrets. 每个人都有自己的秘密。

（三）只能用 that 引导的定语从句

通常只能用 that 引导的定语从句有以下几类。

（1）先行词为 everything、something、anything、nothing、all、little、much、none、the one、one of 等指事物的不定代词和数词。例如：

There is nothing that can prevent her from challenging to climb Mount Qomolangma. 没有什么能阻止她挑战攀登珠穆朗玛峰。

Is there anything that I can do for you? 有什么我能为你效劳的吗？

There is much that I want to tell you. 我有很多话想要告诉你。

Look at the books on my bookshelf. You can find the two that you bought me for my birthday. 看看我书架上的这些书,你可以找到我过生日时你给我买的那两本。

All that glitters is not gold. 闪光的未必都是金子。

> 注：all 指人时，关系代词可用 who 或 that。例如：
> I've told all who/that will attend the meeting. 我已经通知所有与会人员。

（2）先行词既包含人又包含物。例如：

They talked about the persons and things that they remembered at the campus. 他们谈论了他们所记得的大学里的人和事。

He thought of the people and things that had a great influence on him. 他想起了那些对他有极大影响的人和事。

（3）先行词前有 last、first、next、only、very、all、any、few、much、no 及形容词最高级、序数词等词修饰。例如：

You can borrow any book that you want to read in our school library. 你可以在我们学校图书馆借任何你想读的书。

This is the very factory that they visited last summer holiday. 这恰好是他们去年暑假参观的那个工厂。

He was the first one that ate crabs. 他是第一个吃螃蟹的人。

The only person that the boy can depend on is his grandfather. 这男孩唯一能依靠的人是他的爷爷。

It is the longest river that I have ever seen. 它是我见过的最长的河。

(4) 主句以 which、who、what 等词开头，避免混淆。例如：

Who is the girl that is playing basketball? 正在打篮球的女孩是谁？
Which is the bus that you will take? 你要乘的是哪一班车？
What is the factor that causes his failure? 导致他失败的因素是什么？

（四）关系代词同介词连用的几种结构

(1) 介词+which/whom，例如：

He is an experienced driver, from whom much can be learned. 他是一个经验丰富的司机，从他那儿可以学到很多东西。

Our hometown, Jiujiang is a beautiful city, of which we are greatly proud. 我们家乡九江是一个美丽的城市，我们为之感到很自豪。

Lushan Mountain, for which Jiujiang is famous, is beautiful. 庐山很秀丽，九江因庐山而闻名。

The lady to whom he was engaged was an English teacher. 他与之订婚的那位女士是一位英语老师。

> **注：** 介词通常放在定语从句中动词后面，也可以放在关系代词前面，但有些特殊动词短语搭配不能拆分，介词只能放在动词后面，如：look forward to、look for、look after、look into、listen to、take care of 等。例如：
> This is the pen for which you are looking. （×）
> This is the pen that/which you are looking for. （√）这就是你一直在找的那支笔。

(2) 介词+which/whose+名词，例如：

Last month, part of Jiujiang was struck by floods, from whose effects the people are still suffering. 上个月，九江的部分地区发生洪水，人们还在遭受着洪水所带来的影响。

It rained all night and all day, during which time the farmland was flooded. 雨整日整夜地下，期间农田都被淹没了。

I called her by the wrong name, for which mistake I should apologize. 我叫错了她的名字，对此我应该道歉。

The girl was the person from whose room he had stolen the necklace. 那个年轻的女人就是他从其房间偷走项链的那个人。

(3) 名词+of+which/whom，表示"所有格"或"整体与部分关系"，部分（名词）+of+整体（which/whom 指代先行词）。例如：

He's written a novel the hero's name of which I've forgotten. 他写了一本小说，其男主角的名字我给忘了。

She has a daughter the eyes of whom are big and bright. 她有一个女儿，眼睛又大又亮。

The house the walls of which were damaged has now been fixed. 那幢墙被损坏的房子现在已经修好了。

(4) 不定代词+of which/whom/whose+名词，表示"所有格"或"整体与部分关系"，其中用到的不定代词有 some、any、none、both、all、many、a few、few、a little、little、either、neither、one 及百分比等。例如：

There are about 50 students in our class, most of whom like English. 我们班大约有 50 名学生，他们大多数喜欢英语。

These are stories written by Brothers Grimm, one of which was read to me by my mother. 这些是格林兄弟写的故事，其中一个故事我母亲给我读过。

She has two daughters, neither of whom is a teacher. 她有两个女儿，两个都不是老师。

She has many books, none of which is interesting. 她有许多书，但其中没有一本有趣。

She had a teddy-bear, both of whose eyes were missing. 她有一个泰迪熊，它的两只眼睛都不见了。

The factory produces one million articles of clothing every year, 75% of which export overseas. 这个工厂每年生产 100 万件衣服，其中 75% 出口海外。

三、关系副词

关系副词主要有 when、where、why 等，在定语从句中作状语。关系副词经常可以转化为介词+关系代词，其用法如表 20-4 所示。

表 20-4　关系副词及其用法

关系副词	先 行 词	在从句中的作用	说　　明
when (=at/on/in/during+which)	表示时间的名词 day、month、year、moment、occasion 等	时间状语	在限制性定语从句中，关系副词有时可用 that 替代，亦可以省略不用
where (=in/at/on/under+which)	表示地点的名词 place、school、library、country 等	地点状语	
why (=for which)	表原因的名词 reason	原因状语	

（1）when 在定语从句中作时间状语，其先行词为表时间的名词。例如：

I still remember the time when/during which I lived in the countryside. 我还记得我住在乡村的那段时光。

In China, Spring Festival is a special holiday when/on which a whole family are supposed to get together. 在中国，春节是一个全家人应该团聚的特殊节日。

There are occasions when/on which one must yield. 任何人都有不得不屈服的时候。

（2）where 在定语从句中作地点状语，其先行词为表地点的名词。例如：

The hotel where/at which we stayed wasn't clean. 我们住的那家旅馆不干净。

The city where/in which she lives is far away. 她住的城市很远。

China has built its own space station, where/in which Chinese astronauts teach students and answer their questions. 中国建立了自己的空间站，中国宇航员们在空间站里给同学们上课，并回答同学们的各种问题。

（3）why 在定语从句中作原因状语，其先行词为 reason。例如：

This is the reason why/for which I didn't come here. 这就是我没有来这里的原因。

There are many reasons why/for which people like surfing the Internet. 人们喜欢上网的原因有很多。

四、关系词的省略

(一) 关系代词的省略

(1) 关系代词 which/whom/who/that 在定语从句中作宾语(参见"常见关系代词")时,可以省略。

(2) 关系代词 that 在定语从句中作 be 的表语,且先行词是特指时,通常省略,而不用 who/which。例如:

China is not the country (that) it was. 中国已经不是过去的中国了。

The latest mobile phone is not the machine (that) it was when first invented. 最新款的手机已不是最初发明出来时的那种样子了。

> 注:但如果先行词是泛指时,关系代词通常用 which,且不省略。例如:
> He looked like a teacher which he was. 他像个老师,而他也的确是个老师。

(3) 关系代词 that 在定语从句中作补语时,例如:

I'm not the fool (that) you thought me. 我不是你以前所认为的那个傻瓜了。

He is the nicest teacher (that) the students consider him in their school. 他就是学生认为的学校里最好的那个老师。

(4) 主句是 there be 结构或定语从句是 there be 结构,关系代词在从句中作主语,也可省略。例如:

There is some one (who) calls you. 有人来电话找你。

He is the tallest boy (that) there are in his class. 他是他班里最高的男孩。

(二) 关系副词的省略

(1) 关系副词 when 的省略。when 在从句中作时间状语时通常不能省略,但当它用于先行词 day、year、time 等少数几个词后面时,when 可以省略或用 that 代替。例如:

That was the year (when/that) I first met you. 就是那一年我第一次遇见你。

I'll never forget the day (when/that) I joined the Party. 我永远也不会忘记我入党的那一天。

(2) 关系副词 where 的省略。where 在从句中作地点状语时通常不能省略,但当它用于先行词 place、somewhere、anywhere、everywhere、nowhere 等少数几个词后面时,where 可以省略或用 that 替代。例如:

This is the place (where/in which/that) we met yesterday. 这就是我们昨天见面的地方。

Have you somewhere (that) I can sleep for an hour? 你有没有一个可以让我睡上一个小时的地方?

(3) 关系副词 why 的省略。why 在从句中作原因状语,只用于先行词 the reason 后面引导定语从句,通常可换成 that 或 for which,且可以省略。例如:

This is the reason (why/for which/that) the teacher came here. 这就是那位老师来这儿的原因。

Give me one reason (why/for which/that) we should forgive you. 给我一个应当原谅你的理由。

五、关系词的选择

选择关系词时,首先看指代先行词的关系词在从句中充当什么成分;其次,看先行词表示的是人、物、时间、地点还是原因;最后,还要看从句是限制性还是非限制性定语从句。例如:

The day which/that is never forgotten in our hearts is October 1st, 1949, the founding day of the People's Republic of China. 我们心中永远不会忘记的日子是1949年10月1日,中华人民共和国成立的日子。

I'll never forget the time (which/that) I spent on campus. 我永远不会忘记我在校园里度过的时光。

Because of COVID-19, gone are days when/in which the local hotels are full. 因为新型冠状病毒,当地宾馆客满的日子过去了。

The city which/that was mentioned in the news is my hometown, Jiujiang. 那则新闻中提到的城市是我的家乡九江。

The museum (which/that) you will visit tomorrow was built in 1980. 你明天要去参观的那家博物馆建于1980年。

They will fly to Hainan, where/in which they plan to spend the Spring Festival. 他们将飞往海南,计划在那里过春节。

The reason which/that was given by the student is just an excuse for his being late. 这个学生所说的理由只是他迟到的借口。

The reason (which/that) he explained is not true. 他解释的理由不是真的。

The reason (why/for which/that) he didn't come to school was that he was ill. 他没来上学的原因是他病了。

I like the way (which/that) you are using. 我喜欢你们正在使用的那种方法。

I like the way (in which/that) you learn English. 我喜欢你学习英语的方式。

巩固练习

Complete the following sentences by choosing the items marked A, B, C, or D.

1. This is the magazine _____ I copied the paragraph.
   A. that   B. which   C. from that   D. from which

2. The clever boy made a hole in the wall, _____ he could see what was going on inside the house.
   A. which   B. through which C. through that   D. what

3. That is not the way _____ I do it.
   A. /   B. which   C. or which   D. with which

4. Great changes have taken place since then in the factory _____ we are working.
   A. where   B. that   C. which   D. there

5. The place _____ interested me most was the Children's Palace.
   A. which   B. where   C. what   D. in which

6. I can never forget the day _____ we worked together and the day _____ we spent together.
   A. when; which   B. which; when   C. what; that   D. on which; when

7. They arrived at a farmhouse, in front of _____ sat a small boy.
   A. whom   B. who   C. which   D. that

8. This is the reason _____ he didn't come to the meeting.
   A. in which   B. with which   C. that   D. for which

9. The engineer _____ my father works is about 50 years old.
   A. to whom   B. on whom   C. with which   D. with whom

10. I want to use the same dictionary _____ was used yesterday.
    A. which   B. who   C. what   D. as

11. Is oxygen the only gas _____ helps fire burn?
    A. that   B. /   C. which   D. it

12. Li Ming, _____ to the concert enjoyed it very much.
    A. I went with   B. with whom I went   C. with who I went   D. I went with him

13. He talked a lot about things and persons _____ they remembered in the school.
    A. which   B. that   C. whom   D. what

14. In our factory there are 2,000 workers, two thirds of _____ are women.
    A. them   B. which   C. whom   D. who

15. He is good at English, _____ we all know.
    A. that   B. as   C. whom   D. what

16. You're the only person _____ I've ever met _____ could do it.
    A. who; /   B. /; whom   C. whom; /   D. /; who

17. During the days _____, he worked as a servant at the Browns.
    A. followed   B. following   C. to follow   D. that followed

18. I lost a book, _____ I can't remember now.
    A. whose title   B. its title   C. the title of it   D. the title of that

19. The pen _____ he is writing is mine.
    A. with which   B. in which   C. on which   D. by which

20. Last summer we visited the West Lake, _____ Hangzhou is famous in the world.
    A. for which   B. for that   C. in which   D. what

21. Do you know the year _____ the Chinese Communist Party was founded?
    A. which   B. that   C. when   D. on which

22. The way _____ he looks at problems is wrong.
    A. which   B. whose   C. what   D. /

23. I have bought two pens, _____ writes well.
    A. none of them   B. neither of them   C. neither of which   D. none of which

24. I don't like _____ as you read.
    A. the novels
    B. the such novels
    C. such novels
    D. same novels

25. He is working hard, _____ will make him pass the final exam.
    A. that   B. which   C. for which   D. who
26. Do you know the man _____?
    A. whom I spoke   B. to who spoke   C. I spoke to   D. that I spoke
27. I want to use the same tools _____ used in your factory a few days ago.
    A. as was   B. which was   C. as were   D. which
28. John got beaten in the game, _____ had been expected.
    A. as   B. that   C. what   D. who
29. He isn't such a man _____ he used to be.
    A. who   B. whom   C. that   D. as
30. He is not such a man _____ would leave his work half done.
    A. that   B. which   C. who   D. as
31. All _____ can be eaten has been eaten up.
    A. what   B. that   C. which   D. there
32. That is the day _____ I'll never forget.
    A. which   B. on which   C. in which   D. when
33. You can depend on whatever promise _____ he makes.
    A. /   B. why   C. when   D. whose
34. I'm interested in _____ you have said.
    A. all that   B. all what   C. that   D. which
35. Is there anyone in your class _____ family is in the country?
    A. who   B. who's   C. which   D. whose
36. Is _____ some German friends visited last week?
    A. this school   B. this the school   C. this school one   D. this school where
37. The factory _____ we'll visit next week is not far from here.
    A. where   B. to which   C. which   D. in which
38. Smoking, _____ is a bad habit, is, however, popular.
    A. that   B. which   C. /   D. though
39. The reason _____ he didn't come was _____ he was ill.
    A. why; that   B. that; why   C. for that; that   D. for which; what
40. This is the fastest train _____ is going to Nanjing.
    A. that   B. what   C. where   D. /

第二十一章

状语从句

热身训练： 下列句子各有一处错误，请指出并改正。

1. It wasn't long that he joined the job.
2. If I was only a child when I studied in that classroom, I will never forget it.
3. Will you go that our motherland needs us most after graduation?
4. As soon as we arrived, so we dropped the lines into the water.
5. It's been a week after we left your family and we are now back home.
6. We shouldn't do that dangerous experiment if the chemistry teacher is with us.
7. He has such little education that he is unable to find a job.
8. It was not until his mother came in the boy began to prepare his lessons.
9. I am sure I'll meet a kind-hearted man where I go.
10. I have been missing you very much after I went to college a year ago.
11. Hardly had the bell rung than the students took their seats.
12. Because we have come, let's stay and enjoy it.
13. Although we allow tomato plants to grow in the same place year after year, but we have never had any disease or insect attack problem.
14. Since the day went on, the weather got worse.
15. If it's difficult to make her dream come true, she never gives up.

在句子中用来修饰动词、形容词或副词,具有状语作用的从句称为状语从句。状语从句可放在句首或句末,偶尔也可放在句中。根据作用不同可分为以下十种:时间状语从句、地点状语从句、原因状语从句、目的状语从句、条件状语从句、让步状语从句、方式状语从句、结果状语从句和比较状语从句。

一、时间状语从句

（一）when、while 和 as 的用法

（1）when 引导时间状语从句时,意为"当……的时候,这时"。其引导的状语从句可表示一段时间,也可表示点时间,从句中的动词既可以用延续性动词,也可以用短暂性动词,从句的

动作可表示与主句的动作同时发生,也可表示在主句的动作之前或之后发生。例如:

When he arrived, I was cooking lunch. 他到的时候,我正在做午饭。

When he ran to the stop, the bus had gone. 当他跑到车站时,公共汽车已经开走了。(主句和从句动作前后发生,只可用 when)

I'll call you when the bus comes. 当公交车来的时候,我会喊你的。

When he was waiting for the bus, he was reading a book. 他边等车边看书。(从句中 wait 是延续性动词,when 可用 as/while 代替)

I was wandering in the street, when suddenly I caught sight of one of my old friends. 我在街上闲逛,这时突然看见一个老朋友。

(2) while 引导时间状语从句时,意为"当……的时候,在……期间"。它强调主句与从句的动作同时进行(从句与主句的谓语动词都必须是延续性的),或者主句的动作发生在从句动作的进行过程中(主句的谓语动词通常是短暂性的,从句的动词必须是延续性的)。例如:

She felt asleep while she was reading a book. 她在看书的时候睡着了。

She visited many scenic spots while she was in Jiujiang. 她在九江时游览了许多景点。

Strike while the iron is hot. 〈谚〉趁热打铁。

(3) as 引导时间状语从句时,意为"当……的时候,正当……之时,一边……一边……,随着……"。它强调主句和从句的两个动作同时发生(从句和主句的主语可以是同一个人,也可以不是同一个人);或者随着从句动作的发生,主句的动作也跟着发生。例如:

I saw her as she was shopping. 她在逛街时,我看见了她。

She fell down as she came downstairs. 她下楼时摔倒了。

She is walking as she is singing. 她边唱边走。

As she wrapped up some food in a cloth and gave it to the kids, her husband busied himself with preparing coffee for them. 当她用布包起一些食物给孩子们吃的时候,她丈夫忙着给他们准备咖啡。

As autumn comes, the leaves begin to turn yellow. 随着秋天的到来,树叶开始变黄了。

(二) until 和 till 的用法

until 和 till 作为连词,一般情况下可以互换使用。

(1) 用于肯定句时,即 until/till,意为"直到……为止",主句常常要用延续性动词,表示这个动作一直延续到 till/until 所表示的时间为止。例如:

She watched TV until/till her mother came back. 她一直在看电视直到她母亲回来为止。

He will persist until he succeed. 他将坚持不懈直到成功为止。

(2) 用于否定句时,即 not... until/till,意为"直到……(才)",主句常常用短暂续性动词,表示 until/till 所表示的时间一到,该动作就发生。例如:

He couldn't get in until he was given the key. 直到他得到钥匙才能进去。

She didn't go to bed until/till her mother came back. 直到她母亲回来,她才去睡觉。

(3) until 不可用 till 替换的情况有以下三种。

① not until 放在句首用于部分倒装句时。例如:

Not until her mother came back did she go to bed. 直到她妈妈回来,她才上床睡觉。

② not until 在强调句中时。例如:

It was not until her mother came back that she went to bed. 直到她妈妈回来,她才去睡觉。

③ until 放在句首时。例如:

Until I finished my homework, mother didn't let me out. (√) 直到我做完家庭作业,妈妈才准我出去。

Till I finished my homework, mother didn't let me out. (×)

(三) as soon as、once、the moment/instant/minute/second、immediately/directly/instantly 的用法

as soon as、once、the moment/instant/minute/second、immediately/directly/instantly 这些词引导时间状语从句时,意为"一……就……"在从句中可放句首也可放句末,偶尔也可放句中。例如:

As soon as he finished the exam, he went to his grandma's for the summer vacation. 他一考完试就去外婆家过暑假了。

Once you start, you should continue. 你一旦开了头,就应该继续下去。

The moment I received your letter, I set off. 我一收到你的信就出发了。

I informed you the instant I got the examination results. 我一得到考试结果就告知你了。

The second the alarm rang, he woke up. 闹钟一响,他就醒了。

The baby wants his mother to hold him immediately/directly/instantly he sees his mother. 宝宝一看见妈妈就要妈妈抱。

(四) no sooner... than、hardly/scarcely... when 的用法

这两个结构引导状语从句时,也译为"(刚)一……就"。主句常用过去完成时态,从句常用一般过去时态。当 no sooner、hardly、scarcely 等放在句首时,表示强调,主句主语和谓语动词要进行部分倒装。例如:

Jane had no sooner got home than someone knocked at the door.(= No sooner had Jane got home than someone knocked at the door.) 简刚到家就有人来敲门。

He had hardly/scarcely put his clothes in when it started to rain cats and dogs. (= Hardly/Scarcely had he put his clothes in when it started to rain cats and dogs.) 他刚把衣服收进来,天就开始下了倾盆大雨。

(五) every/each time 的用法

在引导状语从句时,every/each time 意为"每次"。从句可放句首或句末。例如:

Every/Each time she went to the nursing home, she would chat with the old to relieve their boredom. 她每次去敬老院,都会陪老人聊天解闷。

They are very enthusiastic every/each time we go to their dormitory. 我们每次去他们寝室,他们都很热情。

(六) any time 和 whenever 的用法

any time 和 whenever 在引导状语从句时,意为"随时,任何时候,无论什么时候/何时"。例如:

Any time/Whenever you come to Jiujiang, you must come to me. 无论你什么时候来九江,一定要来找我。

You only have to ask for it any time (that) you need help. 你任何时候需要帮忙,只要开口就行。

(七) the first/last/next time 的用法

the first/last/next time 在引导状语从句时,意为"第一次/上次/下次"。the last/next time 中的冠词 the 可以省略。例如:

The first time I came here, I had a good impression of it. 我第一次来这儿,就对这儿的印象很好。

I'll take you to Lushan Mountain (the) next time you come to Jiujiang. 你下次来九江的时候,我带你去庐山。

Last/The last time I went to Jingdezhen, I bought several blue and white porcelain cups. 上次去景德镇的时候,我买了几个青花瓷的杯子。

(八) since 的用法

(1) since 引导的时间状语从句的谓语动词为短暂性动词(如 come、go、arrive、leave、begin 等)的过去式,表示"自从该动作开始的那一刻起",主句用现在完成时或现在完成进行时,整个句子可以直接按照字面意思翻译。例如:

She has studied very hard since she came to the class. 自从来到这个班,她学习就非常努力。

The little boy has been crying since his mother left. 自从他母亲离开,这个小男孩就一直在哭。

(2) since 引导的时间状语从句的谓语动词为延续性动词或者静态动词(如 stay、lie、stand、learn、be 等)的过去式,表示"自从该动作或状态的完成或结束时算起",主句用现在完成时或者现在完成进行时,翻译时不能只按照字面翻译,而要译成"否定"意义。例如:

I haven't heard from him since he lived here. 从他不住这儿起,我就一直没有收到过他的信。

此句的意思为:I haven't heard from him since he left here. 自从他离开这儿,我就一直没收到他的信。

It is ten years since I was in the army. 我退伍十年了。

It has been almost 15 years since I was in my hometown. 我离开家乡已经快 15 年了。

注:since+延续性动词/状态动词与 since+短暂性动词的区别如下例句所示。

She has written to me since I was used to living here. (was 为状态动词)从我还不习惯这儿的生活起,她就经常给我写信。

She has written to me since I got used to living here. (got 为短暂性动词)自从我习惯了这儿的生活,她就经常给我写信。

(3) since 引导的时间状语从句的谓语动词为延续性动词或静态动词的现在完成时,表示从句的动作和状态延续到现在,主句用现在完成时或者现在完成进行时,翻译时可以直接按照字面意思理解。例如:

I have seldom heard from her since she has lived there. 自从她去那儿生活到现在为止,我就很少收到过她的来信。

It has been almost 15 years since I have been a teacher. 我当老师快15年了。

(4) "It is+时间段+since..."的句型,意为"从……起,已有多长时间了"。since 引导的从句通常用延续性动词的过去式,表示"这个动作结束的时间有多长了"。例如:

It is five years since he lived here. 他不住这儿五年了。

下列两个句子作比较:

It is five years since he has lived here./It is five years since he started to live here. 他住在这儿已有五年了。

注:对"他好久没学英语了。"这句话的英文翻译进行对错判断。
It is a long time since he studied English. (√)
It is a long time since he didn't studied English. (×)
因为 study 是为延续性动词的过去式,表示从该动作结束时算起。

(九) before/by the time 和 after 等连词的用法

(1) before/by the time 引导时间状语从句时,意为"在……(之)前",表示主句的动作在前,从句的动作在后;by the time 强调从句的动作之前,主句的动作已经完成,所以主句部分要用完成时态。例如:

Before you go to bed, turn off the lights. 你在睡觉前,把灯关掉。
It will be one week before my mother comes back. 我妈还要一周才回来。
She had left for Nanchang just before the job offer arrived. 她恰好在工作通知到达之前去南昌了。
By the time they arrived, we had already left. 他们到达前,我们已经离开了。
By the time they go to bed, we will have already gone. 他们睡觉前,我们已经走了。

注:"It be not long before..."的结构,意为"不久(之后),很快"。例如:
It was not long before she came back. 不久她便回来了。
It isn't long before we have a warm home. 不久我们就有了一个温暖的家。
It won't be long before you pay the price for your cheating. 不久你就会为你的欺骗付出代价。

(2) after 引导时间状语从句时,意为"在……(之)后",表示从句的动作在前,主句的动作在后。例如:

Please tell us your decision after you think it over. 仔细考虑后请把你的决定告诉我们。
After he had finished his homework, he went to bed. 他做完作业后就上床睡觉了。

二、地点状语从句

(一) where 的用法

where 引导地点状语从句,意为"在……地方"。例如:

The school stood where the two roads meet. 这所学校坐落在两条路交汇的地方。
Where there is a big river, there is a big city. 哪儿有大河,哪儿就有大城市。

> 注：where 引导状语从句，在句型"Where there is…, there is… "中表示条件的含义。例如：
> Where there is a will, there is a way.〈谚〉有志者事竟成。
> Where there is love, there is happiness. 只要有爱，就会有幸福。
> Where there is no purchase, there is no sale. 只要没有买，就不会有卖。

（二）wherever/anywhere/everywhere 的用法

wherever、anywhere、everywhere 引导地点状语从句，意为"无论何地，在任何地方"。例如：
Make marks wherever/anywhere/everywhere you have questions. 在任何有问题的地方做出标记。
You can live wherever/anywhere/everywhere you like. 你可以住在你喜欢的任何地方。

三、原因状语从句

（一）because、since/now（that）和 as 的用法

这四个词引导原因状语从句时，都有"因为"的含义。

（1）because 引导的从句语气最强，意为"因为"，是对 why 提出的问题的回答，表示直接的因果关系，多放于主句之后。只有在特别强调原因时，才放于主句之前。例如：
I'm not going there because I don't want to. 我不去是因为我不想去。
Because they were talking in French, we couldn't understand them. 因为他们说的是法语，所以我们听不懂他们在讲什么。
He was angry not because we were late but because we made a noise. 他生气不是因为我们迟到了，而是因为我们吵闹了。

> 注：① because 和 so 不能出现在同一个句子中，句中有 because 就不能有 so，有 so 就不能出现 because。例如：
> I do it because I want to do it. 我这么做是因为我想这么做。
> I want to do it so I do it. 我想这么做，因此我就这么做了。
> ② "not... because..."常常译为"并不是因为"，例如：
> I didn't take a raincoat because it was raining.
> 我不带雨衣是因为下雨。（×）
> 我带雨衣并不是因为下雨。（√）
> The ring is not valuable because the precious stones are set in.
> 这枚戒指值钱并不是因为那些宝石镶在里面。（√）
> 这枚戒指不值钱，因为那些宝石镶在里面。（×）

（2）since 引导的从句语气比 because 稍弱，意为"既然"相当于 now（that），而 as 引导从句的语气比 since 还要弱，意为"由于"，并且这两个词引导从句表述的是很明显的、已知的原因，所以多放于主句前，也可用于主句之后。例如：
Since we have no enough money, we can't buy the car. 既然我们钱不够，就无法买下这辆车了。
Since you don't trust him, you shouldn't work with him. 既然你不信任他，就不应该和他一起

工作。

I left a message as you weren't there. 因为你不在，我就留了个口信。

As it is raining, you'd better take a taxi. 因为下雨，你最好打出租车。

> **注**：for 作为并列连词，连接的是两个并列的分句。for 后面的分句不能放在句首，且和前面的分句要用逗号隔开；for 后面的分句所表达的原因，并非前面分句行为发生的直接原因，而是推断出来的原因，只提供辅助性的补充说明。例如：
> They stay home, for it's raining heavily. 他们待在家里，因为雨下得很大。
> She rarely goes out now, for she is very old. 她现在很少出去，因为她年纪很大了。

（二）seeing (that)、now (that)、considering (that) 和 in that 的用法

seeing (that)、now (that)、considering (that) 和 in that 这几个连词同 as 和 since 意义相近，都有"既然，是因为，鉴于某个事实"的意思，通常用于正式场合中。in that 相当于 because，意为"因为，就在于"。例如：

Seeing (that) she doesn't want to go to school, there's no need to buy school supplies for her. 既然她不愿去上学，那就没有必要为她买学习用品了。

Now (that) you are grown up, you should find a job to support yourself. 你已经长大了，就应该找工作养活你自己。

Considering (that) everyone is here, let's go. 既然大家都到了，我们出发吧。

Men differ from brutes in that they can think and speak. 人不同于兽类就在于/因为人能思考和说话。

四、条件状语从句

（一）if 和 unless 的用法比较

if 和 unless 两个连词都引导条件状语从句。if 表示正面条件，意为"如果"；unless 表示反面条件，意为"除非……否则……；若非，如果不"，相当于"if... not"，但语气较强。例如：

You'll fail the exam if you don't study hard. 如果你不努力学习，你就会考试不及格。

＝You'll fail the exam unless you study hard. 除非你努力学习，否则你会考试不及格。

If it rains, we won't go out. 如果天下雨，我们就不出去了。

If we do not fail Nature, Nature shall never fail us. 人不负青山，青山定不负人。

We won't forgive you unless you admit your mistake. 除非你承认错误，否则我们就不原谅你。

（二）only if 和 if only 的区别

only if 引导的条件状语从句为肯定句，且用陈述语气，意为"只有"。如果从句放句首，主句主谓要部分倒装。if only 引导的条件状语从句多为感叹句，要用虚拟语气，意为"但愿/要是……就好了"。例如：

I will give you a gift as a reward only if you pass the exam.

＝Only if you pass the exam will I give you a gift as a reward. 只有你通过了考试，我才会送你一件礼物，作为奖励。

228

If only you had passed the exam! 要是你通过了这次考试就好了！（虚拟语气）

If only I had enough money, I could buy the book. 要是我有足够的钱就好了,我就能买这本书了。（虚拟语气）

（三）其他连词的用法

（1）providing 和 provided 引导条件状语从句,意为"只要,要是,如果"。例如：

Providing/Provided (that) you don't cry, I will call your mom back. 只要你不哭,我就叫你妈妈回来。

I will work for him providing/provided (that) he hires me. 只要他雇我,我就为他工作。

（2）suppose 和 supposing 引导条件状语从句,意为"假如,假若,如果"。suppose 引导从句时,必须放主句前,而 supposing 既可放主句前也可放主句后。例如：

Suppose/Supposing (that) we don't catch the school bus, what shall we do? 假如我们没有赶上校车,那该怎么办？

Who else can we ask for help supposing (that) they refuse us? 假如他们拒绝我们,我们还能向谁求助呢？

（3）so/as long as 引导条件状语从句,意为"只要"。例如：

So/As long as one keeps calm, one doesn't feel the heat too much. 只要你保持平静,你就不会觉得太热。（心静自然凉。）

You can use my dictionary so/as long as you don't keep it too long. 只要你使用的时间不会太长,你可以用我的字典。

（4）so/as far as 引导条件状语从句,意为"就……（而言）"。但是在表示"只要"时,只能用 as far as,相当于 as/so long as。例如：

So/As far as I'm concerned, it doesn't matter who wins. 就我而言,谁赢并不重要。

I'll try my best to help you as far as I can. 只要我力所能及,我就会尽力来帮你。

（5）in case (that) 引导条件状语从句,意为"假如,如果,万一"。例如：

In case (that) you need help, don't hesitate to let me know. 如果你需要帮忙,随时告诉我。

We can't go in case (that) it rains. 万一下雨,我们就去不了了。

五、方式状语从句

（一）as if/as though 的用法

as if 和 as though 引导方式状语从句,意为"好像,似乎,仿佛"。从句可以用陈述语气,表示(可能)符合事实的情况；也可以用虚拟语气,表示不符合事实或与事实相反的情况。例如：

He walks as if he is drunk.（陈述语气,醉了）

He walks as if he were drunk.（虚拟语气,没醉）

他走起路来就像喝醉了一样。

She is looking at me as if/though she knows me.（陈述语气,她认识我）

She is looking at me as if/though she knew me.（虚拟语气,她不认识我）

她看着我,就好像认识我一样。

He talked to me as if/though he had been a teacher.（虚拟语气,他不是老师）

他跟我说起话来就好像他是个老师似的。
She cried out as if/though she had been bitten by a snake.（虚拟语气，她没被蛇咬）
她大叫起来，好像被蛇咬了似的。

（二）as 的用法

（1）as 引导方式状语从句，意为"按照，如，像"。例如：
You must do as the prophet tells you. 你必须按照先知说的去做。
She performed as the teacher taught her. 她按照老师教的表演了。
When in Rome, do as the Romans do. 〈谚〉入乡随俗。

（2）as 之前可用 just 或 exactly 加强语气，意为"正如"。例如：
Most plants need air just/exactly as they need water. 大部分的植物需要空气，正如它们需要水一样。
We can't live without air, just/exactly as fish can't live without water. 我们离不开空气，就如鱼离不开水一样。

> 注：有时 what 也可以引导方式状语从句，且常可用 as 代替。例如：
> Leaves are to the plants what/as lungs are to the animals. 叶之于植物，犹如肺之于动物。
> An individual is to a country what/as a screw is to a machine. 一个人对于国家的作用，就如同螺丝钉对于机器一样。
> 以上句子还可以用"(just) as... so..."的结构来表示，当 as 位于句首时，引导的从句带有比喻的含义，意为"正如，就像"。例如：
> As/Just as lungs are to the animals, so leaves are to the plants. 叶之于植物，正如肺之于动物。
> As/Just as a screw is to a machine, so an individual is to a country. 一个人对于国家的作用，就如同螺丝钉对于机器一样。

六、让步状语从句

（一）even if/though、though 和 although 的用法

even if/though、though 和 although 四个连词引导让步状语从句，意为"尽管，虽然"。even if 和 even though 的让步语气最强，although 次之，though 最弱。though 可用在倒装句中，although 则不可以。例如：
We'll make a trip even if/though the weather is bad. 即使天气不好，我们也要来一次旅行。
Even if the salary he gives us now isn't high, we are willing to work for him. 即使他现在给我们的工资不高，我们也愿意为他工作。
Though/Although it is heavily raining, the farmers are still working on the farm. 尽管雨下得很大，农民们仍在农场干活。
Hard though he worked, he made little progress. 尽管他工作努力，但进展不大。

（二）while 和 as 的用法

（1）while 引导让步状语从句，其意思相当于 although，所引导的从句必须放在主句前。例如：

While I understand what you mean, I can't approve of you. 虽然我明白你的意思，但我不能赞同你。

While he is old, he is still energetic and dynamic. 虽然他年纪大了，但依然精力充沛，很有活力。

（2）as 引导让步状语从句时，要把表语、状语或谓语动词等放在 as 之前，形成部分倒装。当表语是单数可数名词时，不用冠词。可以和 though 互换。例如：

Much as/though I like English, I don't study it well.（much 为副词，状语）
= Although I like English much, I don't study it well. 虽然我很喜欢英语，但我学得不好。

Successful as/though she is, she isn't proud.（successful 为形容词，表语）
= Although she is successful, she isn't proud. 虽然她很成功，但并不骄傲。

Child as/though he is, he knows a lot.（child 为名词，表语）
= Although he is a child, he knows a lot. 尽管他是个孩子，但懂得很多。

Object as/though you may, I'll go.（object 为动词）
= Although you may object, I'll go. 虽然你可能会反对，但我还是会去。

注：as 引导倒装的状语从句在某些情况下也可表示原因。例如：

Interested as she was in the book, she read it late at night. 因为她对这本书很感兴趣，所以看到深夜。

Actress as she is, she can play the old lady vividly. 因为她是个演员，所以可以把老太太演得惟妙惟肖。

（三）whether or not、whatever、whoever、however、wherever 的用法

连词 whether or not、whatever、whoever、however、wherever 都可以引导让步状语从句，意为"不论/无论/不管……"

（1）whether or not 意为"不论/无论/不管是否"。例如：

Whether or not they come, we will hold a sports meeting. 无论他们来不来，我们都要举办运动会。

Whether you participate or not, we will finish the task. 无论你是否参与，我们都要完成这项任务。

（2）whatever 相当于 no matter what，意为"不论/无论/不管什么"。例如：

We will support you whatever/no matter what you decide. 不管你如何决定，我们都会支持你。

（3）whoever 相当于 no matter who，意为"不论/无论/不管谁"。例如：

Whoever/No matter who asks you, don't reply. 不管谁问你，都不要回答。

（4）however 相当于 no matter how，意为"不论/无论/不管怎样"。例如：

However/No matter how late it is, she will wait for him to come back. 无论多晚，她都会等他回来。

No matter how the U.S. blocks space technology from China, China eventually has its own space station. 无论美国如何阻止空间技术进入中国，中国最终还是拥有了自己的空间站。

（5）wherever 相当于 no matter where，意为"不论/无论/不管何地/哪里"。例如：

In China, they will live happily wherever/no matter where they are. 在中国，无论他们在哪

里,都会生活得很好。

(6) whenever 相当于 no matter when,意为"无论/不论/不管何时"。例如:

Whenever the invaders come, we will fight for our country. 不管侵略者什么时候来,我们都要为祖国而战。

(四) be 的用法

be 引导让步状语从句时,从句的主语和 be 动词必须倒装。例如:

My motherland, be you poor or rich, I love you forever. 我的祖国,无论您是贫穷还是富裕,我永远爱您。

We are friends, be you right or wrong. 不管你是对还是错,我们都是朋友。

七、目的状语从句

(一) so that 和 in order that 的用法

so that 和 in order that 两种连词引导目的状语从句时,意为"为了,以便"。常与情态动词 can、could、may、might 等连用。例如:

China persists in zero COVID-19 policy in order that/so that people can get the greatest protection. 中国坚持新冠清零政策,以使人们能在最大程度上获得保护。

In order that she should/would/might buy fresh vegetable, she came to the market early. 为了买到新鲜的菜,她早早来到菜市场。

She has practiced driving many times in order that/so that she can get her driving license. 为了能拿到驾照,她已练习开车多次。

In order that she can improve oral English well, she always goes to the English corner. 为了练好英语口语,她总是去英语角。

> 注:so that 引导目的状语从句时,so 经常可以省略。例如:
> Speak slowly (so) that we can understand you. 你说慢点,以便我们能听得懂。

(二) in case、lest (that) 和 for fear (that) 的用法

连词 in case、lest (that) 和 for fear (that) 引导目的状语从句时,一般用虚拟语气,从句谓语动词用"(should)+动词原型"。in case 意为"以防,免得,万一",lest 意为"免得,以免",for fear 意为"以防,以免,唯恐,生怕,害怕";in case 也可用陈述语气。例如:

She dared not dress like this lest she (should) be laughed at. 她不敢如此穿衣唯恐被人嘲笑。(虚拟语气)

Wear your mask in case you (should) get infected. 戴上口罩,以防被感染。(虚拟语气)

She is now walking after her son for fear (that) he (should) lose his way home. 她现在正跟在她儿子后面走,生怕他回家迷路。(虚拟语气)

She takes a flashlight in case it gets dark and she can't see the way home. 她带着手电筒,以防天黑了,她看不见回家的路。(陈述语气)

八、结果状语从句

（一）such... that...的用法

such... that...结构引导从句时，意为"如此……以致……"such 后接名词结构，such 放句首表强调时，主句主谓需要部分倒装。例如：

Shirley has such a beautiful garden that she can stay in it all day.
=Such a beautiful garden does Shirley have that she can stay in it all day. 雪莉有一座如此美丽的花园，以致她可以整天待在里面。

They are such advanced chips that the country needs them. 它们是如此先进的芯片，国家需要它们。

It is such snowy weather that we can make a snowman. 如此大雪天，我们可以堆雪人了。

（二）so... that... 的用法

so... that... 结构引导从句时，意为"如此……以致……"。so 后接形容词或副词，并经常用来修饰 much、many、few 和 little（such 后面不可接这些词）。放句首表强调时，主句主谓需要部分倒装。例如：

The math problem is so complex that nobody in our class can solve it.
=So complex is the math problem that nobody in our class can solve it. 这道数学题太复杂了，我们班上没有人能解出来。

He ran so fast at the sports meeting that no one could catch up with him.
=So fast did he run at the sports meeting that no one could catch up with him. 他在运动会上跑得如此之快，以致没人能追上他。

He lost so many points in the game that he was eliminated. 他在比赛中丢了那么多分，以致被淘汰了。

She lost so much money that she couldn't pay for her mother's treatment. 她丢失如此多的钱，以致付不起母亲的治疗费。

He has so few relatives that no one can help him. 他的亲人如此少，以致连个能帮他的人都没有。

He made so little money that his wife had to find a part-time job to support the family. 他挣的钱如此少，以致他的妻子不得不找一份兼职来养家。

> 注：so... that... 和 such... that... 的结构表达同样含义的一句话时，so 后面接形容词再接名词，such 后面直接接名词短语。例如：
> It is so difficult a job that the experienced engineer Jack can't do it.
> It is such a difficult job that the experienced engineer Jack can't do it.
> 这项工作太难了，经验丰富的工程师杰克也做不了。

（三）so（that）的用法

so（that）引导结果状语从句时，意为"以致，因此，所以"。

It's extremely cold today, so (that) rime appears in Lushan mountains. 今天极其冷,庐山出现了雾凇。

> 注:so that 可引导目的状语从句,也可引导结果状语从句。例如:
> ① 引导目的状语从句时,意为"为了,以便",so that 可以用 in order that 代替,放在主句前面或后面均可。例如:
> They departed early (so) that they could catch the company bus. 他们早早出发以便赶上公司的大巴车。
> In order that they could catch the company bus, they departed early. 为了能赶上公司的大巴车,他们早早出发了。
> ② 引导结果状语从句时,意为"以致,因此,所以",只可放于主句后,常用逗号隔开,并且 that 可以省略。例如:
> They departed early, so (that) they caught the company bus. 他们出发得早,所以赶上了公司的大巴车。

九、比较状语从句

(一) than 的用法

(1) "形容词/副词的比较级+than+从句"的结构,意为"比……更……"。例如:
He did better in the exam than I expected. 他考试考得比我预期的好。
Jane earned more money this month than Tim did in the past year. 简这个月赚到的钱比蒂姆过去一年赚的都多。

(2) "not+形容词/副词比较级+than+从句"的结构,意为"不比……更……"。例如:
He doesn't perform better this year than he did last year. 他今年的表现并不比去年好。
He didn't draw the painting just now worse than his classmate did yesterday. 他刚画的这幅画并不比他同学昨天画的画差。

(二) as... as... 的用法

(1) "as+形容词/副词+as+从句"的结构,意为"和……一样"。例如:
She was dressed as pretty as I thought she was. 她打扮得和我想象中一样漂亮。
I hope my son can cherish food as much as I do. 我希望我儿子能和我一样珍惜食物。
You are as smart as I expected. 你和我预想得一样聪明。

(2) "倍数+as+形容词/副词+as+从句"的结构,意为"……是……的几倍"。例如:
Bonnie has done twice as much housework today as she did yesterday. 邦妮今天所做的家务活是昨天做的两倍。
There are ten times as many flowers here as they saw yesterday. 这里的花是他们昨天看到的十倍。
The old man treats me twice as well as he does Jack. 这位老人对待我要比对杰克好上一倍。

(三) not so/as... as 的用法

"not so/as+形容词/副词+as+从句"的结构,意为"不像……那样,不如……"。例如:

Life there is not so/as comfortable as it was last year. 那里的生活不像去年那样舒适。

He doesn't speak English so/as fluently as his English teacher expected. 他英语说得不如他英语老师所期望的那样流利。

He only ate a little food, not as much as his elder sister did. 他只吃了一点点食物，没有他姐姐吃得多。

（四）the+形容词/副词的比较级……，the+形容词/副词的比较级……的用法

"the+形容词/副词的比较级……，the+形容词/副词的比较级……"的结构，意为"越……，就越……"。例如：

The more carefully he thought about it, the clearer it became to him that this was a job for someone with experience. 他想得越仔细，就越清楚这是一份需要有经验的人做的工作。

The bigger they are, the harder they fall. 〈谚〉爬得越高，摔得越重。

The more challenges we face, the more imperative it is for us to break waves and forge ahead. 我们面临的挑战越多，我们就越需要打破僵局，勇往直前。

十、状语从句中的省略

当状语从句的主语与主句的主语一致或是代词 it，且谓语部分含有 be 时，则从句的主语和 be 可以同时一起省略。

（1）时间状语从句。例如：

When (he was) in primary school, he was determined to defend his country. 当他上小学的时候，就立志要保家卫国。

When (it is) cooked, the shrimp turns red. 当虾煮熟时会变红。

The peanuts should be dug out when (they are) ripe. 花生成熟时，就应该被挖出来。

Metals expand when (they are) heated and contract when (they are) cooled. 金属热胀冷缩。

（2）地点状语从句。例如：

Where (they are) needed, the medical staff will go. 哪儿需要医务人员，他们就会去哪儿。

Spend the sum of money where (it is) necessary badly. 把这笔钱花在急需的地方。

Avoid this mistake wherever (it is) possible. 这种错误随处都要避免。

（3）条件状语从句。例如：

If (it is) essential, I will buy a computer. 如果有必要，我会买一台计算机。

Unless (he is) asked, he won't answer. 除非被问，否则他不会说。

If (you are) grateful for her help, you should say thanks to her. 如果你感谢她的帮助，你应该对她说声谢谢。

You may be in legal trouble once (you're) in debt. 一旦你负债累累，你就可能会陷入法律困境之中。

（4）让步状语从句。例如：

Although (she was) very tired, she cooked dinner for the whole family. 尽管她很累，但她还是为全家人做了晚餐。

Even if (I were) asked, I would not answer. 即便有人问我，我也不会回答。

His behaviors, whether (they are) good or evil, make a deep impression on us. 他的行为，无论善恶，都给我们留下了深刻的印象。

（5）方式状语从句。例如：

She opened her mouth as if (she was) to ask for help. 她张开嘴，好像要寻求帮助似的。

She is pulling me as if (she were) catching a life-saving straw. 她拉着我就好像抓住一棵救命稻草一样。

Make sentences as (you are) required. 按要求造句。

（6）比较状语从句。例如：

The cross-talk show yesterday was more wonderful than (it was) expected. 昨天的相声表演比预期的精彩。

The fuel is consumed much faster than (it was) before. 燃料比以前消耗得快多了。

巩 固 练 习

Complete the following sentences by choosing the items marked A, B, C, or D.

1. A survey of transport department has showed that as many as 50% of drivers do not drive cars _____.

   A. like directed   B. as directed   C. as being directed   D. so that directed

2. _____ reason you may give, you ought not to have left homework unfinished.

   A. What   B. No matter   C. However   D. Whatever

3. It was _____ he was ill that he didn't go to school.

   A. since   B. as   C. because   D. though

4. The secretary made a note of it _____ she should forget.

   A. in order that   B. in case   C. so that   D. ever when

5. No matter _____ says no to us, we will return to our motherland.

   A. what   B. whatever   C. whoever   D. who

6. I'll start early _____ I oversleep.

   A. unless   B. though   C. if   D. whether

7. You'll surely make progress _____ you work with a strong will.

   A. unless   B. until   C. as long as   D. as well as

8. He wouldn't give up smoking _____ his doctor told him it was a matter of life and death.

   A. except   B. after   C. until   D. in case

9. I sent the letter early that morning _____ she got it that afternoon.

   A. in order that   B. so that   C. for purpose that   D. in order for

10. I paid only 5 pounds for the book, _____ I expected it would cost.

    A. not as many as   B. not so much as

    C. cheaper than   D. not so expensive

11. He always talks _____ he had been to outer space.

    A. like   B. as if/though   C. because of   D. as

12. He was walking along the sands _____ he saw a big foot-print in the sand.
    A. while   B. when   C. as   D. after
13. Jack was very tired _____ he played tennis all afternoon.
    A. if   B. as soon as   C. because   D. before
14. _____ he finished his work, he left hurriedly.
    A. As soon as   B. As if   C. Unless   D. In order that
15. We are going to have a barbecue _____ it rains.
    A. if not   B. when   C. except that   D. unless
16. _____, I am sure that he is honest.
    A. No matter people say   B. What people say
    C. Whatever people say   D. It doesn't matter people say
17. It won't be long _____ you regret what you've done.
    A. after   B. before   C. since   D. then
18. The price of diamond rings has risen sharply _____ the price of gold rings has gone down.
    A. while   B. as   C. when   D. otherwise
19. It seemed only several minutes _____ he finished this painting.
    A. after   B. before   C. when   D. until
20. Eat less food _____ you want to put on weight.
    A. if   B. unless   C. until   D. as soon as
21. It looks _____ it's going to rain.
    A. that   B. as   C. as if   D. that
22. _____ he is, he will be thinking of you.
    A. Wherever   B. Where   C. Whether   D. What
23. Be careful while _____ the road.
    A. crossing   B. to cross   C. crossed   D. having crossed
24. _____ the film may be, I have no time to see it.
    A. Although exciting   B. No matter exciting
    C. Even if excited   D. However exciting
25. _____ he said he wasn't hungry, he ate the big breakfast.
    A. Even   B. Unless   C. As   D. Although
26. Tired _____ he was, he decided not to trouble her.
    A. as   B. although   C. unless   D. even if
27. _____ you have got used to it, you'll like it.
    A. While   B. On the condition   C. Once   D. Unless
28. We'll never give up _____ they may do or say.
    A. although that   B. no matter how   C. whatever   D. however
29. Generally speaking, _____ according to direction, the drug has no side effect.
    A. when taken   B. when taking   C. when to take   D. when to be taken

30. I'll lend you my car _____ you return it intact.
    A. as long as   B. so far as   C. unless   D. until
31. _____ you begin the work, you must carry it out through to the end.
    A. When   B. Though   C. Sometimes   D. Once
32. I'll get up early, _____ it is dark or light.
    A. however   B. whether   C. if   D. though
33. I'll leave him a note _____ he'll know where we are.
    A. so that   B. so as   C. in order   D. for
34. He is _____ strongly built that he looks _____ he could lift an elephant.
    A. such; as if   B. such; like   C. so; as if   D. so; like
35. Smith has made _____ that we are all surprised.
    A. so much progress   B. such much progress
    C. such a great progress as   D. so fine a progress
36. _____, he is good at drawing.
    A. To be a child   B. A child as he is   C. As a child   D. Child as he is
37. When _____ for his views about his teaching job, Philip said he found it very interesting and rewarding.
    A. asking   B. asked   C. having asked   D. to be asked
38. You'd better do _____ you are required.
    A. like   B. which   C. that   D. as
39. _____ that none of us could follow him.
    A. He spoke very fast   B. So fast he spoke
    C. So fast did he speak   D. Too fast he spoke
40. _____ the baby fell asleep _____ the room.
    A. After; did the mother leave   B. Not until; did the mother leave
    C. Not until; the mother left   D. Soon after; the mother had left

第二十二章

一致关系

热身训练： 下列句子各有一处错误，请指出并改正。

1. For example, Shanghai food, a little bit sweet, differ from Sichuan food that is rather hot.
2. He would ask who we was and pretend not to know us.
3. Earning their own money allow them to spend on anything as they please.
4. My dream school look like a big garden.
5. Suddenly the arrows was flying down at us from the sky — they looked like rain!
6. There exist now a park that has a small river running through.
7. Hard work have made him very ill.
8. A great number of students in this school is League members.
9. Now my friend Ann, together with me, are going to do field study.
10. The classroom is a place for learning and that include learning from textbooks and mistakes as well.
11. Anyone can borrow books if he or she wish.
12. My brother is one of the students who has been chosen to join the force.
13. He looked up at us and said, "I just want to know what the sign say."
14. The early morning barking have been disturbing us as we are often up all night with the baby.
15. My brother as well as I are taking drawing classes from Ms. Pearl.

  一致关系是指句子成分之间或词语之间必须在人称、数、性别等方面保持一致。英语中的一致关系主要是指主谓一致、名词代词一致，另外还有同等成分的一致。

一、主语和谓语的一致

  主谓一致是指主语和谓语在人称和数两方面保持一致，即谓语动词随着主语的人称和数的不同而做相应的变化。一般遵循以下三个原则。

  （1）语法一致原则——语法形式上取得一致。即主语为单数形式，谓语动词用单数形式；主语为复数形式，谓语动词也用复数形式。例如：

  Our monitor sings the best in our class. 我们班长在我们班歌唱得最好。

  My kids are watching TV. 我的孩子们正在看电视。

  The sixth plenary session of the 19th CPC Central Committee has adopted the Party's third resolution on historical issues. 中国共产党的十九届六中全会通过了党的第三个历史决议。

（2）意义一致原则——根据实际意义取得一致。即有时主语虽然在形式上是单数，但实际意义为复数，此时谓语动词须用复数形式。例如：

Mankind long for peace. 人类渴望和平。

The cattle are grazing on the mountain slopes. 牛群正在山坡上吃草。

（3）邻近一致原则——谓语动词的数与靠得最近的主语的数保持一致。例如：

There is one table and four chairs in the room. 房间里有一张餐桌和四把椅子。

Neither you nor I am wrong. 你和我都没有错。

下面介绍几种不同类型主语的主谓一致原则。

（一）并列结构作主语

（1）两个或两个以上不同的人或物，由 and 连接起来并列作主语时，谓语动词用复数。例如：

The Yellow River and the Yangtze River are two "mother rivers" of the Chinese nation. 黄河长江是中华民族的母亲河。

Air and water are essential for our daily life. 空气和水是我们日常生活的必需品。

The hard work and dedication of countless unsung heroes have all added to the great momentum of China's march forward in the new era. 无数平凡英雄拼搏奋斗，汇聚成新时代中国昂扬奋进的洪流。

（2）and 连接两个名词时，若表示同一个人或物，或被视为一个整体时，则谓语动词用单数，例如：

A poet and painter has come to our school. 一位诗人兼画家来我们学校了。

There is a knife and fork on the plate. 盘子里有一副刀叉。

Bread and butter is my favourite breakfast. 黄油面包是我最喜欢的早餐。

Realization of moderately prosperous society in all respects and elimination of extreme poverty is what the CPC has delivered to our people. 全面小康、摆脱贫困是中国共产党给人民的交代。

（3）由 not... but、not only... but also、or、ether... or、neither... nor 等连接的两个或两个以上的并列主语，谓语动词与靠得最近的主语在人称和数上保持一致。例如：

Either she or I am wrong. 要么是她，要么是我错了。

Either you or he was driving against traffic regulations. 不是你就是他违章驾驶。

Neither my sister nor I am coming to the dinner party. 我和我妹妹都不会参加宴会。

Not only the mother but also the children are cleaning the house. 妈妈和孩子们都在搞卫生。

（4）"each/every/no/many a+单数名词+and+each/every/no/many a+单数名词"结构作主语时，谓语动词用单数，这种结构中的第二个 each、every、no、many a 可以省略。例如：

Each boy and (each) girl has a pen. 每个孩子都有一支笔。

Many a boy and (many a) girl has read the story. 许多男孩和女孩都读过这个故事。

Every man, woman and child needs love. 每个男人、女人和儿童都需要爱。

No teacher and no student likes this book. 没有教师，也没有学生喜欢这本书。

（5）主语后面带有 besides、but、except、including、like、plus、accompanied by、along with、as much as、as well as、combined with、in addition to、instead of、no less than、rather than、together with

等引导的短语时,谓语动词按主语的单复数而定,不考虑后面的短语。例如:

Nothing but some books was lost. 除了一些书,其他什么也没有丢。

The teacher along with his students is visiting a factory. 那位老师带着他的学生正在参观一家工厂。

The teacher, rather than the students, is responsible. 应负责任的是老师,而不是学生。

All the team players have left except the coach. 除了教练之外,所有队员都离开了。

Mother together with her children is cooking in the kitchen. 妈妈和孩子们一起在厨房做饭。

(二)集体名词作主语

(1)集体名词 mankind、militia、people、personnel、police、youth、cattle、poultry 等(尤其是有生命的物体)作主语时,谓语动词通常用复数形式。例如:

The police have caught the murderer. 警方已经抓到了杀人犯。

People are enjoying themselves over there. 人们在那边玩得很开心。

A lot of cattle were killed because of his wrong decision. 因他的错误决策许多牲畜被屠宰。

> **注**:当 people 作为"民族", youth 作为"男青年"时,有单数和复数两种形式,谓语动词应与主语单复数形式保持一致。例如:
> He is a youth of twenty. 他是一个20岁小伙子。
> Many English-speaking peoples are fond of the movie. 许多说英语的民族都喜欢这部电影。

(2)集体名词 clothing、equipment、furniture、hardware、information、jewelry、luggage、machinery、merchandise(商品)、poetry、stationery 等(尤其是无生命的物体)作主语时,其谓语动词用单数形式。例如:

The furniture is not hers. 这家具不是她的。

The Chinese stationery enters the overseas market. 中国文具进入海外市场。

His luggage has arrived undamaged. 他的行李完好无损地运到了。

(3)集体名词 army、audience、band、class、committee、couple、crew、crowd、faculty、family、government、group、jury、public、staff、team、troop、union、village 等作主语,若被看作一个整体时,谓语动词用单数形式;若被看作具体成员时,谓语动词用复数形式。例如:

Over half of the staff is female. 半数以上的职工是女性。

Most of our sales staff are working on line now. 我们的销售人员现在大多在线开展业务。

The family is rich. 这个家庭很富有。

My family all like playing basketball. 我的家人都喜欢打篮球。

The committee was set up last year. 这个委员会是去年成立的。

The committee are mostly young people. 这个委员会的成员大都是年轻人。

(三)单复数同形的名词作主语

单复数同形的名词作主语时,根据"意义一致原则"判定谓语动词的单复数形式。常用的这类名词有:aircraft、antelope、crossroads、deer、fish、headquarters、means、series、species、sheep、works 等。例如:

Every possible means has been tried. 每一种可能的方法都试过了。

All possible means have been tried. 所有可能的方法都试过了。

The species of fish are numerous. 鱼的种类繁多。

This species of fish is very rare. 这种鱼很稀有。

There is a sheep under the tree. 那棵树下有一只羊。

There are a flock of sheep near the tree. 那棵树附近有一群羊。

（四）含数量词的名词短语作主语

（1）表示时间、金额、距离、重量等名词复数形式作主语时，通常把它们看作一个整体，谓语动词用单数形式。例如：

Eighty miles has been covered. 已经走了80英里。

Twenty dollars is enough for him. 给他20美元就够了。

Eight hours of sleep is enough. 8小时的睡眠是足够的。

（2）one and a half+名词（复数）、many a+名词（单数）、more than one+名词（单数）等作主语时，谓语动词用单数。例如：

One and a half years has passed since we met last. 自从我们上次见面，一年半的时间过去了。

More than one boy has read the story. 不止一个男孩读了这个故事。

Many a woman has great influence on her husband. 许多女人对丈夫有很大影响。

（3）a kind/list/pair/portion/series/species+of+名词等作主语时，谓语动词往往用单数形式。例如：

A series of questions was asked by the student. 那个学生问了一系列问题。

A pair of 3D vision glasses is needed to see this movie. 看这部电影，需要一副3D眼镜。

A large portion of the test papers has been corrected. 大部分的试卷批改了。

（4）a number of+名词（复数）作主语，谓语动词用复数形式；the number of+名词（复数）作主语，谓语动词用单数形式。例如：

A number of migrant workers are from poor districts. 许多农民工来自贫困地区。

The number of pages in this book is three hundred. 这本书有300页。

（5）分数/百分数+of+名词作主语时，谓语动词的形式按of短语中的名词单复数而定。例如：

Three fourths of the students in the class are girls. 这个班四分之三的学生是女孩。

More than 70 percent of the earth's surface is covered by water. 地球表面70%以上是水。

Over sixty percent of the doctors are women. 百分之六十以上的医生是女性。

（6）half/most/rest/plenty+of+名词"等作主语时，谓语动词形式按of短语中的名词单复数而定。例如：

Half of the fruit is bad. 一半水果是坏的。

Half of the girls are Chinese. 一半女生是中国人。

Most of the students in the class are from the countryside. 这个班大多数学生来自于农村。

The rest of the work is finished. 其余工作都完成了。

Plenty of petroleum is imported from Russia. 大量的石油是从俄罗斯进口的。

Plenty of illegal publications were burnt. 许多非法出版物被焚毁。

（五）不定代词作主语

（1）each、either、neither 等代词作主语时，谓语动词用单数形式。例如：
Each man has his fault. 每个人都有缺点。
Neither of them is satisfactory. 两个都不令人满意。
Each of the twenty guests was given a present. 给 20 位客人每人赠送了一份礼品。

（2）somebody、someone、anybody、anyone、nobody、no one、everybody、everyone、something、anything、nothing、everything 等代词作主语时，谓语动词用单数形式。例如：
No one wants to read such books. 没有人想看那样的书。
Nobody is to blame for it. 这谁也不怨。
Someone is asking to see you. 有人找你。
Everything is ready for the sports meeting. 运动会的一切准备工作都已就绪。

（3）all、some 等代词作主语时，遵循"意义一致原则"，其谓语的单复数形式根据它们所代替的含义来确定。none of+复数名词作主语时，其后的动词单复数均可。例如：
All of the water is gone. 所有的水都用光了。
All of my classmates work hard. 我们班所有同学都很努力学习。
Some of the material seems too high-priced. 有一些材料似乎定价太高。
Some of the plants are dying out soon. 有一些植物很快就要灭绝了。
None of us is/are perfect. 我们没有一个人是完美的。

（4）在 one of+复数名词+定语从句的结构中，定语从句的谓语动词用复数形式；但当 one 之前有 the only、the very 修饰时，定语从句的谓语动词形式与 one 一致，用单数形式。例如：
This is one of the rooms that were damaged in the fire. 这是那次大火烧毁的房间之一。
Mary is one of the youngest girls who play in the band. 玛丽是参加乐队伴奏的最年轻的姑娘之一。
He is the only one of those workers who is able to do this job. 他是那些工人中唯一能做此工作的人。
She is the very one of the women who has received higher education. 她就是那些女子中接受过高等教育的人。

（六）不定式短语、动名词短语以及名词性从句作主语

（1）不定式短语、动名词短语作主语时，谓语动词用单数形式。例如：
Reading books is a good habit. 阅读是一个好的习惯。
Watching TV too much is bad for your eyes. 过多地看电视对眼睛有害。
To see is to believe. 〈谚〉眼见为实。

（2）名词性从句作主语时，谓语动词通常用单数形式。例如：
Who took the books away is unknown. 大家都不知道谁把那些书拿走了。
Whether it will do us harm or good remains to be seen. 这对我们是利还是弊，还有待观察。
Where they will go has not been decided. 他们将去哪里还没有定下来。
What Bloor lacks is confidence and courage. 布卢尔缺乏的是信心和勇气。

（3）当 what 引导的从句作主语表示复数概念时，谓语动词可用单数也可用复数。例如：

What the children want is/are toys. 孩子们想要的是玩具。

What we need is/are more volunteers. 我们所需要的是更多的志愿者。

（七）其他情况

（1）表示衣物或工具等的名词，如 clothes、pants、shorts、shoes、trousers、chopsticks、compasses、glasses、scales、scissors 等由两部分构成的物体，单独作主语时，谓语动词一般用复数；这类词如果与表示数量的单位词连用，谓语动词的单复数由表示数量的单位词而定。例如：

My glasses are broken, so I can't see well. 我的眼镜破了，所以看不太清楚。

Jack's gloves are of good quality. 杰克的手套质量很好。

A pair of trousers was found in the washing machine. 在洗衣机里找到了一条裤子。

Two pairs of scissors are in the drawer. 抽屉里有两把剪刀。

（2）常以复数形式出现的名词，如 goods、contents、stairs、wages、savings、belongings、clippings、earnings、fillings、lodgings、surroundings 等作主语时，通常看作复数，谓语动词用复数形式。例如：

The contents of the story are fascinating. 该故事的内容引人入胜。

High wages often result in high prices. 高工资常引起高物价。

The savings are for your future use. 这些储蓄是供你将来用的。

The workers lodgings are outside the factory. 工人们的住所在厂外。

The surroundings of the library are picturesque. 图书馆周围的环境景色如画。

（3）news 以及表示"学科"的名词 maths、physics、politics、statistics（统计学）等词作主语时，看似是复数形式，其实是表示单一概念，所以谓语动词用单数。例如：

No news is good news. 没有消息就是好消息。

Maths is hard to learn for some girls. 对一些女生来说，数学是很难学的。

Statistics is a branch of mathematics. 统计学是数学的一个分支。

（4）the+形容词/过去分词结构作主语时，如果指一类人或事物，谓语动词用复数形式；如果指某一个人或抽象概念时，谓语动词用单数形式。例如：

The young are mostly ambitious. 年轻人多半有雄心。

The old are more likely to catch cold than the young. 老年人比年轻人更容易感冒。

The wounded was his cousin. 受伤者是他的表弟。

The true is to be distinguished from the false. 真实与虚假应加以区分。

The beautiful is not always the useful. 美丽并不总是有用的。

（5）两个形容词+名词（单数）作主语指两件不同的事物时，谓语动词用复数形式。例如：

The yellow and the red rose are both beautiful. 黄玫瑰和红玫瑰都很美。

The English and the French language have something in common. 英语和法语在某些方面很相似。

（6）如有两个或两个以上的主语，既有肯定又有否定时，谓语动词的形式与肯定的主语一致。例如：

Not his brothers but Tom himself has finished the job. 不是汤姆的兄弟们，而是汤姆自己完成了这项工作。

The parents, rather than the child, are responsible. 应负责任的是家长，而不是孩子。

(7) 在 there be 结构中，be 动词的形式通常按照"邻近一致原则"来确定。例如：
There are three books and one pen on the table. 桌子上有三本书和一支笔。
There is one pen and three books on the table. 桌子上有一支笔和三本书。

二、代词和名词的一致

代词与其所指代或修饰的名词应在人称、数和性别上保持一致。例如：

Jane, Carol and I have been working all day. We are all tired. 简、卡罗尔和我已经工作了一整天。我们都累了。

Each citizen of the country can express his/her opinion freely. 这个国家的每个公民都可以自由地表达他/她的观点。

China has actively pursued its diplomatic agenda despite difficulties and steered the changes of our times. 中国不畏困难，积极推进外交议程，顺应时代变化。

三、平行结构中成分的一致

并列成分应在结构上保持一致。例如：

Swift is athletic and scholarly. 斯威夫特体格健壮，又有学者风度。

You can go with us or meet us at the bookstore. 你可以和我们一同前往或在书店和我们汇合。

He likes singing and dancing. 他喜欢唱歌和跳舞。

Henry was the first to get to the classroom, and the last to leave it. 亨利是第一个到达教室的人，也是最后一个离开教室的人。

四、状语逻辑主语与句子主语的一致

表示时间、原因、条件、伴随情况等状语的逻辑主语必须同句子的主语保持一致。例如：

Walking straight(If you walk straight), you will find the city hall. 径直走，你就会找到市政厅。

Not having received a reply(As he hadn't received a reply), he decided to write again. 由于没有收到回信，他决定再写一封信。

Greatly surprised(As he was greatly surprised), Simon couldn't say a word. 西蒙大吃一惊，一时讲不出话来。

Before being used, the machine must be checked. 机器在使用前，必须检查。

Seen in the broader context of human development and progress, the great rejuvenation of the Chinese nation represents an unstoppable trend. 从人类发展进步的大背景来看，中华民族的伟大复兴呈现出不可阻挡的趋势。

巩固练习

Complete the following sentences by choosing the items marked A, B, C, or D.

1. Each man and each woman _____ asked to help when the fire broke out.
   A. is   B. was   C. are   D. were

2. About 60 percent of the students _____ from the south; the rest of them _____ from the north and foreign countries.
   A. are; is   B. is; is   C. is; are   D. are; are

3. —Are these your sheep?
   —No. Mine _____ on grass at the foot of the hill.
   A. are feeding B. feed   C. is fed   D. is feeding

4. Her family _____ much larger than mine four years ago. Her family _____ dancing and singing when I came in last night.
   A. were; was   B. was; were   C. was; was   D. were; were

5. How and why Jack came to China _____ not known. When and where to build the new library _____ not been decided.
   A. is; has   B. are; has   C. is; have   D. are; have

6. Now Tom together with his classmates _____ football on the playground.
   A. play   B. are playing C. plays   D. is playing

7. Two hundred and fifty pounds _____ too unreasonable a price for a second-hand car.
   A. is   B. are   C. were   D. be

8. All but Dick _____ in Class Three this term.
   A. are   B. is   C. were   D. was

9. War and peace _____ a constant theme in history.
   A. has   B. have   C. is   D. are

10. _____ students are waiting for the lesson to begin.
    A. A number of   B. Many a
    C. The number of   D. The amount of

11. If law and order _____, neither the citizen nor his property is safe.
    A. is not preserved   B. not preserved
    C. are not preserved   D. were not preserved

12. All the students in the class except Xiao Li _____ passed the final examination.
    A. Is   B. has   C. are   D. have

13. One-third of the area _____ covered with green trees. About seventy percent of the trees _____ been planted.
    A. are; have   B. is; has   C. is; have   D. are; has

14. The number of teachers in our college _____ greatly increased last term. A number of teachers in this school _____ from the countryside.
    A. was; is   B. was; are   C. were; are   D. were; is

15. What _____ the population of China? One-third of the population _____ workers here.

    A. is; are   B. are; are   C. is; is   D. are; is

16. Not only he but also we _____ right. He as well as we _____ right.

    A. are; are   B. are; is   C. is; is   D. is; are

17. What he'd like _____ a digital watch. What he'd like _____ textbooks.

    A. are; are   B. is; is   C. is; are   D. are; is

18. He is one of the boys who _____ here on time. He is the only one of the boys who _____ here on time.

    A. has come; have come   B. have come; has come

    C. has come; has come   D. have come; have come

19. Either you or he _____ interested in playing chess. _____ you or he fond of music at present?

    A. are; Are   B. is; Are   C. are; Is   D. is; Is

20. Many a professor _____ looking forward to visiting Germany now. Many scientists _____ studied animals and plants in the last two years.

    A. is; have   B. is; has   C. are; have   D. is; are

21. A knife and a fork _____ on the table. A knife and fork _____ on the table.

    A. is; is   B. are; are   C. are; is   D. is; are

22. The committee _____ congratulations to the new chairperson.

    A. wish to offer their   B. wishes to offer their

    C. wish to offer its   D. that wishes to offer its

23. Three weeks _____ allowed for making the necessary preparations.

    A. is   B. are   C. has   D. have

24. Ignorance and negligence _____ this mistake.

    A. cause   B. have caused   C. has caused   D. are

25. No teacher or no scientist _____ for wages which _____ quite low for the time being.

    A. works; are   B. works; is   C. work; is   D. work; are

26. We each _____ strong points and each of us on the other hand _____ weak points.

    A. have; have   B. has; have   C. has; has   D. have; has

27. My friend and classmate Paul _____ motorcycles in his spare time.

    A. race   B. races   C. is raced   D. is racing

28. The factory, including its machines and buildings, _____ burnt last night.

    A. is   B. are   C. were   D. was

29. Climbing hills _____ of great help to health.

    A. is   B. are   C. were   D. be

30. Time and tide _____ for no man.

    A. wait   B. waited

    C. is waiting   D. has waited

31. The injured in the tsunami _____ good care of by some medical teams.
    A. is taken　　　　　B. are being taken　　　C. are taking　　　　D. is being taken
32. It is not J. K. Rowling but her works that _____ us excited.
    A. makes　　　　　　B. is made　　　　　　　C. make　　　　　　　D. are made
33. On the closet _____ a pair of trousers his parents bought for his birthday.
    A. lying　　　　　　B. lies　　　　　　　　　C. lie　　　　　　　　D. is laid
34. Every means _____ tried since then to solve the problem.
    A. has been　　　　　B. have been　　　　　　C. are　　　　　　　　D. is
35. Neither all of the cookies nor all of the fruit _____.
    A. have been eaten　　B. has been eaten　　　　C. have eaten　　　　　D. has eaten
36. It rained for two weeks on end, completely _____ our holiday.
    A. ruined　　　　　　　　　　　　　　　　　　B. being ruined
    C. being ruining　　　　　　　　　　　　　　　D. ruining
37. The human race has certainly made _____ mark on the earth.
    A. its　　　　　　　　B. their　　　　　　　　C. his　　　　　　　　D. his or her
38. Not the teacher but the students _____ excited.
    A. is　　　　　　　　B. has　　　　　　　　　C. are　　　　　　　　D. have
39. As I have a meeting at four, ten minutes _____ all that I can spare to talk with you.
    A. are　　　　　　　　B. was　　　　　　　　　C. is　　　　　　　　　D. were
40. Having arrived at the station, _____.
    A. it was found that the train had left　　　　　B. the train had left
    C. the train was found left　　　　　　　　　　D. he found that the train had left

第二十三章

附加疑问句

热身训练： 下列句子各有一处错误，请指出并改正。

① There's a new seafood restaurant in the small town, isn't it?
② The price of car used to be a great deal lower than now, wasn't it?
③ It has been a long time since we have talked to Joyce, isn't it?
④ He was disappointed that you did not answer his letter, did you?
⑤ I don't think that the ring is made of diamond, isn't it?
⑥ His wife had the blankets and the curtains cleaned, did she?
⑦ It's my daughter's wedding next week, and I have to do my best for that, do I?
⑧ Birds rarely build nests in our garden, don't they?
⑨ You must have been to the Summer Palace, have you?
⑩ I had to tell the truth, haven't I?

在英语中，附加疑问句也称反义疑问句，由陈述句和附在其后的简略疑问句组成，用于证实说话者所说的事实或观点。附加疑问句中的助动词一般是与陈述部分的动词相对应，附加疑问句的主语一般是与陈述部分的主语相对应的人称代词。

一、附加疑问句的结构

附加疑问句的结构有以下两种形式。
（1）肯定陈述句+否定简略疑问句。例如：
You like winter outdoor swimming, don't you? 你喜欢冬泳，不是吗？
Sophia is modest, isn't she? 索菲亚很谦虚，不是吗？
（2）否定陈述句+肯定简略疑问句。例如：
She doesn't like dancing, does she? 她不喜欢跳舞，是吗？
You haven't finished your work yet, have you? 你还没有完成工作，是吗？

二、附加疑问部分的主语

附加疑问部分的主语与陈述部分的主语有一致和不一致两种情况。

（一）附加疑问部分的主语与陈述部分的主语一致

（1）当陈述部分的主语是人称代词,谓语部分有助动词、情态动词或 be 动词时,附加疑问部分要重复这些词。例如：

He's finished his homework, hasn't he? 他完成了作业,是吗？

You should pay more attention to what your teacher says, shouldn't you? 你应该多注意你老师所说的话,不是吗？

We can't run on the grass, can we? 我们不能在草地上跑,是吗？

（2）陈述部分的主语是 one 时,附加疑问部分的主语可以用 one（正式语体）,也可以用 you（非正式语体）。例如：

One can't be good at everything, can one/you? 没有人样样都精通,是吧？

One should answer for what he does, shouldn't one/you? 一个人应该为他的所作所为负责,不是吗？

（3）以 there be 结构引导的陈述句,其后的附加疑问部分仍用引导词 there。例如：

There is no real freedom in this country, is there? 这个国家没有真正的自由,是不是？

There used to be a shopping mall in the east of this city, didn't there? 这个城市的东边曾经有一个购物商场,不是吗？

（二）附加疑问部分的主语与陈述部分的主语不一致

（1）陈述部分的主语是不定代词 everything、something、anything、nothing 以及指示代词 this、that 时,附加疑问部分的主语用 it。例如：

Everything goes difficultly, doesn't it? 一切进展都很艰难,是吗？

Nothing could make her give up her thoughts, could it? 什么也不能让她放弃她的想法,对吗？

That is what you want to achieve, isn't it? 那是你想要实现的,不是吗？

（2）陈述部分的主语是不定代词 everybody、everyone、somebody、someone、anybody、anyone、nobody、no one、none、neither 等词时,附加疑问部分的主语常用 they,但正式语体中也可用 he。例如：

Everyone knows he's the only person who can do the job, don't they/doesn't he? 每个人都知道他是唯一能做这项工作的人,不是吗？

No one knows exactly how or where he met his end, does he/do they? 没人确切地知道他是在何处又是如何丢掉性命的,是吗？

Neither of them agreed to the plan, did they? 他们俩都不同意这个计划,是吗？

（3）如果陈述部分的主语是动词不定式、动名词短语或其他短语,附加疑问部分的主语常用 it。例如：

To learn skating skills is difficult, isn't it? 学习溜冰技巧很难,不是吗？

Reading about her experiences is very touching to us, isn't it? 读关于她的经历,我们都很感动,不是吗？

Learning how to repair cars takes a long time, doesn't it? 学习怎样修理汽车是要花费很长一段时间的,不是吗？

（4）陈述部分的主语是 such 时,附加疑问部分的主语单数用 it,复数用 they。例如：

Such is the fact, isn't it? 真相就是如此,不是吗？

Such are the books you read during the summer vocation, aren't they? 这就是你暑假看的书,不是吗?

(5) 陈述部分的主语是 each of... 时,如果强调全体,附加疑问部分的主语可用 they、we 或 you;如果强调单个,则可用 he、she 或 it,例如:

Each of these architectural designs has its own disadvantages, didn't they? 每个建筑的设计都有它自己的缺点,不是吗?

Each of the students passed the exam, didn't he? 所有学生都通过了考试,不是吗?

Each of you has brought a present, haven't you? 你们每个人都带礼物来了,不是吗?

Each of the girls must take responsibility for her own action, mustn't she? 每个女孩子都必须对自己的行为负责,不是吗?

三、附加疑问部分的动词

(一) 情态动词与附加疑问句

(1) 陈述部分的动词是 would rather 和 had better 时,附加疑问部分分别用 wouldn't 和 hadn't+主语。例如:

We had better listen to them first in order to show our respect for others, hadn't we? 为了表示对别人的尊重,我们最好先听他们表达,好吗?

You'd better keep quiet when you come back, hadn't you? 你回来时最好保持安静,好吗?

You'd rather not do it, would you? 你宁愿不做,对吗?

(2) 陈述部分的动词是 used to 时,附加疑问部分用 usedn't 或 didn't+主语。例如:

She used to study in Russia, usedn't/didn't she? 她过去在俄罗斯学习过,是不是?

The Blacks used to live in the countryside, usedn't/didn't they? 布莱克夫妇以前住在乡下,不是吗?

(3) 陈述部分有情态助动词 must 表示"义务"时,附加疑问部分用 mustn't。当陈述部分的 must 表示"有必要"时,附加疑问句的谓语动词要用 needn't。例如:

You must be back home by 11 o'clock, mustn't you? 你必须在 11 点前回家,好不好?

He must get to the Central Park on time, needn't he? 他需要准时到达中央公园,是吗?

陈述部分中有 mustn't 表示"禁止"时,附加疑问句部分用 must 或 may。例如:

You mustn't walk on the grass, must/may you? 你不能在草地上走,可以吗?

We mustn't be late, must/may we? 我们不可以迟到的,是吗?

(4) 陈述部分有情态助动词 must 表示对现在的情况进行"推测"时,附加疑问部分用 must 后面的动词相应的形式。例如:

Jenny's parents must be in the living-room, aren't they? 珍妮的父母准在客厅里,对吗?

She must be kind. isn't she? 她一定很和蔼,是吗?

He must be lying to me, isn't he? 他肯定是在对我撒谎,是不是?

当情态助动词 must 表示对过去的情况进行"推测"(must+ have done)时,附加疑问部分用"didn't+主语"(有明确的过去时间状语);或"haven't/hasn't+主语"(没有明确的过去时间状语)。例如:

You must have read the book last week, didn't you? 你上星期一定读了这本书,是吗?

He must have waited here for a long time, hasn't he? 他一定在这里等了很久,是吗?

(5) 陈述部分有 need、dare 时,他们是作实义动词或是情态动词,必须注意区分。例如:

They needn't work long if there are some significant technical improvement, need they? 假如技术上有重大改进的话,他们就不必工作这么长时间,是吗?

A fence needs the support of five stakes, doesn't it? 篱笆需要五根木桩支撑,不是吗?

(6) 陈述部分有情态动词 ought to 时,附加疑问部分中用 shouldn't/oughtn't+主语。例如:

The thief ought to be caught, oughtn't he/shouldn't he? 这个小偷应该被抓起来,对吗?

I ought to make a plan, shouldn't I? 我应该制订一个计划,不是吗?

(二) 否定词与附加疑问句

(1) 陈述部分带有 seldom、few、little、hardly、scarcely、barely、rarely 等半否定词时,附加疑问部分用肯定式。例如:

Few people now remember the sinking of the great passenger ship Titanic exactly 110 years ago, do they? 现在很少有人记得110年前巨大的客轮泰坦尼克号的沉没,是吗?

Birds rarely build nests in our garden nowadays, do they? 现在鸟儿很少在我们的花园里筑巢,对吗?

He scarcely earns enough to keep himself and his family, does he? 他几乎赚不到足够的钱养活自己和家人,是吗?

(2) 陈述部分的动词带否定意义或形容词带有否定意义的前缀或后缀时,附加疑问部分仍用否定式。例如:

He failed/refused to receive her invitation, didn't he? 他没有/拒绝接受她的邀请,是吗?

He was unsuccessful at the end of the battle, wasn't he? 他在战争结束时失败了,是吗?

They dislike discussing things like traffic or weather, don't they? 他们不喜欢讨论交通或天气之类的事情,是吗?

(三) 其他句型的附加疑问句

(1) 陈述句中谓语为 wish 时,附加疑问部分用 may,而且后面都用肯定形式。例如:

I wish to shake hands with your manager, may I? 我希望和你的经理握手,可以吗?

I wish to go there on foot, may I? 我希望步行去那儿,行吗?

(2) 祈使句也可用附加疑问句,谓语形式通常用 will 或 shall(以 let's 开头,用 shall,否则用 will),祈使句的附加疑问部分一般用肯定形式,偶尔也用否定形式。Let me/us 等开头的祈使句,附加部分要用 will you。例如:

Carry this heavy suitcase for me, will you? 帮我拿这个重的行李箱,可以吗?

Remember to specify your size when ordering clothes, won't you? 记着订购服装时要详细说明你要的号码,好吗?

Let's go for a walk, shall we? 让我们一起去散步吧,好吗?

Let us approach the subject from a different direction, will you? 让我们从一个不同的角度来探讨这个题目,好吗?

Have a little more coffee, will you? 再喝点咖啡,好吗?

（3）陈述部分是复合句时，附加疑问部分的主语一般与主句主语一致。例如：

You visited Dany when you were in London, didn't you? 你在伦敦时去看了丹尼，对吗？

She said her son was coming with her, didn't she? 她说她儿子将跟她一起来，是吗？

但如果主句的主语是第一人称，谓语动词是 believe、think、consider、guess、expect、suppose、imagine 等时，附加疑问部分的主语则与从句的主语一致。例如：

I believe that Elizabeth is right, isn't she? 我相信伊丽莎白是对的，对吗？

I don't think he really understands the word at the moment, does he? 我觉得他当时根本连这个词什么意思都不懂，对吗？

I consider that he is fit for the only position of the manager, isn't he? 我认为他适合经理这个唯一的职位，不是吗？

I don't suppose you are coming back today, are you? 我猜你今天不会回来的，不是吗？

（4）感叹句后的附加疑问部分，其动词要用"be"动词的现在时，而且通常用否定形式。例如：

What a funny man, isn't he? 多么有趣的一个人啊，不是吗？

How exciting the soccer game is, isn't it? 多么令人激动的足球比赛啊，不是吗？

（5）陈述部分是并列句，附加疑问部分则需就近和分句的主语和谓语保持一致。例如：

I don't enjoy cold weather in winter, but we have to live with it, don't we? 我不喜欢冬季寒冷的天气，但是我们必须接受，是吧？

Benja has been writing a new history of Europe all year but he should finish it now, shouldn't he? 本杰一整年一直在写一部新的欧洲史，但是现在他应该写完了，是吗？

四、其他有关问题

（1）除了上述两种结构的附加疑问句外，英语中还有一类带感情色彩的附加疑问句，表示惊奇、愤怒、讽刺、不服气等，其形式为前后一致，"肯定+肯定"或"否定+否定"，它们常用 oh、so 等字眼开头，陈述部分和疑问部分要么同是肯定的，要么同是否定的，有的语法学者称为"同向附加疑问句"。例如：

You call this a day's housework, do you? 你这就叫一天的家务活儿，是吗？

Oh, you invited Emily to your birthday party, did you? 呵，你邀请了艾米丽来参加你的生日晚会，是吗？

So he won't pay me the money, won't he? 这么说他不会付钱给我了，是不是？

（2）有时某些固定短语可以代替附加疑问部分，其形式不受陈述部分的制约。例如：

He forgot/didn't forget to turn off the light when he left the room, am I right?/isn't that so?/don't you think?/wouldn't you say? 他离开房间时忘记（没有忘记）关灯，对吗？/不是吗？

巩 固 练 习

Complete the following sentences by choosing the items marked A, B, C, or D.

1. Michel wouldn't become a teacher if it hadn't been for the holiday, _____?

   A. had he   B. would he   C. would it   D. had it

2. No one left here yesterday, _____?
   A. didn't they   B. did they   C. didn't one   D. did one
3. Birds rarely build nests in our garden, _____?
   A. do they   B. did they   C. didn't they   D. don't they
4. You must have been to the Great Wall, _____?
   A. mustn't you   B. must you   C. haven't you   D. aren't you
5. Learning how to repair motors takes a long time, _____?
   A. does it   B. do they   C. doesn't it   D. don't they
6. They must have stayed at home last night, _____?
   A. mustn't they   B. didn't they   C. must they   D. haven't they
7. What a big fish, _____?
   A. is it   B. wasn't it   C. can't it   D. isn't it
8. Let's start out early tomorrow morning, _____?
   A. will you   B. can't you   C. do you   D. shall we
9. There's not much news in today's newspaper, _____?
   A. isn't it   B. is there   C. isn't there   D. is it
10. She doesn't dare to go home alone, _____?
    A. does she   B. needn't she   C. need she   D. doesn't she
11. She is unfit for the position, _____?
    A. is she   B. does she   C. doesn't she   D. isn't she
12. I wish to visit America, _____?
    A. don't I   B. may you   C. may I   D. can I
13. She's been a worker here for many years, _____?
    A. isn't she   B. has she   C. hasn't she   D. is she
14. Mother used to live in a poor village, _____?
    A. used she   B. did he   C. didn't he   D. usedn't she
15. You'd better go at once, _____?
    A. wouldn't you   B. should you   C. hadn't you   D. had you
16. Somebody borrowed my pen yesterday, _____?
    A. did they   B. don't they   C. didn't they   D. do they
17. I don't think you've done it, _____?
    A. do I   B. haven't you   C. don't I   D. have you
18. I suppose you know the meaning of the word, _____?
    A. do you   B. don't I   C. don't you   D. do I
19. Don't forget to phone me, _____?
    A. aren't you   B. do you   C. should you   D. will you
20. Margaret scarcely seems to care, _____?
    A. doesn't she   B. isn't she   C. does she   D. is she
21. Let us do it by ourselves, _____?
    A. don't you   B. will you   C. do you   D. won't you

22. He has to stay here all day, _____?
    A. wasn't he   B. does he   C. was he   D. doesn't he
23. As far as I can remember, Tom used to live here, _____?
    A. used he   B. didn't I   C. usedn't he   D. did I
24. You'd rather I didn't say anything, _____?
    A. wouldn't you   B. did I   C. would you   D. didn't I
25. That's your sister, _____?
    A. is that   B. isn't it   C. isn't that   D. is it
26. You had some trouble finding where I live, _____?
    A. had you   B. didn't you   C. hadn't you   D. did you
27. He has his hair cut every month, _____?
    A. has he   B. doesn't he   C. hasn't he   D. does he
28. You need to come earlier, _____?
    A. should you   B. don't you   C. shouldn't you D. do you
29. Nothing can stop us now, _____?
    A. does it   B. can't it   C. doesn't it   D. can it
30. The nurse said that she was feeling well, _____?
    A. didn't she   B. did she   C. was she   D. wasn't she

第二十四章

there be 句型

热身训练： 下列句子各有一处错误，请指出并改正。

❶ There was six countries in SCO at first, but now the number has increased to eight.
❷ There's no use to wait any longer.
❸ There are plenty of housework to do.
❹ It was too late for there being any buses.
❺ There are a pen and two books on the desk.
❻ She was relying on there to be another opportunity.
❼ Once there living a clever old man.
❽ There will being rain soon.
❾ —How many birds are there in the tree?
　—There are only one bird in the tree.
❿ There is no need worrying.

　　英语中有一种特殊结构"there be"句型，是表示"存在"的句型（存在句），用本身无实义的引导词 there 引出。there 在句中作形式主语，而真正的主语通常是表示不确定的人或事物等名词、代词及其短语，放在 be 动词的后面。句型结构是：There be+真正主语+地点状语或时间状语。在疑问句中，there 和动词 be 要倒装。例如：
　　There is a history of collaboration between the countries. 两国之间有着合作的历史。
　　There is some boiled water in the kettle. 水壶里有一些开水。
　　Are there any people in the hall? 大厅里有人吗？

一、there be 句型中的谓语形式

（一）there be 句型中动词 be 的使用

　　当主语是单数可数名词或不可数名词时，be 的形式为 is/was；当主语是复数可数名词时，be 的形式为 are/were；当主语是由 and 连接的两个或多个并列名词时，be 应与离它最近的主语在数上保持一致，即"就近原则"来选择 be 的单复数形式。例如：
　　Behind every successful man there is a lot of unsuccessful years. 每个成功者的后面，都有许

多不成功的岁月。

There is a coach and some students in the classroom. 教室里有一位教练和一些学生。

（二）there be 句型中的其他谓语动词

除了be动词以外,该结构中的谓语动词还可以是以下几种类型。

（1）某些表示"存在"概念的不及物动词,如 lie、live、remain、stand、stay、exist 等。例如:
Behind the house (there) lies a mountain.
=There is a mountain behind the house. 房子后面有一座山。
There remained just thirty-three dollars. 只剩33美元了。
There stand small torches at the doorway of every household. 每家每户的门口都有小火把。
There exists a social and cultural connection between two countries. 两国之间存在着社会和文化方面的联系。

（2）某些表示"发生,到来"意义的不及物动词,如 occur、appear、enter、come、arrive、follow、emerge、arise、spring up 等。例如:
There occurred a flood in my hometown in 1998. 1998年,我家乡发了一场洪水。
There will follow an interval of fifteen minutes. 随后将有15分钟休息。
At present, however, there appear a lot of errors in the spreading process. 但目前在流传过程中还存在着许多错误。
There often spring up new things in the world with the development of the technology. 随着科技的发展,当今世界经常涌现新鲜事物。

（3）某些固定的词组,如 appear to be、seem to be、happen to be、have to be、be sure to be、be certain to be、be bound to be、use to be、need to be、continue to be、tend to be、be likely to be、be apt to be 等。例如:
There appear/seem (to be) some mistakes in your speech. 你的演讲中好像有一些错误。
There is sure to be a heavy snow tonight. 今晚肯定有一场大雪。
There used to be dinosaurs on the earth in the ancient time. 在远古时代地球上曾经有恐龙。
There seem to be fewer tourists around this year because of COVID-19. 由于新型冠状病毒（COVID-19）,今年的游客似乎更少。
There needs to be more than just passion. 需要的不仅仅是激情。
There are likely to be tensions and personality clashes in any social group. 任何社会团体都容易出现关系紧张和性格冲突。

（三）there be 的时态和语态

（1）there be 结构有现在、过去、完成和将来等时态,一般没有进行时态。例如:
There has been a meeting of the minds. 大家已取得了一致的看法。
There were four tall trees in front of the pond last year. 去年池塘前面有四棵大树。
There is going to be an end to these miseries! 苦日子总有熬出头的时候!
There will be an exhibition of paintings next month. 下个月将举行画展。
There has happened a series of strange things recently. 近来接连发生了许多奇怪的事情。
（2）there be 的被动式多用于正式文体,且常用于 believe、say、consider、expect、think、

report、mean、intend 等动词。例如：

There will be believed to be an official report soon. 相信不久就会有官方的报道。

Nowadays there is considered to be no life on the Mars. 如今人们认为火星上没有生命。

There is said to have been shots fired from both sides. 据说双边都已开火射击。

There is expected to be a severe frost tonight. 预计今晚有严重的霜冻出现。

（四）情态动词与 there be 句型

there be 句型也可以用于由情态动词构成的各种形式。根据需要，在 there 与 be 之间加上情态动词，构成：There will/can/must/may+be…。例如：

There must have been a rain last night, for the ground is wet. 昨晚肯定下雨了，因为地面湿了。

There must be one set of rules and regulations for the whole of the country. 必须有一套适用于全国的规章制度。

There might still be some seats in the theater. 剧院里可能还有空座位。

二、there be 句型的非限定形式

there be 句型的非限定形式是 there being 和 there to be 结构，主要用在书面语中。

（1）两种结构都可作介词宾语，多数情况下用 there being 结构。但若介词是 for，只能用 there to be 结构。例如：

It is impossible for there to be any more opportunities. 不可能再有机会。

This depended on there being a sudden change. 这需要有一个突然的改变。

It was too early for there to be any taxis. 太早了，不会有出租车。

（2）作动词宾语时，一般用 there to be 结构。这类动词主要有 believe、expect、hate、hope、intend、like、mean、refer、want、wish 等。例如：

We expect there to be more discussion about freedom. 关于自由，我们希望有更多的讨论。

The young people believe there to be a great generation gap between the old and the young. 年轻人相信老人与年轻人之间存在很大的代沟。

（3）there being 结构可用作动名词短语，作主语；也可用作分词独立结构，作状语。例如：

There being nothing to do, we went home separately. 由于没有什么事要做，我们就各自回家了。

There not being an index to this book is a disadvantage. 此书没有索引，查找很不方便。

三、there be 句型中的附加部分

there be+名词是 there be 句型的主体部分，位于名词（短语）之后的成分则是它的附加部分。这一附加部分一般有以下几种情况。

（1）there be+名词+状语。例如：

There was a house by the sea two years ago. 两年前海边有一所房子。

There are some girls on the playground. 操场上有几个女生。

（2）there be+名词+形容词/分词/不定式。例如：

There is something important to deal with. 有重要的事情需要处理。

There are some people standing outside the house. 有一些人站在房子外面。

There's a man to show you around the library. 有人带你参观图书馆。

（3）there be+名词+定语从句（从句中关系代词可省略）。例如：

There's something (that) has been on my mind. 有一些事情一直印在我脑海。

Are there any architectures around here (that) I have to take a look at? 这附近还有哪些建筑物是我一定要去看看的呢？

四、there be 句型的惯用结构

（1）There be some/no trouble/difficulty (in) doing sth./with sth.意为"做某事有/没困难"。例如：

There was much difficulty (in) finding his address. 好不容易才找到他的地址。

There is no trouble in translating the article without a dictionary. 即使不用词典翻译这篇文章也不难。

（2）There is no use/good/sense/point (in) doing sth.意为"做某事没有用/没有意义"。例如：

There is no use crying over spilt milk. 牛奶泼掉了，哭也无用。（〈谚〉覆水难收。）

There is no point in learning English without speaking. 学习英语不开口说是没有意义的。

（3）There is no need for sth./to do sth. 意为"（做）某事没必要"。例如：

There is no need to worry about the result of this final exam. 没必要担心期末考试的结果。

"There is no need for anxiety or for hype."he said. 他说："愤怒或者大肆宣扬都是没有必要的。"

（4）there is no doing sth. (=it is impossible to do sth.) 意为"（口语）不可能做……"。例如：

There is no telling what will happen in the future. 未来之事无可奉告。

There is no knowing what he will do next. 无法知道他下一步要做什么。

五、there be 句型其他注意事项

（1）there be 句型的主语是人时，后面常接动词-ing 形式作定语。例如：

Look! There are lots of boys playing soccer over there. 看！那边有很多男孩正在踢足球。

There is a little girl crying in the corner. 角落里有个小女孩在哭泣。

（2）there be 句型的主语是物时，后面常接动词不定式作定语，动词不定式常用主动形式表示被动意义。例如：

There is much housework to do today. 今天有很多家务活要做。

There are a lot of flowers to water. 有很多花需要浇水。

（3）该结构变否定句和一般疑问句时，除系动词 be 外，其他动词借助 do 的不同形式来构成否定句和一般疑问句。构成反义疑问句时，用 there 代替主语构成简单问句。例如：

There usedn't to be a high skyscraper here, used/did there? 这里以前没有摩天大楼，是吗？

There seems to be no limit to his greed, doesn't there? 他的贪婪似乎没有止境，不是吗？

巩固练习

Complete the following sentences by choosing the items marked A, B, C, or D.

1. There _____ a folk music concert in Beijing Opera Theater next week.
   A. is going to have   B. is   C. is going to be   D. will have

2. There is reported _____ a number of the wounded on both sides.
   A. to be   B. will be   C. was   D. being

3. —_____ there anything new in today's *Morning Daily*?
   — No. But there _____ some inspiring stories worth reading.
   A. Is; is   B. Are; is   C. Are; are   D. Is; are

4. _____ appeared to be a war between his heart and his mind.
   A. It   B. What   C. There   D. Where

5. The TV news reports that there _____ a storm the day after tomorrow.
   A. will be   B. has be   C. is   D. was

6. There are a lot of persons _____ for the bus to come.
   A. waiting   B. is waiting   C. waited   D. to wait

7. —Excuse me. Is there a bank near here?
   —_____. It's just between a park and a post office.
   A. Yes, it is   B. No, it isn't
   C. No, there is   D. Yes, there is

8. _____ plenty of water in this river.
   A. There used to being   B. There is used to be
   C. There used to be   D. There is used to being

9. What a pity, my new computer doesn't work. _____ must be something wrong with it.
   A. It   B. There   C. Here   D. That

10. There is little water in the cup, _____?
    A. isn't there   B. aren't there   C. are there   D. is there

11. The radio says _____ a cold day in South China tomorrow.
    A. will be   B. will get   C. there will be   D. there will have

12. There _____ a box of oranges in the room.
    A. is   B. has   C. have   D. are

13. _____ no need for us to discuss the problem again since it has already been settled.
    A. It has   B. There has   C. It is   D. There is

14. There _____ something new in tomorrow's newspaper.
    A. are going to have   B. is going to be
    C. is going to have   D. will have

15. There are five pairs _____, but I'm at a loss which to buy.
    A. to choose   B. for my choosing
    C. to be chosen from   D. to choose from

16. There is no use _____ the olive branch now.
    A. to offer   B. offer   C. to offering   D. offering
17. If the storm had happened in the day time, there _____ many more deaths.
    A. would have been   B. would be   C. had been   D. were
18. Look! _____.
    A. Here the bus comes   B. There does the bus come
    C. The bus come here   D. Here comes the bus
19. The teacher was waiting for _____ to be complete silence.
    A. it   B. what   C. there   D. where
20. Let's deal with the problem quickly. _____ seems to be little time left now.
    A. There   B. We   C. It   D. That

第二十五章

倒装与强调

热身训练： 下列句子各有一处错误，请指出并改正。

1. Bach died in 1750, but it was not until the early 19th century when his musical gift was fully recognized.
2. That was by making great efforts that she caught up with other students.
3. The shocking news made me realize how terrible problems we would face.
4. Only when Lily walked into the office does she realize that she had left the contract at home.
5. It was after he got what he had desired which he realized it was not so important.
6. Knocking at the door before you enter my room, please.
7. After I visited Beijing, I told my wife how a beautiful city it was!
8. It doesn't matter if they want to come to your party, is it?
9. The flowers his friend gave him will die unless watering every day.
10. Much although I have traveled, I have never seen anyone who's as capable as John.
11. Help others whenever you can or you will make the world a nice place to live in.
12. You didn't use to like him much when we were at school, didn't you?
13. Starting out right away, or you'll miss the train.
14. It was in New Zealand which Elizabeth first met Mr. Smith.
15. If Joe's wife doesn't go to the party, neither would he.

一、倒装结构

英语句子中的主语通常位于谓语之前，但有时为了强调或句子结构的需要，把谓语的一部分或全部移到主语前面，这就形成倒装句。

（一）部分倒装

只把谓语中的一部分（如助动词、be 动词或情态动词等）放在主语前，称为部分倒装。

1. 疑问句

（1）助动词/be 动词/情态动词+主语。例如：

Do you know how the word is spelt? 你知道这个词怎么拼写吗？

How soon will the tourists be back to the hotel? 游客多快返回酒店？

（2）特殊疑问句中，如果疑问词作主语或修饰主语，不用倒装。例如：

Who invented the telephone? 谁发明了电话？

How many people took part in the campaign for the civil rights? 多少人参加了民权运动？

2. 以 so、neither 和 nor 开头的句子

以 so、neither 和 nor 开头的句子，表示前面所说的情况也适用于另一人或事。so 用于肯定句，neither 和 nor 用于否定句。so/neither/nor+助动词/be 动词/情态动词+主语。例如：

Tom likes climbing the hill. So do I. 汤姆喜欢爬山，我也喜欢爬山。（口语中常用"Me too."）

Peter is a bit nervous, and so am I. 彼得有点儿紧张，我也有点儿。

Society has changed and so have the people in it. 社会变了，人也跟着变了。

I cannot drive. Neither can Jim. 我不会开车，吉姆也不会。

I don't know when to leave. Nor does Anna. 我不知道什么时候离开，安娜也不知道。

Job never laughed. Nor did he ever lose his temper. 乔布从来不笑，也从不发脾气。

注：① so 开头的句子如果表示对前面所说的情况加以肯定，不用倒装。so+主语+助动词/be 动词/情态动词，意为"的确，确实"。例如：

—Henry works hard. 亨利学习很努力。

—So he does, and so do you. 他确实是很努力，你也一样的。

② 表示后者与前者有两种情况一样时，需用 so it is/was with sb. 结构，不用倒装。例如：

Mabel is young and strong. So it is with his brother. 梅布尔年轻、工作努力，他兄弟也一样。

Sarah can speak Japanese and speaks well. So it is with Bede. 莎拉会说日语并且说得很好，比德也一样。

3. only+状语放在句首

Only+副词/介词短语/状语从句+助动词/be 动词/情态动词+主语。例如：

Only then did Amy realize that she was lost. 直到那时艾米才意识到自己迷路了。

Only by working hard can we reap a bumper harvest. 只有通过辛勤的劳动才能收获丰硕的成果。

Only through vigorous and determined endeavor can we fulfill our responsibility to history, prove worthy of our times and live up to people's expectations. 我们唯有踔厉奋发、笃行不怠，方能不负历史、不负时代、不负人民。

Only if you eat the correct foods will you be able to keep fit and stay healthy. 只有饮食合理，才能保持身体健康。

Only when one is away from home does he realize how nice home is. 只有离开家时，才会意识到家庭的温暖。

注：当 only 位于句首修饰主语时，不用倒装。例如：

Only the doctor can save his life. 只有这个医生才能救他的命。

4. 否定意义的副词（not、seldom、little、hardly、never、rarely、nowhere 等）放句首

Not…/Seldom/Hardly/Never/Nowhere/…+助动词/be 动词/情态动词+主语。例如：

Not a single egg did I eat today. 我今天一个鸡蛋也没吃。

Never shall I forget the day when we first met. 我永远不会忘记我们初次见面的那一天。
Hardly could she believe her own eyes. 她几乎不敢相信自己的眼睛。
Seldom have I read a novel so touching as this. 我很少读到如此动人的小说。
Scarcely did Mara speak about the difficulties in her work. 玛拉极少谈起自己工作中所遇到的困难。

> **注**：上面的否定是否定整个句子，需倒装；如果是局部否定（如对主语进行否定等），则不倒装。例如：
> Not everyone can do things perfectly. 不是所有的人都能把事情做得十分完美。

5. 否定介词短语置于句首

At no time/By no means/In no way/Under no condition/… +助动词/be 动词/情态动词+主语。例如：
At no time will China be the first to use nuclear weapons. 中国决不会最先使用核武器。
By no means will we change the plan. 我们绝不改变计划。
In no way can we allow this to go on. 我们绝不允许这样的事再继续下去了。
Under no circumstances should we give up hope. 我们绝不放弃希望。

6. 否定结构（not until...、no sooner、hardly/scarcely、not only 等）置于句首

Not until… /No sooner/Hardly/Scarcely+助动词/be 动词/情态动词+主语。例如：
Not until yesterday did I meet Allan. 直到昨天我才遇见艾伦。
No sooner had we got there than it became dark. 我们一到那里，天就黑了。
Scarcely had we reached home when it began to rain. 我们刚到家，就开始下雨了。
Not only does the sun give us light, but (also) it gives us heat. 太阳不仅给我们光，而且给我们热。

> **注**：not only… but also 连接并列主语时，不用倒装。例如：
> Not only his parents but also his friends watched his performance. 不仅他父母，他的朋友们也观看了他的表演。

7. 方式状语、频度状语位于句首

以方式副词（well）或频度副词（often、many a time）开头的句子。Well/Often/Many a time+助动词+主语。例如：
Often did we persuade him not to smoke. 我们经常劝他不要吸烟。
Many a time have I climbed that mountain. 我曾多次爬过那座山。
Well do I remember the place where we first met. 我清楚地记得我们初次见面的地方。

8. 虚拟条件句

含有 were、should 或 had 的虚拟条件句，省略 if 时，条件句倒装，结构为 were/should/had+主语。例如：
Had he taken my advice, he might have succeeded. 他要是采纳了我的建议，可能就成功了。
Were I in his position, I wouldn't do it that way. 如果我在他的位置，我不会那么做的。
Should it rain tomorrow, the sports meeting would be put off. 如果明天下雨，运动会就延期。

9. 让步状语从句

(1) as 引导让步状语从句时,必须倒装。表语(名词、形容词、分词)/状语(副词)/谓语(动词)提前。名词(不带冠词)/形容词/分词/副词/动词+as+主语+……。though 引导的可倒装也可不倒装。例如:

Woman as/though she is, she is brave. 她虽是女流,却非常勇敢。

Difficult as/though the task was, we managed to accomplish it in time. 虽然任务很艰难,但我们还是设法如期完成了。

Much as I like the shirt, I won't buy it. 尽管我很喜欢这件衬衫,但我不会买的。

Search as they would, they could find nobody in the house. 尽管他们在房子里到处搜寻,但什么人也没发现。

Our country, big as it is, also has its list of priorities. 大国之大,也有大国之重。

(2) 动词原形+疑问词+主语+情态动词。这个句型相当于 no matter what/where/when… 引导的让步状语从句。例如:

Do what you will, we'll always support you. 无论你做什么,我们都会支持你。

Go where you will, you cannot succeed without effort. 无论你到哪里,不努力都不可能成功。

Come when you will, you will find him in the library. 你无论什么时候来,总会在图书馆找到他。

(3) be+主语+(or 连接的)两个并列表语,相当于 whether… or… 引导的让步状语从句。例如:

Be he friend or enemy, the law regards him as a criminal. 无论他是敌是友,法律认为他是罪犯。

Be it cheap or dear, I will take it. 不管它是贵还是便宜,我都要买。

I think of the joys of reading, be it a letter, or a book, or some subject for deep thought. 我想起了阅读的快乐,不论它是一封信、一本书或某个让人深思的话题。

The business of each day, be it selling goods or shipping them, went quite smoothly. 每天的业务,不管是售货还是运货,都进展得相当顺利。

(4) be+名词/代词+ever so+形容词,相当于 no matter how 引导的让步状语从句。例如:

Be a man ever so successful, he should not be proud. 一个人无论多么成功,也不应该骄傲。

Be it ever so late, I must finish the task. 无论时间多晚,我都必须完成这项任务。

Home is home, be it ever so homely. 家总是家,不管它多么简陋。

10. 比较状语从句

(1) 出现在 than 后的结构中,than+助动词/be 动词+主语。例如:

Jack spends more than does his brother. 杰克花钱比他兄弟花得多。

Actions speak louder than do words. 〈谚〉行胜过言。

Students with rich imagination are more likely to succeed than are those with poor imagination. 想象力丰富的学生比想象力差的学生更有可能获得成功。

(2) the more…, the more… 结构,形容词/副词比较级提前。例如:

The harder you work, the happier you'll feel. 你越努力工作,就越觉得快乐。

The bigger they are, the harder they fall. 块头越大,摔得越痛。(〈谚〉爬得越高,摔得

越重。)

The more challenges we face, the more imperative it is for us to break waves and forge ahead. 我们面临的挑战越多,我们就越需要打破僵局,勇往直前。

11. 表示感叹和祝愿的句子

表示感叹和祝愿的句子也常用倒装。例如:

What a clever boy Bill is! 比尔是多么聪明的男孩啊!

How happy we are to see you! 看见你我们真高兴呀!

May our country enjoy prosperity! 愿国家繁荣昌盛!

12. 宾语前置或后置

(1) 有时为了强调宾语或衔接上文,将宾语前置。例如:

This I'll never forget. 这件事,我将永远不忘。

Whether it is true or not, I don't care. 是真是假,我不在乎。

The past one can know, but the future one can only feel. 过去的我们可以知道,但未来的我们只能感受。

(2) 宾语过长时,往往把宾语放在状语或宾语补足语的后面。例如:

I'll take with me whatever might be needed in this trip. 我会带着旅途中可能需要的一切物品。(状语之后)

Don't consider possible what really is impossible. 不要把根本不可能的事当成可能的。(宾语补足语之后)

13. 以 such 开头的句子

such 位于句首需倒装。例如:

Such a difficult problem do I have to face. 我必须面对这个难题。

Such was Albert Einstein, a simple man of great achievements. 这就是爱因斯坦,一个成就卓著而又简单的人。

14. 以 so/such(...that)开头的句子

以 so/such(...that)引导的结果状语从句时,若 so/such 位于句首,需要倒装。so(+形容词/副词)/such+be 动词/助动词+主语。例如:

So interesting is the book that all the students like it. 这本书是如此有趣,以至于所有的学生都喜欢它。

So fast did he run that we couldn't catch up with him. 他跑得非常快,我们赶不上。

Such was his surprise that George stood wordless for some moments. 乔治大吃一惊,站在那儿半天说不出话。

(二)全部倒装

把整个谓语全部都放在主语前,称为全部倒装。全部倒装包括以下几种情况。

1. 表示方向的副词开头的句子

以 down、up、in、out、off、away 等表示方向的副词开头,谓语动词是 go、come、run、rush 等表示位置转移的动词。例如:

Up went the plane. 飞机起飞了。
Down fell an apple from the tree. 树上掉了一个苹果下来。
In came the children, talking. 孩子们边走边说进来了。
Over turned the bottle. 瓶子一下子翻过来了。
Out rushed the miners. 矿工们冲了出去。

注：如果主语是代词,则不能倒装。例如：
Away it flew. 它飞走了。
Out they rushed. 他们冲了出去。

2. 介词短语开头的句子

有时为了强调或上下文衔接,将介词短语前置。结构为:介词短语+谓语+主语。例如：
Under the big tree stood some people, talking and laughing. 大树下站着一些人,有说有笑的。
Around the Bali hu Lake have sprung up many new buildings. 八里湖周边许多新的建筑拔地而起。
In the middle of the lake lie two small islands. 湖的中央有两个小岛。

3. 以引导词 there 开头的句子

用于 there be/remain/appear/stand/live… 等结构,主语实际上是在动词的后面。例如：
There are some trees in the garden. 园子里有几棵树。
There stands a stone bridge over the river. 河上有一座石桥。
There appeared a star from behind the cloud. 云层后面出现了一颗星星。

4. 以 here、there、now、then、next 开头的句子

以 here、there、now、then、next 开头的句子,谓语动词多为 be、go、come 等。例如：
Now comes your turn. 现在轮到你了。(习惯说法)
Then came a wonderful surprise. 然后奇迹出现了。
Next came a man in uniform. 接着来了一个穿制服的人。
There goes another quarter. 又过了一刻钟了。

注：主语为代词时,以 there 或 here 开头的句子不倒装。例如：
There it is. 它在那边。
Here she comes. 她来了。

5. 表语前置的句子

为了表示强调或保持句子平衡或上下文的衔接,常将表语部分提前。表语(形容词/介词短语/分词等)+系动词+主语。例如：
More important still is the question of how we should stay cool-headed and not be affected by any distractions in a volatile world. 更重要的问题是我们应该如何在这个动荡的世界里,保持冷静、不受任何干扰。
Opposite our school is a modern hospital. 我们学校对面是一所现代化的医院。
Seated on the grass are a group of young men playing the guitar. 坐在草地上的是一群弹吉他的年轻人。
Gone are the days when we played happily on the beach together. 我们一同在海滩上快乐地

玩耍的日子一去不复返了。

Hanging on the wall is a painting by Xu Beihong. 墙上挂的是一幅徐悲鸿的画。

Facing the square is the famous Bell Tower. 面对广场的是著名的钟楼。

6. 直接引语之后的引述句

当直接引语的一部分或者全部位于句首时,引述句通常倒装。例如:

"Go on, apply for the job." said Lily. 李莉说:"去吧,去申请那份工作。"

"Why is that?" asked the student, "Can't we choose B?" 这个学生问:"那是为什么?我们不能选择 B 吗?"

但如果引述句的主语是人称代词,则一般不倒装。例如:

"Who will attend the meeting?" he asked. "谁去参会呢?"他问道。

二、强调结构

强调是为了突出句中的某个成分而采用的一种修辞手段。在英语中,说话者为了突出某些重要信息,可以通过词汇、词组和句型等方式来对所表述的内容进行强调。

(一) 词汇词组强调

1. very、only 等形容词

用 very、only 等形容词来强调名词或名词词组。例如:

You are the very person Alan wants to see. 你正是艾伦想要见的人。

You must do the work from the very beginning. 你必须从头开始做这项工作。

You can borrow only one book at a time. 你一次只能借一本书。

2. even、just、simply、right、really 等副词

用 even、just、simply、right、really 等副词来加强谓语或状语。例如:

Our campus is simply too beautiful. 我们的校园简直太美了。

Put the table right in the middle. 就把桌子放在中间。

Things turned out just as I expected. 事情正如我所预料的那样。

This is really the book that I want to borrow. 这就是我想要借的书。

3. even、still、much、far、by far、a great deal、a lot 等词语

用 even、still、much、far、by far、a great deal、a lot 等词语来加强形容词或副词的比较级。例如:

This new road is far better than the old one. 这条新路比旧的要好得多。

He runs much faster than Jack. 他跑得比杰克快得多。

It's cold today, but it'll be still colder tomorrow. 今天很冷,但明天会更冷。

Tom is a great deal better today. 汤姆今天好多了。

4. 助动词 do

"助动词(do/does/did)+动词原形"结构,可用来强调祈使句或陈述句中的谓语。通常只有一般现在时和一般过去时两种时态,该结构无疑问、否定形式。例如:

Do come on time next time. 请下次务必按时来。

Do be more cautious later on. 今后务必更谨慎些。

They did come early this morning. 他们今天早晨确实来得挺早。

He does go fishing every Sunday. 他的确每个星期天都去钓鱼。

5. on earth、in the world、under the sun、the hell、the devil 等词组

on earth、in the world、under the sun、the hell、the devil 主要用在疑问词之后加强语气,表示"究竟,到底"。例如:

What on earth do you mean by that? 你到底是什么意思啊?

What the devil did you do that for? 你做那件事究竟为了什么?

How the hell can he deal with such a matter? 他到底如何处理这件事?

Where under the sun could I have put my eyeglasses? 我到底把眼镜放到哪里了?

6. good and、nice and 等结构

good and/nice and/lovely and/fine and/sweet and 等+形容词或副词结构相当于 very/completely/thoroughly+形容词/副词。例如:

The book is good and useful. 这本书非常有用。

The eggs are lovely and fresh. 这些鸡蛋非常新鲜的。

The old man looks nice and healthy. 老人看上去很健康。

He usually drives fine and carefully. 他开车通常非常小心。

7. a bit、at all、in the least、possibly、simply、just 等词语

a bit、at all、in the least、possibly、simply、just 可用来加强否定意义。例如:

I do not understand you at all. 我一点也不明白你的意思。

I can't possibly drink any more. 我无论如何也喝不下了。

Mr. Smith is not in the least satisfied with my work. 史密斯先生对我的工作一点也不满意。

This piece of work simply isn't good enough. 这项工作做得实在不够好。

Alan is not a bit stupid. 艾伦根本不笨。

注:not a bit (=not at all) 一点也不; not a little (=very much) 非常。例如:
She was not a bit fond of tea. 她一点也不喜欢喝茶。
She was not a little fond of tea. 她非常喜欢喝茶。

8. 重复同一词语

句子中的某个词重复使用来表示强调。例如:

Business is business. You have to pay the bill. 公事公办,你还是要付账的。

He read the paper again and again. 他一遍又一遍地看了那篇论文。

You are my lifelong friends and friends! 你们是我一生的知己好友!

The competition became keener and keener. 竞争变得越来越激烈。

9. 使用重叠形式

有时反复使用 and 以示强调,或用 and 连接同义词、近义词、反义词表示强调。例如:

The shark is cruel and greedy and strong and clever. 鲨鱼既残忍、贪婪又强壮、聪明。

We have to find ways and means of securing ourselves better. 我们不得不寻找各种方法更好

地保护自己。

She kept still and motionless for a while. 她有一会儿一动不动。

I sometimes wonder why life is always full of ups and downs. 有时候我想知道生活为什么总是充满了起起落落。

(二) 句型强调

1. it is... that... 引导的强调句型

(1) "It is+强调部分+that/who+其他部分"是最常见的强调句型,可以强调除谓语以外的各种句子成分。例如:

Jack found a book in the dining room yesterday. 昨天杰克在餐厅发现一本书。

It was Jack that/who found a book in the dining room yesterday. 昨天在餐厅发现一本书的人是杰克。(强调主语)

It was a book that Jack found in the dining room yesterday. 杰克在餐厅里发现的是一本书。(强调宾语)

It was in the dining room that Jack found a book yesterday. 昨天杰克发现一本书的地方是餐厅。(强调地点状语)

It was yesterday that Jack found a book in the dining room. 杰克在餐厅发现一本书是在昨天。(强调时间状语)

分析以下句子,各强调哪一部分。

It is the unexpected that always happens. 意外事情常发生。

It is a doctor that he is now. 他现在是一位医生。

It was green that they painted all the walls. 他们把墙漆成了绿色。

It is from the sun that we get light and heat. 我们是从太阳那里得到热能。

It was slowly that he drove the car into the garage. 慢慢地,他把车开进了车库。

It was not until midnight that he got home. 直到午夜他才回家。

It is not only fine feathers that make fine birds. 仅靠美丽的羽毛成不了美丽的鸟。

被强调的部分也可以是从句。例如:

It is what he said that is very encouraging. 正是他所说的话鼓舞人心。

It was who had borrowed my pen that I forgot. 到底是谁借了我的笔,我记不起来了。

It was where we now stand that we first met. 我们第一次见面的地方就是现在所站的位置。

It is because I am new that he distrusts me. 就因为我是新来的,他就不信任我。

> **注:** 强调句型中的主谓一致。强调主语时,that/who 后面的动词需和被强调部分在人称和数上一致。例如:
>
> It is I who am able to speak Japanese. 会讲日语的人是我。
>
> It is you that are responsible for his safety. 是你该对他的安全负责。
>
> It is Bright who is best at mathematics in our class. 我们班数学学得最好的是布莱特。
>
> 强调句型中的 that/who 在非正式的文体中可以省略。例如:
>
> It was his brother you saw. 你见到的是他的弟弟。(省略 who)
>
> It was the headmaster himself spoke to me. 是校长亲自和我谈了话。(省略 who)
>
> It was last week this happened. 这是上周发生的事情。(省略 that)
>
> It was in the library I noticed it. 我是在图书馆注意到的。(省略 that)

（2）强调句型用于一般疑问句中，强调结构用"Is/Was it... +that/who... "形式。例如：

Was it you that lost a watch yesterday? 是你昨天丢了手表吗？

Was it yesterday that he bought a new telephone? 他是昨天买了新手机吗？

Was it on this island that he found the rare bird? 他是在这个岛上发现的那种珍稀鸟类吗？

Was it because he was too busy that he refused to go to the party? 他是因为太忙才不愿参加派对吗？

（3）强调句型用于特殊疑问句中，强调结构用"疑问词+is/was it+that... "形式。例如：

Who was it that saved the drowning child? 是谁救了那个落水的孩子？

Why is it that you wish to leave? 你究竟是为什么想要离开？

When was it that he graduated from Peking University? 他是什么时候从北京大学毕业的？

Where was it that you met Wang Lin? 你是在哪里碰到王林的？

（4）强调句型用于感叹句中，强调结构用"What/How... it is/was that..."形式。例如：

What remarkable intelligence it was that you have displayed! 你表现出的是多么杰出的才智啊！

How wonderful a speech it was that Ira made! 艾拉作了一个多么精彩的演讲啊！

（5）强调句型与情态动词连用，强调结构用"It+情态动词+be... that/who..."形式。例如：

It must be your girlfriend that you are waiting for. 你等待的人一定是你女朋友。

It might be tomorrow that the news will be broadcast. 这则消息或许是明天播出。

It can't be Emily that you met in the theatre. 你在剧院遇到的不可能是埃米莉。

（6）强调句中的 not... until 结构。强调由 not... until 引导的时间状语时，要注意将 not 前移。"It was not until... that... "意为"直到……才……"。例如：

It was not until the 19th century that heat was considered as a form of energy. 直到19世纪，热才被人们认为是一种能量形式。

It is not until we have lost our health that we know its value. 等到我们失去健康，才知道健康之可贵。

把 not until 置于句首，用倒装句同样起到强调的作用。例如：

I didn't get your letter until yesterday. 直到昨天我才收到你的信。

→It wasn't until yesterday that I got your letter.

→Not until yesterday did I get your letter.

He won't go away until you promise to help him. 直到你答应帮助他，他才会离开。

→It is not until you promise to help him that he will go away.

→Not until you promise to help him will he go away.

（7）强调句型和一些主从复合句结构相似，区分的方法是：去掉"It is/was... that"后剩下的词仍能组成一个完整句子者，就是强调句型；否则就是主从复合句。例如：

It was in the evening that he got home yesterday. 他昨天是傍晚时分到家的。

It was evening when he got home yesterday. 他昨天到家的时候已经是傍晚了。

It was slowly that the old lady walked in the park. 老太太在公园里慢慢地走着。

It is desired that we get everything ready by tonight. 希望我们在今晚以前把一切都准备好。

It was the fact that encouraged all of us. 这就是那个事实，让我们所有人备受鼓舞。

It is a fact that he didn't read the book. 他没读那本书，这是事实。

2. "what... is/was..." 结构表示强调

"what 从句+be+被强调成分"结构,通常称为"假性分裂句"。多用来强调谓语动词,有时也可以强调宾语。例如:

What she did was (to) go over her lessons. 她所做的事是复习功课。

What the professor did this morning was to interview some foreign scholars. 教授今天上午所做的事就是接见了一些外国学者。

What I am doing is teaching him a lesson. 我是在给他一个教训。

What he brought to me was a bunch of flowers. 他带给我的是一束花。

3. wh-ever 疑问强调句型

疑问词后加上 ever,如 whatever、whenever、wherever、whichever、whoever、whomever、whosever、however 等词可以表示强调,意为"究竟,到底"。例如:

Whatever/What ever are you going to do this afternoon? 今天下午你究竟要干什么?

Whenever/When ever shall we go to Shanghai? 我们究竟什么时候去上海?

However/How ever did you come along here in such a short time? 在如此短的时间内,你究竟是如何过来的?

Wherever did you get that book? 那本书你究竟是从哪儿得来的?

4. 倒装结构表强调

倒装结构常用来表示强调。例如:

Little does he care whether we live or die. 他丝毫不关心我们的死活。

Not a single book did he read that week. 他那一周一本书也没读。

So sudden was the attack that we had no time to escape. 袭击来的非常突然,我们来不及逃跑。

Under no condition can visitors be allowed to walk on the grass. 任何情况下游人都不能践踏草地。

巩 固 练 习

Complete the following sentences by choosing the items marked A, B, C, or D.

1. We have been told that under no circumstances _____ the telephone in the office for personal affairs.

   A. may we use   B. we may use   C. we could use   D. did we use

2. We laugh at jokes, but seldom _____ about how they work.

   A. we think   B. think we   C. we do think   D. do we think

3. Most foreign students don't like American coffee, and _____ .

   A. I don't too   B. either don't I

   C. so do I   D. neither do I

4. Jane won't join us for dinner tonight and _____ .

   A. neither won't Tom   B. Tom won't either

   C. Tom will too   D. so will Tom

5. _____ to win that she practised day and night.
   A. Such was her desire   B. Such her desire was
   C. So was her desire   D. So her desire was

6. Only when he reached the tea-house _____ it was the same place he'd been in last year.
   A. he realized   B. he did realize   C. realized he   D. did he realize

7. When changing lanes, a driver should use his turning signal to let other drivers know _____.
   A. he is entering which lane   B. which lane he is entering
   C. is he entering which lane   D. which lane is he entering

8. Not until he left his home _____ to know how important the family was for him.
   A. did he begin   B. had he begun   C. he began   D. he had begun

9. Not only _____ polluted but _____ crowded.
   A. was the city; were the streets   B. the city was; were the streets
   C. was the city; the streets were   D. the city was; the streets were

10. Distinguished guests and friends, welcome to our school. _____ the Anniversary this morning are our alumni (校友) from home and abroad.
    A. Attend   B. To attend   C. Attending   D. Having attended

11. So sudden _____ that the enemy had no time to escape.
    A. did the attack   B. the attack did
    C. was the attack   D. the attack was

12. _____, Simon offered to carry the heavy box onto the third floor for her.
    A. As tired he was   B. As he was tired
    C. Tired as he was   D. So tired was he

13. In no other restaurant _____ such bad service as in this one.
    A. I have experienced   B. have I experienced
    C. I never experienced   D. I had experienced

14. No sooner _____ than he realized that he should have remained silent.
    A. the words had spoken   B. the words had been spoken
    C. had the words spoken   D. had the words been spoken

15. Little _____ about her own safety, though she was in great danger herself.
    A. did Rose care   B. Rose did care
    C. Rose does care   D. does Rose care

16. So badly _____ in the accident that he had to stay in the hospital for a few weeks.
    A. did the man injure   B. was the man injured
    C. the man injured   D. the man was injured

17. If you have a job, _____ yourself to it and finally you'll succeed.
    A. do devote   B. don't devote   C. devoting   D. not devoting

18. _____ she first heard of the man referred to as a specialist.
    A. That was from Stephen   B. It was Stephen whom
    C. It was from Stephen that   D. It was Stephen that

19. John opened the door. There _____ he had never seen before.

  A. a girl stand   B. a girl stood   C. did a girl stand   D. stood a girl

20. John's success has nothing to do with good luck. It is years of hard work _____ has made him what he is today.

  A. why   B. when   C. which   D. that

21. _____ will I ask them for money.

  A. By all accounts   B. From all accounts   C. On no account   D. Of no account

22. Try _____ she might, Sue couldn't get the door open.

  A. if   B. when   C. since   D. as

23. _____ she would have been able to pass the exam.

  A. If she studies more   B. Should she study more

  C. If she studied more   D. Had she studied more

24. _____ by keeping down costs will Power Data hold its advantage over other companies.

  A. Only   B. Just   C. Still   D. Yet

25. Never _____ such an effort to save whales from extinction.

  A. there has been   B. has there been   C. there being   D. there to be

26. —Have you seen the film *Under the Hawthorn Tree*?

  —Of course, I have. It was in our village _____ it was made.

  A. that   B. how   C. when   D. which

27. _____ where we can have Chinese food.

  A. Next to it another restaurant is   B. Another restaurant it is next to

  C. Next is another restaurant to it   D. Next to it is another restaurant

28. Soon _____ a new development _____ had far-reaching effects.

  A. come; that   B. came; that   C. came; what   D. comes; that

29. At the meeting place of the Yangtze River and the Jialing River _____ , one of the ten largest cities in China.

  A. lies Chongqing   B. Chongqing lies

  C. does lie Chongqing   D. does Chongqing

30. For a moment nothing happened. Then _____ all shouting together.

  A. voices had come   B. came voices

  C. voices would come   D. did voices come

31. Hot objects emit more visible rays than _____ cold objects.

  A. do   B. emit   C. such   D. that

32. _____ that I could hardly see it.

  A. So small was the mark   B. So the mark was small

  C. Such small was the mark   D. Such the mark was small

33. It was _____ he came back from Africa that year _____ he met the girl he would like to marry.

  A. when; then   B. not; until

  C. not until; that   D. only; when

34. Earthquakes are not common in this region, almost never _____.
    A. they occur　　　B. do they occur　　　C. they do occur　　　D. are they occurring
35. Hearing the dog barking fiercely, away _____.
    A. fleeing the thief　　　　　　　　B. was fleeing the thief
    C. the thief was fleeing　　　　　　D. fled the thief
36. On her finger I saw the _____ ring I had given her twenty years ago.
    A. only　　　B. very　　　C. just　　　D. sole
37. —Can I buy stamps here?
    —Well, we _____ sell them, but we haven't got any at the moment.
    A. can　　　B. were to　　　C. do　　　D. will
38. _____ as it was at such a time, his work attracted much attention.
    A. Being published　　B. Publishing　　C. Published　　D. To be published
39. —Is everyone here?
    —Not yet... Look, there _____ the rest of our guests!
    A. come　　　B. comes　　　C. is coming　　　D. one coming
40. _____ she realized it was too late to go home.
    A. No sooner it grew dark than　　　　B. Hardly it grew dark that
    C. Scarcely had it grown dark than　　D. It was not until dark that

第二十六章

独立结构

热身训练： 下列句子各有一处错误，请指出并改正。

❶ The book writing in English, it will be more popular.
❷ Sam sat alone, head bending.
❸ We redoubled our effort, each man worked like two.
❹ Arrived at the spot, they were all standing in surprise face to face, eyes wide open.
❺ As the white skirt on you, you look smarter.
❻ The work doing, we went home.
❼ The girl stared at him, he didn't know what to say.
❽ There was no bus, we had to go home on foot.
❾ When and where to build the new factory are not decided yet.
❿ The writer and singer are here.

　　独立结构的特征有两个：一是有自己的逻辑主语，和句子的主语不一致；二是它没有限定形式。这类结构与句子的主要部分多用逗号隔开，有时也可用破折号。可表示时间、原因、条件、伴随状态和补充说明等。

一、独立结构的形式

（一）独立结构的基本形式

（1）名词/代词+名词。例如：
His first shot failure, he fired again. 他第一枪没打中，又打了一枪。
His book now a bestseller, he felt pleased with the world. 他的书成了畅销书，他对一切都满意了。
The strong winds uprooted lots of trees, most of them willows. 狂风把许多树连根拔起，其中大多数是柳树。

（2）名词/代词+形容词。例如：
He turned to me, his eyes sleepy. 他转向我，眼里充满倦意。
Ann sat down on the ground, her face pale with great pain. 安坐在地上，痛苦得脸色发白。

Angus stared at the picture, his mouth open. 安格斯盯着画看,嘴巴张得大大的。

（3）名词/代词+副词。例如：

The class over, we had a discussion. 下课后,我们进行了讨论。

The TV on, nobody seems to be watching it. 电视机开着,但似乎没人在看。

Nobody in, Bader decided to come again in the evening. 没人在家,巴德决定晚上再来。

（4）名词/代词+介词短语。例如：

Bede stood under the tree, his eyes on Bertha's back. 比德站在树下,眼睛望着伯莎的背影。

A girl came in, book in hand. 一个少女进来了,手里拿着书。

The old woman sat down, traces of tears still on her cheeks. 老太太坐了下来,面颊上还带有泪痕。

（5）名词/代词+动词不定式。例如：

Benge is leaving for the conference next week, all expenses to be paid by his company. 本奇下周去参加一个会议,所有费用由他的公司支付。

Many trees, flowers, and grass to be planted, our newly-built school will look even more beautiful. 种上许多树、花和草后,我们新建的学校看上去将更加美丽。

（6）名词/代词+现在分词。例如：

Weather permitting, we'll go outing tomorrow. 如果天气许可的话,我们明天去郊游。

Other things being the same, copper heats up faster than iron. 其他条件相同的情况下,铜比铁热得要快。

（7）名词/代词+过去分词。例如：

The job finished, we went home. 工作结束后我们就回家了。

This done, we felt relaxed a lot. 做完此事,我们感觉轻松多了。

The workers worked still harder, their living conditions greatly improved. 因为工人们的生活条件大大改善,他们工作更加努力了。

（二）with 引导的独立结构

介词 with 的宾语后带有名词、形容词、副词、介词短语、不定式、分词等,也可看作独立结构。

（1）with+名词/代词+名词。例如：

The workforce is made up of 400 workers,(with) most of them women. 这些劳工由 400 人组成,其中大部分是女性。

She died with her son yet a pupil. 她去世的时候,儿子还是个小学生。

（2）with+名词/代词+形容词。例如：

John likes sleeping with the window open. 约翰喜欢开着窗户睡觉。

A middle-aged woman entered the clinic, with her face pale. 一位中年妇女走进了诊所,脸色苍白。

（3）with+名词/代词+副词。例如：

Lynch left the classroom, with the lights on. 林奇离开了教室,灯还开着。

The child entered the room with his dirty shoes on. 那孩子穿着脏鞋子进了房间。

（4）with+名词/代词+介词短语。例如：

John was watching TV with a book on his head. 约翰头上顶着一本书看电视。

With tears of joy in her eyes, Selma saw her daughter marry. 塞尔玛眼里含着高兴的泪水,看着女儿出嫁。

（5）with+名词/代词+动词不定式。例如：

The little boy looks sad, with so much homework to do. 有这么多作业要做,小男孩看起来很难过。

With the meeting to begin in an hour, I had no time to think about other things. 会议一个小时后开始,我没有时间去考虑别的事情。

（6）with+名词/代词+现在分词。例如：

The girl hid her box without anyone knowing where it was. 女孩把盒子藏了起来,没有人知道它在哪里。

With the dog barking outside, he couldn't concentrate on the book. 由于外面狗在叫,他不能专心读书。

（7）with+名词/代词+过去分词。例如：

With nothing left in the cupboard, Linda went out to get something to eat. 因为家里橱柜里没有吃的了,琳达出去买些吃的。

With all the doors and windows shut, I slept the whole afternoon. 关上了所有的门窗,我整整睡了一个下午。

（三）"there being+名词/代词"的独立结构

"there being+名词/代词"的独立结构中,名词或代词是现在分词 being 的逻辑主语。例如：

There being no further business to discuss, we all went home. 没有别的事讨论,我们都回家了。

There being a taxi available, Barber was able to get to the airport before the plane took off. 因为有出租车,所以巴伯在飞机起飞前赶到了机场。

二、独立结构的句法功能

独立结构一般用于正式语体,位置比较灵活,可以出现在句首或句末,主要用作状语,表示时间、条件、原因、方式或伴随等。

（1）表示时间。例如：

The homework finished, Baker went to sleep. 作业完成后,贝克就去睡觉了。

The PE class over, they went back to the classroom again. 上完体育课后,他们又回到了教室。

My shoes removed, I entered a room, treading cautiously on the soft tatami matting. 我脱掉鞋子后,走进房间,小心翼翼地踩在软软的榻榻米床上。

（2）表示条件。例如：

Weather permitting, we will go outside fishing tomorrow. 如果天气许可,我们明天外出钓鱼。

Such being the case, you have no grounds for dismissing him. 如果情况如此,你没理由解聘他。

More time given, we would have done a better job of it. 如果给予更多的时间,我们会做得更好的。

（3）表示原因。例如：

The boy leading the way, we have no trouble finding the strange cave. 由于那个男孩带路,我们很容易就找到了那个奇怪的洞穴。

The last bus having gone, we had to take a taxi home. 末班车已出发,我们只好打的回家。

The storm drawing near, the workers decided to stop working. 暴风雨即将来临,工人们决定停止工作。

（4）表示方式或伴随状态。例如：

The hunter entered the forest, gun in hand. 那位猎人提着枪走进了森林。

The children returned, their faces covered with sweat. 孩子们回来了,满脸是汗。

Jim took his ticket and marched proudly up the platform, the people falling back respectfully. 吉姆拿着车票,昂首阔步走向月台。人们似乎很尊敬他,纷纷向后退去。

（5）表示进一步解释或补充说明。例如：

We have doubled our efforts, each man working like two. 我们加倍努力,一人干两人的活。

Bamboos grow up straight and thin, with branches at the top. 竹子长得又长又细,顶端长着枝杈。

There are two beautiful dresses, each having its own characteristics. 有两条漂亮的连衣裙,每条都有各自的特色。

巩 固 练 习

Complete the following sentences by choosing the items marked A, B, C, or D.

1. He lay on his back, his hands _____ under his head.
   A. crossing   B. crossed   C. to cross   D. having crossed
2. All flights _____ because of the terrible weather, they had to go there by train.
   A. having been canceled   B. had been canceled
   C. having canceled   D. were canceled
3. _____, copper heats up faster than iron.
   A. Other things to be equal   B. To be equal to other things
   C. When other things equal   D. Other things being equal
4. _____, we will go camping this weekend.
   A. Permitted by the weather   B. Weather permitting
   C. Weather to permit   D. Weather permits
5. Silver is the best conductor of electricity, copper _____ it closely.
   A. followed   B. following   C. to follow   D. being followed
6. Such _____ the case, it's very difficult to judge whose statement is true.
   A. was   B. were   C. being   D. be
7. She felt nervous, with so many eyes _____ on her.
   A. fix   B. fixing   C. fixed   D. to fix

8. All things _____, the planned trip will have to be called off.
   A. considered   B. be considered
   C. considering   D. having considered

9. So many people _____, the meeting had to be put off.
   A. were absent   B. being absent   C. been absent   D. had been absent

10. He felt more uneasy with the whole class _____ at him.
    A. to stare   B. stare   C. stared   D. staring

11. The decision _____, the next problem was how to make a good plan.
    A. had been made   B. having been made   C. having made   D. were made

12. This essay _____ the issue of manners, with particular attention _____ to table manners.
    A. deals with; being paid   B. deals with; paying
    C. dealing with; to pay   D. to deal with; paid

13. _____ left before the deadline it doesn't seem likely that John will accomplish the job.
    A. Although such a short time   B. It is such a short time
    C. With so short time   D. With such a short time

14. With time _____, living conditions in the countryside are greatly improved.
    A. progress   B. progressed   C. progressing   D. has progressed

15. Everything _____ into consideration, they ought to have another chance.
    A. to take   B. take   C. to be taken   D. taking

16. An expert _____ to help them tomorrow, they are sure to work out the problem.
    A. will come   B. coming   C. to come   D. having come

17. The meeting _____ over, he went to pick up his son directly.
    A. to be   B. is   C. was   D. being

18. Here are two volumes, the third one _____ next month.
    A. comes out   B. came out   C. coming out   D. to come out

19. With his son _____, the old man felt unhappy.
    A. to disappoint   B. to be disappointing
    C. disappointing   D. being disappointed

20. —Come on, please give me some ideas about the project.
    —Sorry. With so much work _____ my mind, I almost break down.
    A. filled   B. filling   C. to fill   D. being filled

21. John received an invitation to dinner, and with his work _____, he gladly accepted it.
    A. finished   B. finishing   C. having finished D. was finished

22. _____, I had to ask for two days' leave.
    A. Mother being ill   B. Mother ill
    C. As mother was ill   D. A, B and C

23. The thief stood before the policeman _____ admitting what he had done.
    A. with his dropping head   B. dropping his head
    C. raising his head   D. with his head down

24. Winter _____, it is time to buy warm clothes.
    A. has come on   B. is coming on   C. coming on   D. comes on
25. The old man lay on his back at the corner of the street, his eyes _____ and his hands _____.
    A. close; tremble   B. closed; trembling
    C. closing; trembling   D. closed; trembled
26. With nothing _____ to burn, the fire became weak and finally died out.
    A. leaving   B. leave   C. left   D. to leave
27. It was a pity that the great writer died _____ his works unfinished.
    A. for   B. with   C. of   D. from
28. I couldn't do my homework with that noise _____ on.
    A. to go   B. went   C. going   D. goes
29. _____ two exams to worry about, I have to work really hard this weekend.
    A. Because of   B. With   C. As for   D. Besides
30. Tom came home, _____.
    A. a dog following him   B. a dog followed him
    C. being followed him   D. a dog was followed him

第二十七章

as 的用法

热身训练： 下列句子各有一处错误，请指出并改正。

① With the weather is so bad, we have to delay our journey.
② Much for I like you, I couldn't live with you.
③ With time goes on, he will understand what I said.
④ It is known to everybody, the moon travels round the earth.
⑤ He is not such a fool which he looks.
⑥ Do that the Romans do when in Rome.
⑦ He is famous to a singer.
⑧ Don't do anything silly such like marrying him.
⑨ Take so things as you need.
⑩ I've never heard such a story that he told.

一、as 用作副词

as 用作副词时，表示"同样地，一样地"等意思。在"as… as…"结构中，第一个 as 是副词，第二个 as 是连词。例如：

Bloor runs as fast as I do. 布卢尔跑得和我一样快。

This is the law of jungle, as old and as true as the sky. 本法则就是森林法则，像上苍一般古老正确。

This dictionary is not as useful as you think. 这本字典不如你想象的那样有用。

二、as 用作介词

as 用作介词意为"作为……，当作……"等。
（1）表示主语的身份、用途、作用等。例如：

Allen works as a tour guide. 艾伦做导游工作。

Zhong Nanshan is a famous person as a doctor. 作为一名医生，钟南山很出名。

As a child, Sarah was sent abroad. 莎拉小时候就被送到了国外。

（2）用在宾语后，引出宾语补足语。其结构为：及物动词+名词/代词+as+名词/形容词/动名词/分词。常见的此类及物动词有：accept、acknowledge、classify、consider、define、describe、look on/upon、recognize、regard、see、take、think of、treat、use、focuse on 等。例如：

People consider/regard/look upon the boy as a second Einstein. 人们认为那个男孩是第二个爱因斯坦。

We have focused on development as the solution to all problems. 我们一直把发展作为解决所有问题的方法。

We accepted the story as true. 我们认为那个故事是真实的。

They treated me as being one of their own children. 他们把我当作他们自己的孩子。

They considered the problem as settled. 他们认为问题已经解决。

三、as 用作关系代词

（一）as 与 such 或 the same 连用

此时构成 such... as，the same... as 结构，引导限定性定语从句。意为"和/像……一样的人或事物"。例如：

Mabel is no longer the same as he was. 梅布尔不再是过去的他了。

Bloor made the same mistake as you did in the last exam. 在上次考试中，布卢尔犯了跟你一样的错误。

Bader bought such a pen as I lost last week. 巴德买了一支和我上周丢失的一样的笔。

It was not such a good job as she had read about in the advertisement. 这份工作并不像她在广告上看到的那样好。

（二）as 引导非限制性定语从句

用来代替整个主句，意为"像……那样，正如……"。例如：

As we all know, he is a good teacher. 众所周知，他是一位好老师。

Benge lives a long way from work, as you know. 本奇住得离工作单位远，这你是知道的。

Metals have many good properties, as has been stated before. 如前所述，金属有许多好的性能。

As we speak, three Chinese astronauts are on duty outer space; our fellow compatriots overseas are still working very hard. 正如我们所说，三位中国航天员正在浩瀚太空"出差"，我们海外的同胞仍在辛勤耕耘。

这种带有 as 的非限制性定语从句，常见的固定结构有 as we know/as everybody knows/as is known to all/as far as we know/concerned（众所周知）、as may be imagined（可以想象出来）、as might be expected（可以预料到的）、as I can see（如我所见）、as has been pointed out（正如已指出的）、as you will find out（正如你会发现的）、as often happens（正如常常发生的）、as is often the case（情况常常如此）。例如：

As anybody can see, they were telling a lie. 正如每个人所见，他们在说谎。

As is known to the United States, Mark Twain is a great American writer. 美国人都知道，马克吐温是一位伟大的美国作家。

He is absorbed in work, as he often was. 他正在全神贯注地工作，和他往常一样。

(三) as 表示"如……一样，……也如此"

表示"如……一样，……也如此"时，as 等于 and so，指一种情况也适用于另外的人。as 后的句子要倒装。例如：

Bloor can speak English and Japanese, as can Job. 布鲁尔会说英语和日语，乔布也会。
Iris worked hard, as did her husband. 艾丽丝工作很努力，她的丈夫也是如此。
They go to the concerts frequently, as do I. 他们常去听音乐会，我也一样。

四、as 用作连词

(1) 引导时间状语从句，表示"当……时，随着……，一边……一边"的意思。例如：
The students took notes as they listened. 学生们边听课边做笔记。
As my grandmother sang those old songs, tears ran down her cheeks. 当我奶奶唱起那些老歌时，眼泪顺着她的脸颊流了下来。

(2) 引导原因状语从句，意为"因为，由于"。例如：
As Job was absorbed in the problem, he forgot to eat dinner. 由于乔布全神贯注于这个问题，他忘了吃饭。
The year 2022 was a critical year for the Chinese people as they strove with confidence toward the second centenary goal. 2022 年是中国人民意气风发向第二个百年奋斗目标进军的关键之年。
As you make your bed, you must lie on it. 自己铺的床，就得自己睡。(〈谚〉自作自受。)

(3) 引导让步状语从句，as 意为"尽管，虽然"。可以用 though 替换，要用倒装结构，表语/状语/谓语动词提到句首。例如：
Little boy as he is, he knows a lot. 尽管他是个小男孩，但他还是知道很多。(**表语为单数名词时，省略冠词 a/an**)
Difficult as the work was, they finished it in time. 尽管工作很困难，他们还是及时完成了。
Hard as he studied, he couldn't pass the exam. 尽管他学习很努力，但考试还是没过。
Try as he might, Tom could not get out of the difficulties. 不管怎样努力，汤姆还是摆脱不了困境。

> **注**：这种倒装结构有时也表示原因，但表示原因时，as 不能用 though 替换。例如：
> Tired as I was, I went home and had a rest at once. 我因为太累了，所以就马上回家休息了。

(4) 引导方式状语从句，as 意为"如……那样，依照"；(just) as..., so... 的意思是"正如……，也……"例如：
I finished the work as my teacher told me to. 我按老师的要求完成了工作。
When in Rome, do as the Romans do. 〈谚〉入乡随俗。
Just as we sweep our rooms, so we should sweep backward ideas from our minds. 正如打扫房屋一样，我们也应该清除头脑中落后的思想。
As water is to fish, so air is to man. 我们离不开空气，犹如鱼儿离不开水。

（5）引导比较状语从句，常见的形式有：as... as, not as/so... as 等（第一个 as 是副词，第二个 as 是连词）。例如：

Tom is as excellent as his father. 汤姆和他的父亲一样优秀。

The number of students in our class is twice as large as that of theirs. 我们班的学生要比他们班多一倍。

Mary studies as hard as I do, but the result is not as good as me. 玛丽和我一样努力学习，但她的成绩不如我好。

五、含有 as 的习惯用语

常用的含有 as 的习惯用语有：as against（与……比较）、as a matter of fact、as a result、as a whole（整体看来，总体上）、as follows、as for（至于，关于）、as if/though、as it is（事实上）、as it were（可以说）、as/so long as（只要）、as opposed to（与……不同）、as regards（至于，关于）、as soon as、as to、as usual、as expected（像预期的一样）、as well（同样地，也）、as well as（既……，又……）等。例如：

As a result, he failed. 结果，他失败了。

Broadly speaking, the risks are as follows. 大体上说，风险大致如下。

As a matter of fact, she doesn't want to do that thing. 事实上，她不想做那件事。

As against last month, the profits increased by 10%. 和上个月相比，利润增加了 10%。

In spite of falling natality, the population as a whole went up. 尽管出生率在下降，人口总数还是上升了。

The teacher's attempts at enlightenment failed; I remained as confused as before. 教师虽尽力开导却劳而无功，我仍像以前一样糊涂。

巩 固 练 习

Complete the following sentences by choosing the items marked A, B, C, or D.

1. I thought things would get better, but _____ it was, they were getting worse.
   A. before   B. because   C. as   D. after

2. _____, he does get irritated with her sometimes.
   A. As he likes her much   B. Much that he likes her
   C. Though much he likes he   D. Much as he likes her

3. We will give you such data _____ will help you in your work.
   A. as   B. which   C. that   D. what

4. A square is usually defined _____ a rectangle with four equal sides.
   A. as   B. like   C. to be   D. being

5. I wish I could tide you over. _____, I am unable to help.
   A. As it is   B. As it was   C. As it were   D. As it will be

6. The professor paused as if _____ his students to ask questions on the point he had just made.
   A. expected   B. expecting   C. expect   D. to have expected

7. Change your mind _____ you will, or you will gain no additional support.
   A. although   B. even if   C. as   D. even though
8. Tired _____ she was, I decided not to disturb her.
   A. though   B. like   C. as   D. while
9. Sophia was not unconscious, _____ could be judged from her eyes.
   A. such   B. as   C. it   D. that
10. He was, _____, intoxicated by the soft air and sunshine of spring.
    A. as though   B. as it were   C. as things are   D. as ill
11. _____ last year, the number of our students increased by 50 percent.
    A. As to   B. As for   C. As regards   D. As against
12. We cannot expect her to do the homework _____ look after the children.
    A. as long as   B. as far as   C. as well as   D. as well
13. We can surely overcome these difficulties _____ we are closely united.
    A. as well as   B. as much as   C. as long as   D. as far as
14. She is _____ you are likely to find.
    A. as a nice woman as   B. as nice a woman as
    C. such a nice woman that   D. so nice a woman that
15. _____ is often the case with children, Tom was completely better by the time the doctor arrived.
    A. As   B. What   C. So   D. That
16. This Sunday, _____ Mrs. Martin will go to church.
    A. as a whole   B. as usual   C. as such   D. as follows
17. Careful surveys have indicated that as many as 50 percent of patients do not take drugs _____ directed.
    A. like   B. which   C. so   D. as
18. It is generally believed that teaching is _____ it is a science.
    A. much as an art as   B. as much an art as   C. an art as much as   D. as much as an art
19. He had failed to visit her _____ promised.
    A. that   B. as   C. like   D. which
20. _____ I admire David as a poet, I don't like him as a man.
    A. Only if   B. If only   C. As much   D. Much as
21. I wonder why you don't do it as _____ and it's the third time you have done so.
    A. told you   B. be told   C. told to   D. you told
22. _____ I explain on the phone, your request will be considered at the next meeting.
    A. What   B. When   C. After   D. As
23. That is _____ problem _____ can't be worked out by any of us.
    A. a such difficult; that   B. so difficult a; that
    C. such a difficult; as   D. a so difficult; as
24. _____ is generally accepted, economical growth is determined by the smooth development of production.
    A. What   B. That   C. It   D. As

25. _____ time went on, Einstine's theory _____ right.
    A. With; proved   B. As; be proved
    C. With; be proved   D. As; was proved to be
26. He will surely finish the job on time _____ he's left to do it in his own way.
    A. as if   B. even if   C. so long as   D. so that
27. Do come to my party, and bring your sister _____.
    A. as good   B. as a whole   C. as well   D. instead
28. It's useless trying to argue with the sort of him. You might _____ go and stand upon the beach and argue with the sea.
    A. as well   B. also   C. as if   D. as well as
29. That is _____ problem _____ none of us can work it out.
    A. a such difficult; that   B. so difficult a; that
    C. such a difficult; as   D. a so difficult; as
30. All the gifts must be mailed immediately _____ in time for Christmas.
    A in order to have received   B. in order to received
    C. so as to be received   D. so as to be receiving

第二十八章

否定结构

热身训练： 下列句子各有一处错误，请指出并改正。

❶ I didn't see neither of you.
❷ You not hardly ever come to see us.
❸ I don't believe she knows it, doesn't she?
❹ It's a very toughing story, I don't believe you will read it with being moved to tears.
❺ Don't begin with asking for advice.
❻ None job is easy enough for him to do.
❼ The students went on strike, but no the teachers.
❽ A flag is not more than a piece of cloth. It stands for a national people and their land and their history.
❾ I don't think he can do the work well, can't he?
❿ It is ever too old to learn.

英语中的否定结构通常用否定词（如 not、no、never、nobody、no one、nothing、nowhere、neither、nor 等）或者半否定词（如 hardly、barely、rarely、scarcely、seldom、few、little 等）来表示。

一、否定词 not 的位置和用法

（1）若谓语部分含有系动词、助动词或情态动词，就直接把 not 放在这些词后面构成否定句。例如：

They haven't come back from the disaster area. 他们还没有从灾区回来。
I can't hear a word. 我根本听不见。
I'm not American; I'm Canadian. 我不是美国人，我是加拿大人。

（2）若谓语部分没有系动词、助动词或情态动词，则通过加助动词 do 的具体形式和 not 来构成否定句。例如：

Oil and water do not mix. 油和水不相融。
Pure gold does not dread fire. 真金不怕火炼。

（3）祈使句否定时，直接在动词原形前面加"Do not/Don't"。例如：

Do not/Don't be late next time! 下次别迟到。
Do not/Don't press us for an answer. 别逼我们回答。
（4）不定式、动名词和分词等否定时，直接把 not 放在它们的前面。例如：
Try not to get your shoes wet. 尽量别弄湿了鞋子。
Not being tall is not a serious disadvantage in life. 个子不高在生活中并不是一个严重的不利条件。
Not knowing how to do it, he asked his coach for help. 他不知怎么做这件事，就向他的教练寻求帮助。

二、否定的方式

否定分为全部否定、部分否定、双重否定等多种方式。

（一）全部否定

全部否定可以用表示完全否定的词 no、not、none、never、neither、nor、nobody、nowhere、nothing 等构成。例如：
Nobody was killed in the earthquake. 地震中没有人丧生。
No one told me that the meeting was put off. 没有人告诉我会议推迟了。
Nothing beats home cooking. 什么也比不上家里做得好吃。
Neither of you will be allowed to attend the party. 你们两个都不能参加晚会。
None of my friends know/knows about the plan because it is a secret. 我的朋友都不知道这个计划，因为这是机密。
My glasses are nowhere to be found. 到处都找不到我的眼镜。

（二）部分否定

部分否定的含义是"不都是，不全是"，主要由表示全体意义的代词或副词如 all、both、every、each、everyone、everything、everywhere、everybody 等与 not 搭配来构成。例如：
Not all birds can fly.（All birds can't fly.）并不是所有的鸟都会飞。
Everybody wouldn't like it. 并非每个人都喜欢它。
Not every relationship will endure. 不是每段感情都会长久。
All that glitters is not gold.〈谚〉闪闪发光的未必都是金子。
Both of them are not hard-working students. 他们俩不都是勤奋学习的学生。

（三）几乎否定

由 barely、few、little、hardly、rarely、scarcely、seldom 等半否定词与谓语动词肯定式连用构成，语气比较弱，也称"半否定"。例如：
I hardly ever go to concerts. 我很少去听音乐会。
Lynch has few friends here, so he feels lonely. 林奇这里没什么朋友，所以他感觉寂寞。
I can speak little French. 我几乎不怎么会说法语。
Mill seldom, if ever, buys goods online. 如果说米尔在网上购物的话，那次数也是很少的。

(四) 双重否定

由 not 加上具有否定意义的词构成。双重否定相当于肯定,用来表示强调或表示委婉的说法。例如:

Man can't live without air. 人没有空气便不能生存。
It's never too late to learn. 〈谚〉活到老,学到老。
Nothing is impossible. 一切皆有可能。
You can't make something out of nothing. 〈谚〉巧妇难为无米之炊。

(五) 接续否定

接续否定也称追加否定,它是对前面的否定句,再进一步补充否定。例如:

Even grown-ups can't lift it, to say nothing of children. 连大人都举不起来,更不用说孩子了。
Tom can't afford to buy a bike, much less a car. 汤姆连自行车都买不起,更别说买车了。
She doesn't like music, still less dancing. 她不喜欢音乐,更不用说跳舞了。

(六) 特指否定

谓语动词被否定称为一般否定,其他非谓语成分被否定称为特指否定或局部否定。例如:

He likes watching TV, but not often. 他喜欢看电视,但不经常看。
I told her not to go out by herself at night. 我叫她晚上别独自出去。
It is a good idea not to tell her the bad news. 不告诉她那个坏消息是对的。

(七) 转移否定

转移否定是指某些复合句,否定形式上出现在主句部分,但否定意义实际上转移到从句部分的现象。

(1) 主要用于表示"判断、看法"的动词,如 assume、believe、expect、guess、imagine、reckon、suppose、think 等。例如:

I don't believe that Jim will lose the game. 我相信吉姆不会输掉这场比赛。
I don't think Angell is a good teacher. 我认为安吉尔不是一个好老师。
Most of the students don't suppose the monitor is capable of his job. 大部分学生认为班长不能胜任他的工作。

(2) appear、feel、seem、sound 等系动词的否定形式,也常有否定意义后移的现象。例如:

The weather doesn't look very promising. 天气看起来不会太好。
Your idea doesn't sound great. 你的主意听起来不是很好。
It doesn't look like it's going to rain. 天好像不会下雨。

(3) 在 not... because 句型中,有时出现否定的转移现象。例如:

He did not come to the hospital this morning because he was sick. 他今天早上来医院并不是因为他生病了。
She doesn't teach because she is interested in teaching. 她教书并不是因为她对教学感兴趣。
The engine didn't stop because the fuel was finished. 引擎并不是因为燃料耗尽而停止运转

（八）多余否定

多余否定指的是有些句子,否定词 not 可有可无,即有无 not 意思不变,这个否定词是多余的,通常不译出来。例如：

I want to know if it will (not) rain tomorrow. 我想知道明天是否会下雨。

I'm not sure if he could (not) come back. 我不确定他是否能回来。

I wonder if I should wear a coat (or not). 我不知道我该不该穿外套。

三、肯定形式表示否定意义

用肯定形式表示否定意义一般有以下几种情况。

（一）具有否定意义的句型

(1) more than... can/could（超出……的,非……所能）。例如：

The problem is more than you can handle. 这个问题你处理不了。

The pain is more than I can stand. 痛得我受不了。

Don't bite off more than you can chew. 不要贪多嚼不烂（不要好高骛远——凡事量力而行）。

(2) 比较级+than+不定式,意为"明白事理而不至于……"。例如：

He is more considerate than to sit idle while others are busy. 他是个很体贴的人,绝不会看别人忙碌而自己游手好闲。

I am clever enough to have more sense than to tell him about our plan. 我很聪明,不至于把我们的计划告诉他。

You ought to know better than to be cheated. 你应该明白事理不要上当受骗。

(3) the last...+不定式/定语从句（the last 意为"最不可能,最不合适,决不会"等）。例如：

He is the last one to get here. 他决不会到这儿来。

He is the last person I want to meet in school. 他是我在学校里最不想碰见的人。

That's the last thing I'd expect you to do. 那是我最不期望你做的事情。

(4) too... to...（太……以致不能）例如：

She is too young to tell right from wrong. 她还太小,不能分清是非。

George is too full to eat any more. 乔治太饱了,再也吃不下任何东西。

The child is too tired to go further. 那小孩太累不能再走了。

注：① too 与 anxious、apt、eager、easy、ready、willing 等连用时,它表示肯定的意思。例如：

We are too eager to do so. 我们太渴望这样做了。

She is too willing to pay the price I ask. 她非常愿意照我的要价付钱。

② only/all/but too... to...意为"极,非常",表示肯定的意思。例如：

The children are but too glad to play together with their teacher. 这些孩子非常高兴和他们的老师一起玩。

He's only too excited to see you. 他见到你很激动。

（5） have yet to+动词（相当于 have not yet+过去分词）。例如：

I have yet to decide which team I choose to join. 我还没决定我加入哪个队伍。

I have yet to figure out what to do next. 我还没想好接下来该怎么做。

（二）含有否定意义的词和短语

含有否定意义的词和短语有动词型、名词型、形容词型、副词型、连词型、介词型及其他习惯用语型等。

（1）动词型有 avoid、cease、decline、deny、doubt、escape、exclude、fail、forbid、ignore、lack、miss、neglect、refuse、reject、resist、overlook、wonder、get rid of、give up、live up to、keep/protect/prevent/stop...from...等。例如：

They failed to pass the last CET-4. 他们没有通过上次的大学英语四级考试。

The students lived up to their teachers' expectations. 学生没有辜负他们老师的期望。

The Coast Guard have given up all hope of finding the two divers alive. 海岸警卫队已放弃了两名潜水员生还的全部希望。

She quitted her job to join her husband's campaign. 她辞了工作，以参加丈夫的竞选活动。

（2）名词型有 absence、failure、denial、refusal、ignorance、lack、shortage、reluctance、exclusion、loss 等。例如：

What was the real reason for your absence? 你缺席的真正原因是什么？

He was in an entire ignorance of what was being done. 他完全不知道正在做的事情。

Exclusion of air creates a vacuum in the bottle. 瓶子里的空气排出后就产生真空。

Lack of current capital seemed the reason why they defeated their business. 缺少流动资本似乎是他们的企业告败的原因。

（3）形容词型有 absent、different、ignorant、reluctant、free of/from、far from、safe from、short of、clear of/from、foreign to、alien to、blind to、deaf to 等。例如：

Dishonesty is foreign to his nature. 弄虚作假并非他的本性。

She was blind to the silent worship in his eyes. 她没有发觉他眼里流露出的无声的敬慕之情。

I'm short of cash right now. 我眼下正缺钱。

（4）副词型有 barely、hardly、little、rarely、never、scarcely、seldom、otherwise、in vain 等。例如：

It became obvious that all her complaints were in vain. 很明显她所有的抱怨都是白费口舌。

We rarely agree on what to do. 我们很少在要做的事情上看法一致。

I've got hardly any money. 我几乎身无分文。

I think it will rain this afternoon, but Jenny thinks otherwise. 我认为下午会下雨，但詹妮认为不会。

（5）连词型有 before、unless、rather than 等。例如：

I'll do it now before I forget it. 趁我还没忘记的时候就做。

You can't imagine how moving the story is, unless you read it. 除非你读了这个故事，不然你想象不到这个故事有多么感人。

The sweater she bought was beautiful rather than cheap. 她买的这件羊毛衫与其说便宜不如说它漂亮。

（6）介词型有 above、against、before、below、beside、beyond、but、but for、except、off、past、without、instead of、regardless of、in spite of、at a loss、out of the question 等。例如：

I'll take the job regardless of the pay. 不管报酬多少我都要这份工作。

Life without the Internet had no savour, was tedious, insupportable. 没有网络的生活平淡无趣、单调沉闷,让人难以忍受。

The islanders use a system of barter instead of money. 岛上的居民实行的是以物易物,而不是用货币。

（7）习惯用语型有 anything but（绝对不）、leave much to be desired（很不完善）、much/still/even less（更不用说）、other than（不同于,除了）、to say nothing of/not to speak of/not to mention/let alone（更不用说）等。例如：

That kind of person is anything but a Marxist. 那种人根本不是马克思主义者。

Schooling and hospitals also leave much to be desired. 学校教育和医院也有很多不尽如人意的地方。

He can't discipline himself, much less set a good example for his children to follow. 他不能以身作则,更不用说做孩子们的榜样。

I don't know any French people other than you. 除了你,我不认识别的法国人。

四、否定形式表示肯定意义

有些句型和短语尽管形式上看是否定的,但意义上却是肯定的。

（一）带有肯定意义的句型

（1）cannot (help) but do sth.、cannot keep from、cannot refrain from、cannot help doing sth.、have no choice/alternative but to do sth.（不得不,不能不,不禁要）。例如：

Black can't but tell the teacher the truth. 布莱克不得不告诉老师真相。

We couldn't keep from laughing, when Jane finished the story. 当珍妮讲完这个故事,我们忍不住笑起来了。

We had no choice but to do what we were asked. 出于无奈,我们只得按要求做。

People cannot refrain from recalling their contribution to the development of the Chinese culture and traditions. 他们为弘扬中华传统文化作出的贡献,人们是不会忘记的。

（2）cannot… too (over/enough)（无论如何也不过分）。例如：

Firms can't be too cautious about hiring new workers. 公司雇用新员工越谨慎越好。

While you are doing your homework, you can't be careful enough. 当你做家庭作业时,你越仔细越好。

I cannot over emphasize how important this first step is. 这第一步实在是太重要了。

（3）cannot wait to do（迫不及待地做,急于做）。例如：

The children can't wait to see their mother 孩子们渴望见到他们的母亲。

We are very hungry and can't wait to have dinner. 我们很饿,急着吃饭。

（4）否定词+until/till/before/unless/but（that）等。例如：

Draw not your bow till/before your arrow is fixed. 箭搭好了再拉弓。（〈谚〉不打无准备之战。）

There is no one but knows him. 人人都认识他。
No one believes but that Selma will succeed. 人们相信塞尔玛会成功。

（5）否定词+比较级（+than），否定词+so+形容词+as，表示肯定，相当于最高级。例如：
I couldn't feel more hungry. 我感觉饿极了。
I've never seen a nicer bird than this one. 我从没有见过比这更美的鸟。
Nobody is so well qualified for the position as he. 没有人比他更适合这个职位。
No one is so blind as those that won't see. 有眼无珠的人最眼瞎。

（二）反问句

形式上是否定疑句，但实质上并不表示疑问，而表示强烈的肯定。例如：
Who does not know the story? 人人都知道这个故事。
Can't we just stand here? 我们就站在这儿吧。
Isn't the answer obvious? 答案很清楚。
What does not he know? 他无所不知。

（三）具有肯定意义的短语

常见的有 in no time、none but、not half、nothing but、none/no other than，nothing else than、leave nothing to be desired 等。例如：
It isn't half windy today. 今天风好大。
Last evening Mond did nothing but repair his telephone. 昨晚蒙德只修理了手机。
His lecture left nothing to be desired. 他的演讲非常成功。
She is none other than Professor Wang. 她正是王教授。
She'll have them eating out of her hand in no time. 她很快就会让他们俯首帖耳的。

五、容易混淆的否定结构

1. no more than 与 not more than

no more than 指确定的数目，强调"少"，译为"只不过，仅仅，才"；not more than 陈述客观事实，意为"不超过，不多于"。例如：
There is room for no more than three cars. 这地方只能停放三辆车。
This main avenue is not more than eight feet wide. 这条主干道的宽度不超过八英尺。

2. no less than 与 not less than

no less than 强调数目之多，意为"多达，高达"，相当于 as much/many as，与 no more than 意思刚好相反；not less than 陈述客观事实，意为"不少于"。例如：
Briefly, no less than nine of our agents have passed information to us. 简而言之，至少已经有9位我们的代理商将信息传递给了我们。
Write a narrative of not less than 300 words. 写一篇不少于300字的记叙文。

3. no better than 与 not better than

A is no better than B 表达 A 和 B 都很坏（差）；而 A is not better than B 只是客观地进行比较，意为"A 不比 B 好（强）"。例如：

Her English is no better than mine. 她的英语跟我一样差。

John is not better than Tom. 约翰并不比汤姆好。

Jim is no more careful than you. 吉姆和你都不仔细。

He who listens to truth is not less than he who utters truth. 聆听真理的人并不亚于说出真理的人。

4. not a bit 与 not a little

not a bit 表示"一点也不"(not at all); not a little 意为"非常,很"(much)。例如:

Benge is not a bit brave. 本奇一点儿也不勇敢。

Tom is not a little brave. 汤姆非常勇敢。

5. I am no... 与 I am not a/an...

I am no...意为"我绝不是……""我不善于……""我不是……的材料"等,说话人在职业上可能是……,也可能不是……; I am not a/an...表示"我不是……"(在职业上),表明身份。例如:

I am no doctor. 我绝不是做医生的料。

I am not a doctor. 我不是医生。(表明身份)

Simon is no lawyer. 西蒙不懂法律。

Bertha is not a lawyer. 伯莎不是律师。(表明身份)

巩固练习

Complete the following sentences by choosing the items marked A, B, C, or D.

1. Little _____ about his own safety, though he was in great danger.
   A. does he care   B. did he care   C. he cares   D. he cared

2. _____ got into the room, _____ the telephone rang.
   A. He hardly had; then   B. Hardly had he; when
   C. He had not; than   D. Not had he; when

3. —The boys are not doing a good job at all, are they?
   —_____.
   A. I guess not so   B. I don't guess   C. I don't guess so   D. I guess not

4. Tom kept quiet about the accident _____ lose the job.
   A. so not as to   B. so as not to   C. so as to not   D. not so as to

5. —I don't like chicken _____ fish.
   —I don't like chicken, _____ I like fish very much.
   A. and; and   B. and; but   C. or; and   D. or; but

6. _____ a reply, he decided to write again.
   A. Not receiving   B. Receiving not
   C. Not having received   D. Having not received

7. We couldn't eat in a restaurant, because _____ of us had _____ money on us.
   A. all; no   B. any; no   C. none; any   D. on one; any

8. They were all tired, but _____ of them would stop to take a rest.

    A. any   B. some   C. none   D. neither

9. Both teams were in hard training; _____ was willing to lose the game.

    A. either   B. neither   C. another   D. the other

10. I agree with most of what you said, but I don't agree with _____ .

    A. everything   B. anything   C. something   D. nothing

11. _____ he comes, we won't be able to go.

    A. Without   B. Unless   C. Except   D. Even

12. —You can't finish the book in less than an hour, I suppose?

    —_____.

    A. Yes, I'm sure I can   B. No, hardly

    C. Sorry, I can't   D. I don't think I can't

13. It's impossible for all the people to get jobs because _____ of them are not fit for them.

    A. none   B. all   C. not all   D. every one

14. Never _____ forget the days when _____ together with you.

    A. Shall I; I lived   B. Shall I; did I live

    C. I shall; I lived   D. I shall; I lived

15. For _____ students, their teacher's advice is more important than _____ of their parents'.

    A. few; one   B. a few; that   C. a little; some D. a lot; many

16. He didn't like coffee _____ tea, but water.

    A. and   B. or   C. but   D. with

17. —I haven't found any money, though I've searched the drawer bottom up.

    —Then, I'm afraid there is _____ left.

    A. nothing   B. no one   C. none   D. neither

18. By no means _____ to your parents.

    A. is the first time you are lying   B. this is the first time you have lied

    C. this is the first time you tell a lie D. is this the first time you have lied

19. The purpose of the new plan is to make life easier, _____ it more difficult.

    A. not make   B. not to make   C. not making   D. do not make

20. —It is a long time since I saw my sister.

    —_____ her this week.

    A. Why not visit   B. Why not to visit

    C. Why not visiting   D. Why don't visit

21. Is there a law _____ spitting in the streets in this country?

    A. against   B. towards   C. from   D. for

22. I must be getting fat. I can _____ do my trousers up.

    A. fairly   B. hardly   C. nearly   D. seldom

23. I know nothing about the young lady _____ she is from Beijing.

    A. except   B. except for   C. except that   D. besides

24. —Must I turn off the gas after cooking?
    —Of course. You can never be _____ careful with that.
    A. enough   B. too   C. so   D. very

25. He never said that he was good at English, _____?
    A. was he   B. wasn't he   C. did he   D. didn't he

26. As I know, there is _____ car in this neighbourhood.
    A. no such   B. no a   C. not such   D. no such a

27. —I'd like some more cheese.
    —Sorry, there is _____ left.
    A. some   B. none   C. a little   D. few

28. —Shall I give you a ride as you live so far away?
    —Thank you. _____.
    A. It couldn't be better   B. Of course you can
    C. If you like   D. It's up to you

29. The dog seems very quiet now, but he still _____ go by.
    A. dare not to   B. dare not
    C. does not to dare   D. dares not

30. —So comfortable a bed!
    —Yes. We can never find _____ one.
    A. a better   B. the best   C. a worse   D. the worst

31. —She looks upset.
    —Yes, I'd rather I _____ her the bad news.
    A. didn't tell   B. don't tell
    C. hadn't told   D. wouldn't tell

32. —Why hasn't our English teacher been invited to the English Evening being held here now?
    —She _____ an important article when I found her and she _____ it.
    A. had written; didn't finish   B. was writing; hasn't finished
    C. wrote; hasn't finished   D. was writing; hadn't finished

33. My dictionary _____. I have looked for it everywhere but still _____ it.
    A. has lost; don't find   B. is missing; don't find
    C. has lost; haven't found   D. is missing; haven't found

34. _____ I had done it I knew I had made a mistake.
    A. Hardly   B. Directly   C. Mostly   D. Nearly

35. In my opinion, what he told us just now about the affair simply doesn't make any _____.
    A. idea   B. meaning   C. sense   D. point

36. _____ you don't like him is none of my business.
    A. What   B. Who   C. That   D. Whether

37. I don't have a job. I would find one but I _____ no time.
    A. had   B. didn't have   C. had had   D. have

38. The customer didn't choose _____ of the coats and went away without looking at a third one.

  A. both   B. all   C. any   D. either

39. It must be he that has stolen Mr. Smith's purse, _____?

  A. hasn't he   B. isn't he   C. mustn't it   D. isn't it

40. I don't think he could have done such a stupid thing last night, _____?

  A. did he   B. could he   C. do I   D. hasn't he

第二十九章

标点符号与分隔现象

一、标点符号

标点符号是书面语中用于标示句子或词组之间停顿的一种符号。常用的英语标点符号有十二种,如表29-1所示。

表29-1 常用的英语标点符号

标 点 名	符号	标 点 名	符号
句号(Full Stop)	.	问号(Question Mark)	?
感叹号(Exclamation Mark)	!	逗号(Comma)	,
冒号(Colon)	:	分号(Semicolon)	;
连字符(Hyphen)	-	破折号(Em Dash)	—
括号(Parentheses)	( )	引号(Quotation Marks)	(双)" ";(单)' '
撇号(Apostrophe)	'	省略号(Ellipses)	…

注:英语标点中没有汉语的书名号、顿号,书名常用斜体字,文章标题常用引号标示。

(一) 句号的用法

(1) 用于陈述句或语气不太强烈的祈使句末尾。例如:
We have a great admiration for her courage. 我们非常钦佩她的勇气。
Be careful of what you are doing. 做事要小心。
(2) 用于某些缩略词之后。例如:
Mr.、Mrs.、Dr.、Prof.、a.m.、kg.、pron.、Dec.、M.A.(Master of Arts 文科硕士)等。

注:在英语中,有些缩略词常省略句号,如:UN(联合国)、USA(美国)、UK(英国)、CPC(中国共产党)、WWⅡ(第二次世界大战)、MIT(麻省理工学院)、UNESCO(联合国教科文组织)等。

(3) 用于不期待对方回答,形式上是疑问句,实质上是表示请求、规劝等意义。例如:
Will you please give me a cup of tea. 请给我一杯茶。
May I use your computer for a moment. 我借用一下你的计算机。

(二) 问号的用法

（1）用在疑问句的末尾。例如：

Which of the questions are more difficult? 哪些问题比较难？

How will you solve the problem? 你将如何解决这个问题？

（2）用在陈述句末，表示疑问，此时句子用升调。例如：

You've studied Japanese? 你学过日语？

You mean you're also from Japan? 你是说你也来自日本吗？

(三) 感叹号的用法

（1）用于感叹词、感叹句之后。例如：

What fine weather it is! 多好的天气呀！

How hard he works! 他学习多努力啊！

My god! I left my umbrella on the bus. 天啊！我把雨伞落在公交车上了。

（2）用于祈使句，加强祈使语气。例如：

Get out! 出去！

Don't be so self-satisfied! 别这样自满！

Stop probing! 别刨根问底了！

（3）用于祝福语、口号等之后。例如：

May you succeed! 祝你成功！

Long live the People's Republic of China! 中华人民共和国万岁！

（4）用于其他词、短语或句子后，表示强烈的感情或引起注意。例如：

Help! I can't swim. 救命啊！我不会游泳。

Oh! we'll miss the plane. 我们赶不上飞机啦！

The exams came to an end at last! 考试终于结束了！

(四) 逗号的用法

（1）分隔句子中并列的平行成分。例如：

Tokyo, Shanghai, New York, Beijing and London are the five largest cities in the world. 东京、上海、纽约、北京和伦敦是世界上5个最大的城市。

Keep calm, take your time, concentrate and think twice before you do. 保持镇定，慢慢来，集中精力，三思而后行。

He is a very lovable man, kind-hearted, easy to get along with and always ready to help others. 他是一个很可爱的人，心地善良、容易相处，总是乐于助人。

（2）分隔并列连词连接的两个或两个以上的独立分句。例如：

He is clever, but he can't be trusted. 他很聪明,但是不可信任。

We must leave now, or we can't catch the train. 我们必须马上动身，否则就赶不上火车了。

The length of your education is less important than its breadth, and the length of your life is less important than its depth. 教育的长度不如其广度重要，生命的长度不如其深度重要。

（3）分隔放在句首或插在句子中间的状语从句（或其省略形式）。例如：

When the bell rings, stop writing. 铃响,就不要再写了。

If you're ever in Beijing, come and look me up. 一旦你到北京,可得来看我。

This medicine, taken in time, can be very effective. 这种药如果及时服用会很有效。

(4) 分隔放在句首或插在句子中间的某些其他形式的状语。例如:

To make sure to get there on time, I left an hour early. 为了确保能准时到达那里,我提前一个小时出发了。

In spite of their good intentions, most parents do not really understand their children. 大部分家长虽然好心,但他们并不真正了解自己的孩子。

I needn't, therefore, give you a route map. 因此我不必给你交通路线图。

(5) 分隔作状语的分词短语。例如:

Seeing his brother hurt, Tom ran to help him. 汤姆看到弟弟受伤了,就跑过去帮他。

Given enough time, I will accomplish the task. 给我足够的时间,我就能完成这项工作。

(6) 分隔作状语的独立结构。例如:

The task finished, Tom had a two-month leave. 任务完成后,汤姆休了两个月的假。

The day being fine, we decided to go swimming. 天气很好,我们决定去游泳。

She entered the office, her nose red with cold. 她走进办公室,鼻子冻得通红。

(7) 分隔非限制性定语从句、同位语或附加说明的词语。例如:

The old man has a son, who is in the army. 那位老人有一个儿子,在部队工作。

Her hobby, collecting stamps, brings her many friends. 她集邮的爱好给她带来许多朋友。

Jenney has to get up early, particularly on weekends. 珍妮必须早起,尤其是周末。

(8) 分隔附加疑问句或选择疑问句。例如:

Bloor worked very hard, didn't he? 布卢尔工作很努力,不是吗?

Which mobile phone do you prefer, the golden one or the silvery one? 你更喜欢哪个手机,金色的还是银色的?

(9) 分隔直接引语和引述语。例如:

Mary said, "Let's go skiing." 玛丽说:"我们去滑雪吧。"

"Wait a minute," Tony exclaimed, "I'm nearly ready." 托尼喊道:"等一下,我快准备好了。"

"Only a fool," Jack said, "would continue like that." 杰克说道:"只有傻瓜才那样做下去。"

(10) 用于日期或地址等后面。例如:

The meeting will be held at 2 p.m., October 20nd, in Classroom (No.) 405, 4th floor, Southeast Building. 会议定于10月20日下午2时在东南大楼4楼405室召开。

His address is 118 Nanjing Road, Shanghai, China. 他的地址是中国上海市南京路118号。

(11) 分隔呼语(美国用法中多用冒号)或末尾客套语之后。例如:

Good morning, Miss Annie! 安妮小姐,早!

Harry, shall we go shopping this weekend? 哈利,我们周末去逛街好吗?

You are warmly welcome, new schoolmates! 热烈欢迎新同学!

Dear Dr. Smith, (英国)/Dear Dr. Smith: (美国) 亲爱的史密斯博士:

Yours sincerely, (英国)/Sincerely yours: (美国) 你忠实的:

(12) 用于 oh、yes、no、excuse me、well、sorry 等之后。例如:

Yes, I saw him just now in the meeting-room. 是的,我刚刚在会议室看到他。

Well, perhaps you are right. 嗯,可能你是对的。

Excuse me, which is the way to the subway station? 请问地铁站怎么走?

(五)冒号的用法

(1)用于列举的事物前。例如:

Please buy me some fruits: apples, oranges and bananas. 请给我买些水果:苹果、橘子和香蕉。

There are two articles in modern English: the indefinite article and the definite article. 现代英语中有两种冠词:不定冠词和定冠词。

(2)解释或说明上文。例如:

This is her plan: go shopping. 这就是她的计划——逛街。

My mother taught us one important rule in life: always be honest. 母亲教给我们一条重要的生活原则:永远要诚实。

(3)正式文体中可以用在引述语之后。例如:

Shakespeare said: "Neither a borrower nor a lender be." 莎士比亚说:"既不要找人借钱,也不要借钱给人。"

A Chinese proverb says: "Blood is thicker than water." 中国有句谚语:"血浓于水。"

(4)用于书名或文章的主标题和副标题之间。例如:

Stylistics: A Practical Coursebook《实用文体学教程》

Japan: earthquake aftermath《日本:地震后果》

Learning strategy: Having A Positive Attitude《学习策略:拥有积极的态度》

(5)表示时间、比赛的比分等。例如:

16:45/4:45 p.m. 下午四点四十五分

The library is open on Saturday from 8:30 a.m. to 11:30 a.m. 周六图书馆开放时间是8:30—11:30。

Wang Lin beat Li Ping 15:12 in the Badminton Game yesterday. 昨天羽毛球比赛,王林以15比12击败李平。

(6)在通知等应用文中,用于表示时间、地点、人物、主题等。例如:

Speaker: Professor Peter 演讲人:皮特教授

Topic: Culture and Communication 主题:文化与交流

Time: 2:00 p.m. 时间:下午两点

Place: Lecture Room 4 地点:第四演讲厅

(六)分号的用法

分号表示的停顿比句号短,比逗号长。

(1)用于并列分句之间,替代并列连词 and、but、or 等。例如:

It was a spring evening; the air was warm and fresh. 那是春天的一个夜晚,空气温暖宜人而清新。

People make history; unusual people make history interesting. 人类创造历史;不平凡的人让历史变得有趣。

（2）常与连接性副词 however、besides、nevertheless、also、otherwise、so、therefore、hence 等一起使用（放在这些词语之前），以表明子句之间的紧密联系。例如：

You must take more exercise; otherwise you will get too fat. 你必须多锻炼，否则你会发胖的。

I realize I need more exercise; however, I need to have a rest first. 我意识到自己需要多练习，但我需要先休息一下。

He works hard; so he has obtained good results in scientific experiment. 他工作努力，因此他在科学实验方面已取得了良好的成绩。

（3）连接两个或两个以上并列的已有逗号的内容，以避免歧义。例如：

When I started, the sky was clear; but before I had covered two kilometers, it began to rain. 我动身时天空明净无云，但走了不到两公里路就开始下雨了。

The guests were Professor Lee, my teacher; Jim, my classmate; and Tom, my best friend. 客人是我的老师李教授，我的同学吉姆和我最好的朋友汤姆。

（七）连字号的用法

（1）用于复合词中。例如：water-melon（西瓜）、father-in-law（岳父、公公）、ex-husband（前夫）、self-esteem（自尊）、brand-new（全新的，崭新的）、up-to-date（最新的）、five-year-old（五岁的）、ten-ton（十吨的）、six-foot（六英尺的）、in-coming and out-going（进进出出的）等。

（2）用于两地名、数字或时间之间，译为"至"。如：in the academic year 2021–2022（2021—2022 学年）、during the years 2002–2022（在 2002—2022 年期间）、Beijing-Shanghai Flights（北京至上海的航班）、pages12-52（12 页到 52 页）等。

（3）用于单词移行。用于一个词的一部分要移行，一般按音节间断开单词加连字号。例如：birthday 可断为 birth-day 不可断为 birt-hday。不要把单个字母留在行尾或行首。注意一页中最后一个单词不能使用连字号将其置于两页。

（八）破折号的用法

（1）表示话语突然中断、意思突然转折或迟疑犹豫。例如：

"And may I ask—"said Tom, "but I guess it's better for you to ask him about it."汤姆说，"我可以问——不过我想还是你问他比较好。"

I was offended—no, enraged would be more accurate. 我很生气——不，更准确地说，是我被激怒了。

"I—I—I rather think—maybe—Amy has taken it.""我……我……我想，或许……是艾米拿了。"

（2）用于插入语的前后（相当于一个括号）。例如：

During my vacation—I must have been insane—I decided I would ski. 假期中，我准是疯了，我竟然决定去滑雪。

When I left the town—a day never to be forgotten—I began my new life. 当离开镇子——我难以忘怀的那一天，我开始了新生活。

（3）表示解释或补充说明。例如：

Shanghai—one of the largest cities in China—has an area of 6100 square kilometers and a population of over sixteen million. 上海——中国最大城市之一，面积为 6100 平方千米，人口

1600 多万.

It's an environmental issue—that's not a small matter. 这是个环境保护的问题,这不是一件小事。

(4) 总括前面列举的若干事物或引出被强调的词语。例如：

New houses, larger schools, more sheep, more pigs and chickens—everywhere we saw signs of prosperity. 新房子,扩建的学校,更多的羊、猪、鸡,我们到处都看到一片繁荣景象。

Men were shouting, women were screaming, children were crying—it was chaos in the war. 男人呼喊,女人尖叫,孩子们哭泣——战争中一片混乱。

(5) 表示引文的来源。例如：

With this faith, we will be able to hew out of the mountain of despair a stone of hope. —Martin Luther King 有了这个信念,我们将能从绝望之巅劈出一块希望之石。——马丁·路德·金

（九）括号的用法

(1) 表示插入的或附加的解释成分。例如：

the Li Zicheng Uprising (late Ming Dynasty) 明末李自成起义

William Shakespeare (1564—1616) wrote many beautiful sonnets. 莎士比亚(1564—1616)写了许多优美的十四行诗。

He thinks that modern music (anything written after 1900) is rubbish. 他认为现代音乐(即1900 年后创造的音乐)都不堪入耳。

(2) 标示数字或字母编号。例如：

to take courses in (a) mathematics, (b) English, (c) history and (d) geology. 学习(1)数学,(2)英语,(3)历史,(4)地质学等课程。

(3) 表示可省略或可供选择的内容。例如：

It seems (to me) that Jerry is asking too much. (我看)杰瑞似乎问得太多了。

The well-known play of William Shakespeare's *Romeo and Juliet* was so good (that) many young people asked to see it a second time. 莎士比亚的名剧《罗密欧与朱丽叶》非常好,以致许多年轻人要求再看一遍。

Please indicate the course(s) you would like to attend. 请注明你想去听的课程。

注：括号会削弱强调作用,因此,如果要强调插入的句子成分,则要用破折号。例如：

In the whole world there is only one person he really admires—himself.

在整个世界上,他真正崇拜的只有一个人——他自己。

（十）引号的用法

(1) 用于直接引语。例如：

Longfellow wrote, "Life is real! Life is earnest!" 朗费罗写道:"生活是真实的! 生活是严肃的!"

"Tell me," I said, "How you know all that." 我说,"告诉我,你是怎样知道事情的全部情况的。"

(2) 表示引起读者注意的词语或读者不熟悉的特殊词语。例如：

What's the difference between "differ" and "differentiate"? "differ"和"differentiate"有什么区别？

"SOS" is a message for help from a ship or aircraft when in danger. "SOS（紧急求救信号）"是当船只或飞机遭遇危险时发出的求救信息。

（3）用于文章、小说、电影、歌曲、节目等标题。例如：

Chapter Three is entitled "*Man and Nature*". 第三章标题是《人与自然》。

Tolstoy's "*War and Peace*" is a great novel. 托尔斯泰的《战争与和平》是一部伟大的小说。

> 注：如果引语中又有引语，常加单引号。例如：
> Mr. Zhang asked, "Who said ' Give me liberty or give me death ' ?" 张老师问："谁说过'不自由毋宁死'？"

（十一）撇号的用法

（1）构成名词的所有格。例如：

Li Ping's bicycle 李平的自行车　　　*The Emperor's New Clothes*《皇帝的新装》

the twins' bedroom 双胞胎的卧室　　　three weeks' journey 三个星期的旅程

（2）用于构成字母、数字的复数形式。例如：

during the 1990's 在 20 世纪 90 年代

How many A's have you got? 你得了几个 A？

There are two f's in the word "differ". 单词"differ"中有两个"f"。

（3）用于表示字母的省略。例如：I've、don't、it's、can't、o'clock、needn't、rock'n'roll（rock and roll）等。

（十二）省略号的用法

（1）用于表示词语的省略（句尾用省略号时，加上句号共计 4 个点）。例如：

We are not living for material stuff, not money, not fancy clothes, not authority.... 我们活着不是为了物质、金钱、昂贵的衣服、权力等.

... the book is lively... and well written. ……该书行文生动……写得很好。

（2）表示说话中断或犹豫。例如：

"If that the way you think... just go back to school." he said.

"如果你那么想……那就返回学校吧。"他说。

Let me see... I think it's 83568888. 让我想想……我想是 83568888。

（3）表示段落或整行词句的省略，须使用一整行黑点。例如：

....

二、分隔现象

英语句子成分不仅排列次序有一定的规律，而且相对位置也比较固定。但有时，为达到某种修辞效果、保持句子结构平衡避免头重脚轻、强调或突出某一成分、表达生动活泼或使上下文衔接紧凑等，把本应放在一起的两个成分分隔开来，这种结构称为"分隔结构（split structure)"。常见的分隔结构有以下几种情况。

(1) 主语与谓语的分隔。例如：

Coal and oil, for instance, hold energy for us to use. 例如,煤和石油中有我们可使用的能源。

The castle, surrounded by high walls, was little known to the outside world. 那座城堡四周是高高的围墙,鲜为外界知晓。

Our country, big as it is, also has its list of priorities. 大国之大,也有大国之重。

(2) 谓语动词与宾语的分隔。例如：

We should make clear which of them is primary and which secondary. 我们应该搞清楚这两者哪个是主要的,哪个是次要的。

Don't put off till tomorrow what should be done today. 今日事,今日毕。

(3) 定语从句与其先行项的分隔。例如：

The day will come when Mond realizes his ambition of becoming a writer. 总有一天,蒙德会实现成为作家的抱负。

Mary made the girl laugh who had cried just a moment ago. 玛丽让刚才还哭的女孩笑了。

(4) 介词短语与其所修饰的名词的分隔。例如：

There is no report to us of any accident. 我们没有收到发生事故的报告。

The story is told of his great success in business in Australia. 传说他在澳大利亚经商获得了巨大成功。

Difference still remains between town and country. 城镇和乡村之间的差异仍然存在。

(5) 不定式短语与其所修饰名词的分隔。例如：

Tom has few opportunities in Japan to meet interesting people. 汤姆在日本很少碰到有趣的人。

The time has come to make the final decision. 做最后决定的时候到了。

(6) 分词短语与其所修饰名词的分隔。例如：

A man appeared wearing a yellow jacket. 一个穿黄色夹克的人出现了。

There are many people on the platform waiting for the train. 月台上有很多人在等火车。

Now a new material has been developed, made of aluminum, which is covered with a layer of polyester. 现在已经研制出一种新材料,它是用铝制成的,上面涂了一层聚酯。

(7) 同位语与其先行项的分隔。例如：

An order came from the headquarters that we should get to the airport before dawn. 司令部来了命令,我们要在天亮前到达机场。

There were two nice children in the family by that time, a little boy and a baby girl. 那时他家已经有了两个可爱的孩子:一个小男孩,一个女婴。

(8) 谓语部分被分隔。例如：

Jerry's bad luck was, however, not finished. 然而,杰瑞的厄运并未结束。

John had, according to his wife, given up smoking before their child was born. 据约翰的妻子说,孩子出生之前,他就戒烟了。

Your eyes are, if I may say so, very much alive. 你的双眼,如果我可以这么说的话,真的是炯炯有神。

（9）固定搭配的分隔。例如：

Man is capable, particularly in childhood, of distinguishing minute changes in audio frequency. 人特别是在幼年时期，能够分辨音频的细微变化。

Devote some of your leisure, I suggest, to cultivating a love of reading. 我建议你利用空闲时间培养对阅读的爱好。

Putin has served for some years as president of Russia. 普京多年来担任俄罗斯总统。

（10）介词和宾语的分隔。例如：

He is angry about, to tell the truth, the decision to close the school. 说实话，他对关闭这所学校这一决定感到气愤。

It is bad for, in my opinion, the children to read such books. 我认为孩子们读这样的书不利于成长。

（11）宾语和其补足语的分隔。例如：

Sunshine can help the people who have been sick get well more quickly. 晒太阳能帮助生病的人康复得更快些。

Mr. Smith proved himself, despite his youth, to be a man of the world, and a practised talker. 史密斯先生尽管年轻，却老于世故，善于辞令。

巩 固 练 习

请指出下列句子中的分隔现象。

（1）His habit, getting up early in the morning, remains unchanged.

（2）He once again imparted to us his great knowledge, experience and wisdom.

（3）Any living thing, however small or simple it may seem, is far more complex than anything that has no life.

（4）Some little boys caught sight, yesterday, of a lot of frogs, which were hopping cheerfully around a pond.

（5）This, I think, is a very good way to raise our theoretical level.

（6）An order has come from Berlin that no language but German may be taught in the school.

（7）They saw two workers repairing the instrument who designed it.

（8）Tim, upset by the manager's use of insulting language, decided to leave the job.

（9）The thought came to him that maybe he did not turn off the switch.

（10）The day has come when we no longer need to carry cash around with us.

（11）I don't suppose anything happens that he doesn't foresee.

（12）The search goes on constantly for new and better material to lower costs.

（13）Arrangements have been made to install safety devices on all machines.

（14）Bees, as soon as they secure the foundation, begin to work at the building of the comb.

（15）Today doctors can find out by means of X. rays whether a patient has TB.

（16）All the bees that had been to the distant feeding place were doing a completely different dance, a wagging dance.

（17）They have, so far, attended classes regularly. They've worked hard.

(18) It has two stomachs in its body, one for itself, and one for carrying food to "the folks back home."

(19) The earth, in travelling around the sun, meets many of such fragments.

(20) Many countries, for example, Mexico and Japan, have a lot of earthquakes.

参考文献

[1] Michcel Swan. Practical English Usage：the 2nd edition［M］. Oxford：Oxford University Press,1995.
[2] Thomson AJ, Martinet AV. A Practical English Grammar：the 4th edition［M］. Oxford：Oxford University Press,1986.
[3] 埃克斯利 CE,埃克斯利 JM. 综合英语语法[M]. 洪清盾,等译. 石家庄：河北人民出版社,1984.
[4] 薄冰. 薄冰英语语法指南[M]. 北京：外语教学与研究出版社,2006.
[5] 崔校平. 英语语法难点精解[M]. 北京：外语教学与研究出版社,2002.
[6] 贺立民. 贺氏英语语法全书[M]. 广州：中山大学出版社,2003.
[7] 黄国文,肖俊洪. 大中学生简明英语语法词典[M]. 广州：广东教育出版社,1999.
[8] 江澄子. 大学英语六级考试全真题详解(增补本)[M]. 北京：世界图书出版公司,2005.
[9] 陆谷孙. 英汉大词典(缩印本)[M]. 上海：上海译文出版社,1993.
[10] 夸克,等. 英语语法大全[M]. 王国富,贺哈定,等译. 上海：华东师范大学出版社,1989.
[11] 全国大学英语四、六级考试委员会编. 大学英语六级考试历年实考试卷详解[Z]. 上海：上海外语教育出版社,1999.
[12] 全国大学英语四、六级考试委员会编. 大学英语四级考试历年实考试卷详解[Z]. 上海：上海外语教育出版社,1999.
[13] 汤普森. 牛津现代高级英汉双解词典[M]. 牛津大学出版社,北京：商务印书馆,1992.
[14] 王国栋. 大学英语深层语法[M]. 北京：清华大学出版社,2005.
[15] 王敏,裘正铨. 实用大学英语语法教程新编[M]. 北京：北京理工大学出版社,2018.
[16] 亚历山大 LG. 朗文英语语法[M]. 雷航,等译. 北京：外语教学与研究出版社,1991.
[17] 张道真. 张道真实用英语语法(最新版)[M]. 北京：外语教学与研究出版社,2004.
[18] 张维. 英语疑难词典(修订版)[M]. 北京：外语教学与研究出版社,2002.
[19] 张向阳. 实用大学英语语法教程[M]. 南京：东南大学出版社,2012.
[20] 章振邦. 新编英语语法教程[M]. 上海：上海外语教育出版社,2000.
[21] 赵振才. 英语常见问题解答大词典[M]. 哈尔滨：黑龙江人民出版社,1998.

本书参考答案